COMPUTER SUPPORTED
COOPERATIVE WORK

Also in this series

CSCW in Practice: An Introduction and Case Studies
(ISBN 3-540-19784-2)
Dan Diaper and Colston Sanger (Eds.)

Computer Supported Collaborative Writing
(ISBN 3-540-19782-6)
Mike Sharples (Ed.)

CSCW: Cooperation or Conflict?
(ISBN 3-540-19755-9)
Steve Easterbrook (Ed.)

CSCW and Artificial Intelligence
(ISBN 3-540-19816-4)
John H. Connolly and Ernest A. Edmonds (Eds.)

Duska Rosenberg and
Chris Hutchison (Eds.)

Design Issues
in CSCW

Springer-Verlag
London Berlin Heidelberg New York
Paris Tokyo Hong Kong
Barcelona Budapest

Duska Rosenberg, BA, MA, DipCAI, PhD
Department of Computer Science
Brunel University
Uxbridge
Middlesex UB8 3PH, UK

Christopher Hutchison, MSc, PhD
Faculty of Technology
Kingston University
Penrhyn Road
Kingston upon Thames
Surrey KT1 2EE, UK

Series Editors

Dan Diaper, PhD
Department of Computer Science
University of Liverpool
PO Box 147, Liverpool L69 3BX, UK

Colston Sanger
GID Ltd
69 King's Road
Haslemere, Surrey GU27 2QG, UK

ISBN 3-540-19810-5 Springer-Verlag Berlin Heidelberg New York
ISBN 0-387-19810-5 Springer-Verlag New York Berlin Heidelberg

British Library Cataloguing in Publication Data
A catalogue rocord for this book is available from the British Library

Library of Congress Cataloging-in-Publication Data
A catalog record for this book is available from the Library of Congress

Typeset from authors' disks by The Electronic Book Factory, Fife, Scotland.
Printed by Athenæum Press Ltd, Gateshead, England
34/3830–543210 Printed on acid-free paper

Preface

One of the most significant developments in computing over the last ten years has been the growth of interest in computer based support for people working together. Recognition that much work done in offices is essentially group work has led to the emergence of a distinct subfield of computer science under the title Computer Supported Cooperative Work (CSCW). Since the term was first coined in 1984, there has been growing awareness of the relevance to the field of, and the valuable contributions to be made by, non-computing disciplines such as sociology, management science, social psychology and anthropology. This volume addresses design issues in CSCW, and – since this topic crucially involves human as well as technical considerations – brings together researchers from such a broad range of disciplines.

Most of the chapters in this volume were originally presented as papers at the one-day seminar, "Design Issues in CSCW", held at the Department of Trade and Industry (DTI), London, on 17 March 1992, one in a series of DTI-supported CSCW SIG seminars.

We would like to express our gratitude to the series editors, Colston Sanger and Dan Diaper, for their useful comments on, and suggestions for revisions to, the final draft of the manuscript; to Linda Schofield, our editor at Springer, for her continued encouragement throughout the preparation of the manuscript; and, finally, to our respective families for their support and patience over so many months.

London
June 1993

Duska Rosenberg
Chris Hutchison

Contents

List of Contributors... xv

1 Introduction
D. Rosenberg and C. Hutchison............................... 1

2 Computer Supported Cooperative Work:
A Framework
A. Dix 9

3 Capturing Interactions: Requirements for CSCW
D. Murray and B. Hewitt....................................... 27

4 Situation Theory and the Design of Interactive
Information Systems
K. Devlin... 61

5 Patterns of Language in Organizations: Implications
for CSCW
C. Hutchison 89

6 Coordination Issues in Tools for CSCW
R. Procter, A. McKinlay, R. Woodburn and
O. Masting 119

7 Software Engineering Design: A Paradigm Case of
Computer Supported Cooperative Working
C. Boldyreff... 139

8 Where Are Designers? Styles of Design Practice,
Objects of Design and Views of Users in CSCW
M. Hales.. 151

9 Coping with Complexity and Interference: Design
Issues in Multimedia Conferencing Systems
M.A. Sasse, M.J. Handley and N.M. Ismail 179

10 The Role of Replication in the Development of Remote CSCW Systems
S. Scrivener, S. Clark and N. Keen 197

11 Computer Supported Conflict Management in Design Teams
M. Klein 209

12 ShareLib: A Toolkit for CSCW Applications Programming Using X Windows
M. Winnett, R. Malyan and P. Barnwell 229

13 Adapting a Design History Editor for Concurrent Engineering
D. Jenkins 241

14 "Nouvelle Design": A Pragmatic Approach to CSCW Systems Building
P.T. Hughes, M.E. Morris and T.A. Plant 271

References 293

Subject Index 309

Name Index 315

Contents

List of Contributors xv

1 Introduction
D. Rosenberg and C. Hutchison 1

2 Computer Supported Cooperative Work:
A Framework
A. Dix 9
  2.1 Introduction 9
  2.2 Cooperative Work 10
    2.2.1 Cooperation 10
    2.2.2 Work 11
    2.2.3 Communication through the Artefact 13
    2.2.4 Understanding: Soft and Hard Artefacts 14
    2.2.5 Deixis 15
  2.3 Computer Support: Communication 16
    2.3.1 Computer Mediated Communication 16
    2.3.2 Anti-CMC 18
  2.4 Computerized Artefacts of Work 19
  2.5 Non-Computerized Artefacts 21
    2.5.1 Prosthesis 21
    2.5.2 Implications for Design 22
    2.5.3 Success Story: Bar Codes 25
  2.6 Summary 25

3 Capturing Interactions: Requirements for CSCW
D. Murray and B. Hewitt 27
  3.1 Design Issues for CSCW 27
    3.1.1 The Life-Cycle Framework 30
  3.2 Ethnographic Study of Office Work 31
  3.3 Case Study of a Technical Publications Unit 33
    3.3.1 Organizational Description 35
    3.3.2 Authors' Views on their Work 36
    3.3.3 Life History of a Job 37
    3.3.4 Job Conditions 39
    3.3.5 Interaction Episodes 43

3.4 The Analysis.. 46
    3.4.1 Strategy 46
    3.4.2 Classification of Activities 46
3.5 Conclusions.. 55
    3.5.1 What the Authors Want.................................. 55
    3.5.2 What the Analysis Found 56
    3.5.3 In Conclusion... 58

4 Situation Theory and the Design of Interactive Information Systems
K. Devlin... 61

4.1 Introduction 61
4.2 Information 62
4.3 On Mathematics, Metaphor and Design 65
4.4 Situation Theory: A Review 69
4.5 Normative Constraints and Cognition............................ 75
4.6 Information, Situations and Design 79
4.7 Multimedia and Multi-User... 81
4.8 The Role of Situation Theory 83
4.9 Conclusion 86

5 Patterns of Language in Organizations: Implications for CSCW
C. Hutchison 89

5.1 Introduction 89
    5.1.1 Aims.. 89
    5.1.2 The Sopwith Case Study................................. 91
5.2 Four Models of Linguistic Support for
      Collaborative Work 93
    5.2.1 Language and Information 93
    5.2.2 Sociometric Analysis..................................... 95
    5.2.3 Style Checkers: Form versus Content.................... 102
    5.2.4 Language and Reality: An Overview of Systemic
          Functional Linguistics 105
    5.2.5 Language, Information and Organizations............. 109
5.3 Conclusions.. 114
Appendix A 114
    A.1 The Message from Leyland.................................... 114
    A.2 How the *Sunday Times* Rewrote It 115
Appendix B... 116
    B.1 Alcatraz on the Third Floor or Communications
          and Information Free of Time and Space
          (CIFTS!).. 116

6 Coordination Issues in Tools for CSCW
R. Procter, A. McKinlay, R. Woodburn and O. Masting 119

6.1 Introduction 119
6.2 Early Experiences with CSCW 120
6.3 Cognitive Issues in CSCW 121
6.4 Conversation Analysis 122
    6.4.1 Turn Management in Conversations 123
    6.4.2 An Example of Conversation Analysis 124
6.5 Coordination in CSCW 128
6.6 Studies of Turn Management in CSCW 131
6.7 Discussion 133
6.8 Concluding Remarks 135
Appendix A 136
    A.1 Annotated Bibliography 136

7 Software Engineering Design: A Paradigm Case of
Computer Supported Cooperative Working
C. Boldyreff 139

7.1 Introduction 139
    7.1.1 What is Design Theory? 140
    7.1.2 Is Design a Natural Phenomenon? 141
    7.1.3 A View of Design from Cognitive Science 142
7.2 Use of Abstract Representations 143
    7.2.1 Implications for Design Methods and Tool
         Support 143
    7.2.2 Philosophical Issues: Are they relevant? 144
    7.2.3 The Role of Concepts in Structuring Knowledge 145
7.3 The Design Frameworks Approach 145
7.4 An Approach to Design-for-Reuse 146
    7.4.1 Considerations Regarding the Use of Frameworks
         in Design 147
7.5 Conclusions 150

8 Where Are Designers? Styles of Design Practice,
Objects of Design and Views of Users in CSCW
M. Hales 151

8.1 Design as Technique, as Social Function and as Politics .. 153
8.2 Three Interpretations of the Significance of "Users" 155
8.3 Users as Clients: The "Specify and Deliver" Style 156
8.4 Users as Codesigners: The "Reflect
    and Reinterpret" Style 158
8.5 Users as Actor–Constructors: The
    "Enable and Empower" Style 161
8.6 Where are Designers? The Geo-
    Economic "Location" Problem 165
8.7 Taking Design with Us 170

9 Coping with Complexity and Interference: Design Issues in Multimedia Conferencing Systems
M.A. Sasse, M.J. Handley and N.M. Ismail 179

9.1 Introduction 179
9.2 The CAR Multimedia Conferencing System 180
9.3 Design Principles 182
    9.3.1 WYSIWIS 183
    9.3.2 Seamlessness 184
9.4 Design and Usability Issues 184
    9.4.1 Screen Clutter 185
    9.4.2 Unexpected Events 187
    9.4.3 Notification of Events 187
    9.4.4 Floor Control 189
    9.4.5 Pointers 190
9.5 Discussion: Design Principles for
       Multimedia Conferencing 192
9.6 Conclusions 194

10 The Role of Replication in the Development of Remote CSCW Systems
S. Scrivener, S. Clark and N. Keen 197

10.1 Designing for the Future 197
    10.1.1 The System Designer as Creative Problem
        Solver 197
    10.1.2 The Difficulty of Exchanging Creation for
        Facilitation 198
    10.1.3 Single-User Product Innovation 198
10.2 Designing for the Present: Replication 199
10.3 An Experiment in Replication 200
    10.3.1 The ROCOCO Station 201
    10.3.2 User Interface 202
10.4 Evaluating the System 203
    10.4.1 The LookingGlass 203
    10.4.2 An Investigation of the LookingGlass in Use 205
10.5 Conclusion 207

11 Computer Supported Conflict Management in Design Teams
M. Klein 209

11.1 The Challenge: Supporting
       Collaboration in Design Groups 209
11.2 Contributions and Limitations of Existing Work 210
11.3 The Design Collaboration Support System 212
    11.3.1 Describing Design Actions and Rationale 213
    11.3.2 Detecting Conflicts 219
    11.3.3 Resolving Conflicts 223
11.4 Evaluation and Future Work 225

12 ShareLib: A Toolkit for CSCW Applications Programming Using X Windows
M. Winnett, R. Malyan and P. Barnwell 229

12.1 Introduction 229
12.2 Existing Applications 230
12.3 Other Similar Work 230
12.4 What Programming Support Should Provide 231
    12.4.1 Features of CSCW 231
    12.4.2 Tailorability 232
12.5 Design of ShareLib: Architecture 232
    12.5.1 A New Level of Abstraction 232
    12.5.2 Features and Tailorability Provided by the
             CSCW Layer 234
12.6 Design of ShareLib: Implementation 235
    12.6.1 The X Window System 235
    12.6.2 ShareLib as a Layer above X Windows 236
12.7 Example Implementation: The Telepointer 237
    12.7.1 Writing Xlib Applications 237
    12.7.2 The Telepointer Type 237
    12.7.3 Initializing the Telepointer 238
    12.7.4 Processing Telepointer Events 239
    12.7.5 Floor Control 239
    12.7.6 Drawing the Telepointer Pixmap 239
12.8 Summary and Further Work 239

13 Adapting a Design History Editor for Concurrent Engineering
D. Jenkins 241

13.1 Introduction 241
    13.1.1 Motivation 241
    13.1.2 Starting Point 242
    13.1.3 Outline of the DHE Work 243
13.2 Design History Editor 247
    13.2.1 Inherent Difficulties with Current Approaches ... 247
    13.2.2 Conventional Logbooks and Hypertext 248
    13.2.3 The Impact of Prescription 249
13.3 User Requirements of the Design History Editor 250
    13.3.1 Page Emulation 250
    13.3.2 Representation of Finer Structure 251
    13.3.3 The Lemma 256
13.4 Technology 262
    13.4.1 The SMART Frame Server 263
    13.4.2 The Blackboard Architecture 265
    13.4.3 Managing Knowledge Assets 266
    13.4.4 Khoros 267
13.5 Technology Transfer 267
13.6 Concluding Remarks 269

14 "Nouvelle Design": A Pragmatic Approach to CSCW Systems Building
P.T. Hughes, M.E. Morris and T.A. Plant............................ 271

    14.1 Introduction.. 271
    14.2 Background.. 272
    14.3 Conversation Analysis 273
    14.4 User Centred Design.. 275
    14.5 Requirements Capture → Structured Observation 278
        14.5.1 Basic System Functionality 278
        14.5.2 Prototyping... 279
        14.5.3 Evaluation.. 279
        14.5.4 Subject Selection 282
        14.5.6 Types of Data....................................... 282
    14.6 System Specification → Analyse Observations 284
        14.6.1 Aims of Analysis Phase 284
        14.6.2 Data Analysis 285
    14.7 Build and Release → Review, Interpret, Modify 286
        14.7.1 Aims of this Phase 286
    14.8 Application of the Design Process................................. 287
        14.8.1 Programme 287
        14.8.2 Evaluation.. 288
    14.9 Summary and Conclusions 290

References.. 293

Subject Index.. 309

Name Index 315

Contributors

Peter Barnwell

School of Computer Science and Electronic Systems, Kingston University, Kingston upon Thames, Surrey KT1 2EE, UK

Cornelia Boldyreff

School of Engineering and Computer Science, University of Durham, South Road, Durham DH1 3LE, UK

Sean M. Clark

Department of Computer Studies, University of Technology, Loughborough, Leicestershire LE11 3TU, UK

Keith Devlin

Saint Mary's College of California, PO Box 3517, Moraga, CA 94575-3517, USA

Alan Dix

School of Computing and Mathematics, University of Huddersfield, Queensgate, Huddersfield HD1 3DH, UK

Mike Hales

Centre for Business Research, University of Brighton, Falmer, Brighton BN1 9PH, UK

Mark J. Handley

Department of Computer Science, University College London, Gower Street, London WC1E 6BT, UK

Betty Hewitt

Cognitive Systems Group, Risoe National Laboratory, PO BOX 49, DK 4000, Roskilde, Denmark

Philip T. Hughes

BNR Europe Ltd, London Road, Harlow, Essex CM17 9NA, UK

Chris Hutchison
School of Information Systems, Kingston University, Kingston upon Thames, Surrey KT1 2EE, UK

Nermeen M. Ismail
Department of Computer Science, University College London, Gower Street, London WC1E 6BT, UK

David Jenkins
Department of Computing and Information Systems, University of Paisley, High Street, Paisley PA1 2BE, UK

Nicola Keen
Department of Computer Studies, University of Technology, Loughborough, Leicestershire LE11 3TU, UK

Mark Klein
Boeing Computer Services, PO Box 24346, Seattle, WA 98124-0346, USA

Ron Malyan
School of Computer Science and Electronic Systems, Kingston University, Kingston upon Thames, Surrey KT1 2EE, UK

Oliver Masting
Department of Computer Science, University of Edinburgh, King's Buildings, Mayfield Road, Edinburgh EH9 3JZ, UK

Andy McKinlay
Department of Maths and Computer Science, University of Dundee, Dundee DD1 4HN, UK

Michele E. Morris
BNR Europe Ltd, London Road, Harlow, Essex CM17 9NA, UK

Diane Murray
Department of Sociology, University of Surrey, Guildford GU2 5XH, UK

Tony A. Plant
BNR Europe Ltd, London Road, Harlow, Essex CM17 9NA, UK

Rob Procter
Department of Computer Science, University of Edinburgh, King's Buildings, Mayfield Road, Edinburgh EH9 3JZ, UK

Duska Rosenberg

Department of Computer Science, Brunel University, Uxbridge, Middlesex UB8 3PH, UK

Martina Angela Sasse

Department of Computer Science, University College London, Gower Street, London WC1E 6BT, UK

Stephen A.R. Scrivener

Design Research Centre, University of Derby, Kedleston Road, Derby DE22 1GB, UK

Maria Winnett

School of Computer Science and Electronic Systems, Kingston University, Kingston upon Thames, Surrey KT1 2EE, UK

Robin Woodburn

Department of Electrical Engineering, University of Edinburgh, King's Buildings, Mayfield Road, Edinburgh EH9 3JZ, UK

Chapter 1

Introduction

D. Rosenberg and C. Hutchison

Computer Supported Cooperative Work (CSCW) is, as its name indicates, concerned with the ways in which people work *together* and with the ways in which computer systems can be designed to support the collaborative aspects of work. It is through developing an insight into what makes people behave as they do in the organizational context that we hope to explain the nature of the interaction between computers and their users in the workplace, and ensure that the application of computers in human activities is successful. Indeed, one of the major objectives of CSCW is to create a design approach that puts technology into its proper perspective; that is, not a central place in design *per se*, but a place determined by considerations of the ways in which technological artefacts are used by human groups in work organizations.

Consequently, computer system design and the study of group behaviour in the human and social sciences are properly brought together in the context of CSCW. The disciplines in both areas come with a distinguished history of rich repertoires of analytical techniques. Therefore, it seems reasonable to suppose both that CSCW design falls naturally within the topics for which a social science approach is appropriate, and that systems design can similarly be extended to guide the development of computing systems not only for use by individuals, but also by groups of cooperating users. The point of convergence between the contributing disciplines is the shared emphasis on the understanding of collaborative work, rather than more narrowly on the ability to develop increasingly complex new technology.

Given this emphasis of CSCW and its essential interdisciplinary nature, one of the fundamental problems that arises in relation to design, and which is addressed throughout this volume, concerns the formulation of design perspectives most suitable for CSCW. Yet the formulation of such perspectives is itself dependent upon an understanding of the issues arising from the paradigm shift from technology-orientated to people-orientated design. What is distinctive about the chapters in this volume is that they address this issue by examining the implications, both theoretical and practical, of such a shift. We start with the recognition that if we want to support human collaboration in the workplace, we have to focus our attention not only on designing a computer system, but also on designing the way in which that computer system influences both the nature and the form of the user's work.

Indeed, CSCW points to the fact that human beings work together, not always cooperatively, but always socially – that is, in relation to others. It is therefore one of the goals of this book to show how a design perspective centred on work has stimulated the search for new theoretical and research frameworks, which in turn guide the selection of design principles and influence the development of tools, techniques and methods for CSCW.

The recognition of both the need and the opportunity for computer systems to support human collaboration has not only brought to light the limitations of systems designed for single users, but has also motivated a wider scoping of interdisciplinary research to include the nature of human organizations, and especially the interpersonal communication that takes place within them, the processes that influence the effectiveness of collaboration in the workplace and other factors that are commonly subsumed under the terms of user requirements capture (e.g. Norman and Draper 1986). The systematic study of user requirements in CSCW has already been established as a major objective of CSCW theory and method, research and development, as discussed and published throughout the CSCW community in volumes such as ACM 1986, 1988 and 1990, in the activities of the CSCW SIG in the UK, as well as in Japanese government-sponsored projects into the development of new models of software architectures.

The consequences of adopting such a people-orientated view of design form the core of the contributors' work. This encompasses considerations of theoretical underpinnings for CSCW design, aspects of CSCW methodology and the associated development of analytical frameworks (cogently discussed by Dix, in Chapter 2). The design perspectives presented in this volume illustrate the variety of topical approaches to CSCW design, from their motivation in philosophical orientation and reliance on the contributing scientific disciplines (as presented, for example, in the work of Murray and Hewitt (Chapter 3), Devlin (Chapter 4), Hutchison (Chapter 5) and Procter et al. (Chapter 6)), through the quest for understanding collaboration, conflict and interdependence in the context of design activities (presented, in particular, by Boldyreff (Chapter 7) and Hales (Chapter 8)), to the development of analytical tools needed for investigations of the significant phenomena associated with cooperative work practices (presented in the work of Sasse et al. (Chapter 9), Scrivener et al. (Chapter 10) and Klein (Chapter 11)). While all of the chapters in this volume are focused on the issues relating to the role of technology in the workplace, some also illustrate the very technologies, tools and methods that are evolving as distinctive characteristics of CSCW design (described by Winnett et al. (Chapter 12), Jenkins (Chapter 13) and Hughes et al. (Chapter 14)).

Thus the common theme throughout this volume is that of a significant shift of emphasis in CSCW design away from the technology itself and towards the people who use this technology at work. Indeed, Dix looks at significant elements of the cooperative work situation and develops a framework for examining specific areas for computer support. He uses this framework to examine different aspects of CSCW and to consider the impact of various computer systems on cooperation in the workplace. He makes the important point that system development should take a broader view of cooperation as the basis for the design of systems to support cooperative work, so that their impact on cooperation is considered even when the systems themselves are not specifically designed as CSCW applications. His intricate analysis of the term "computer supported cooperative work" leads Dix to conclude that "work" should be at the centre of CSCW design.

In the spirit of the interdisciplinary nature of CSCW, Chapters 3–6 illustrate complementary perspectives to understanding the nature of cooperation at work: respectively, ethnographic, formal, linguistic and cognitive. In the first of these, Murray and Hewitt are concerned with the details of capturing and analysing requirements for CSCW systems. They assess why requirements capture and analysis for CSCW systems differs from that for more traditional IT systems, and discuss how to gather data through observational and related studies, debating where and how such techniques could fit into the life-cycle model of software engineering and design. They highlight the issues involved in understanding both cooperative and conflicting patterns of communication between those engaged in collaborative activities, and show how they are developing a methodology to define more clearly the relationship between work contexts and types of computer support for group working. They summarize some of their investigative work into the organizational contexts in which such systems might be used, focusing on interaction-based studies of office settings, and present a case study of "knowledge workers" engaged in authentic information processing tasks. The authors investigate methods of translating their tacit knowledge into requirements statements, assessing views of the organization through the participants' eyes, as contrasted with more formal views of the organization as a business.

Devlin presents a formal framework adapted to the requirements of CSCW design, and looks to the need for conceptual tools in the analysis and design of "interactive information systems". He approaches CSCW from a different perspective – that of the study of information within the interdisciplinary framework provided by situation theory, which began as an attempt to provide a mathematical foundation for situation semantics, a natural language semantics developed by Barwise and Perry during the early 1980s. Since then, the theory has developed into a general framework for the study of information, as described in his book, *Logic and Information*. In his contribution to this volume he outlines the way in which the ideas developed there, and elaborated further in the study of cooperative action and the provision of the framework for the description of conflict resolution (references for which are provided), may be of use in the design of interactive information systems and, in particular, systems designed for CSCW.

The importance of conceptual tools in this context is also highlighted by Hutchison, who, sharing with other contributors the view that communication is the essence of cooperative work, considers the significant role it plays in organizational behaviour and group activity. Standard computer based tools tend to acknowledge communication in the workplace only at a superficial, effectively content-free, level; instead, CSCW design emphasizes the need to look beyond the surface into the underlying conventions that collaborating agents use for generating shared meanings and mutual understandings, where technology is only one of the media for communication. Since organizational work depends crucially on the sharing and exchange of meanings, it is by definition collaborative; but meanings are shared only by virtue of there being public codes and conventions for the generation and interpretation of messages. Of the many codes and conventions learned and used by organizational members, the most basic and important are those tied to the use of language. His chapter thus outlines some views of the role of language in cooperative working, and argues that language issues are properly design issues.

Within a cognitive framework, Procter et al. base their work on conversation analysis, in particular on its techniques for describing shared understanding and coordination. When people work together in groups they have to establish and maintain a shared understanding, or common ground, allocate tasks and coordinate individual activities. Group members must therefore not only respond to the cognitive demands of their individual tasks, but also cope with the demands of communicating with others. In conventional circumstances, where group members are copresent, they have recourse to a complex of informal acts of communication that are generally referred to as "social presence". Social presence supplements explicit channels of communication, providing a means for group members to signal their intentions, and anticipate and resolve conflicts. In combination with the affordances of the physical workspace, social presence is a low cost way of sustaining common ground and coordination, and thus of situating the activity of the group as a whole.

The attenuation of social presence, typical in computer mediated communications, together with the substitution of the physical workspace by a virtual one, means that collaboration awareness is more difficult to sustain in CSCW tools where group members are not copresent. Procter et al. examine the extent to which conversation analysis, with the insights it is able to provide concerning the practical coordination of conversational "work", may be applied to the problem of coordination in CSCW.

Thus, people-orientated design is different from technology-orientated design in several crucial ways. One concerns the nature of design itself; another is focused on the role of the user *vis-à-vis* that of the designer; a third concerns the kinds of tools and techniques that are needed to support systems design in this context.

As regards the nature of design, Boldyreff considers software engineering design as an example of CSCW, suggesting that this recognition provides a starting point for improving the process of design in software engineering. In her view, software development as an engineering process can usefully draw upon the results of studies in design theory, and, in particular, results from cognitive science applied under the umbrella of design theory can provide insights into how the cooperative working of software designers can be better supported by computers. Since, in this context, the activity of design is itself amenable to being designed, the potential exists to develop theories of design with the possibility of radically changing the nature of existing design practice.

Hales also examines the activity of design but focuses on the role of the user. He points out that the view of the user significantly influences design styles, and he identifies three styles. Firstly, in the technology-orientated paradigm of design the user is a significant factor, but only in so far as he or she motivates the design by providing user requirements and evaluating the outcomes. Secondly, in an understanding-orientated paradigm users know things which must be active in design. They must be co-designers, they must both learn and also show what they know; so must "official designers". Thirdly, in a management- or power-orientated paradigm users must be given support to continue to design – in a real, if different, sense – after "the designers" have finished, and in this way technology issues gradually merge with organizational issues. Moreover, managers must negotiate the balance of power between the two. Hales suggests that all three design styles are visible in the emerging CSCW field, but that political awareness and accountability (intrinsic aspects of the third style) are very underdeveloped in the CSCW community. In principle, a mix of all three styles is called for.

The issue of the role of the user is pursued further in the work of Scrivener et al., who develop a method for finding out what goes on in the workplace and discuss new ways of distributing authority and responsibility between the designer and the user in the design process. They focus on the need to minimize externally defined change and stimulate an internally regulated change process. In support of this, they advocate initial "replication" of the workspace so that users will be able to achieve with new media what it is already possible to achieve with existing media. Remote CSCW applications offer possibilities for investigating the potential of such replication, since a primary motivation for these applications is to allow pre-established group work practice to persist or to occur where it would otherwise not have been possible. They define the usability goals of replication and describe the development of a system intended to replicate a workspace, in which product designers work face to face using pen and paper. Evaluation of the replication suggests that it meets its design objectives and provides a workspace that is accessible, useful and stimulating for designers to inhabit. They conclude that the challenge for the system designer is to be creative and inventive in finding ways of stimulating and supporting the evolution of the workspace as new opportunities for augmentation and enhancement are recognized by its inhabitants. The role of the system designer will shift from defining new workspaces and work practices, to creating environments in which new workspaces and work practices can be defined.

Similarly, Sasse et al. recount the design and usability issues they encountered during a project to build a multimedia conferencing system. These issues tend to arise mainly from two sources: the complexity involved in handling the system, and the continual interference users experience when interacting with the system and with each other. Sasse and colleagues found that the design principles that have been suggested (such as WYSIWIS and seamlessness) offer only partial solutions to these problems. Generally, the complexity and interference experienced by users can be reduced by imposing certain constraints on the way in which users interact with the system and with each other. Imposing any of these constraints, however, results in reduced flexibility of user–system interaction, as well as more rigid protocols on user–user interaction, and is bound to make the system less acceptable for some groups of users and some tasks. They therefore suggest that such constraints should be agreed and implemented by the user group prior to undertaking a collaborative project. In this way, user and task characteristics can be originated by the user group rather than be imposed on users by including such constraints in the design of the system interface.

Klein considers the design of complex artefacts as fundamentally a cooperative process where occurrences of conflict in designer teams play a central role. Effective tools for supporting the conflict management process, however, are still lacking. These tools, in general, do not support task-level interaction or encode significant expertise about how to detect and resolve conflicts. Klein's chapter describes an implemented computer based system called DCSS (the Design Collaboration Support System) for supporting conflict detection and resolution among cooperating human and machine based design agents that avoids these limitations. Design agents describe their design actions and rationale to DCSS in terms of a task-level model of the cooperative design process; human designers use a direct-manipulation graphical interface for this purpose. DCSS uses a body of domain-independent expertise to help the agents to detect and resolve conflicts among them. The system has been used successfully by human designers to design local area networks in cooperation with other human and machine based designers. This chapter describes DCSS's underlying model and implementation, gives examples of its operation, and evaluates its strengths, weaknesses and potential for future growth.

So how do we go about developing the tools and systems that are built in the spirit of the new design orientation? In the context of distributed, synchronous CSCW, Winnett et al. address the design problem from the technologist's point of view, and describe a toolkit to support CSCW applications using the X Window system as a programming environment. The toolkit aims to allow designers to concentrate on the design issues of CSCW and to incorporate the insights provided by social scientists into the ways in which people work together in groups. It achieves this by hiding the lower level implementation details from the designer, while still allowing the application to be tailored to users' needs where required. The authors suggest that the toolkit should comprise a number of key features such as shared windows and telepointers, with parameters that allow design flexibility and tailorability, and describe the implementation of the toolkit as a layer of functionality above X Windows.

In another example of a tools-centred CSCW design, Jenkins describes an adaptation of an existing system, seeing its extension to deal with the requirements of concurrent engineering as requiring the provision of domain-specific CSCW. By describing the requirements of the engineering designer, he shows that understanding these requirements is a key CSCW design issue. A brief survey of the technological resources available show that these do not constrain the development of CSCW. Rather, cultural issues dominate, and because of this the maturity of engineering design endeavours is a significant factor in ensuring the success of the design process as a whole.

Finally, all the strands presented in some detail in the previous chapters are synthesized into an integrated perspective of people, theory and system building by Hughes et al. They argue that apart from the benefits of the technology, building CSCW systems is providing valuable insights into the collection of human activities that we call design. New features and directions are emerging for these design activities – which they call nouvelle design. Using their shared window system work for the EuroCoOp project as an example, they illustrate the important perspectives on CSCW design in the practical enactment of nouvelle design.

Taken together, there emerges from the different chapters in this volume an awareness of possibly inherent problems in established systems design methodologies and practices. These may not be apparent when we design conventional, stand-alone, single-user systems, where work as an inherently *social* process is not an issue. Yet, as the contributions show, the social nature of work *is* an issue that must be addressed in the context of

CSCW, and it is precisely this shared concern that constitutes the common focus of this volume.

The shared view of work as a social process underpins, in the first place, the fundamentally interdisciplinary nature of CSCW and, in the second place, the search for appropriate design perspectives. In these regards also the contributors are in agreement. They illustrate the interdisciplinary nature of CSCW design by showing how it is motivated in inter-disciplinary theory and accomplished in design practice. Although the authors come from different disciplines and describe different experiences of design in the context of CSCW, their work speaks of the results of successful collaboration between the social sciences and technology, and between academic and industrial research, that has become a distinctive feature of CSCW. In this context, the specific issue regarding the place and the role of technology in both users' workplaces and in the design activity thus becomes that of establishing the right balance between technology-orientated and people-orientated design. By pointing out the limitations of conventional systems analysis and design, this volume points the way to the formulation of design perspectives appropriate to CSCW.

Chapter 2

Computer Supported Cooperative Work: A Framework

A. Dix

2.1 Introduction

This chapter presents a framework for considering different aspects of Computer Supported Cooperative Work (CSCW) and different CSCW systems. We are also able to look at systems not normally regarded as having a CSCW element, and consider their positive and negative impacts on cooperation. The aim of the framework is to enhance understanding of existing areas, and hence both to develop them and also to suggest new avenues for research and development. We shall place existing concepts such as computer mediated communication, deixis and communication through the work itself within the framework. We shall also consider many familiar shared tasks from both CSCW and non-CSCW systems, including meeting rooms, shared editing, piano moving and bar codes. The significance of this work is not in the particular examples presented, but in the structure within which they sit.

Although the original purpose of this framework was rhetorical, it has also become a potent tool for design. In Miles et al. (1993) the framework is used to structure the issues surrounding the design of a synchronous–asynchronous group editor. In addition, in Dix et al. (1993) it has been used to structure an introductory survey of groupware systems. Other surveys have been based around the ubiquitous time–space matrix and functional decomposition (e.g. Rodden 1991). This framework deals with the participants and entities in a cooperative work situation and their relationships. It does not explicitly address temporal issues or the physical location of the entities, and it therefore complements the standard time–space matrix. The most similar work is probably Lim and Benbasat's framework, which also concentrates on participants and entities (Lim and Benbasat, 1991); however, their approach is based around the computational entities. The emphasis in this chapter is upon the work situation and those objects which – computerized or not – contribute to cooperative work.

The chapter will proceed by dissection. We take the phrase "computer supported cooperative work" and pull it apart – looking, firstly, at cooperation, then at cooperative work and finally at various forms of computer support. This sort of dissection is not really a particularly valid form of analysis. CSCW obviously has a meaning over and above the particular words of which it is composed. My only excuse is that it is useful and draws out the points that I wish to make. In particular, it helps us to focus on the importance of work – the purpose of cooperation. Also, having started from the words "computer supported cooperative work", one feels somewhat justified in using the resulting framework in a normative fashion, to criticize systems that fail to address important areas.

2.2 Cooperative Work

2.2.1 Cooperation

The word "cooperation" suggests two or more participants communicating with one another (Fig. 2.1). Interpersonal communication is a complex and interesting subject in its own right. For example, conversational analysis and speech-act theory both look at the structure of utterances within normal conversation. For discussion of the role of the former in CSCW, see Procter et al. and Morris et al. (this volume), and for the latter see Winograd and Flores (1986), who used speech-act in the design of the Coordinator message system. At an entirely different level, information theory measures the raw capacity of channels (Shannon and Weaver 1949), and between these extremes, the author has himself studied other temporal properties of channels (Dix 1992). Important as communication is, the purpose of this chapter is to show that it is but one part of the study of cooperative work.

Part of the job of communicating is coming to a mutual understanding about the subject of conversation. This need not be an agreement about matters of substance, but at least a sufficient understanding about each other's positions. Indeed, communication can be viewed as the process of

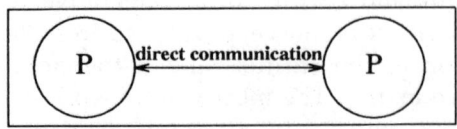

Fig. 2.1. Anti-CMC.

establishing mutual understanding; Clark and Brennan (1991) refer to this understanding as "common ground". Understanding can thus be seen as an aspect of communication, but, in addition, it will be presented below as a facet of work.

Important as they are, communication and shared understanding are only a beginning. When we talk of cooperation, we need to know what we are cooperating over, what we are communicating about. Cooperation is never just communication; it is communication with a purpose. That purpose is work.

2.2.2 Work

Work takes many forms: the production of goods (for example, by farmers and factory workers), the use of those goods in service (e.g. by bus drivers), intellectual work (management and academia) and entertainment.[1] This work is carried out with, or is performed upon, various artefacts of work: tractors and turnips, business plans and books. These artefacts are denoted A in Fig. 2.2. The artefacts of work are controlled and acted upon by the participants, who are also able to perceive the state of the artefacts. This control and observation is denoted by arcs between the participants and the artefacts in Fig. 2.2.

Sometimes an artefact is shared between the participants; that is, they both exercise an element of control and observation of the same thing, for instance (and we shall return to this example several times), when moving a large object such as a piano. In other cases, the different participants each have control of different artefacts.

The sharing of artefacts is not necessary for cooperation. In the simplest case, only one participant is in contact with the artefacts (Fig. 2.3); for example, a timetable enquiry. Here, the enquirer asks for the time of the

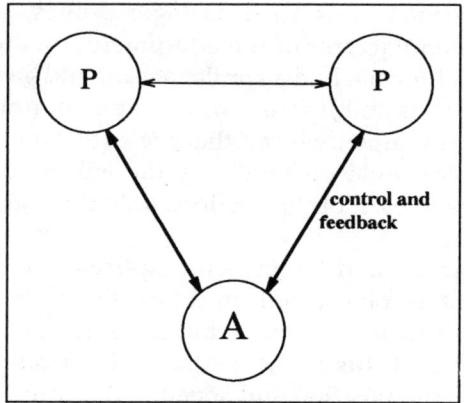

Fig. 2.2. Shared artefacts of work.

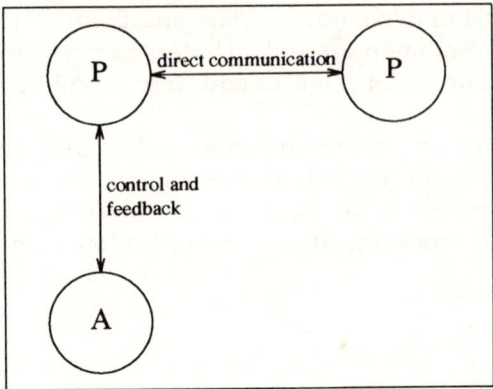

Fig. 2.3. One participant controls artefacts.

train, whereupon the officer looks up the time in the timetable (paper or electronic) and relays the information back to the enquirer. Another example is in expert–novice situations, where the novice is in physical control of the work and is advised by the expert. Sometimes this is for the purposes of instruction. In these cases, the aim of the work is establishing understanding and skill in the novice; the artefact of work is a tool to that end.

There are also many expert–novice situations where there is little or no didactic element. A short while ago, a colleague who had a problem with a computer program telephoned me. While we talked he recompiled the program several times and tried various experiments, eventually finding the bug. The telephone is not the best instrument for such remote debugging; ideally, one would like direct contact with the target system. However, despite this, the exercise was surprisingly successful.

I was once at the novice end of a similar, but slightly different, form of interaction. This time the artefacts were a piece of complex electronic equipment and various tools such as logic probes, ammeters and an oscilloscope. The manufacturer of the equipment, on the other end of the telephone line in California, had a similar set-up and gave us instructions, performing similar tests on his (working) equipment until the fault in ours was found. In this example, we see that we each had control of distinct artefacts of work. We could observe only the effects of our own actions, and had knowledge of each other's actions only through our conversation (Fig. 2.4).

Sometimes the picture may be further complicated, since one participant may have control of an object, but no direct observation of it. The other participant may be able to observe it, but have no control except through the first. An example of this is the control of large ships; the captain on the bridge observes the position and speed of the ship, but has to exercise control via the sailors in the engine room.

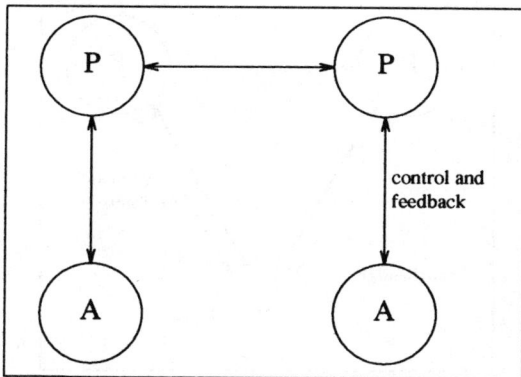

Fig. 2.4. Participants control different artefacts.

In general, a work situation will include all types of artefacts, some shared between all participants, some controlled and observed by just one or a group. Normally, those with control will also receive feedback relating to their actions, but – as in the case of the ship – not always.

To denote this generic situation, we will use the original diagram (Fig. 2.2), with arcs between both participants and the artefacts. However, we should remember that this does not imply that all such artefacts are shared, and certainly not that all participants have equal access and control of all artefacts. It also emphasizes that even where there is not shared control of the artefacts, the artefacts are the shared focus of the work, and, furthermore, that the work is the focus of the cooperation.

2.2.3 Communication through the Artefact

Where an artefact is shared, that artefact is not only the *subject* of communication, it can also become a *medium* of communication. As one participant acts upon the artefact, the other observes the effects of the action. We can call this observation by the other participants "feedthrough". Just as each participant receives feedback as to their own actions, they receive feedthrough as to the actions of their colleagues. Because of this feedthrough, the participants are able to communicate through the artefact (Fig. 2.5). Consider, for example, two people moving a piano: as one of them lifts or shifts her end the other will feel the movement in the piano and shift his hold correspondingly. No words need be spoken; the actions are eloquent enough.

Communication through the artefact can be very powerful, as the piano moving example demonstrates. The communication medium is obviously well suited to the task in hand. How successful it is depends on the nature of the task: solid physical objects are obviously particularly well suited. At

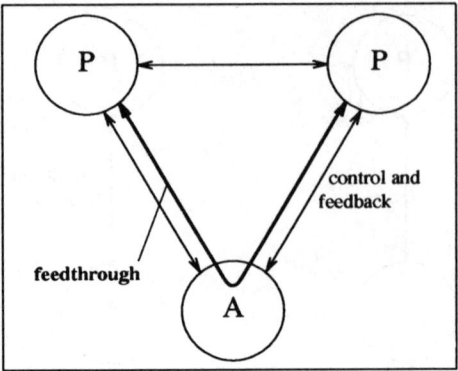

Fig. 2.5. Communication through the artefact.

the other extreme, if there are no shared artefacts there is no possibility for communication through the artefact. In between these extremes are shared artefacts that are more or less tightly knit.

Imagine our piano movers again: let's call them Sue and Keith. Now they have finished getting the piano into the house and are bringing in the mattress. This time, as Sue moves her end Keith does not feel what has happened because the mattress bends in the middle. Each gets feedback as to their own actions and tends to pace their work in relation to that feedback. However, there is little feedthrough informing them of the other's actions.

To simplify the situation, imagine two people, blindfold and silent, holding opposite ends of a solid pole. They could communicate using simple Morse code, and develop quite a speed at it. Now swap the pole for a "slinky" spring. Possibly, one could feel the waves propagate through it, but the pace of communication, and particularly the pace of interaction, would drop significantly. The pole and the piano are examples of tightly knit artefacts where feedthrough is almost as strong as feedback. The slinky spring and the mattress are less tightly knit; feedthrough is far weaker.

2.2.4 Understanding: Soft and Hard Artefacts

We have already mentioned understanding in the light of communication for cooperation. This may take two major forms. Firstly, there is understanding about the work. This is most closely tied to the communication itself, and is a means to the completion of the work. On the other hand, understanding may be a goal of the work. This is the case in academic work: one communicates to share or discover some understanding of a domain, and understanding is the sole purpose of the work. We may thus see understanding as a form of artefact of work (Fig. 2.6).

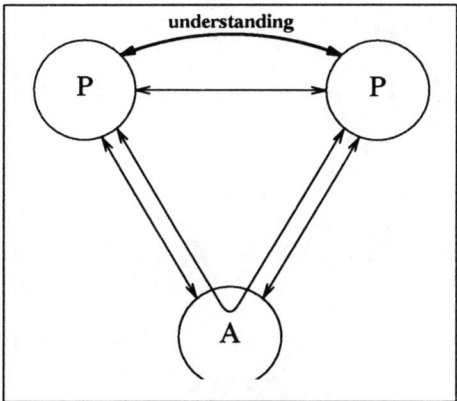

Fig. 2.6. Shared understanding.

Understanding and other "intellectual-ware" may be seen as soft artefacts, as opposed to the physical or hard artefacts. It is often the case that during the process of intellectual work one externalizes the understanding in some form; for example, by the production of academic papers, management reviews, use of a whiteboard or demonstrations using models or computer simulations. This representation of soft artefacts as hard ones may merely be the communication medium where the real aim is the understanding itself, or may be seen (as with the production of a shared paper) as a primary goal of cooperation. Furthermore, the existence of the external reified form may serve to facilitate understanding among the participants.

2.2.5 Deixis

As we have seen, cooperation cannot be seen as communication alone, but as communication with a purpose. In particular, it is communication about work and about the artefacts of work. During this process the participants will use various means to refer to the particular artefacts – this is deixis. Deixis is shown in Fig. 2.7 as an arc from the communication to the artefacts of work.

In conversation where the artefacts of work are present, one is able to indicate the different objects by pointing, or even just by movement of the eye. These indicative movements may be accompanied by phrases such as "put that one there" or "let's use this". If one is writing, using a telephone, or just talking about the objects when they are elsewhere, deixis is more difficult, and one is forced to use more complex expressions such as "turn the left-hand knob with the red dot on it". This is not confined to physical objects: in academic papers, one cites other papers, and organizations usually have sophisticated labelling schemes to enable them to refer to specific letters, bills, people and so on.

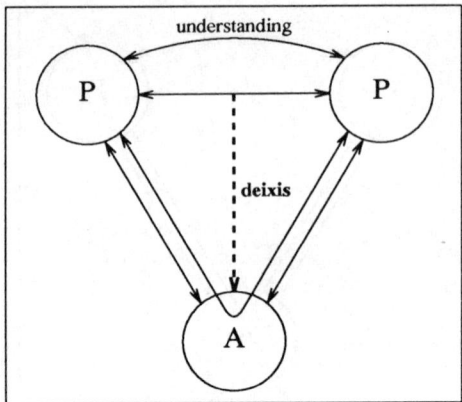

Fig. 2.7. Deictic reference.

2.3 Computer Support: Communication

We can use the diagrammatic representation of cooperative work shown in Fig. 2.8 to investigate different aspects of CSCW. For any CSCW system, we can ask precisely which aspects are computerized.

We shall move through Fig. 2.8 looking at the different arcs (representing communication or control) and see what sort of systems computerize these arcs. We begin at the top of the diagram, with the interparticipant communication and the establishment of understanding. In later sections we shall look at the artefacts of work, whether or not they are themselves computerized, and at the results of automating the control of the artefacts.

Looking at Fig. 2.8, we see that cooperative work has many facets. If the term "CSCW" is at all meaningful, we should expect that any system or discussion that claims to address CSCW should relate to the larger picture, not just to one aspect or another. This may not be entirely fair; part of the valid study of any discipline is the study of quite specific aspects of it. It is at least useful, however, to assess any particular system in the light of the whole – does it support cooperative work? This can then be a touchstone with which to judge the various approaches to CSCW that emerge as we focus on the specific areas of the framework.

2.3.1 Computer Mediated Communication

The participants themselves are assumed to be human, so the first candidate for computer support is the communication between the participants (Fig. 2.9).

Many systems fall into this category: email, bulletin boards and some electronic conferencing systems, for example. There are many important

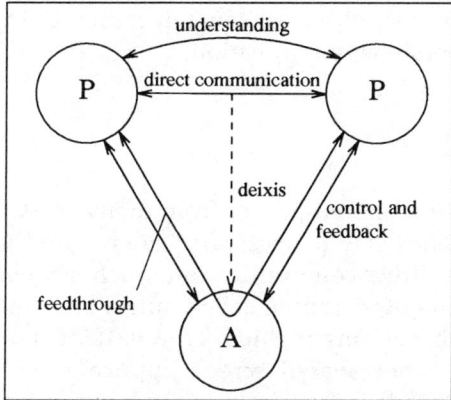

Fig. 2.8. Candidates for computer support.

issues in this area: how to compensate for lack of face-to-face meetings (heaven forbid substitute) or how to improve existing communication-at-a-distance, such as letters.

If we stay just with this arc, we are talking about Computer Mediated Communication (CMC), not CSCW. That is not to say that CMC is not a part of CSCW. It is a valid CSCW activity in the same way as, say, screen design is part of Human–Computer Interaction (HCI). However, it does make one wonder about the very large place CMC has in the CSCW literature.

A CMC system will have an impact on the cooperative work situation, whether or not it is designed with that intent. The introduction of new media has profound effects on the nature of conversation. Different conversational structures encouraged by the media, perhaps branching conversations, or the permanence of the media will be more or less useful for different activities and may change the whole social dynamics of the conversation (Clark and Brennan 1991). Thus, while the role of CMC as such is debatable, the impact of CMC is most definitely a central CSCW issue.

There is another set of CSCW systems that goes beyond CMC: the ideas-generating kind, typified by various forms of electronic meeting rooms such as Colab (Stefik et al. 1987b). These systems include the support of mutual understanding as well as communication. The activities that they support have understanding as their principal or sole activity. Understanding is the artefact of work. These systems can then justifiably

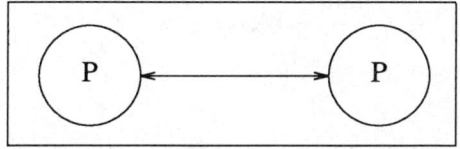

Fig. 2.9. Computer mediated communication.

be called CSCW systems with a (or several) capital C, in that they support cooperation, not merely communication.

2.3.2 Anti-CMC

So, despite the feeling one might get from many "CSCW" systems, CMC is not sufficient. Neither is it necessary: many good CSCW systems do nothing to support direct communication. Such systems, which have no communication element, could be called anti-CMC systems (Fig. 2.10).

Examples of such systems include Timbuktu (Farallon 1987), ShrEdit (CSMIL 1989) and other shared screen applications. These systems all implicitly assume that the participants will have some additional means of communication: face-to-face, audio or audio/visual. Indeed, there is no particular reason why such systems could not be combined with an on-line electronic conferencing system. Nevertheless, the systems in themselves only support a shared artefact. There is, of course, communication through the artefact: the participants can read each other's typing and share a focus of attention. Indeed, there have been attempts to use such systems as the sole means of communication, but this is not their design intent.

The electronic meeting rooms are similar in some ways to shared screens. However, the emphasis in the meeting rooms is that the shared surface is the focus for establishing common understanding and externalizing that understanding. It is, therefore, explicitly supporting communication, even though additional (verbal and non-verbal) forms of communication are expected. On the other hand, the emphasis of ShrEdit is on the document as an artefact; the establishment of common understanding is a side effect of collaborative editing.

The anti-CMC systems have been introduced here as an example to show that a CSCW system need not be a CMC system. The example of

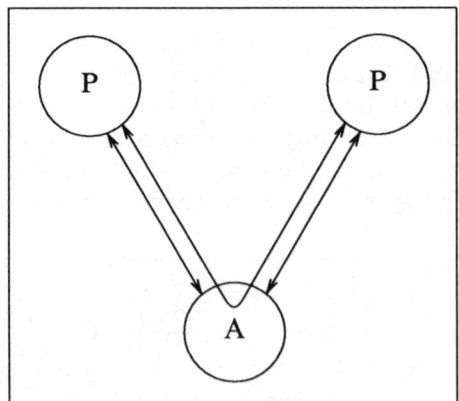

Fig. 2.10. Communication.

ShrEdit is one where the artefact of work is computerized. We look at general issues of the computerization (and not) of artefacts in Sections 2.4 and 2.5.

In Dix (1991), I examined the distinction between communication via messages as compared to using shared data. At first sight these categories appear to correspond to the direct communication between the participants (which is often message based) and through the shared application objects. This is, however, an oversimplification. Looking at direct communication, systems such as bulletin boards and electronic whiteboards act as direct interpersonal channels, but are a shared information source. On the other hand, the movement of another participant's cursor in a closely coupled shared editor clearly acts through the artefact, and yet may act as a message. This should, therefore, again be seen as a closely related but distinct categorization of communication.

2.4 Computerized Artefacts of Work

So, we have seen that the communication between the participants, about the work, may or may not be computerized. If we look down the diagram to the artefacts of work (Fig. 2.8), these too may or may not be computerized. This in itself is not a CSCW issue, but one about automation in general. However, if the artefacts are part of a cooperative work situation (as are most), then we must look at the impact of automation on cooperation.

We have already seen one example of an electronic artefact, the document in ShrEdit. Other examples come from virtually any area of computing: databases, spreadsheets, financial information, stock control, anywhere where the participants' focus of work is on the computer.

The final example, stock control, is interesting because it reminds us that, although the computerized artefacts are the local focus of work, they are often (probably always) a means to an end. If one looks deep enough there are physical artefacts of work behind the electronic ones. Stock control systems remind us by their name that they are for the efficient recording of physical stock. At some different level of analysis we may prefer to think of the stock control systems as a communication medium about the stock, or as medium of control of the stock.

Traditionally, cooperation has not been a major concern in the computerization of work objects. They were either centralized in a Data Processing (DP) department or, more recently, individual property. To the extent that they fitted within a cooperative framework, this was an externally imposed, organizational framework, and not an attribute of the systems themselves.

Systems can be built that recognize that they are part of a wider, group context:

- *Support for sharing:* it is now accepted that information systems, especially databases, are likely to be shared between various members of an organization. Both databases and network file systems, are built with a range of locking mechanisms designed to minimize the effects of this sharing. The intention is to stop damage to the data or confusion of the users from inadvertent sharing. They thus support sharing, but not cooperation.

- *Environments for cooperation:* a long-term aim is to look towards environments where the sharing of information is a focus for communication and cooperation. This means not having a conferencing window where one can communicate, but having communication as a seamless part of the electronic environment. In particular, we need support for deixis, within the electronic medium, with references from conversations to artefacts, and notes attached to the artefacts themselves.

We have started along this path in the design of a "group editing environment" (Miles et al. 1993). Attaching conversations to sections of a document makes the document a focus for cooperation as well as the outcome of the work. However, if similar mechanisms of cooperation are to become an integral part of all systems, the whole architectural design may have to change. Locking mechanisms introduced to deal with clashes between users must be rethought completely to support cooperation between users. These mechanisms must become pervasive if users are to be allowed to cooperate over their work, rather than periodically use special cooperative applications. By analogy, we would find it rather difficult if we were only allowed to talk to our colleagues in special "cooperation rooms" and not allowed to take in any of our normal working equipment and papers with us.

There are examples of systems that move towards the ideal of an environment for cooperation. The Quilt co-authoring tool (Leland et al. 1988) allows email messages to contain navigable references to documents, and automatically posts email upon certain changes to the database. Quilt, of course, addresses a specific task. However, more generic tools must cope with the fact that most applications are not group aware.

Despite the limitations imposed by existing single-user applications, some progress can be made. Some commercial email systems allow enclosures – the inclusion of arbitrary application objects such as spreadsheets or documents. These enclosures can be navigated by the recipient invoking the appropriate application. At the interface level, shared window systems such as SharedX (Gust 1988) allow users to use single-user applications cooperatively.

The computerization of artefacts of work may allow sharing of data where there was none before. This then becomes a focus for cooperation and, of course, allows communication through the artefact. For instance, a shared calendar system, such as that described by Beard et al. (1990), makes information that was previously isolated in individual diaries available to the group. Network based object linking such as *publish and subscribe* under Apple's System 7 operating system will allow and encourage sharing of data between different applications and users. Although these facilities are not really group aware at the moment, one can imagine them evolving to include specific group features, while third party applications gradually adapt. Within research systems DistEdit (Knister and Prakash 1990) is a good example of this approach, as it supplies an underlying group text object which existing editors can be relatively easily adapted to support.

2.5 Non-Computerized Artefacts

Despite the current emphasis away from traditional manufacturing industry towards financial, clerical and information jobs, the ultimate end of most of these is physical. We eat bread, not EPOS, and fly in aeroplanes, not flight control systems. As an information technologist (that's what my job title says I am), one is hardly used to moving outside the electronic and magnetic medium, and yet that is where real life is lived.

If the artefacts of work themselves are not computerized, how is the process of cooperative work supported by computer? Firstly, we may use electronic means to talk about the real world. For instance, a shipping company may use email (but more likely fax!) to discuss cargo details. With no added connection to the job at hand, this is CMC pure and simple. In addition, one may have electronic representations of the real world, as with the stock control system. But, as we noted previously, if the focus of work is the stock itself, then the stock control system begins to become a means of communication. It does differ from the simple email system in that it is a medium of communication that directly supports the task. That is, it is an embodiment of understanding of the task.

Moving on from the communication about and understanding of the artefact, we have two more candidates for computerization: the communication with the artefacts (control and feedback) and deixis (reference to the artefacts). We will look at these below. However, to some extent, the stock control system can be said to support deixis, as it creates an electronic counterpart of the physical artefact, which can then be used as a focus for communication about the artefact.

2.5.1 Prosthesis

Extending the meaning of the word, I use prosthesis to mean the automation (whether mechanical or electronic) of the control of the artefacts of work. Blurring the computerization/mechanization distinction somewhat, we can look at various examples of prosthesis. The forklift truck is a good example. Rather than lift boxes directly, the driver lifts them indirectly using the truck. For a slightly more high-tech example, there are many situations, such as handling radioactive material or working on the sea bed, where it is dangerous or impossible to work directly. Often mechanical arms are used, where a mechanical arm in the dangerous environment follows the movements of a control arm moved by the operator.

These aids are, of course, very necessary, but they are clearly not the same as directly handling the objects. In particular, there is a loss of feedback and feedthrough:

- *Feedback:* the operators rarely have any tactile feedback of their actions. Instead, they must rely on visual feedback. In remote situations, even the visual contact is mediated by television cameras, which remove many of the clues (e.g. stereo vision) of direct visual contact. This in itself is a problem for individual operator control of the environment. In this respect, it is likely to be recognized and some attention paid to it.

- *Feedthrough:* as well as experiencing the effects of our own actions, we experience the effects of others' actions on the environment. If two users cooperate using prostheses, then in addition to their individual feedback being reduced, they will also lose the feedthrough through the artefact. That is, their ability to communicate through the artefact is reduced. This effect is much less likely to be recognized than simple loss of feedback.

Compare two people moving an object, say a piano, by hand with the same people moving it with the aid of two (small) forklift trucks. The tasks will be very different for many reasons: the piano is heavy, the forklifts do not have many degrees of freedom. However, if you listen to the carriers other differences become apparent. In the manual case, much of the time you hear very little (except grunts). As they manoeuvre the piano round corners, one of them (probably the one in front) may tip it and the other, feeling the movement, will move in concert. With the forklift trucks (over the roar of the engines), the carriers tell each other their intentions, and perhaps rely more on visual feedback as well. This is an oversimplification: in both cases they would talk about strategic decisions, such as "shall we tip it on end to go through the door?". The difference is most apparent at the tactical level of minor movements.

In the above example, we saw the principal effect of replacing direct control with prosthesis. Communication *through* the artefact was replaced by communication *about* the artefact.

2.5.2 Implications for Design

Realizing that prostheses may reduce feedthrough can guide us in our design of systems where the control of artefacts, or the artefacts themselves, is computerized. For an example, compare a traditional filing cabinet containing paper files with the equivalent system on database. This is an example where the whole artefact is automated; however, some of the most important points are due to the effect of prosthesis.

Consider first the original paper system. Imagine that you go to the filing cabinet to retrieve a file, and discover that it is missing. Depending on the urgency, you may either leave it until later, or look for the file on a colleague's desk. In either case you will have obtained useful information: in the former, that someone else had an interest in the same file; in the latter, who that person was. In addition, in the latter case, you would have an opportunity to discuss the mutual interest in the record. In both cases, the physical nature of the record acted as a communication mechanism registering interest about the particular record. Even if the record were not in use, a paper record lends itself to the addition of *ad hoc* comments as a communication between different users of the record.[2] Also, the very act of going to a central filing cabinet may form the locus for less directed, perhaps social, communication.

If these informal channels of communication are recognized by the organization, they may be formalized and official mechanisms introduced for recording interest and relevant information. However, it has been repeatedly noticed that, however well such formalization is done, the informal contacts within an organization are crucial to its running. Indeed, the formalization of such channels may stifle the very informal communication it is meant to capture. With the trend towards flatter management structures, this factor can only increase in importance.

The equivalent database system loses these informal channels of communication almost entirely. Locking mechanisms exist, but, as we have previously noted, these are aimed at preventing the problems of users concurrently accessing data, rather than treating this as an opportunity for cooperation. They do at least give some indication (as did the empty filing cabinet) that someone else is interested. But, whereas with paper records one might expect the record to be out of the filing cabinet for several hours or even days, the typical database transaction will take minutes or seconds to complete, so the likelihood of users noticing concurrent access is minimal. Furthermore, multiple readers of files are not usually locked, and thus users concurrently referencing the same file will be unaware of one another's interest. Note how this is a result of loss of feedthrough. In the paper case the actions of one user upon the file (removing it to read or update) had an effect upon the other users. The electronic database has removed this feedthrough, and thus the resulting communication through the artefact.

Of course, one usually regards the lack of a wanted file as a problem for the users. Thus database systems attempt to give the illusion that there is only one user. The very success of this illusion is the problem from a cooperative work standpoint. The challenge for the designer of such a system is how to maintain the advantages of the electronic database, but at the same time provide some replacement for the informal channels of communication focused on the file as an artefact. For instance, you could imagine a system whereby you brought files that you were interested in from the database onto your (electronic) desktop. The file would also remain in the database but with an indication for subsequent users that you were accessing it. As in the group editing environment, conversation areas could be associated with individual files. In line with our previous comments, one would hope that such a mechanism would be integrated with the whole communication and cooperation environment.

A similar story could be told about process control systems. In a manually controlled plant, as you go to operate a valve you notice the state of other bits of equipment, and perhaps talk to other workers who are nearby. Special circumstances are obvious, such as other workers engaged in maintenance. The electronic control room divorces the worker from this contact. Feedback is supplied by sensors, and indications of maintenance by written reports. Somehow, this lacks the immediacy of physical presence, and the paucity of feedback is recognized as a problem. Improved interfaces are suggested as solutions (including aspects of virtual reality) and some plants have included microphones at strategic points to capitalize on the important role of aural feedback.

These attempts to improve feedback for the individual operator may have positive effects on the feedthrough between operators. However, the control system designer should be making explicit provision for communication to replace that lost by the introduction of electronic prosthesis. For example, this may suggest the redundant replication of information for different operators, so that they have indications of one another's activities – even where these are not obviously relevant.

Indeed, there may be an opportunity for improving the communication through the artefact compared to the manual situation. Such plants are by their nature complex. Manipulating controls in one part of the plant may have effects in a distant area. Also, most of the activity is inside sealed tanks and pipes, and one is aware of this only indirectly via dials and sensors. The way to control the pressure in a tank, say, may be via a valve positioned in another area. The operator would need to read the pressure dial on the tank, go to the valve, adjust it and then return to obtain the new reading. The process is further complicated by the various delays in pipes and stabilizing of reactions. Thus, the feedthrough (and feedback) in such a plant may already be poor. An electronic control room could help by presenting both physical and logical views of the plant. Representation of copresence (as suggested for the database) could be used to initiate conversation between operators focused on logically connected areas.

In both examples – the database and process control – potential solutions have been posed for the loss of feedthrough introduced by prosthesis. However, the particular solutions are not as important as the general design issue of loss of communication through the artefact, and how we can compensate for its loss.

2.5.3 Success Story: Bar Codes

So having seen how the introduction of prostheses can cause problems for cooperation, it is time for a more positive slant, in fact, a CSCW success story – bar codes. Now, I think it fair to say that bar codes are rarely regarded as an aspect of CSCW. However, they form a focus for cooperation between many workers.

If one considers the production, distribution and sale of goods, vast numbers of workers are involved. Bar codes form an important locus for much of this activity. If we begin at a supermarket chain, goods are scanned on the shelves and as they pass through the tills. This information is used to help in the restocking of shelves from the store room and for stock control within the local store. Furthermore, the resulting information is used centrally by the chain's management to control shipping of stock to different stores and in order to develop suitable purchase policies. Information flows the other way too, as bar codes are used to communicate pricing information to the tills.

The level of international cooperation in the production of bar codes is amazing, especially when compared with other computer standardization. A bar code can identify the country, producer and product line. It can then be used to refer to the product, from its manufacture or packing in a factory, right through to the till where it leaves the marketing system.

The level of cooperative activity is perhaps rather diffuse compared to, say, shared editing, but the sheer scale more than compensates for this. Bar codes should surely be seen as an important case study in CSCW.

Where exactly do bar codes fit into the CSCW framework? The important artefacts of work are physical – the goods and products. However, their usefulness is greatest when many of the soft artefacts – stock control systems, sales and purchase ledgers etc. – are computerized. The bar code is a form of deixis relating the physical artefacts and the logical artefacts which describe them. Arguably, this deixis arc is the most important in the CSCW framework, because it relates the world of work to the world of communication – it allows us to talk about the things with which we are working.

2.6 Summary

We began by looking at various elements of a general cooperative work situation. This framework has enabled us to examine specific areas for computer support and place existing systems by what aspects of the framework they cover. In particular, we have seen how CMC should be seen as just one element in a cooperative work situation, and as an element that should be integrated into a general "environment for cooperation". We have discussed the importance of communication through the artefact and seen how this can be lost by automated prostheses with their loss of feedthrough. Finally, we saw how bar codes could be regarded as an important example of CSCW in that they aid deixis.

The general message is that systems to support cooperative work should take a larger view of cooperation, and that systems not specifically designed to support cooperation should consider their effects on cooperative work.

If we look at the term "computer supported cooperative work", we see that work comes at the end. The take-home message is that work should be at the centre of CSCW.

Acknowledgements   The author is funded by SERC Advanced Fellowship B/89/ITA/220. The author also wishes to thank his colleagues on the "conferencer" project and all those who have commented on previous drafts and oral presentations of this work.

Notes

1 I'm not sure where politics fits into this spectrum: surely not under intellectual labour? Perhaps entertainment?
2 In Dix (1990b) I discuss the importance of such annotations in ensuring the correct use of personal information.

Chapter 3

Capturing Interactions: Requirements for CSCW

D. Murray and B. Hewitt

This chapter is concerned with the details of capturing and analysing requirements for Computer Supported Cooperative Work (CSCW) systems. Technological factors and the increasing viability of communication networks have led to the design and implementation of products ranging from schedulers and diary managers through email and conferencing systems to the provision of shared workspaces and techniques for supporting synchronous collaboration in writing and meetings. We assess why requirements capture and analysis for CSCW systems differs from that for more traditional Information Technology (IT) systems and discuss how to gather data through observational and related studies, debating where and how such techniques could fit into the life-cycle model of software engineering and design. We highlight the issues involved in understanding both cooperative and conflicting patterns of communication between those engaged in collaborative activities, and show how we are developing a methodology to define more clearly the relationship between work contexts and types of computer support for group working. We summarize some of our investigative work into the organizational contexts in which such systems might be used, focusing on interaction based studies of office settings, and present a case study of a set of "knowledge workers" who manipulate information. We investigate methods of translating their tacit knowledge into requirements statements, assessing views of the organization through the participants' eyes as contrasted with more formal views of the organization as a business.

3.1 Design Issues for CSCW

Many researchers have attempted to identify just what is meant by CSCW. Greenberg (1991) defines it as a scientific discipline that motivates and validates groupware design, and defines groupware as products specifically designed to assist groups of people working together. Kuutti (1991a) sees CSCW as work by multiple active subjects sharing a common objective and supported by information technology. Engelbart and Lehtman (1988) regard CSCW as the study and development of systems to encourage organizational collaboration. Behind all the definitions lies a concern with supporting individuals who share resources to work collaboratively together to some common end. We believe that an additional set of user requirements based on the social nature of work must be captured and analysed appropriately for the design process to be effective.

Requirements Capture and Analysis (RCA) is a broad term covering the mechanisms of investigating and interpreting activities undertaken in office or work situations to support technological change for work activities. Organizations can be viewed from many perspectives: for example, as static, normative and well-structured entities with predefined sequences of action and hierarchical structures, or as entities whose function is dynamically constructed and interpreted by those who work in them. RCA techniques have traditionally not included investigation of such aspects of the social world, and we propose that the technique of participant observation is useful as a means of achieving this. Analysis of work settings through observation and ethnographic analysis leads to a realization of the real-life experience of day-to-day work activities that may not be amenable to other more structured forms of analysis and which gives insight into what users of CSCW system need to make their work effective.

One of the most important considerations for any type of RCA is simply where to begin and where to end. If data gathered at the beginning of the process is insufficient or inadequate, then, however good the analysis method, the resulting specification will be insufficient and possibly unworkable. The specification and design of computer or IT systems begins with acquisition of relevant data from many different sources, and proceeds by a process of integration, distilling and transforming this data in stages to achieve a final specification. DeMarco (1978) defines systems analysis as the study of some business area or application, the end product of which is a document containing a detailed specification of a new system, the document being a more or less formal model of system functionality. Office based computer systems are traditionally designed to meet organizationally imposed criteria (such as automating manual processes, providing increased functionality, adhering to systems standardization policies or promoting efficiency), and most general systems analysis methodologies follow a data driven approach, where the role of the user is not often explicitly identified. Some of the methodologies of modern systems analysis practice do consider work settings and user needs, preferences and requirements, and do consult users throughout at least part of the design process, when it is recognized that such user input is necessary. Nevertheless, the prime emphasis remains on what the system to be designed will actually do and how the processes individuals engage in will be automated.

Since requirements analysis focuses on individual activities, and divides these into distinct tasks that pass information between processes, problems with data collection can be caused by being unclear as to the data to collect, the level of detail it should be collected at, and how to ensure important information is not being overlooked. Statements such as, "First, collect your data . . ." (Yourdon 1989) and, "Starting from the terms of reference . . ." (SSADM 1986) tend to appear as guidance to analysts but specific collection methods or skills are not detailed. Because of differing emphases and starting points, different data collection methods will tend to yield different requirements. In general, the design phase is concerned with how to build one or more computer systems with appropriate functionality and usability, but the focus on system functionality rather than with those who are to use it is changing. Methodologies such as Ethics (Mumford 1983a), ORDIT (Harker et al. 1991), Multiparty Specification (Finkelstein and Fuks 1989) and CORE (Mullery 1979) have developed mechanisms for modelling users. Human–Computer Interaction (HCI) and task analysis support users as individuals but CSCW systems are primarily concerned with support for collaboration, communication and coordination between and within groups of individuals.

In CSCW applications, it is important to note that users interact with others *through* the system as well as *with* the system. We contend that information about the environment shared by a group working together should be known by all users, to foster a shared awareness and to allow users to monitor each other's work. Investigations of how groups of co-workers achieve this in non-computerized settings will assist in the design of shared applications and will influence the interface paradigms chosen for the final applications. Users who work together, and those targeted by future CSCW systems, operate within a social medium, and the social world is a complex one, consisting of explicit and implicit roles, collaboration, conflict and negotiation. Although the design emphasis moves from the individual to the needs of a cooperating social group, members still retain their individuality and are likely to have at least some conflicting goals within an overall collaborative framework. We need to know and understand how users interact both as individuals and as group members and to identify the knowledge they have of the way in which procedures are carried out. Much of this information is tacit, so data capture techniques must look beyond explicitly documented tasks, roles and jobs. The question that we face is: how can informal interactions be both captured and analysed?

If effective CSCW applications and systems are to be designed then we must aim at capturing elements of the social world of work, looking outside tasks and set procedures at what is happening, both in the environment and between individuals. We suggest that social systems and individual behaviour within groups are complex, and that a requirements analysis methodology must be able to reduce complexity to a manageable form, while retaining critical features, and able to illuminate those features common to many different social systems. By concentrating only on methods of data collection that identify activities, tasks and the processes linking them, aspects of the social structure of an organization may be ignored. Since the CSCW systems we envisage are likely to support multiple copresent users, analysing only tasks and individuals in isolation does not sufficiently reflect what we take the real requirements to be.

3.1.1 The Life-Cycle Framework

The traditional way of addressing the specification and design of computer systems is to make use of the software life-cycle model. Many variants of the basic iterative "waterfall model" exist: that illustrated in Fig. 3.1 is a generalized version, not tied to any one specific analysis methodology, although the model has been adapted to meet the needs of many different systems analysis techniques. There are several stages to all life-cycle models: requirements definition, analysis, specification, logical design and physical design form one common theme. In an iterative approach the design phase can be modified by different levels of analysis detail: by both summative and formative evaluations, by user participation in a user-centred design framework or by building and testing prototypes.

The basic question is how to analyse and model the requirements of a CSCW system and then how to achieve integration with the life-cycle framework. Although Fig. 3.1 looks as though it is purely a sequential model, this is not the intention. It shows the point at which participant observation and analysis could usefully have an impact. Fig. 3.2 shows an expansion of the requirements analysis stage that identifies how ethnographic modelling can inform the specification phase. Sited within

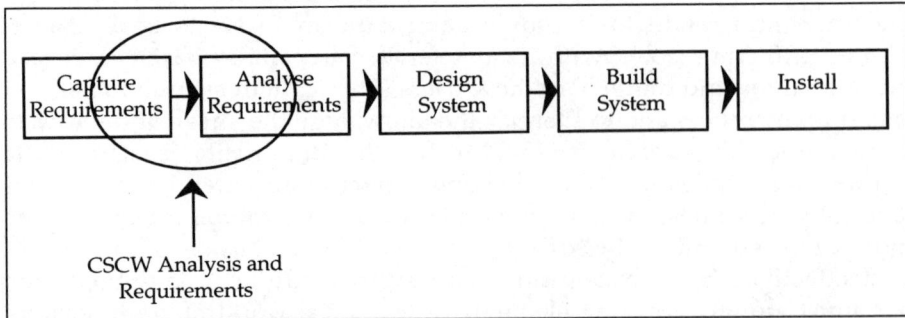

Fig. 3.1. A systems life-cycle model.

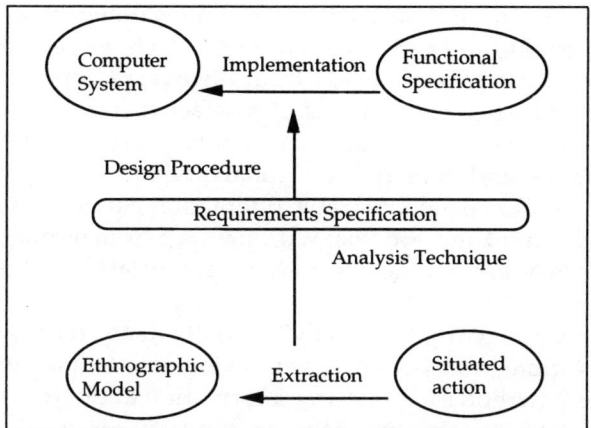

Fig. 3.2. Ethnographically informed requirements specification.

the real-life world of work and taking into account the activities and situated learning (Lave and Wenger 1991; Suchman 1987) that underlie a view of work in practice, the elements that can be extracted and noted by an ethnographic perspective are refined into a "model" of real-world actions. A suitable analysis technique that marries such observations and the type of data (Bentley et al. 1992) that can be collected can then be chosen to advance the requirements specification and implementation phases.

3.2 Ethnographic Study of Office Work

Section 3.3 describes a case study that employed ethnographic observation to determine some essential features of collaborative work (such as a shared system of meanings and the mechanisms of forming coalitions). We carried out studies in real offices and observed employees in the process of carrying out their jobs. As part of the rationale for our work, we felt that one of the major requirements of this type of ethnographic study is to document the basic structure and *raison d'être* of the organizational activity being investigated. We started the process of finding sites for study by deciding that small groups working towards production of some artefact to specific, relatively short, time scales would give a good indication of what some knowledge workers do. We felt that sufficient information about a small set of processes could be achieved by detailed data analysis in an intensive study, together with additional interviewing and the running of focused discussion groups. The task to be undertaken by the knowledge workers was more difficult to determine: it could not be merely repetitive in the sense of a production line, although viewed at a higher, more process-orientated level, the actual activity could be repetitive (e.g. as in the production of a newsletter that can have a generalized production procedure, although each issue will consist of a different set of activities, chosen from an overall repertoire). Finally, a process of producing certain types of artefact that adhered to a format and was ruled by a set of guidelines or quality procedures was identified as being a suitable candidate. An additional obvious feature of a study site was that there should be demonstrable interaction between disparate parts and between different individuals, with passing of material (in whatever form) from one to another, together with the potential for technology based group working.

Observing people acting "normally" in their usual settings (as in participant observation), and perhaps even taking a small part in their work, is not a common method for gathering information about the requirements of a computer system in the software industry. It is a method that originated in studies by anthropologists of remote cultures, developing a set of techniques that involve non-intrusive *in situ* observations. Only a few researchers have investigated real-life work situations in a modern office or operations contexts (Anderson and Sharrock 1992; Bentley et al. 1992; Button 1992; Dubinskas 1988; Harper et al. 1989; Heath and Luff 1990; Hughes et al. 1992a, b; Kling and Scacci 1982; Kraut et al. 1991; Linde 1990; Nardi and Miller 1990; Reder and Schwab 1990; Rogers 1992). The technique, however, has disadvantages as well as advantages: it generates huge volumes of data that make for difficulties in analysis; analysis methods are not well codified; what one observes is not under the researcher's direct control; important but rare events (like disasters) may not be observed at all; and guidelines on ways of carrying out such work are seemingly *ad hoc*.

The advantages are that a detailed understanding of the actual social organization of the work setting (not just what it is supposed to be like), detailed knowledge of what data people actually use in their jobs and where they obtain it (not just what they are supposed to know), and knowledge about the procedures that are actually carried out (not just the way things are supposed to work) can be obtained through close observation. Participant observation provides the "experience of moving from outside to within the organisation" (Woolgar 1990), from being an external observer to one intimately involved with the production of work and able to make assessments from a different perspective than more usual analyses. *In situ* observation allows social, cultural and other factors to be directly recorded and the subsequent analysis to be freed from retrospective reconstruction. It also behoves the observer to pursue "analytic scepticism about claims and knowledge" (Woolgar 1990). It has been said that "work" is socially organized and ethnography functions within this context: situated judgements are made, together with "structures of relevance reproduced as a pattern" (Hughes et al. 1992b). Suchman (1991a) regards technologies as instances of material practice and sees the ethnographic approach as informing the reading of a scene in a real-world technological context. She identifies participation structures that can provide accountability of actions, and highlights as an aspect of investigation the manner in which situated learning and the acquisition of competence occurs. A pervasive theme is normative rules and actions leading to observable rules, these coming into existence originally as a communicative resource for the members of the society being studied. Hughes et al. (1992b) asks, "In what form do you require the society to be represented in order to extract, isolate or verify the source of analysis?". We believe that the ethnographic model or representation of the world that can be derived (see Fig. 3.2) is just such a means of representing relevant aspects of social context to be used in the analysis.

In representing workplace social organization for the design of collaborative systems we must illuminate underlying patterns of interaction and demonstrate that knowledge to designers. CSCW systems will only be effective if they support actual work practices as they are constructed by participants and not just the officially sanctioned and documented ones. One intended outcome of the work we are engaged in is to clarify the requirements capture procedure in such situations and to derive recommendations for the future.

3.3 Case Study of a Technical Publications Unit

Field studies of two sections within larger organizations have been carried out: the first is a technical writing and authoring group, the second, a graphic design studio. Both adhere to the study requirements identified in Section 3.2. Data from the former, a Technical Publications Unit (TPU), is more comprehensive at this stage, and this is the site we report in detail here.

The TPU is part of a large UK company and was visited twice prior to a field study visit, the objectives being to identify the organizational and task aspects of work carried out by technical authors and editors. The TPU comprises a number of groups specializing in providing technical authoring services for different market segments. Initially, two of the four work groups were observed, to get a better "feel" for what the unit as a whole did and to determine which group might be best observed in more detail. For the study itself, five team members from one of these project groups were observed in the process of carrying out their daily work. Staff were interviewed, and material on their general activities and projects was collected. Observation, note taking, schematics, audio tape recordings of interactions and photographing of locations and collaborations were followed by structured interviewing of the individuals in the group. Tape transcripts and field notes were made, and documents and examples of standard forms used by staff were collected. It was not possible to follow up with focused discussion groups, as originally planned, because of time constraints within the organization itself.

Beforehand, some thought was given to what features of collaborative work were being sought. Besides identifying typical activities, interaction episodes and fixed versus spontaneous procedures, we expected to collect data on the physical constraints in the work environment, individual workspace organization and the way in which physical documents progress by means of document histories and differing viewpoints by those involved in their production. We also expected that the collection of visual records would assist in analysing and informing the process of historical justification of actions. We believe that data on socially constructed activities of the following type could be collected and that instances of such activities could provide an insight into the work activity and be identified in the subsequent analysis:

- Traces or a history of passage left behind in the physical world by a document or specific activity, setting up cues that can be read by participants but not readily explained or easily discerned.

- Communication codes that demonstrate shared interpretations, not only of language and jargon, but of actions such as the siting of artefacts to indicate the relative importance.

- "Snapshots" of communication episodes which might otherwise be missed because of brevity, location (in passing, in the corridor) or because they are embedded within another activity.

- An awareness of the implied procedures that underpin the way in which work is carried out and that allow the use of shared information resources such as filing systems (the knowledge of how it is organized, why an item is placed "just there", and where to find other items). Such information is usually difficult to express but must be learned by novices (and not just by explanation, but also by demonstration and observation).

- Tacit knowledge, which, like expert knowledge, is difficult to quantify, describe and identify objectively but which gives a "feel" for the work, for anticipating what is to come next, for allocating time and resources, and for personal and implicit group organization.

- Social organization observed *in situ*, and which may differ substantially from the "official" expectations drawn from job descriptions and organization charts.

While this is not an exhaustive list, and others have identified their own requirements (Bannon and Schmidt 1989), it provided a starting point, with some guidance on which documents to collect and how to limit fruitless attempts to watch everything that was happening in a small project group. Such bounding seems to be necessary when looking for specific traces of activity and indications of communication episodes.

3.3.1 Organizational Description

The comments below come from ethnographic field notes and serve as an introduction both to the work that these technical authors and editors undertake and to the social and physical environment in which it takes place.

The parent company is a large national one with sites in various parts of the country. The TPU is the company's own internal production facility for technical documentation, providing authoring and writing of manuals and documentation for both hardware and software. The TPU is a relatively small group in the technical publishing world, with about half of its staff providing technical authoring services, the remainder providing support services, keyboarding and editing. Many of its customers are long-term clients, who return for updating of previous jobs (re-editing and amendment of existing material) or who initiate new jobs. The specific services the TPU offers are: technical authorship and editing; project management of all aspects of technical publishing; creative design; desktop publishing (DTP); electronically produced graphics; illustration; typography and typesetting design and specification; print design and specification; advice on corporate identity and image; naive user testing and video recording. They produce user and engineering guides, *aide memoire* cards, quick reference guides, reference handbooks and product manuals.

Staff are organized hierarchically under a manager and deputy manager. There are three support staff for the whole unit. Only the manager has a personal secretary. There are four project teams, all containing team leaders and deputies and each working in distinct areas. Each team is a set of five specialists under the management of a team leader, who assigns task leaders and determines who will process each job. A team leader is responsible for a set of projects and a number of staff, reporting to the unit managers. Three staff are project managers, responsible for a particular technical area. Project managers and team leaders are also themselves technical authors. There are nine technical authors and four junior staff, designated as technical editors and keyboarders/editors. The assignment of tasks to individuals is variable: project managers tend to work on the same technical area or large project over a long time. Influenced by current resources and work activities, other editing and authoring jobs are allocated to authors within each team depending on what stage the job was at when it was originally brought into the unit (i.e. whether it is new text to be written, or amendments to existing text, or styling and document production). Such tasks may range from simple styling of electronic text, to rewriting a user's text from a paper copy, to creating a set of manuals for a new product. All undertake activities such as "proofing", which is the process of document checking for typographical errors, inconsistencies and adherence to style. Although the tasks of both groups (authors and editors) appear similar, the staff make distinctions among themselves that help to sustain their professional identity. Some activities and job allocations are dependent upon age and experience and some on whether the staff are permanent or contract staff. The three general categories they distinguish are:

- *Technical authoring:* writing from an engineering specification.
- *Technical writing:* producing documents from existing text.
- *Editing:* "styling", that is, producing and editing a document to fit the "house style", using Word Processing (WP) or DTP systems to make the user's text fit into agreed formats.

The organization has a set of quality procedures, with specific guidelines being laid out for members of the TPU to adhere to (e.g. the procedure to be followed when a new job is tendered, or the archiving strategies). This is to ensure a level of consistency among the activities of the whole unit and to present a coherent interface to clients and customers. Within this structure, the technical authors and writers have two main tasks: "to size the job", write and "almost style" a document, or to provide technical editing together with DTP. Editors and keyboarders take on the styling activities, producing the final versions of documents. These activities take up almost all of the authors' time, the remainder being occupied by liaison and communication episodes, client briefings and general paperwork. The unit also employs a varying number of contractors for specialist typesetting and production work or for tasks such as styling a document from a client's text. Such contractors may be of three types: long-term contractors who work in specific job areas over a time; short-term replacement staff; and external contractors for specific activities. Long-term contractors are included within the staff numbers listed above: they mainly comprise editors, keyboarders and authors.

3.3.2 Authors' Views on their Work

In discussion with both authors and the manager of the unit, it was stressed that all staff, permanent or not, need very good interpersonal skills besides obvious writing and production capabilities because of their close liaison with clients. In keeping with the professional distinctions alluded to above, technical authors must also have an appreciation of engineering or computer processes, because much of their work is in interpreting both clients' and end users' needs. Below are quotations elicited from authors on how they view the work they undertake, on their identification of some of the constraints under which they work, and on what they themselves regard as the skills and qualities needed to carry out their work effectively. These quotations provide "cameo" insights into the way in which they think about clients, customers and their own professional attitude to their "trade". Such comments indicate that they see themselves as "professionals", with a specific set of skills and requirements, forming a distinct social community within the company but linked by profession to other technical publication units in similar technology based organizations, as evinced by gossip with contractors and other authors.

TPU management see their unit's function as being, "custodians of the external style of the Company". A technical author states that he needs, "a technical background for his work and has to have engineering knowledge and skills". The individual who produces manuals for both documentation and training purposes confirms that they are used in two ways during the overall training process: "The training loop works two ways: manuals are used as training material (alpha trial), and as beta trial at implementation". A technical author says, "There is a difference in the person paying for the documentation from the end user of that documentation. This is most important. It [the process] depends on how 'professional' you want to be. What is important is quality control". Technical authors state, with feeling, "Customers have a tendency to change things which an author has written". The technical authors have "design authority" and "ownership" (for the manual and its "look and feel", not for the technical content). They additionally talk about the "authoring" versus the "run" mode and state that, "There is often a difference between the software version of a product and the manual that is being written: the one lags behind the other and changes made to the software are not always told to the authors, are undocumented and do not get into the final version of the manual".

3.3.3 Life History of a Job

There are a number of mechanisms for producing a manual or technical document. The following paragraphs illustrate the life history of one such job. It is a composite description of a longer term process, but all stages were observed (albeit being undertaken by different authors) during the study itself. It is important to note that technical authors continually stress that technical knowledge and a basic understanding of the underlying technology are necessary to write good user guides and documentation.

One author in the team has responsibility for producing documentation both for technical reference by maintenance engineers and as training manuals for new engineering staff. This is his only activity. He usually has the actual equipment he is working on scattered around the floor and under nearby desks, together with test equipment. When he was observed at the beginning of the study, he was working on two new manuals, with a further one in the pipeline and another that he termed a "tester" for a future piece of hardware. When working on the creation of a new manual for a new product, he follows a fairly set procedure. The equipment itself is sent to him from the engineering section of the company. He may or may not recognize it as being similar to a model he has worked on before. He describes the type of equipment he works on as "essentially pieces of hardware with some software" and spends much of his time testing and examining the equipment. When he receives an item of equipment, after opening the package and inspecting the written documents and labels that arrive with it, he first installs it, then tests it to see "how it works". At this stage, he makes notes on the PC or on paper, but then claims that he rejects these as being of "no further use" in producing the documentation itself, perhaps because the equipment is broadly similar to what he has been working on for a number of years and each piece has only minor modifications. If a manual has to be written from scratch, standard company practice is to use an alpha test site for initial testing of the first prototypes. He also keeps a photographic record as the equipment is being dismantled (he takes his own or uses those provided by the manufacturer), or speaks into a Dictaphone, or occasionally uses a video at test sites. The photographs can be used by illustrators to produce diagrams for the final manuals, or to record disassembly for comparison with other pieces of similar equipment.

If text for a new manual exists, it may arrive in a number of ways: in disk format (which may then have to be converted), as a user's written or typed text (which is then keyboarded into computer format), as a user's notes (which must then be expanded and written), or as an existing manual (which then has to be changed). When working on the editing of existing manuals the author takes a printout of the computer file and then manually marks it up. A variety of different mark-up techniques are used, usually chosen by individual preference. The include the use of red dots (in pen) at certain sections of the text, underlining and crossing out, rewriting of text, insertion of new pages or stuck-on notes, or taking notes on separate sheets. If a new manual is required, the text is written by him but this process was not directly observed. The manual is printed out as a first draft and sent to the user or client for inspection and comments after the author's own proofing.

The next stage is a validation phase, consolidating and resolving comments made at a meeting with the client. Sometimes clients have a tendency to change already written text: this often provokes an adverse reaction from authors. The process of producing drafts until a final version is reached can be reiterated a number of times, but, in practice, very few iterations occur because of time and costing constraints and because of the skills of the staff. Once an acceptable draft has been achieved, styling and text manipulation is passed on to the keyboarders or editors. The author observed liaised very closely with the design studio for the production and selection of appropriate diagrams and illustrative material but this is not mandatory. The final selection of illustrations was carried out by him in a "pasting" process when he selected photographs to fit specific captions and sections in the manual. When a final version is agreed with the client, the document is finally styled and the process of printing, copying and binding takes place.

There are a number of structures and strategies for documenting the production stages of a draft manual, authorizing passing of control of the disk file and paper copies, maintaining records of what changes have been made and agreed, and backup and storage of the final copy. Most of these rely on the existence of the "job file", a folder (coloured in different shades) holding a record of all written communication and transactions on a specific job. The outside of the file has a movement record that shows who has been in possession of the file. When a job is in process, it is stored in the filing cabinet with other active jobs; when complete, it is filed as a closed job.

3.3.4 Job Conditions

Besides drawing a picture of what it is that technical authors do, we can identify some of the conditions under which they work and how this affects the way in which tasks are carried out.

Resources

The computer resources used in the TPU are PCs and the Ventura DTP system, together with laser writers and printers. A photocopier and a fax machine, to which everyone has access, are sited in the shared resource area. Other resources are paper-orientated: job files, stationery, standard forms, or computer files that are used to produce standard letters and quotations. An "information centre" contains a record of past jobs, sample layouts, company style documents and the like. Project groups have filing cabinets near their own workspace areas. In the filing cupboard used by the team, files in the centre are live jobs and those in the cabinet are closed. There is storage space for individual in-trays, which are stored there at the end of each day or when someone is absent. Staff must use the official forms provided in the company style (see following paragraph) and must adhere to the company's "clear desk" policy: this does not allow any material to be left on desks at the end of a working day. All work in progress must be locked away, so any cues given by the physical layout of papers on desks and positioning for immediacy are necessarily lost at the end of each day. Although authors may employ such cues during their daily work, they must collect all paperwork together and file it in a single tray before going home. Company policy demands that all computers are also switched off to prevent unauthorized viewing of screens and malicious reading of data.

Corporate Style

The corporate style is the "image" of the company as presented to the outside world, personified by the logo and colours. This is instantiated in the documents produced by the TPU, and written guidelines for the precise format to be adhered to have been produced in some detail. A new corporate style has just been designed and is a matter of some importance because the company is attempting to bring it to bear on all products and services, in conjunction with the concept of "quality". The definitive house style has not yet been finalized. The TPU continue to use the style they themselves developed and are currently trying to fit all new and previous work (in different formats) into the current style. This has constraints on the authors, especially when the style to be used is in such a transition phase, but may allow them to operate more efficiently when it is finalized since it gives distinct parameters for the way in which text must be laid out and provides a shared notation for identifying document versions and categories. The notation is also used for identifying past jobs, as a form of archival shorthand.

Physical Layout

The office space is open plan, divided by screens to make up a number of work group areas: filing cupboards are used as room dividers (Fig. 3.3). There are only two enclosed spaces: the manager's office and the resource area (the door to which is always left open). The situation appears a little cramped but the overall effect is tidy and harmonious. Chairs are on castors to facilitate rapid movement from one desk to another. Everyone in the unit has a telephone, a computer and keyboard and a desk of their own. Each desk has personal memorabilia on it, a PC, a set of three linked in-trays, a small overhead open cupboard attached to the partitions and three desk drawers underneath.

In the team being studied, four people face divider screens, which means that they have their backs to each other (Fig. 3.4). They are the team leader, his deputy, a project leader and a keyboarder. The fifth individual is a technical author, whose desk is on the other side of one of the partitions. This group has two shared printers/laser writers that are connected to the computers and a switch box (also switched from another team's machines). They are in such close proximity that muttered comments and telephone conversations can be overheard easily, but the layout

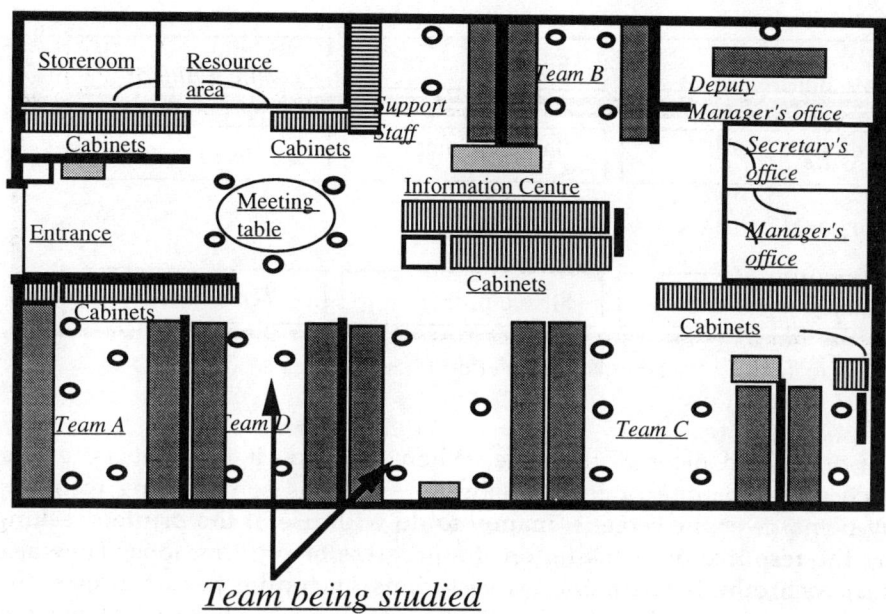

Team being studied

Fig. 3.3. Layout of the office area.

may give them some feeling of personal space and privacy. Monitoring of what is happening to the other members of the group (whether they are at their desks, in a meeting, on the telephone, absent elsewhere in the unit or outside) is continual. When wishing to talk to another author, they either call out or move their chair to the other's desk. One obvious constraint is that the author who works on equipment manuals on the other side of the partition is physically closer to (though separate from) another group, but this does allow him space to spread his equipment around without impinging on the others and, incidentally, to have access to his own coffee-making facilities. He is the one who works least with the others in the team but, if need be, he can simply walk around the partition. The sightlines for the other four and their opportunities to view what the others are working on are good. The keyboarder does most work for the project leader and they share the same row of desks. The team leader and his deputy do likewise. He is furthest away from the filing system but is also furthest away from the distractions of passers-by. Since he is the one who has most access to the confidential Management Information System and there are no screen savers, this is, perhaps, by design.

Atmosphere and Noise Levels

Some individuals, when on the telephone, can be heard from almost everywhere in the room but the general noise level is low and voices

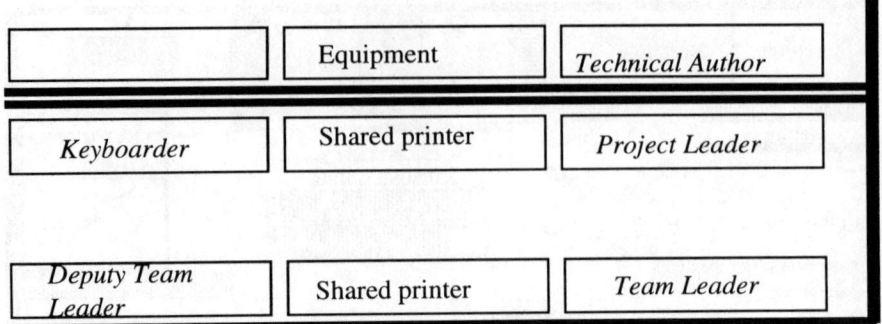

Fig. 3.4. Layout of the team's working area.

are not raised most of the time. When they are, it is for social events such as lunch time or informal breaks. There is some calling to others by name, over the screens, mainly to do with use of the printers, asking for the resource or checking on the progress of printing jobs. They also hear each other's telephone conversations, including personal ones, but seem to have developed a facility for ignoring or filtering out what is not essential. This general chit-chat goes on throughout the day, but in very brief episodes, and does not seem to be disturbing. Rather, it fosters the sense of community that the unit, and the team in particular, have. Quite a lot of chat is addressed to support staff, who move around the groups frequently, or to the deputy manager as he passes by. The manager himself does not walk among the staff in the office in the same fashion. For longer talks or discussion, individuals move over to another person's desk or space, go outside into the corridor, or go to the table underneath the notice board. Here, they have a degree of privacy not afforded within the office itself.

Telephones ring frequently and are answered quickly with polite standard greetings. No call transfers or conference calls were made and it is company policy that answering machines are not used: instead, people take messages for others using a group pickup facility and then place the messages somewhere obvious. When doing so, they write a memo or note, which is placed in the in-tray, or leave a Post-it note on a desk or screen. When the person returns, they may call or walk over to tell him or her about the message. There is some noise from printers and keyboarding: some people type loudly, hammering at the keys. Individuals seem to be able to "close themselves in" on their own spaces and ignore external interruptions and noise. People take their lunch breaks as job and work dictates and, when eating at their desks, read a book and "close themselves off" for a time, or make phone calls or visits. They obviously hear what is happening when comments go back and forwards, and attend to them as they feel necessary.

3.3.5 Interaction Episodes

Interaction takes many forms, both formal (following procedures in standard practices or guidelines) and informal (conversations in passing and muttered comments). The unit has relationships to a greater or lesser degree with many parts of the company itself, with their clients and customers, with consultants and with specific individuals on the site. Staff in the team have interactions with other members of their own group, such as when they are shown aspects of a piece of software, or when a discussion occurs between a technical author and the keyboarder. Multiple interactions are most often instructions, comments on the progress of a job, or tidying-up activity at the end of the day. There is also some discussion between authors, other TPU members and management.

Staff talk to each other very regularly, both about job-related aspects and personal matters. Because of the physical set-up of the room, they call or talk over screens or go to a desk to have a conversation or to look at what is on a screen or in a document. When individuals in the same work group interact they tend to do so by calling out to each other to attract attention, or by moving to the other person's desk. There is much activity, with people being free to move around and most having to visit other parts of the TPU, the design studio or clients frequently. Informal interpersonal interaction concerns activities such as lunch arrangements and is shown in the use of the corridors outside. The unit is a non-smoking area: staff must go outside to have a cigarette, where they may meet others (from the TPU or from the design studio upstairs) and discuss current jobs in passing.

Interactions with Clients

A major part of an author's time (and, partly, that of editors) is spent in dealing with clients. These may be long-term clients (as in the case of the project manager who works on a specific project) or new potential clients, or merely the current client. Most interaction is by holding meetings, sending letters or faxes, or on the telephone. There were no examples of activities such as email messages or telephone conference calls. Examples of standard letters were collected as part of the data gathering exercise. The following discussion centres on telephone and face-to-face meetings.

When on the telephone, authors take notes (generally concisely on notepads) and look at the document they are discussing while they are talking. They generally have such documents open on the desk in front of them, and it is assumed that the other partner will do the same. While talking, they have an alert posture and speak clearly and often quite loudly. They may make notes on the document itself when they talk through a particular document (e.g. "on page x, half-way down the page, section xx") page by page, marking changes to be made to the text. This is usually when a commissioning person in the TPU is talking to a consultant who has tendered to undertake the editing, or when an author is discussing with the client a specific document in production. Other telephone calls are concerned with estimates, tendering, quotations and costing procedures; with checking on deadlines and time scales; with arranging delivery and production dates; and with meeting arrangements. There are occasional troubleshooting or information checking calls.

Meetings with clients within the TPU follow a standard pattern. Visitors will be collected from visitor reception, if necessary; otherwise they will arrive at a prearranged time. There is little speculative visiting because of security constraints: clients tend not to arrive without prior arrangement. It is unusual to have a meeting at an individual's desk, presumably because of the open-plan nature of the office and because of the existence of the meeting table, described below. Most clients arrive with a specification or a specific instruction in mind, to discuss one or more particular jobs. Visitors are seated at a meeting table located at the entrance to the unit, in front of the resource area and the entrance doors. There does not seem to be a formal booking system in operation. The table is round, normally with five chairs in place. Its location means that all staff can see that a meeting is taking place, especially the manager or his deputy, so those individuals do not specifically have to be informed of what is happening. They often are, as part of the process of keeping them informed of future potential work, but the evidence of the meeting table seems to provide an additional informal source of consolidation of what is known by other, more formal, means (for example, through the system of job initiation).

Authors usually take written notes, and some samples were collected; there was no evidence of tape recording or other means of data collection. The client frequently brings the document to be written or styled and discussion revolves around this. Supporting material is gathered in the form of previous job files and history of interactions with that client, or with similar jobs in the past. Illustrative examples can be fetched from the nearby information centre to demonstrate examples of house style and previous publications produced in similar formats or with similar requirements. Such meetings can last from 5 or 10 minutes to almost an hour, and happen at least once a day. Contractors are briefed in these sessions, and supporting items such as equipment and technical specifications are provided for individuals to examine and comment upon. A specific set of procedures is followed after the meeting if the job is to be taken on and a quotation for the client provided. This activity is a major part of the team leader's (or deputy's) work. Other communication is through visiting the client (if on site), having scheduled a meeting to discuss requirements or to clarify points of change or amendments to be made. Staff also go to meetings in London, at other company sites or at the offices of external customers. Frequently two people will attend these off-site meetings (one of them being the team leader or his deputy). They report back verbally to their team leader and the manager, and make a note in the official job file on specific jobs.

Interactions within the Company

The TPU interacts with other sections physically located nearby and within the publicity structure for specific purposes: the publicity section (for advice and work with them), the reprographics section (for copying), the printing section (for final printing and binding), the DTP section (for styling). Such interaction is on both formal and informal levels, and occurs frequently every day. By formal, we mean the processes involved in the transfer of specific jobs to another section (such as the DTP and reprographics sections for styling and production of documents, or the library, information and translation services). Such processes follow a specific pattern, involving official "handing off" of jobs with filling in of appropriate paperwork. These types of activities are frequent and have set limits, with little additional information requiring to be passed on. Informal interaction, on the other hand, tends to be on a personal level with individuals in design and production, most especially with staff in the design studio, to check progress on work in hand, future scheduling and decision making on specific jobs. This is characterized not by paperwork but by personal communications, by visits to the studio itself and by frequent telephone conversations between the two. The design studio appears to function as an extension of the workplace society of the unit, and procedures for passing on work are less structured and more amenable to rapid change and negotiation. Meetings with designers can also take place without premeditation because of the physical proximity, and authors were seen to go off with a designer they had met in the corridor outside or to start a conversation with a visiting designer, engaged in a job for another author or group. Our use of the term "informal" can be seen as distinguishing opportunistic meetings and as being an aspect of cooperation through everyday activity, and will be described in greater detail in Section 3.4.

There is also interaction with other facilities (travel authorization, personnel or salaries). One major interaction is with the security services, since visitors to the site must be notified in advance, usually over the telephone. Interaction at a formal level within the company involves attendance at briefing sessions for information dissemination. The meeting that took place during the study lasted for about one hour. Only the full-time staff attend such meetings, contractors remaining behind in the unit, where there was a marked relaxation and change of atmosphere, although work still continued. It was only then that the number of contract staff working in the TPU was identified.

For paper-based communications, there is a set of internal publications and newsletters, together with notice boards in the unit itself and in the passageway outside. People occasionally went to look at what was on the notice boards. Included on these were citations for standards of work and achievement targets met by groups and individuals. No internal memos were noted during the study period.

3.4 The Analysis

3.4.1 Strategy

Transcriptions of the audio tape recordings were made and indexing of documents and photographs by activity, location and communication episodes took place. Authors' own notes, "to-do" lists and notations on documents were catalogued and linked to these indices. Field notes were transcribed and a document describing the ethnographic study was produced (Gilbert et al. 1991). The transcripts were subjected to scrutiny and encoded in a variety of forms to assist in identifying patterns and activities. Originally, text fragments were collated together by activity and a functional decomposition of TPU work activities was made (Gilbert et al. 1991). However, described only in the form of linear text, the totality of the data is confusing, does not match easily with functional decompositions and is unsuitable for translation into user requirements or needs. Therefore, it was recast as a hypertext document to act as a "guide" to the data collected, allowing a set of different viewpoints on the activities to be made evident and highlighting the links between the disparate sets of information gathered. This was not entirely successful, partly due to the limitations of the technology and packages used and partly because the linkages to be made were too complex and subtle to be captured in such a restricted format. Investigation into sets of computer based qualitative analysis tools (many of them hypertext applications) and other potential new types of software for achieving time based analysis, derived from video storyboarding, is now in progress. It is hoped that this will allow greater flexibility, especially along the time dimension, but a major problem of navigation and of providing set routes through the data will remain.

3.4.2 Classification of Activities

Finally, a complex database incorporating text fragments, field note observations and categorization of observed collaborative activities was constructed. The categories used, together with the major parameters identified as being of relevance, are listed below. Although this list is specific, its general nature (as in meetings, discussions, general chat and social interactions) can be seen, and it is being used as the basis for categorizing the second set of case study transcripts.

- Discussing job specification/quotation
  - meeting around table (public)
  - 2+ people (staff and contractor)
  - duration: long or short
  - content: technical
  - with document/artefact/examples
  - notes taken (informal)
- Discussing work with client
  - meeting around table (public) or client's office (private)
  - 2+ people (staff and client)
  - initial consultation for requirements or checking drafts/new instructions
  - duration: long or short
  - content: technical
  - with document/artefact/examples
  - notes taken (informal)
- Telephone call
  - staff and caller
  - usually at desk
  - duration: usually short, occasionally extended
  - content: technical
  - with document/artefact/examples
  - occasional notes taken (informal)
- General discussion
  - 2+ staff
  - short duration, may be very brief
  - usually acknowledgement given
  - usually at desk, or in passing
  - calling over screens
  - private (but may be overheard)
  - artefacts such as letters, screen views, sometimes to pass on to others
  This can be subdivided into: information seeking, information passing, position/information checking, scheduling/administrative requests, working together/teaching
- Dealing with resources: requests, status and return
  - 1+ staff, need artefact/shared resource
  - very brief, acknowledgement given
- Informal "constructed" communications
  - 1+ staff, difficult to quantify, sometimes artefact
- Interaction with ethnographer
  - 1 person, explanatory
- Chat
  - 2+ people, talk, social interactions

Discussions and talk between participants took place along a number of conversational style dimensions: either businesslike or conversational/familiar with colleagues; usually businesslike or occasionally conversational with clients and contractors; brief, familiar, short duration chat or comment with colleagues; self-commentary when working alone, and explanatory commentary to the ethnographer.

"Authoring" as an Activity

The major activity of writing is a solitary process, when authors sit at their computer screens to type in text or at their desks to mark-up documents, or to check manuals for layout and typographical errors, with little concurrent communication with others. This is probably because each author works on an individual job: technical writing is not, after all, a process that occurs collaboratively in the sense of having multiple authors. Jobs that the authors write are passed on to the keyboarder in the group for processing and formatting, and for subsequent insertion of user amendments.

Collaborative Activity

Collaborative activity is demonstrated by the strategies used by individuals to monitor background noise and passers-by, to interweave tasks by taking note of ("glimpsing") others' work, activities, communications and movements, to engage in private discussions or telephone calls versus public activities amenable to others (including the delineation markers for the point at which such actions switch from one to the other), and to evolve and use shared communication "codes".

One example is in the way in which the siting of the central table is important in allowing client meetings and contractor briefings to be made visible so that the manager knows without being explicitly informed which contractors are working for the group and the jobs being tendered for by different teams. This allows him to gauge the level of future work and may have implications for scheduling activities. The duration of the meeting and the strategies used for estimating workload, time to be spent and subsequent costs can be extracted both from incidental glimpses at the table and the state of the documentation that the authors and contractors deal with.

Another is the manner in which interaction between the keyboarder and the project manager takes place: he (the project manager) can see by the paperwork on the keyboarder's desk which part of the document she is editing, how work on one particular manual is progressing and amount of time still to be spent on it. He can hear her comments (directed both at herself and for him to overhear) on any problem areas in formatting (such as tables or complex layouts) that are likely to impact on the time originally estimated for the work. He can then schedule his own work to avoid overloading her, or, conversely, can pressurize her to complete specific tasks. The team leader, because of his proximity, and the need to pass her desk on his way to other parts of the office, can similarly gauge what is happening and estimate which future jobs to pass to her, and when to do so. There are no case conferences or set periods during the day in which such information is routinely discussed and exchanged as explicit commentaries. Rather, interweaving of tasks is linked into glimpses of others' work in such a fashion. Linkage between project management work undertaken by the team leader and his deputy is similarly structured, as they are essentially working as a two-person team on this activity.

Organizational Cooperation

Cooperation in organizations through everyday actions is achieved in numerous types of collaborative enterprises: most activities are not face-to-face meetings or the direct addressing of an individual. Moreover, they are heavily influenced by location. "Organizational strategies" are instantiated by constructions such as those listed below, and are demonstrated by examples of conversation and interactions:

- Group filing systems and historical record keeping to institutionalize and utilize "organizational memory".

- "Institutional" talk, restricted language, jargon, assumed procedures and means of giving rationales and justifications for actions or procedures.

- Socially constructed communications (scribbles etc.), desk ephemera, circulation of documents (not official), notice boards and charts, official communications.

- Meta-group organization of physical artefacts and constructs.

- Fail-safe procedures, security and archiving requirements.

Group filing systems in modern organizations act as a form of "group memory" and embody such characteristics as straightforward historical record keeping, fail-safe procedures and archival/security requirements. They form a classification, revealing objects in the world, but are essentially a social activity concerned with shared information that is not individually owned. They show what counts as being important and what follows on in the implicit knowledge needed by group members if they had to reclassify or re-implement the system if it were lost. They may also be regarded as a communication medium, masquerading as hidden organizational and indirect activity. However, like most office activities, maintenance of such systems is a collaborative enterprise, being at the same time too complex for one person and highly volatile. The process by which others learn categorizations and "how the system works" is an example of situated learning, and this is demonstrated in the following example:

> Author (A): Does Jim [the manager] still need to know about [name removed] invoices or what? That's fine, it's just that on the invoices.
> Deputy (K): I'll get one, a record of that.
> Author (A): If you copy that . . . to put in your job file.
> Deputy (K): Yes, the project file, not for me.
> Author (A): So Jim wants to get rid of that copy then?
> Deputy (K): Yes, it's in the project file.
> Author (A): Copies to . . . copies sent . . . . Right, reformat that, we'll just tap it. Right, that's it then. It doesn't go to them, it, the only thing this does, this will go to Bella and she will send it out. There you go. You feel you want that off.
> Deputy (K): I'll get a copy of that and the one we just done, the previous one.
> Author (A): All you do, just add a page onto it, you can, there is copies of all the pages in the file, but if you delete the first few lines it makes the file a bit smaller.
> Deputy (K): That's all you do for that menu?
> Author (A): You've got to, and she sends it off. They need to know that. Yes. All she's going to do is send that figure out. That should be it, Ken. Just check it.

The features to be noted are a demonstration of the procedures followed for charting and keeping track of current jobs, notifying other members of the unit of actions undertaken and the implicit passage of information as demonstrated by clues within a document format. A(uthor), the project leader, and K(en), the deputy team leader, are sitting together, side-by-side at the author's desk, Ken having rolled his chair over. They are both looking at the author's computer screen, opened to a WP application. The author is editing an invoice to a contractor, a new task that he has asked Ken to check over with him. Looking at something on the screen, he asks if Jim, the deputy manager, needs to have a paper record of jobs being undertaken as instantiated in the invoice he is producing. The implication is that Jim needs to know details of ongoing work and costs for budgetary control purposes since his name appears in the cc: field. The invoice is a copy of a standard file and they are double-checking that the process that is assumed to be in operation is still valid for this particular invoice. This has been signalled by the presence of Jim's name in the file and indicates that in other circumstances Jim would indeed receive an internal copy. The answer, as Ken shakes his head followed by a comment, is that Jim does not, but that Ken, in his capacity as costing and management information reporting, will get a copy of it as it works its way through the system ("I'll get one, a record of that."). Despite passing on this information with its implication of an underlying process in action, he is offered a current copy of the paperwork, presumably as a marker for future reference. The author assumed that this will go into Ken's personal file of current jobs, but Ken makes it clear that he will file it in the actual file for this particular project (subsequently stored in the filing cabinets in a marked suspended folder), to differentiate it from something that he is engaged in here and now: there it will serve to provide a record of what has been sent out and a trace of a set of unseen activities. This clarifies to Ken that there is a record of the transaction in a location where Jim might be expected to look and to which he has immediate access. It also has the effect of being one less piece of paper that Jim has to have on his desk ("So Jim wants to get rid of that copy then?"). The author re-edits the document and, since authors do not post material out themselves, the invoice is prepared for the next stage. It will be sent to Bella, one of the support staff, who will enter details where Ken can access them – "the record" referred to earlier in the conversation – and arrange for it to be sent out. The discussion then easily elides into the editing procedures and commands needed to edit this type of document. Background information is transferred *in situ*, as a part of learning about the invoicing process itself.

The next example shows how the formal established procedure is subverted by the participants to achieve the desired goal, demonstrating in the process how intervention in passing by the manager can resolve issues without them being explicitly brought to his attention:

Author (A): Okey-doke. Right, I'll get a D-number for that and get Ken to contact you. This we class as a new enquiry then, and what will happen now, I've filled a job spec. in, it will be recorded with Linda in Commercial, she will give me a D-number, it will go to Ken and he will then estimate it and put it through the system.

Question: And where are you going to put this?

Author (A): This now I will give to Linda to get a job number and when I get it I will put it in Ken's in-tray along with all the spec. information. This again is just a simple process, this will take the form of the next D-number in line.

Support (L): The latest one was 123 wasn't it?

Author (A): I don't know.

Support (L): I can't give you a D-number. I'm not allowed to.

Author (A): I'll get one off. You can't have a D-number without a project number. Distribution must have a, that's still ongoing isn't it, that must have a project number.

Support (L): 124

Another [in passing]: It's on the board in the other room – was it 9876?

Author (A): 4321, that's the job for [name removed] OK. There is no security project. I can't get the D-number off now. Got it mate? Jim [manager], got a new job come in, come from [name removed] from [name removed] an information security code. Martin suggested it would have the same project code as the [name removed] as it's the same people. Do we note 2-ll – and Linda tells me it can't be 4321 – is that what we had?

Manager (J): No [name removed] here – I don't know the actual code.

Author (A): Yeah. I went to get a D-number and Linda tells me you've got to sign it because it's 4321. It's Ken's job. Right. Can you pass it on to Linda? Thank you.

A(uthor), the project leader, is finishing a telephone conversation at his desk with a new client. He is explaining what the next stages in the process are: that he must get an authorization code number for the job to be entered into the system and to start an official record. The explanation seems very straightforward ("This again is just a simple process"): transfer the information to one of the support staff, get the next job number in sequence and then pass it on to Ken, the deputy project leader, who will make an estimate of costs for this job and start the sequence of job allocation. The obvious place to put this information is in Ken's in-tray, where he will pick it up the next day. However, allocation of numbers is not straightforward after all since the job, being part of another one, is an exception case and must be tied in with a project number. Both the author and Linda, one of the support staff, are standing beside Linda's desk at this point. Another author, Martin, from a different team, is passing at the time and suggests a resolution to the difficulties: to look at the shared job allocation board which one of the support staff, Rita, uses to show which manuals and completed jobs are being shipped out this week, and to identify the correct project code number from that. He has made the connection between the comments made and the need to link it with an existing project. The author identifies a project number from memory (the resort of examining the resource allocation board has not been taken up) but this does not resolve the question of the D-number. The discussion then moves onto specific technicalities of just who the customer is, and Jim, the manager, who has overheard the talking, walks over to investigate. He is immediately asked to resolve the situation and clarify procedures. He then takes over the paperwork because it is an exception case and Linda's inability to offer a D-number has the implication to the author that Jim must sign it and deal with it directly in a different fashion from normal. However, he also provides the background information as to where to send the new job when it has been allocated an appropriate code to bring it back into the normal system.

The following example demonstrates both how the established procedure should work and the rationale given for archiving, together with the way in which such shared systems are organized. It also, in passing, touches on what some of the systems of collaborative information are and what "styling" means to these authors in the context of the company style described earlier.

> Author (A): Right, I'm going to get some hard copy identification sheets. Now, each pile of papers we get we, like, if it's being worked with it's alright, we know what's going out, but if it's going to go away now we like to know what it is and what it was, so I'm going to get a yellow sheet now, which is in the cupboard there, which tells me what these two piles of paper are, one being the customer's comments and the other one being the corrected sheets, which will then go in the job tray pile.
>
> Question: Do you keep all versions normally?
>
> Author (A): Yes, yes, and what happens when the job is closed we archive

those and keep them for six months. They then go to a central archiving place and after so many, I can't remember the exact amount, but a certain amount of time they get destroyed.

Question: Basically, you don't throw anything away?

Author (A): No, because if he comes back to us and says, "Well, look, we gave you this, that and the other on this" I can say, "No you didn't, it's here, look!". We don't throw much away at all. I'll just go and get two forms. First of all the title is what the product is, there is no publication number in this case because he has his own. The Issue Number is the issue number that is on the foot of the page which is (number removed), the number of disks is one, the job number (number removed), software used is Ventura, it's A4, customer facing.

Question: What does that mean?

Author (A): This tells us what the format is – it's an A4 book that we are doing, as opposed to A5, 2/3 A4 or Filofax. The style is either customer facing or internal. The customer facing one at the moment is the style that we have here, which is basically the old internal style that has been developed, and that is an internal style, and that is a different style to this, it's, internal style has a lot of, the top and bottom ruling lines are different, the footers differ in respect. In fact what you have here is a, this is, if you look at this, this is the internal style, and as you can see this one has "in confidence" in caps but it has a single head and bottom footer rule, slight variations in the issue number, they are now using 1.0 whatever, and these style sheets are all produced, these have been produced here locally and set up with all the fonts in them, and everyone's computer has got them in the style file, and all you do is load that style file into the document and it's there already. Down the left-hand side, this, the initial one, the customer group is from the first draft, so what I'll put there is what it is, the first draft, and it is the customer's review, so I shall just sign that and date it.

The next example highlights an implicit procedure, expected to be known to all TPU staff, of "sizing" the job to be done and shows that it is very dependent on the physical artefact itself and the particular ways in which authors touch and examine their constructions to yield what is to them crucial information:

> 1st Author: That's better – another version – this is 1983. It's tremendous. Is it single-sided as well? No, it's doublish – double where needed.
> 2nd Author: Date received, 21st. Estimated printed pages, is it sixty, eighty? Can I leave you to sort it out? Guessed – I thought you'd run your finger through it.

The following example shows how the understood scope of each other's work allows the authors to take action on what appear to be minimal cues and how activities are progressed by common knowledge, with a justification that will be understood by all:

> Author (A): He seems to recall it, having looked when he moved over. But I've told him basically what the job's about and that Jim will be in touch with him. So that was passed on. So there doesn't seem any point in trying to retrieve the files out of archive, seems a waste of time. I've briefed Ken on the job that we talked to yesterday. I've given Ken a quick brief on that and I'll liaise with him further when Jim actually gives him the job. He'll obviously not know much about it, I'll liaise with him then.

Question: So Ken's got the . . .
Author (A): I don't know whether he has or not. I don't know whether I gave him a note, I put them all on Jim's thing. Oh no, they went to Jim, he hasn't got them yet, no. He hasn't got those yet. But when he does I'll be there to help him out. So that's that one done. I've got a thing for Rita which I received yesterday, a rates return, the only reason I took it on really because I know how she does the things, so I'll give her it and explain what it is.
Question: That came in yesterday?
Author (A): This came in yesterday but it came in as a fax, not to anybody in particular, Martin picked it up and saw it was rates, knew that I did rates and it's no problem really just giving it to Rita. Right. I'll just give this to Rita. This came in yesterday, Rita. It's from (name removed). He was questioning the 1 and 2 bit that we sent him, he said it looks exactly the same as the one that's in the book. I said, "Ah, it will until Mike", that it will do up to a certain point and then he'll start getting odd pages because there is no even ones. So anyway basically he couldn't understand why he had been sent it because it looked exactly the same. So he's now done his changeovers.

The author is discussing what to do about a new job he has just been discussing on the telephone. He says that he has briefed the Ken, the deputy team leader, about future work to be expected. However, what he means by briefing is that he has written the information and sent it to Ken, placing it in an appropriate position that he now cannot immediately recall because the context has been lost. When he goes to look at where he thinks the note should be (in Ken's in-tray), it is not there and he then recalls that it was not a straightforward job and had to go via the deputy manager first and that he has sent the information to him instead. The context has been recalled and he makes a comment to himself that he will deal with it when the paperwork has progressed through the system. He then deals with the next piece of paperwork: a rates allocation that should have been directed to Rita, one of the support staff. This material came to him by a round-about route since the original fax was not addressed to a specific person but another author took it, recognized the type of work it was and passed it on to him as being the most appropriate person ("Martin picked it up and saw it was rates, knew that I did rates"). He himself knows that his responsibility for this job has moved on to Rita and walks over to give it to her, explaining just what it is: information that the other author could not know in sufficient detail.

A final example is the communication codes that seem to have been developed for use between group members: the siting of notes for others, the exact positioning of artefacts such as "Post-it" notes, the placing of messages or new mail, and the muttered commentary on jobs in hand all serve to inform the team not only of visible activities but also to attach a specific shared meaning derived from the similarity of their work activities:

Author (A): That was a message for Chris. He will pick this up tomorrow, probably get in touch with the contractor that he's decided he's going to do it, and ask him to supply dates to us.

Question: Where do you leave messages?
Author (A): I shall leave this – ordinarily I would just put it on his desk if he was here or in his in-tray but he's not here so I'll file it in his in-tray within the cupboard that's locked up when he comes in in the morning.

The author is explaining his rationale for the exact siting of a message for the team leader. This code is implicit and dynamic, acting as a means of binding the team together in a social group and externalizing their membership of the group of authors and editors who make up the TPU.

3.5 Conclusions

For a CSCW system to work well within the organization the models of the social and the technical subsystem that are developed must be integrated, so that it is possible to formally specify many of the requirements needed for such systems.

An interesting comparison to be made is to ask users about the needs they perceive and what type of future systems they might wish to have. The following is a "shopping list", derived specifically from questioning and interviewing TPU staff. This "wants" list is quite similar to what we might expect a standard analysis to derive. In the following section we try to define what types of feature have been uncovered by the ethnographic study as being important to the functioning of the unit and essential in constructing how technical authors work. We believe that it is these features that must be supported by the introduction of new technology, especially one that will exploit the ability of the authors to work together as a coherent group.

3.5.1 What the Authors Want

The authors believe that it is essential to have access to high quality workstations with windowing capacities if visual and image based inter-action is to be considered. A specific requirement they have is for design capacities such as "exploded diagrams". The quality of displayed images, either as graphics or as video overlays, is crucial for the production of good documentation: the quality needs to be at least as good as is available with paper based illustrations or photographs. A similar need is identified for the quality of output: laser writers and colour printers are required to produce documentation of print quality. For technical authoring in particular, great emphasis is placed on the quality of screen displays (the WYSIWYG interface for DTP, for example) and so a good quality interface is essential. The actual interface style does not appear to be a matter of great importance just now (i.e. whether icon-based in a graphical direct manipulation environment, or command and menu-based) but this is another area of further investigation. What is important is that a windowing based system is used to allow multiple views of a document, with added functionality of audio-visual links if available.

Voice links by telephone are thought to be adequate, as they are used extensively at the moment. An audio-visual link may be useful in certain circumstances, most specifically between a technical author and the design studio when producing manuals with a high illustrative content. This suggestion was not thought to be significantly better than the current communication mechanisms of telephone and being able to visit the individual in person. Voice annotation in text documents may be a useful option when editing and amending text in both first draft and final draft stages. It could be a substitute for the current practice of talking through a document on the telephone, describing areas on the page and individual words and paragraphs, or for the process of annotation that is normally carried out at the moment by marking in coloured pen, pasting amendments or rewrites on top of already written text, or using additional written notes and Post-it notes.

3.5.2 What the Analysis Found

The aims of the analysis were manifold: firstly, to give indications of circumstances in which CSCW tools would be effective for a certain type of organization or business activity; secondly, to provide commentaries on activities showing how people use technology to achieve something they cannot otherwise do; and, thirdly, to give insight into the features we described earlier as being crucial to CSCW implementations. Such features are concerned with aspects of group organizational memory; are examples where individuals coordinate actions without explicitly recognized communication; are implied assumptions, behaviours and the societal "ethos" illuminating hidden organizational and indirect activities; are identifying objects and artefacts that are social products. They may be demonstrated by identifying social roles, relationships and the interplay of the different personalities; in the modes of communication used between group members; in the impact of the shared artefacts (an office design of furniture, trappings and physical layout); in behaviours that demonstrate evidence of the organization being "constructed" by participants to their own ends in defiance of the formal organizational model; in "satisficing" behaviour, and in the predominance of the individual over the collective and the personal over the impersonal. Aspects concerned with the predominance of paper in designated sequences of activities to ensure both immediacy and traceability, with identifying the recipients of particular information, and the idea of "inside" the group or unit versus "outside" (both physically and socially) are important to the way in which work is achieved. The idea of a setting was devised to explain when and where such examples could be formalized so that it could be incorporated into more formalized descriptions of tasks and activities. It is an identified point at which other factors influence the work carried out and impinge on how the authors carry out their work. A setting is an activity that focuses communication, allowing meaning to be described as situated activity. A setting is a structured time-bound episode constrained by the observer, the task activities, organizational norms and rules, informal norms, the language, communication media and codes used and the physical environment and location. Below are initial examples of what the settings for a range of activities within the TPU may be:

- Client briefings in the TPU:
  - *Task activity:* to obtain the parameters for a job (such as editing, format, technical and budgetary and time constraints).
  - *Organizational norms:* the formal procedures carried out (e.g. form filling, setting in motion the estimating process, recording on a new job file, allocation of reference numbers, checking with previous jobs from the same client). The technical author who is to do the work is normally present. Preset time limits are usually in place.
  - *Informal norms:* authors make use of note-taking; the use of artefacts to illustrate specific features and ease of access to prior examples of work in the information centre; the opportunity to ask the manager for input; a specific closure and checking of actions to be undertaken; impressions of the unit given through "professional" behaviour by adherence to quality procedures; the client's opportunity to view the activities of the rest of the unit and the output and productivity graphs kept on the wall beside the meeting table; the client may also be able to move easily to discussion or checking of other jobs in progress, or to exchange information with other visitors (usually if contractors are present).
  - *Communication media:* formal language and technical terminology; explication of points is permissible in discussion, perhaps some friendly chat as greeting behaviour and on meeting closure; notes and drawings may be used to communicate information; examination of the physical artefact frequently employed to estimate the graphic design needs; comparisons with previous documents in order to adhere to stylistic requirements.
  - *Physical location:* meeting table in view of the whole unit.
- Discussion between two authors:
  - *Task activity:* to give guidance on how to create invoices from standard forms. This is a new activity for one of the authors: the other already knows how to do it.
  - *Organizational norms:* two people working together in a recognized fashion.
  - *Informal norms:* sitting close to each other in a cooperative positioning;

descriptions of the process underlying the activity and what the implication of various fields in the form show; learning or novice training taking place is the ostensible reason but information on what the process means to the parties involved is also being communicated.

– *Communication media:* informal language and brief comments, with a wealth of underlying shared meaning attached; the ability of both to view what is on a screen and to refer to it, knowing that the other will recognize the item being discussed.

– *Physical location:* an author's own desk and computer screen. One of the authors has rolled his chair over side-by-side with the other so that both can view the screen. Only one author has access to the keyboard.

- Informal "chat":
  – *Task activity:* one author has gone outside to the corridor to have some coffee and a cigarette.
  – *Organizational norms:* recognized break in work activities; meeting with others from the unit and the design studio.
  – *Informal norms:* general chat and fortuitous co-location leads on to a question by a designer on a job in progress and the relevant author answers in passing, but then decides to go upstairs to look at the design and answer the question directly even though he is currently engaged in another activity: the interleaving of tasks by opportunistic meeting rather than by a telephone request or having to visit the author at his desk.
  – *Communication media:* bantering language, informal chat.
  – *Physical location:* the corridor outside the TPU office space.

3.5.3 In Conclusion

There is obviously much future work that could be undertaken at this study site. This will involve the collection of much more specific data on some of the following aspects, in an attempt to gain a deeper understanding of features of the work of a technical authoring section. Some features of note that could be followed up on the specifics of technical authoring can be distinguished from those with a wider relevance.

Technical authoring specifics:

- Version control and responsibilities
- Job scheduling and allocation
- Tendering and bidding support
- Analysis of the "job file" and movement record
- Stylesheets (how to agree on a common style)
- Ephemera details: how does this structure work or relate to "glimpses"?

Of wider potential relevance:

- Information-checking telephone calls
- Informal interaction outside the office
- Expert-to-novice training
- Task pace
- Cross-national comparisons and input from professional organizations
- Errors and recovery procedures
- Designated authority and responsibilities

From the perspective of this study, we may ask just what ethnographic analysis can contribute to the design of future IT systems. We expect that our work will lead directly to guidance as to the appropriateness of CSCW systems for a particular work group or organization, and will give indications of the kind of features that should be provided. We can also try to integrate ethnography as a technique by focusing on what it does give, which is the experience of moving from outside to within an organization. The ethnographer can then adopt a number of potential roles vis-à-vis the design process. One is that of being a translator between cultures, a "bridging mechanism" between the needs of users and the hidden processes that facilitate their daily work, and the needs of the software designer and analyst who looks at the task implications of such users' work. In being a "reflector" of reality, the ethnographer may act as a "surrogate user", and could usefully be employed as part of a multidisciplinary design team, bringing skills which we believe to be necessary when analysing how people work together in groups.

Acknowledgements   The work reported here has been undertaken as part of the Theories of Multi-Party Interaction (TMPI) project in conjunction with Queen Mary and Westfield College, University of London and sponsored by British Telecom. Thanks are due to project members for comments on this text and to the staff at the study sites for their assistance, forbearance and good humour.

Chapter 4

Situation Theory and the Design of Interactive Information Systems

K. Devlin

4.1 Introduction

> If you want to design a system to be used by people, start off by examining the way they work and tailor the system to their needs.

Although this general design principle expresses self-evident common sense, it is frequently ignored, as witnessed by Norman's woeful list of poorly designed artefacts (1990). In the case of computer systems, technology-orientated – as opposed to people-orientated – design was understandable in the days when computer hardware was expensive and scarce, when computer memory was in short supply, when computer processing was relatively slow, and when computer programming was still closely wedded to the machine architecture. But today, the successful development of computer engineering techniques and computer science has meant that greater attention can be paid to the human side of systems development, and, indeed, in recent years, we have seen a significant shift in this direction (see, for example, Carroll 1991).

What this shift (or broadening) of emphasis has meant in practice is that the business of designing an information system has become much more an interdisciplinary team effort, requiring input from sociologists and psychologists (and quite often from linguists and philosophers), in addition to the more traditional systems design disciplines of computer science and systems engineering.

By far the greatest problem facing such an interdisciplinary team is communication within the group. Each discipline has its own distinctive methodology and use of language, and each has distinctive practices for evaluation and validation of work carried out within the discipline.

The work presented here can be regarded as an attempt (more precisely, as part of an attempt) to develop a conceptual framework linking these various disciplines, a form of lingua franca, if you will.[1]

I should perhaps end this introduction with a remark about the role of theory in such a human-centred an activity as design. Designers are well known to carry out their craft with little or no "concern" for theory (see, for instance, Carroll 1991, p. 47). But what this means is that design is a holistic, creative process, involving both experience and considerable trial and error, rather than something that can be codified by some theory (this is not to say that a design team may not adopt one of a number of design methodologies – see, for instance, many of the chapters in Carroll 1991). But just because designers often make little or no explicit use of a theory does not mean that that theory is not important to the design process. Indeed, theory is crucial to design, since the entire approach to and way of thinking about a particular domain are conditioned by the various pertinent theories of which designers are aware.

For instance, electrical engineers may not make much explicit use of physics or mathematics in the course of a particular design process, but their entire approach – right down to the way in which they think of electricity – is conditioned by the physics and mathematics they learned at school and college.

Likewise, mechanical engineers make constant, *implicit* use of Newtonian mechanics (among other theories) in the design of some mechanical systems. They cannot fail to make such use, since, again, their whole way of thinking is grounded in their learning of these theories as part of their professional training. (It should be noted that the professional training of electrical and mechanical engineers always includes a considerable grounding in physics and mathematics.)

It is, I believe, at the *education* stage that theory is most important, since the basic theories we learn and become familiar with contribute to the way in which we conceptualize and approach a task such as design.

In the case of the design of interactive information systems, the theories that are most likely to play a significant (educational) role in conditioning and influencing the designer's approach are theories in sociology, psychology, linguistics, computer science, philosophy and informatics – of which the last is, I believe, the least well developed, and is the discipline in which situation theory may be found.

The case I try to make in this chapter (see, in particular, Section 4.8) is that situation theory provides the designer of an interactive information system with a cohesive, system-wide conception of information flow that is particularly well suited to user-orientated design, in that it provides a conceptual framework and an associated set of metaphors that encourage good design practice.

4.2 Information

Imagine yourself suddenly transported back in time to (say) the Iron Age. You meet a local ironsmith, and ask him, "What is iron?" What kind of answer are you likely to get? Very probably, your craftsman would point to various artefacts that he had made, and inform you that each of them was iron. But this is not what you want. What you want to know is just what it is that makes iron *iron* (and not some other substance that may or may not look quite like iron). What, then, does your Iron Age man do in response to your persistent questioning? He is an acknowledged expert on ironship, his products sell well, and he knows a good piece of iron when he sees it. And yet he is unable to supply you with the kind of answer you are seeking. Indeed, he has no frame of reference within which to even begin to understand what it is you are asking! To give the kind of answer that would satisfy you, he would need to know all about the molecular structure of matter – for that, surely, is the only way to give a precise definition of iron (or maybe there are other ways, ways that require theories we ourselves are not aware of? This possibility merely strengthens the point I am trying to make). But not only is your man not familiar with molecular theory, he probably does not even conceive of the possibility of such a theory!

To anyone trying to understand the nature of information in today's Information Age, the situation must surely seem not unlike that facing your Iron Age man. That there is such a thing as *information* cannot be disputed. After all, our very lives depend upon it: upon its gathering, storage, manipulation, transmission, security and so on. Huge amounts of money change hands in exchange for information. People talk about it all the time. Lives are lost in its pursuit. Vast commercial empires are created in order to manufacture equipment to handle it. Surely, then, it is there. But what exactly is it? The difficulty in trying to find an answer to this question lies in the absence of an agreed, underlying theory upon which to base an acceptable definition. Like the Iron Age man and his stock in trade, Information Age man can recognize and manipulate "information", but is unable to give a precise definition as to what exactly it is that is being recognized and manipulated.

The above two paragraphs are based on the opening of the first chapter of my monograph (Devlin 1991). They were used there to help motivate a fundamental analysis of the nature of information, a task commenced (or more precisely, continued) in that volume. They apply, quite obviously and clearly, to the design of information systems. Today's information system designer is in very much the same position as that Iron Age artisan.

We have, as yet, no comprehensive theory of information, nor indeed anything approaching a reasonable conception of what information *is* (or may be regarded to be). So how is it possible for us to design and construct, as we do, the numerous information systems upon which our lives so clearly depend? As I tried to indicate in the opening section, there is nothing new, or surprising, in this state of affairs. Design and construction do not depend on theory and understanding. At least, up to a point they do not, for surely no one can deny that mankind was able to do far more with iron once a proper theory had been worked out. Indeed, the artefacts constructed during the Iron Age bear little more than a superficial resemblance to the kind of things built in the industrial and technological ages, when designers and engineers could draw on a large and growing wealth of scientific knowledge.

In today's Information Age, we are still having to work with no more than odd fragments of what may one day be a fully worked out theory of information. The results of trying to build information systems in the absence of a proper scientific framework are familiar to us all, in the form of systems that simply do not work in the way they were intended. That so many of the systems we use every day can in fact be used at all, is a consequence not so much of good design but of the enormous degree of resourcefulness that we, as human users, may bring to bear when we encounter the system.

A particularly graphic illustration of this problem is provided by Suchman's account (1987) of the major problems that can arise in a system as simple as a help facility for a photocopying machine. As Suchman explains, the problem lies in the mismatch that can, and frequently does, arise in practice between the user's intentions and expectations and the designer's anticipation of those intentions and expectations. (The issues are too detailed to summarize here, but I strongly urge anyone who thinks that the design of something as "simple" as an on-line help facility for a photocopier is not an inordinately difficult task to examine Suchman's evidence.)

Another kind of problem, described by Winograd and Flores (1986, p. 165), arises when there is confusion between the ways in which the designer and the user each view the system, resulting in the user experiencing a loss of transparency, such as when the user of an email facility is faced with some mysterious system message, of value only to the system support staff, such as:

MAILBOX SERVER IS RELOADING.

The user's world of activity comprises people in various locations, people to whom messages need to be sent and from whom messages should be received. The appearance of a message about mailbox servers is an intrusion of issues from a quite different domain, and as such is inappropriate. The computer system and its operation should simply mediate the user's communication tasks, and as such ought to be transparent to the user.

In each case, the problem boils down to one of the different contexts in which designer and user view the system. In the case of the email system, where the user–system interaction is fairly straightforward, good design should be able to overcome the kind of designer–user mismatch just mentioned. By looking at the system from the user's viewpoint, the designer could realize that a more appropriate error message would be:

TEMPORARY TECHNICAL DELAY. WILL ATTEMPT TO DELIVER YOUR
MESSAGE TO [name] AGAIN IN FIVE MINUTES

The kind of problem Suchman describes, on the other hand, seems far
less easily resolved; the degree of human–machine interaction involved
in something even as seemingly simple as an on-line help system for a
photocopier already presents the designer with enormous challenges that
we do not, as yet, know how to overcome.

4.3 On Mathematics, Metaphor and Design

How, then, do we set about developing a theoretical underpinning for
design that might begin to help us overcome some of the problems
Suchman describes, for instance? More specifically, is it even possible
to provide a formalizable framework, based on a mathematical ontology,
that encompasses both machine and human action? Such a framework
would, of course, bridge the gap that separates the starting position for
system design – namely a real-world situation with all its complexity
– from the final, formal system specification, which ideally should be
capable of rigorous verification. And this would seem to imply a theory
based on mathematics. So we may rephrase our previous question as: is
it possible to capture some of the complexity of the real, populated world
with sufficient mathematical precision to yield the formality of a system
specification?

Well, first of all we need to be clear about what is meant by the
word "mathematics". Present-day mathematics evolved in eras when
quantization was paramount: commerce, architecture, cartography, engineering and the laboratory sciences all required numerically-based tools
for measurement and computation. In contrast, the kinds of issue I am
proposing to deal with here require radically different mathematical
tools, based on descriptive rather than numerical concepts. For, while
much of present-day mathematics already plays an essential role in
the design and construction of information systems, attempts that have
been made to utilize numerically-grounded techniques to handle issues
such as common sense and default reasoning, vague predicates, context
dependency, evolution of context and natural language understanding
and generation have met with little success. These issues are essentially
descriptive and *qualitative*, and are not amenable to techniques that are
ultimately *quantitative*. Put bluntly, what on earth have such issues got
to do with numbers?

What is required, then, is *qualitative* or *descriptive* mathematics, not
a *quantitative* theory. Although mathematics has always had qualitative
aspects, the quantitative aspects have hitherto dominated, particularly in
applications. Indeed, so fundamental has been number and measurement
to most of mathematics over its 5000 year history, that a great deal

of the mathematics that has been used in, say, computer science and linguistics has had to be developed almost from scratch, with those applications in mind, largely based on mathematical logic, one of the few purely qualitative branches of classical mathematics. Likewise, the work described in Devlin (1991), Sacks (1972) and Devlin and Rosenberg (in preparation) involves mathematical techniques that had to be tailor-made for those applications.

Such descriptive mathematics is outlined later in this chapter. In the meantime, let me ask the following fundamental question: what exactly would it mean to *understand* the nature of information, a development that I have claimed will improve our ability to design interactive information systems?

By way of analogy, what conceptual tools does the electrical engineer bring to bear on the design of an electrical circuit? Electricity is, after all, quite like information in some respects: although we can measure it in various ways and can observe some of its effects, we cannot see it or touch it. How does the human mind cope with something as effectively abstract as electricity?

The answer, surely, is by means of a metaphor, or at least an understanding that is rooted in metaphor.[2] Most commonly, at least in my experience, the metaphor used is that of flowing liquids. As children, we all become familiar with water, and in particular with its flow properties. This familiarity is achieved in an intimate and tactile manner, as we play in it, wash in it, swim in it, shower in it, pour it through tubes and from container to container, and observe it flow from the tap, having passed through the water pipes in our homes. By direct feel we learn to distinguish low pressure from high, the effect of squeezing together the end of a garden hose, and so forth. Based on such childhood experiences, we can then readily conceptualize electric current flowing through a wire as similar to water flowing through a pipe, with amperage corresponding to the diameter of the pipe and voltage corresponding to pressure. Indeed, this is a standard way for middle or high school teachers to try to explain the behaviour of electric current.

Once this basic "flowing liquid" metaphor has been adopted, the next step in our understanding of electric current comes from observing those points at which the behaviour of electricity differs from that of the metaphor; for instance, we learn that electric current is not subject to gravity in the way water is. Then, subsequently, we may merge, or even replace, the simple water metaphor with another one, namely of particles "flowing" along the wire. (The principal initial metaphor alternative to water flow is that of marbles rolling down a tube. Some readers of this chapter may in fact have started with such a metaphor.) At this stage, the metaphor may become fairly sophisticated, since "particles" (a defined notion) called "electrons" constitute a significant part of the metaphor used by physicists in order to study the universe. At this level, the metaphor is essentially a mathematical one. Sophisticated physicists do not claim (at least in public!) that electrons are billiard-ball-like particles whizzing along; rather they work with mathematical equations that "describe" the "motion" of these entities. And at this point, we have now entered the realm of science and engineering, where the practitioners work with a mixture of physically-rooted metaphor and abstract mathematics.

At the level that is, I suggest, most appropriate to the system designer or the engineer, *understanding* a certain phenomenon amounts to:

1. The construction of a suitable metaphor.
2. The identification of the points where the metaphor fails.
3. The construction of a suitably detailed description of the phenomenon; a description based on the metaphor but sufficiently abstract to transcend the limitations that the metaphor imposes.

In the cases of the metaphors we utilize to understand scientific and technical phenomena, the abstract description is usually in mathematical terms or else in scientific terms that are themselves rooted in mathematics.

Successful educational tools and software systems often make ingenious use of metaphors that throw us back to the everyday physical world with which we are so familiar. The windows (=pages), desktop, document, folder, filing cabinet, trashcan display of the Apple Macintosh (Fig. 4.1) is now a classic example of such a metaphor. Another excellent example is provided by the mathematics package Stella (Fig. 4.2), which allows the user to construct, manipulate and solve differential equations using a "water flowing through pipes" metaphor. And, of course, the very talk of *information flow*, *flow charts*, etc. is itself a metaphorical way to approach communication and computation. (It was this metaphor that led me to introduce the term *infon* to denote an "item" of information in Devlin (1991).)

The key, then, to the development of a theory of information of the kind proposed above is, I claim, to find the appropriate metaphor, to evolve a sense of the limitations of that metaphor and, finally, to develop an abstract mathematical theory of information that is based on, but not bound by, the metaphor. The more basic and fundamental is that metaphor, the better will be our understanding, and the better equipped we will be to design information systems.

Information is a highly nebulous concept, as the discussions in Devlin (1991) make clear. The same hundred-pulse signal in a wire can be meaningless on Monday, used to encode (or represent) your name on Tuesday, and signal the launch of a nuclear missile on Wednesday. We have theories that can handle the representations and the signals – the storers and carriers of information – but the information itself, that which is stored as a representation or carried by the signal, remains beyond the reach of those theories, a highly abstract phenomenon that only the mathematics can pick up.

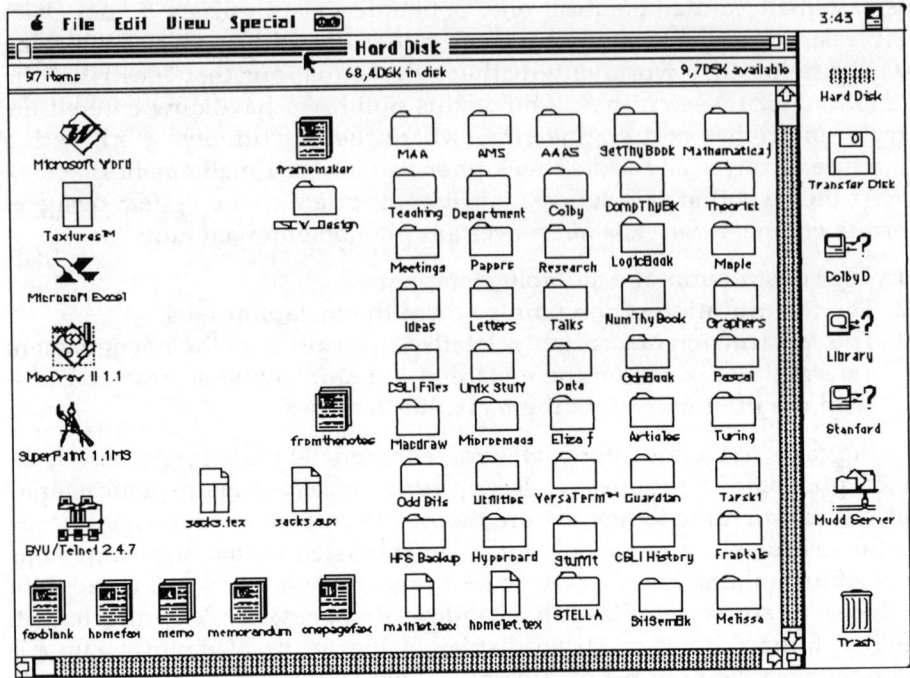

Fig. 4.1. A Macintosh screen.

Thus, the only way for an engineer to be able to design a potentially useful information system is to adopt appropriate metaphors. By this, I mean to imply that the engineer should be aware of all three of the requirements listed above for productive metaphor use. For, given the metaphor domain alone, it is unlikely that a system could be built, let alone verified for reliability. And, given the mathematics alone, it is

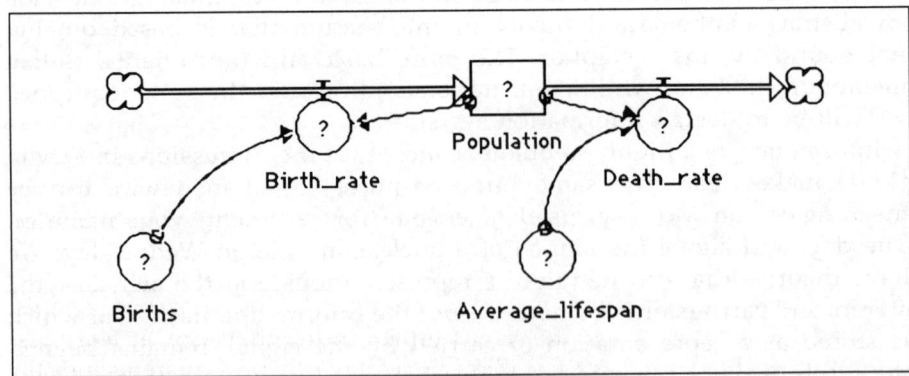

Fig. 4.2. Stella.

doubtful the designer would know where to begin, and even less likely that a usable system would result. Put simply (and therefore somewhat naively), we *think* in terms of metaphors, *design* using a combination of metaphor and accompanying (mathematical) theory, and *verify* and *build* using mathematics.

The remainder of this chapter presents a brief overview of a metaphor–theory combination that, I believe, is an appropriate one for the design of interactive information systems.

4.4 Situation Theory: A Review

This section amounts to a technical summary of the relevant parts of Devlin (1991), and may be skipped by readers familiar with situation theory as described there. Readers unfamiliar with situation theory who simply wish to gain an overall view of the potential for applications of situation theory to design may also prefer to skip this section on first reading, and refer back to it when necessary.

Situation theory is a mathematical theory designed to provide a framework for the study of information. In the situation theoretic treatment of cognition, information processing and communication, recognition is made of the partiality of information due to the finite, *situated* nature of the agent (human, animal or machine) with limited cognitive resources. Any real agent must employ necessarily limited information extracted from the environment in order to reason and communicate effectively.

The theory takes its name from the mathematical device introduced in order to take account of context and partiality. A *situation* can be thought of as a limited part of reality. Such parts may have spatiotemporal extent, or they may be more "abstract", such as fictional worlds, contexts of utterance, problem domains, mathematical structures, databases or UNIX directories. The status of situations in the ontology of situation theory is equal to that of (say) individuals, the distinction between the two being that situations have a *structure* that plays a significant role in the theory whereas individuals do not.

The basic ontology of situation theory consists of entities that a finite, cognitive agent individuates and/or discriminates as it makes its way in the world: spatial locations, temporal locations, individuals, finitary relations, situations, types and a number of other "higher order" entities. The objects (known as *uniformities*) in this ontology include:

- *Individuals:* objects such as tables, chairs, tetrahedra, cubes, people, hands, fingers etc. that the agent either individuates or at least discriminates (by its behaviour) as single, essentially unitary items; usually denoted in our theory by $a, b, c \ldots$

- *Relations:* uniformities individuated or discriminated by the agent that hold, or link together specific numbers of, certain other uniformities; denoted by $P, Q, R. \ldots$
- *Spatial locations:* denoted by $l, l', l'', l_0, l_1, l_2$, etc. These are not necessarily like the "points" of mathematical spaces (though they may be so), but can have spatial extension.
- *Temporal locations:* denoted by $t, t', t_0 \ldots$. As with spatial locations, temporal locations may be either points in time or regions of time.
- *Situations:* structured parts of the world (concrete or abstract) discriminated by (or perhaps individuated by) the agent; denoted by $s, s', s'', s_0 \ldots$.
- *Types:* higher order uniformities (see later) discriminated (and possibly individuated) by the agent; denoted by $S, T, U, V \ldots$.
- *Parameters:* indeterminates that range over objects of the various types; denoted by $\dot{a}, \dot{s}, \dot{t}, \dot{l}$, etc.

The agent-relative framework that "picks out" the ontology is referred to as the *scheme of individuation* (appropriate for a study of that agent vis-à-vis information flow).

The intuition is that in our study of the activity (both physical and cognitive) of a particular agent or species of agent, we notice that there are certain regularities or *uniformities* that the agent either individuates or else discriminates in its behaviour.

For instance, people individuate certain parts of reality as *objects* ("individuals" in our theory), and their behaviour can vary in a systematic way according to spatial location, time and the nature of the immediate environment ("situation types" in our theory).

Information is always taken to be information *about* some situation, and is taken to be in the form of discrete items known as *infons*. These are of the form:

$$\ll R, a_1, \ldots, a_n, 1 \gg, \quad \ll R, a_1, \ldots, a_n, 0 \gg$$

where R is an n-place relation and $a_1, \ldots, a_n$ are objects appropriate for R (often including spatial and/or temporal locations). These may be thought of as the informational item that objects $a_1, \ldots, a_n$ do, or do not, stand for, respectively, in the relation.

It should be stressed that in terms of our theory, infons are semantic objects in a mathematical theory, not sentences in some language that require interpretation.

The class of *compound infons* is constructed from the infons by closing under operations of conjunction and disjunction and bounded existential and universal quantification (over parameters).

Infons (or compound infons) are "items of information". They are not things that are themselves true or false. Rather, a particular item of information may be true or false *about a certain part of the world* (a "situation").

The view taken of relations is a fairly sophisticated, realist one that regards them as abstract objects having a definite and often intricate structure. In particular, there are in general very definite restrictions (called *appropriateness conditions*) upon what kinds of entities may and may not fill the various *argument roles* of a given relation, and certain *minimality conditions* that stipulate which collection of argument roles must be filled in order to obtain an infon with that relation as head.

For example, the relation *eating* has argument roles for the eater, the thing eaten, the time of the eating and the location of the eating; the only things that are eligible to fill the role of the eater are animate individuals, the thing eaten must be some edible substance, the time role can only be filled by an appropriately sized temporal location, the location role by an appropriately sized spatial location. The minimality conditions require that at least one of the eater and the thing-eaten roles must be filled to produce an infon.

Given a situation, s, and an infon σ we write:

$$s \models \sigma$$

to indicate that the infon σ is "made factual by" the situation s, or, to put it another way, that σ is an item of information that is true of s. The official name for this relation is that s supports σ. The facticity claim $s \models \sigma$ is referred to as a *proposition*.

It should be noted that this approach treats "information" as a *commodity*; moreover, as a commodity that does not have to be "true". Indeed, for every positive infon there is a dual negative infon that can be thought of as the "opposite" informational item, and both of these cannot be "true".

One of the basic ideas of situation semantics is the relational theory of meaning. This assumes that any information carried by a meaningful utterance or signal is information *about* some part of the world, that is to say, about a situation. Then the *meaning* of an expression ϕ, denoted by $\|\phi\|$, is defined to be a relation between two situations, the one in which expression is uttered (or the signal propagated) and the one it describes. The relational theory thus provides a conceptual scheme to express the way in which the agent may utilize information in the circumstances of utterance (or of signal propagation).

To give an extremely simple example, consider a spoken utterance of the English language sentence:

$(\|\Phi\|)$: "I am a logician."

The meaning of this sentence provides a link between the utterance, u, and a proposition, p. The situation u and the proposition p are related by $\|\Phi\|$ if and only if there is an individual a and a time t such that:

1. *a* is the speaker in *u*;
2. *t* is the time of *u*; and
3. *p* is the proposition that *a* is a logician at time *t*.

This example shows, in particular, how the first person singular pronoun works: the meaning of the word "I" *relates* (identically in this case) the subject of the described circumstances to the speaker in the utterance.

Clearly, this view of meaning is radically different from that given by those semantic enterprises that view the meanings of expressions as set-theoretic objects that can be described independently of the uses of the expression, such as Tarski's definition of model-theoretic truth in classical logic or Montague semantics for natural languages.

Sentence meanings are one particular instance of what are known as *constraints*, which I turn to next. This requires a brief review of some technical material in Devlin (1991) concerning types.

The *types* of the theory are defined by applying two type-abstraction procedures, starting with an initial collection of *basic types*. The basic types correspond to the process of individuating or discriminating uniformities in the world at the most fundamental level. These are the *basic types*:

- TIM: the type of a temporal location
- LOC: the type of a spatial location
- IND: the type of an individual
- REL: the type of an *n*-place relation
- SIT: the type of a situation
- INF: the type of an infon
- TYP: the type of a type (see below)
- PAR: the type of a *parameter* (see below)
- POL: the type of a polarity (i.e. the "truth values" 0 and 1)

For each basic type *T* other than PAR, there is an infinite collection of *basic parameters*, used to denote arbitrary objects of type *T*.

We generally use the less formal notation $\dot{l}$, $\dot{t}$, $\dot{a}$, $\dot{s}$ etc. to denote parameters (in this case of type LOC, TIM, IND and SIT, respectively).

Given an object, *x*, and a type, *T*, we write:

$$x : T$$

to indicate that the object *x* is *of* type *T*.

Most uses of parameters require what are known as *restricted parameters*, the range of which is more fine grained than that of the basic parameters. In essence, the mechanism for constructing restricted parameters enables us to make use of parameters restricted to range over any relevant domain. See Devlin (1991) for details.

There are two kinds of type-abstraction, leading to two kinds of types.

Firstly, there are the *situation-types*. Given a SIT parameter, s, and a compound infon σ, there is a corresponding *situation-type*:

$$[\dot{s} \mid \dot{s} \models \sigma]$$

the *type* of situation in which s obtains.

This process of obtaining a type from a parameter, $\dot{s}$, and a compound infon σ, is known as *(situation-) type abstraction*. We refer to the parameter s as the *abstraction parameter* used in this type abstraction.

For example:

$$[\text{SIT}_1 \mid \text{SIT}_1 \models \ll\text{running}, \dot{p}, \text{LOC}_1, \text{TIM}_1, 1\gg]$$

where $\dot{p}$ is a parameter for a person, denotes the type of situation in which someone is running at some location and at some time. A situation s will be of this type just in case someone is running in that situation (at some location, at some time).

As well as situation-types, our theory also allows for *object-types*. These include the basic types TIM, LOC, IND, RELN, SIT, INF, TYP, PAR and POL, as well as the more fine-grained uniformities described below.

Object-types are determined over some initial situation. Let s be a given situation. If x is a parameter and σ is some compound infon (in general involving x), then there is a type:

$$[\dot{x} \mid s \models \sigma],$$

the *type* of all those objects x to which x may be anchored in the situation s, for which the conditions imposed by s obtain.

This process of obtaining a type from a parameter $\dot{x}$, a situation s, and a compound infon σ, is known as *(object-) type abstraction*. The parameter $\dot{x}$ is known as the *abstraction parameter* used in this type abstraction.

The situation s is known as the *grounding* situation for the type. In many instances, the grounding situation s is "the world" or "the environment" in which we live (generally denoted by w in my account). For example, the *type* of all people could be denoted by:

$$[\text{IND}_1 \mid w \models \ll\text{person}, \text{IND}_1, \dot{l}_w, \dot{t}_{now}, 1\gg]$$

Constraints, the facilitators and inhibitors of information flow, are abstract links between types of situation. They may be natural laws, conventions, logical (i.e. analytic) rules, linguistic rules, empirical, law-like correspondences, or whatever. Their role in the information chain is quite well conveyed by the use of the word *means*. For instance, consider the statement:

smoke means fire.

This expresses a constraint (of the natural law variety). What it says is that there is a law-like relation that links situations where there is smoke to situations where there is fire. If T_{smoke} is the type of situations where there is smoke present, and T_{fire} is the type of situations where there is a fire, then an agent (e.g. a person) can pick up the information that there is a fire by observing that there is smoke (a type T_{smoke} situation) and being aware of, or *attuned to*, the constraint that links the two kinds of situation, denoted by:

$$T_{smoke} \Rightarrow T_{fire}$$

(This is read as "T_{smoke} involves T_{fire}".)

As a constraint that holds "because the world is that way", this constraint is one that holds regardless of the presence or absence of any cognitive agent, and is an instance of what is referred to as a *nomic constraint*. For an example of a non-nomic constraint, consider:

FIRE means fire.

This describes the linguistic constraint:

$$T_{utterance} \Rightarrow T_{fire}$$

that links situations (of type $T_{utterance}$) where someone yells the word FIRE to situations (of type T_{fire}) where there is a fire. Awareness of this constraint involves knowing the meaning of the word FIRE and being familiar with the rules that govern the use of language.

The three types just introduced may be defined as follows:

$$T_{smoke} = [\dot{s} \mid \dot{s} \models \ll smokey, \dot{t}, 1 \gg]$$
$$T_{fire} = [\dot{s} \mid \dot{s} \models \ll firey, \dot{t}, 1 \gg]$$
$$T_{utterance} = [\dot{u} \mid \dot{u} \models \ll speaking, \dot{a}, \dot{t}, 1 \gg \wedge \ll utters, \dot{a}, FIRE, \dot{t}, 1 \gg]$$

The use of the same parameters in the types T_{smoke} and T_{fire} means that the constraint:

$$T_{smoke} \Rightarrow T_{fire}$$

functions by constraining the situation in which there is smoke to be a situation in which there is fire. The use of different parameters u and s in the types $T_{utterance}$ and T_{fire} means that the constraint:

$$T_{utterance} \Rightarrow T_{fire}$$

simply guarantees that an utterance of the word FIRE is linked to there being some situation in which there is a fire. The utterance situation and the fire situation may be quite separate. The use of the same time parameter t in all three types means that there is no time slippage in either case. The smoke and the fire are simultaneous, and so are the utterance and the fire.

In general, then, parameters keep track of the various informational links that are instrumental in the way constraints operate.

Notice that constraints links types, not situations. On the other hand, any particular instance where a constraint is utilized to make an inference or modify behaviour will involve specific situations (of the relevant types). Thus, constraints function by relating various regularities or uniformities across actual situations.

4.5 Normative Constraints and Cognition

In our discussion of Sacks (1972), Rosenberg and I (Devlin and Rosenberg 1993) introduced a kind of constraint slightly different from the ones described in the previous section. Known as *associative links*, these new constraints connect not just situation-types but object-types as well. Associative links concern the way in which an agent cognitively encounters the world.

Consider a constraint $U \Rightarrow V$, where:

$$U = [\dot{x} \mid u \models (\dot{x})\,], V = [\dot{y} \mid v \models_\tau (y)]$$

for some grounding situations u, v and compound (parametric) infons σ, τ. This constraint provides an "associative link" between objects of type U and objects of type V, in that an agent that is aware of, or attuned to, this constraint will, when it encounters an object x of type U as *an object of type U* and, under the same circumstances encounters an object y of type V, will regard, or encounter, y as *an object of type V*.

To take an example that figures significantly in the discussion in Sacks (1972), there is a constraint:

$$T_{\text{baby}} \Rightarrow T_{\text{mother}}$$

that obtains in certain circumstances (i.e. in certain situations), such that, if these appropriate circumstances prevail, and if A is attuned to this constraint and encounters an object B of type T_{baby} and an object M of type T_{mother}, and furthermore, encounters B as an object of type T_{baby}, then A will in fact encounter M as an object of type T_{mother}.

Associative links are an important special case of what we call *normative constraints*. These are informational constraints that guide the normal behaviour of agents.

As entities within the situation-theoretic ontology, constraints are just infons of a certain kind. The "official" way to denote the infon $S \quad S'$ is:

$$\ll \Rightarrow, S, S', 1 \gg$$

(or ≪involves, S, S', 1≫). This observation at once raises the question: when we speak of a constraint *prevailing*, what situation supports the relevant infon?

Well, consider first the *smoke means fire* constraint. Call it C_1. This constraint is a certain regularity in the world, a systematic linkage between situations of the two types T_{smoke} and T_{fire}. But what is the ontological status of this systematic linkage other than a situation? (See Devlin (1991), pp. 69–85 for a discussion of the nature of situations.) And it is precisely this situation that supports C_1. I denote this situation by *Support* (C_1).

In general, any nomic constraint C will comprise a systematic, informational link between pairs of situations, situations of types T and T', respectively, and, as a systematic regularity in the world, this linkage will constitute a situation, which we denote by *Support* (C). This situation will include, in particular, the relevant causality between situations of type T and those situations of type T' to which they are linked. Moreover:

$$Support\ (C) \vDash C$$

and *Support* (C) is in a sense the "minimal" situation that supports C.

To take another example, let C_2 be the linguistic constraint that links utterances of the word FIRE to instances of fire in the world. Although one could take the supporting situation to be that very regularity that connects uses of the word FIRE to instances of fire, this would amount to reducing language to a whole bag of isolated words and connections. More reasonable is to take the supporting situation in the case of a linguistic constraint such as C_2 to be the entire language situation; that is to say, the complete collection of rules, norms, and practices that constitutes the English language.

Turning now to the associative links, let C_3 be the constraint:

$$T_{baby} \Rightarrow T_{mother}$$

This links the two concepts of babies and mothers. What supports it? Well, it is one of the constraints that could be said to be part of the "world of families". But the "world of families" constitutes a situation, the situation that comprises everything that is part and parcel of being a family. This situation is captured within our framework as $oracle(T_{family})$. (Intuitively – and very roughly – speaking, the *oracle* for any object a is the situation that comprises everything in the world of "direct relevance" to a. See Devlin (1991), section 3.5, for details.) It is this oracle situation that supports the constraint in this case:

$$oracle(T_{family}) \vDash T_{baby} \Rightarrow T_{mother}$$

Notice that the above discussions assume a very general notion of a "situation" as an aggregate of features of the world that constitute an *aspect* of the world, an aspect that may be physical, possibly located in time and/or space, or abstract, perhaps consisting of systematic regularities in the world, as in the case of nomic constraints, or maybe arising from the intentional activity of cognitive agents, as in the case of language or social conventions.

Plans constitute another example of a highly abstract form of situation relevant to the present study. According to the theory proposed by Bratman (1987), and outlined in Devlin (1991, section 7.6) , human agents are planning creatures that are able to regulate their activities according to plans of future activity. The agent does not necessarily *follow* a particular plan in the sense of acting according to specific *rules*, but as long as it remains active, the plan will influence and guide activity. Bratman discusses this approach to intentional activity in some detail, but his approach is entirely descriptive; he does not attempt to provide a formal mechanism to capture his theory. In Devlin (in preparation), I propose that plans be treated as situations, and that an agent acting according to a plan amounts to it regulating its behaviour by means of the constraints supported by that situation.

Now, according to the basic picture outlined above, an agent will act and reason in accordance with various constraints, constraints that obtain in the context in which that agent is situated. But a given situation will, in general, support a great many constraints, many of them quite possibly of a minor and, to a large extent, irrelevant nature as far as the agent's current activity is concerned. How is the agent to choose? Although this question is largely one of psychology rather than situation theory, we can give a partial answer.

A situation supporting a constraint, or more generally any kind of infon, is, of course, simply a matter of rendering that infon true, i.e. informationally supporting it. But for many situations, in particular the ones that arise as contexts for cognitive activity, there is a "hierarchy" of constraints, with some constraints being closely bound up with the nature of the situation *as a situation*, and others less closely bound to that situation. We shall refer to constraints that are closely bound up with a particular situation as being *salient* to that situation. The more salient is a constraint C within a given supporting situation s, the more likely is an agent for whom s is a context to be guided by C.

For example, in real-world, environmental situations, the constraint that links smoke to fire is a highly important one, crucial to the agent's survival, and as such is, under normal circumstances, likely to be the most salient in any situation in which there is smoke. On the other hand, one can imagine that a group of people has established a constraint whereby a smoke signal indicates that the enemy is approaching, and for the members of that group, their context is such that the most salient constraint is the one that links smoke to an approaching enemy. Since the behaviour of an agent is most likely to be influenced by the most salient constraints in its current context, different contexts can bring different constraints into play.

To take another example, the situation $oracle(T_{family})$ supports many constraints concerning family relationships and the way in which members of a family behave towards each other, including constraints that, while undoubtedly guiding and influencing an agent's behaviour, do so in a highly peripheral way as far as purposeful activity is concerned, such as the constraint that a family member is human, that husbands are male, etc. On the other hand, some constraints are particularly salient to this situation, in particular those that concern the family relationships that bind the family together as a family, such as the associative link that says a mother is the mother of a child, a husband is the husband of a wife, etc. Thus, an agent for whom a current context is the family situation, is likely to readily associate babies with mothers. This particular example, the focus of a classic paper in the early literature on ethnomethodology (Sacks 1972), is discussed at length in Devlin and Rosenberg (1993).

Again, the purposeful behaviour of an agent who is following a certain set of *plans* can be regarded as acting in accordance with constraints supported by the relevant plan-situations. This example is taken up in detail in my paper (Devlin, in preparation).

In thinking about cognitive behaviour in situation-theoretic terms, I find it particularly helpful to make use of the metaphor of "living in a situation". Situations are an attempt to capture, within a rigorously defined ontology, the role played by context in reasoning and communication. Now the key feature of context – what makes it a *context* – is that it guides the flow of information *from without*; it does not play an explicit role. For example, in the case of everyday activity, the way you behave in the home situation differs significantly from your behaviour at work, and is different again from the way you act when in a concert hall. Each situation carries with it a distinctive set of rules and norms of behaviour, which situation theory treats as constraints. Again, in the case of communication, you make use of different linguistic constraints depending on whether you are speaking to a small child, to your family or at work, and different constraints again when speaking a foreign language. Now in each of these cases, you do not make explicit use of any *rules* (except perhaps on very special occasions which need not concern us here); the context does not play an active role in your activity, it simply *establishes* the appropriate constraints. During the course of any particular situated activity, you may be thought of as "living in the world" that constitutes the context for that activity.

Notice that there is no reason to suppose that you are restricted to "living in" just one situation at a time in this manner. The high degree of abstraction allowed for situations enables us to use the theory to capture many different aspects of behaviour at any one time. When playing a game of cards with some friends, for example, your behaviour will be guided by the formally specified rules of the game, the linguistic rules governing English language, and the social rules and norms that guide group behaviour when among friends. According to the "living in a situation" metaphor, you may thus be described as simultaneously living in three different situations here.

One of the future challenges facing situation theory is to develop structural connections between situations to help to explain the way that purposeful behaviour results from the confluence of constraints supported by a number of distinct situations.

According to this picture, then, to be competent in a particular language, for example, amounts to having a familiarity with a certain abstract situation, to "know one's way around that situation". Speaking or understanding a particular language can be regarded as "cognitively living in" the appropriate linguistic situation, in the same way that finding one's way around one's home can be regarded as physically living in that home situation. Learning a new language involves becoming familiar with another linguistic situation, learning to find one's way around that situation. Adjusting one's way of speaking and understanding from American English to British English involves identifying the small number of differences between the situation that comprises the rules and practices of American English and the situation comprising the rules and practices of British English.

Likewise, since plans may be treated as situations we can regard following a plan in the same way that we regard communicating in a particular language or finding one's way around one's home; namely as "living in" a certain situation. Devlin (1991), Sacks (1972), Devlin and Rosenberg (1993) and Devlin (in preparation) all include further discussions of the nature of constraints that are relevant to the present chapter.

4.6 Information, Situations and Design

The communication scenario that has hitherto motivated most of the development of situation semantics is the one illustrated in Fig. 4.3, namely one person talking to another using natural language. However, since the development has been restricted almost entirely to natural language *utterances*, with no use made of such aspects of human–human communication as facial expression or gestures, practically everything that has been said applies equally well to various other forms of communication involving single-agent to single-agent communication, such as a telephone conversation between two people, the interaction between a person and a personal computer, the sending and receipt of a letter or other written document, or the storage and retrieval of information using diagrams and charts, all of which are illustrated in the typical office scene shown in Fig. 4.4.

Of course, most instances of everyday reasoning involve a constant

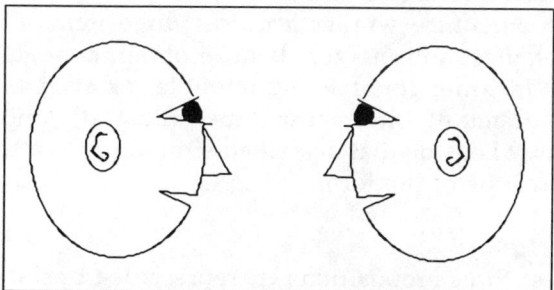

Fig. 4.3. Natural language conversation.

Fig. 4.4. A stand-alone, single-user information system.

switching between different kinds of representation and communicative media. The worker in Fig. 4.4 will most likely handle information that is assembled or merged from several, or indeed all, of the sources shown, together with the information already stored in his head. And during the course of his morning's work, the chances are he will also engage in a number of face-to-face exchanges, as depicted in Fig. 4.3. So where, exactly, is the *information* that forms the focus of his activities? In particular, when our man *merges* information from two or more sources, say diagrammatic, written language and speech, just what exactly is it that gets merged, and what is the product of that merger?

In order to answer fundamental questions of this kind, it seems necessary to distinguish between *information* and *representation*, treating the information stored by means of a certain representation or carried by a particular signal as an abstract entity separate from the representation or signal. This is precisely what is done in situation theory, where the infons provide the basic, representation-independent notion of "information" and the constraints, or rather certain of them, capture the link between representation and represented information.

For instance, in Fig. 4.4, let C denote the wall chart situation; that is to say, C is that aspect of the world that supports all the constraints by virtue of which C stores the information for which it is designed. Similarly, let M be the computer situation and D the document situation.

Suppose that our office worker acquires three items of information, one from each source, and merges them to obtain a single, further item of information. In order for it to be possible, or even to make sense, to merge these items of information, they must all concern the same *described situation*.[3] Let s be that described situation. Then the three items of information will be of the form:

$$s \vDash \sigma_1, \quad s \vDash \sigma_2, \quad s \vDash \sigma_3$$

The fact that these three propositions are represented by the wall chart, the computer and the document, respectively, is captured by the propositions:

$$C \models p_1, \quad M \models p_2, \quad D \models p_3$$

where p_i is the infon $\ll \models, s\ s_i, 1 \gg$. The merged information will then be of the form:

$$s \models \sigma_1 \wedge \sigma_2 \wedge \sigma_3$$

The fact that the user may well arrive at this merged information quite effortlessly, and indeed be unaware of having obtained it by a process of merging from different representations at all, is reflected in our "living in a situation" metaphor by saying that in the course of this process, the user is (cognitively) "living in" the three situations C, M and D, and thus acts according to the constraints that are salient in those situations.

4.7 Multimedia and Multi-User

Fig. 4.5 provides a graphical illustration of the system–agent information links utilized by the individual in the multimedia office system depicted in Fig. 4.4. (Actually, in order to avoid an overcomplicated diagram, I have omitted the wall chart and the possibility of other office personnel.) Viewed in this abstract fashion, it is clear that a typical modern office worker functions in a complex information network, moving constantly from one representation medium to another. Such complexity would surely be too great for any theory of information that does not distinguish representation from the information it represents. Situation theory, on the other hand, is tailored to handle such a set-up. For a particularly well-developed account of multirepresentational reasoning

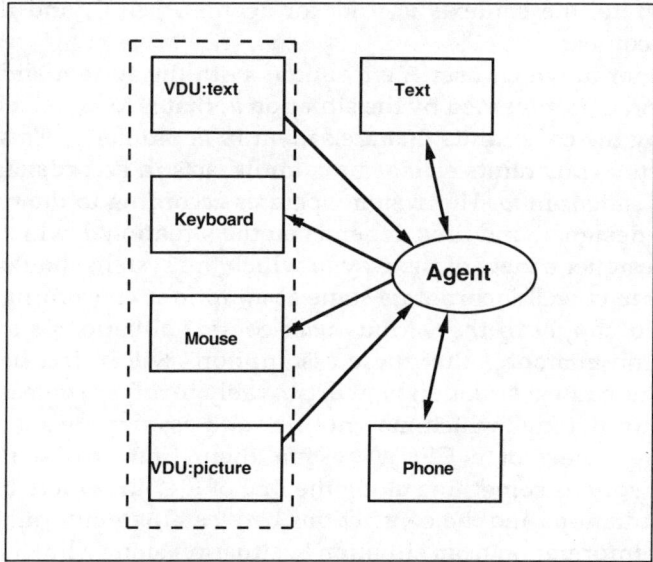

Fig. 4.5. A hypermedia system.

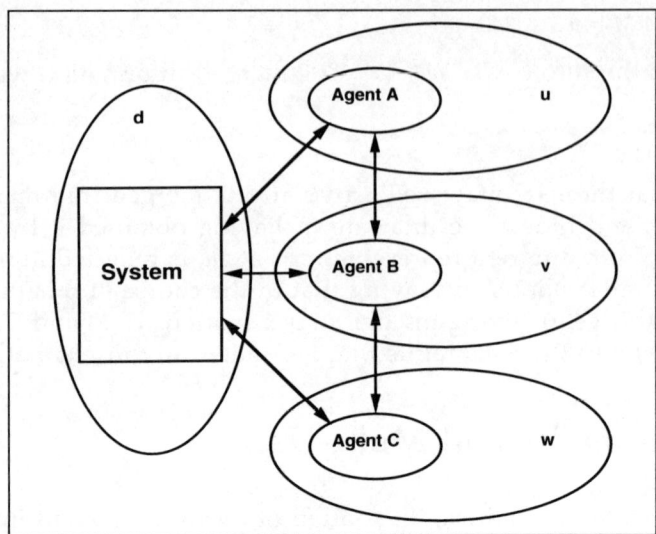

Fig. 4.6. A CSCW system.

within a restricted domain in mathematics, see Barwise and Etchemendy (1991), which presents a detailed situation-theoretic analysis of reasoning using the educational software tool Hyperproof. See also the more complex CSCW information system illustrated in Fig. 4.6 – more complex because the interface between each user and the system may itself be multimedia (by "system" I mean the computer system; that is, I exclude the users).

In Fig. 4.6, I have also drawn in a crucial feature that, for simplicity, I left out of Fig. 4.5; namely, the various contexts in which the different parties operate, the contexts u, v, w for agents A, B, C, and the system designer's context d.

The manner in which user A encounters both the system and the other agents, B and C, is governed by the situation u; that is to say, A's behaviour is guided by the constraints that are salient in u. Similarly, B's actions are guided by the constraints salient in v, and C acts in accordance with the constraints salient in w. The system operates according to the rules specified by the designer, and thus depends on the situation d, which is essentially the designer's view of the way in which the system should function. Although d may well incorporate some assumptions concerning the types that "should" apply to the various user-context situations such as u, v, w, there is no guarantee that these assumptions will in fact be satisfied. Likewise, A's context situation, u, will probably involve type-assumptions about each of B and C which may not be valid assumptions, and so on.

The overall view of a CSCW system then, from the standpoint of situation theory, is something along the line of Fig. 4.7, where the ellipses represent situations and the connections between them information links. The flow of information from situation to situation along a link is mediated by the constraints salient in the various context situations. The salience of a constraint in a particular situation is denoted by drawing the link within the appropriate ellipse. A constraint not enclosed within a situation is one that prevails generally, independent of context.

It should be noted, however, that the picture shown in Fig. 4.7 is a highly simplistic one, and in particular is unrelated to Fig. 4.6. In practice, the topology corresponding to a given information system will be far more complex. In particular, I have not included in this picture any information links between the larger situations that themselves act as contexts for constraints, although such connections play a role in even fairly simple real-life examples, such as the one described by Devlin and Rosenberg (1993). Ultimately, one would expect to make use of mental conceptualizations of figures that are not capable of two-dimensional representation.

Constraints operate at the level of *types*, with situation s providing information about situation s' by virtue of situation s being of type T and situation s' being of type T'. Since infonic information is discrete and capable of precise stipulation, and since situation-types are determined by infonic information and are therefore themselves capable of precise stipulation, the lack of extensional precision concerning the situations themselves plays neither a positive nor a negative role in this framework – the focus of the theory lies elsewhere.

Coupled with the "living in a situation" metaphor, the above situation-theoretic framework should, I believe, prove as useful in the design of interactive systems as it has, already, in the analysis of the use of social knowledge in communicative interaction (Devlin and Rosenberg 1993).

4.8 The Role of Situation Theory

Of course, it is the case that usable systems do get designed, without the use of the kind of methodology I am proposing here. So what exactly can the designer hope to gain by heading off and learning about situation theory? Why bother?

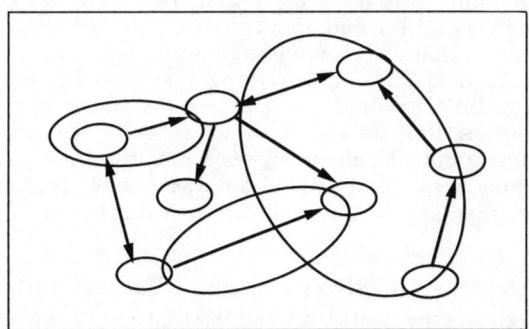

Fig. 4.7. A situation-theoretic network for a CSCW system.

The answer is partly the one given earlier: the resourcefulness of the human user often serves to hide quite severe design limitations. But also, the fact is that designers too can be pretty resourceful, and do on occasion make a very good job of anticipating the context(s) from which the user(s) will approach the system. But without an appropriate theory to guide the development, this process will inevitably be very much a hit-or-miss affair. The role I am proposing for situation theory here is to lessen that hit-or-miss aspect, assisting resourceful designers by providing them with a collection of intellectual design tools appropriate for the task of designing such a system.

That this is possible depends on the very feature of situation theory that newcomers to the field generally find most troublesome, namely the nature of situations.[4] Situations do not have the extensional definiteness normally expected of mathematical objects.

But, for all the unease that situations create for the beginner, their very "extensional vagueness" is both necessary and to be expected if situation theory is to be capable of dealing with context in real-world activity. For, as Suchman (1987) emphasizes, context generally defies an extensional definition. To illustrate this observation, she writes as follows (the Garfinkel work to which she refers concerns a task that Garfinkel set his students in an experiment):

> Garfinkel's aim was to press the common-sense notion that background knowledge is a body of things thought but unsaid, that stands behind behaviour and makes it intelligible. The request was that the students provide a complete description of what was communicated, in one particular conversation, as a matter of the participants' shared knowledge. Students were asked to report a simple conversation by writing on the left hand side of a piece of paper what was said, and on the right hand side what it was that they and their partners actually understood was being talked about. Garfinkel reports that when he made the assignment:
>
> > *Many students asked how much I wanted them to write. As I progressively imposed accuracy, clarity, and distinctness, the task became increasingly laborious. Finally, when I required that they assume I would know what they had actually talked about only from reading literally what they wrote literally, they gave up with the complaint that the task was impossible.* (p. 317)
>
> The students' dilemma was not simply that they were being asked to write "everything" that was said, where that consisted of some bounded, albeit vast, content. It was rather that the task of enumerating what was talked about itself extended what was talked about, providing a continually receding horizon of understandings to be accounted for. The assignment, it turned out, was not to describe some existing content, but to generate it. As such, it was an endless task. The students' failure suggests not that they gave up too soon, but that what they were assigned to do was not what the participants in the conversation themselves did in order to achieve shared understanding. (pp. 46–47)

Situation theory takes seriously the issue of background situations that cannot be specified extensionally, and seeks instead to achieve mathematical precision elsewhere. Just because there is no possibility of specifying a situation *extensionally*, it does not follow that situations cannot figure in a rigorous theory. It simply means that, in many instances, the question of extensional specification is not an appropriate one.

But this is not a new phenomenon. Mathematicians, and those who use mathematics, often work with objects for which certain questions of specification cannot be answered. For instance, most scientists, econo- mists and engineers use the real numbers, yet apart from the rational numbers, no real number can be specified exactly in terms of a decimal expansion. *Some* irrational real numbers have an *alternative* specification – for example, $\sqrt{2}$, π, e – but for most irrational numbers all that can be done is supply lower and upper bounds of sufficient accuracy. And yet, once someone is sufficiently familiar with the real number system, this lack of precision does not cause any great difficulties. Indeed, the theory of the reals has been sufficiently well developed *around* this "problem" that, almost by definition, the issue of the decimal representation of a real number hardly ever arises; the reals are handled in different ways, precision being achieved in an alternative fashion.

Analogously, although extensional specification of situations is not possible, this does not mean that we cannot develop a precise calculus for handling situations, and, indeed, this is one of the main aims of current situation theory. Along with the development of that formal framework should come a familiarity with situations, including an awareness, at first conscious but subsequently tacit, of their extensional imprecision. It is in this way that situation theory aims to offer the social scientist or the designer a formal framework that incorporates in its formality the inherent imprecision of context.

For instance, Millar (1992) makes use of situations in order to organize and analyse the data she obtained in her study of the resolution of conflict in a workplace undergoing major change. Again, in her study of cooperative work involving a photocopier, Suchman (1987) makes frequent reference to "situations", and although she was not using this word in the technical sense of situation theory, everything she says is consistent with such an interpretation, and indeed, I believe that by reformulating her analysis in the more formal framework of situation theory, it can be made more precise.

This is precisely what Rosenberg and I do in Devlin and Rosenberg (1993), where we recast a classic ethnomethodological analysis of coopera- tive action in formal, situation-theoretic terms. Although the situations we use are, by their very ontological nature, "extensionally imprecise", we achieve precision elsewhere, and are able to focus on various key features of the (highly contextual) data that can be handled precisely, thereby obtaining a more precise analysis. Indeed, we believe we have uncovered imprecision in the original, Sacks analysis – the sort that situation theory allows us to correct.

Likewise in the design process. A designer who starts with the simple picture of a CSCW system as in Figs 4.6 and 4.7, who is sufficiently familiar with the nature of situations, will be forced, at every stage in the design process, to take account of the influence, and the imprecision, of context. This awareness is not something that will have to be consciously imposed; rather, it is implicit in the metaphor that situation theory provides, as the designer goes from the collected, on-site data through the various stages of the design process that lead to the finished product.

As situation theory develops further, we can expect to provide an increasing number of formal tools that the social scientist or the systems designer can make use of. In the meantime, simply the adoption of the framework of situation theory as an analytic and design methodology should prove beneficial. By adopting an initial situation-theoretic metaphor as in Figs 4.6 and 4.7, and coupling this with the additional metaphor of "living in a situation" (where the living might be cognitive rather than physical), the designer does not need to "take account of contextual factors", since the relevant contexts are part and parcel of the metaphor that governs the entire approach.

Thus, the incorporation of contextual features into the design becomes transparent, the metaphor allowing the designer to make use of ordinary experience in the everyday, physical world of rooms, houses, cities and parks. This approach of providing people with a simple, everyday metaphor has, of course, proved hugely successful in the design of personal computer interfaces (Fig. 4.1) and technical software systems (Fig. 4.2). The proposal I am making here is that the adoption of situation theory as an analytic and design framework will provide the anthropologist and the system designer with similarly powerful metaphors.

4.9 Conclusion

One of the goals of good system (or tool) design is transparency of use, the provision of physical or software tools that can be used in a "ready-to-hand" fashion. This is often achieved by means of a metaphor, creating a familiar (and appropriate) look and feel to something new. In this chapter I suggest that the same goal of transparency of use be applied to the conceptual tools used in the design process itself, and that this can likewise be achieved by the adoption of suitable metaphors. In the case of interactive computer systems, the metaphor is often an everyday, physical one, mediated visually by graphics. For the interactive information system design process, I suggest that situation theory can lead to a metaphor that is likewise rooted in the everyday, physical world, mediated by mathematics.

In this chapter, I have argued in favour of the adoption of situation theory as a framework for design on the following grounds:

- It forces the designer (by virtue of the nature of situations) to work with context and with the enormous imprecision and lack of predictability that context entails.

- It forces the designer (by virtue of the way that constraints operate) to take constant account of the complexity of inference and information flow.

- It forces the designer (by virtue of the nature of infons and propositions) to realize that the actual information used or processed in any instance is almost always partial and incomplete.

- It forces the designer (by virtue of the way it handles meaning) to take constant account of indexicality.

It achieves these ends by confronting the issues of vagueness, imprecision, partiality, and indexicality head-on, incorporating them into its formality. In addition, by using a situation-theoretic framework throughout the design cycle, to frame the initial data collection process, to organize the data and formalize its analysis, to carry out the actual design work, and to provide formal verifications for the design, the designer will be working within a single framework, guided by powerful metaphors rooted in the everyday world.

Acknowledgement An earlier version of this chapter was circulated as a technical report of the Center for the Study of Language and Information, Stanford University, Stanford, California, USA, reference CSLI Report 92-171, Summer 1992.

Notes

1 I say "regarded" here, since the main motivation behind situation theory is the development of a scientific theory of information. For this purpose, areas such as natural language semantics and Computer Supported Cooperative Work (CSCW) systems design are highly relevant phenomena that both guide the development of the theory and provide application domains to test its efficacy.

2 Indeed, according to Lakoff and Johnson (1980), all human understanding is metaphorical in nature. The argument I present here is intended to be independent of the veracity of that claim, although if their claim is accepted, then most of my argument on the role of metaphor in design becomes informationally superfluous.

3 The term *described situation* is one that I adopt from Devlin (1991). I mean the focus or target situation.

4 This does not apply to the fairly simple notion of situations developed by Barwise and Perry (1983), but it does occur with some of the kinds of situation mentioned in this chapter and elsewhere in the current literature on the subject.

Chapter 5

Patterns of Language in Organizations: Implications for CSCW

C. Hutchison

5.1 Introduction

5.1.1 Aims

In this chapter I outline four (of many possible) views of the role of language in cooperative working. My intent is neither to be exhaustive nor profound, but rather to simply draw attention to the central part that language plays in group work and consequently to highlight its relevance to the design of Computer Supported Cooperative Work (CSCW) systems. I take it as uncontroversial that interpersonal (and intergroup) communication is a *sine qua non* of all organizational work, that the importance of communication in the operation and hence behaviour of the organization is now well understood (e.g. Farace et al. 1977; Francis 1987; Kanter 1989; Kotter 1978; Manning 1971; Mintzberg 1979; Putnam and Pacanowsky 1983; Robb 1990), and thus hope to show that attention to the issues raised below (although they may at first sight seem tangential to "hard" CSCW, namely the design and evaluation of groupware) is highly pertinent, and arguably crucial, to CSCW as a discipline concerned with "the study and theory of how people work together, and how the computer and related technologies affect group behaviour" (Greenberg 1991, p. 1). On that understanding, more useful than a *technology-centred* distinction between single-user and (paradigmatically synchronous distributed) group-user systems might be a *task-orientated* distinction between single-agent and multi-agent problem solving, where that problem solving is supported by computers.

Underpinning the work in which I have been involved has been the view that organizations, in the most general sense, are in large part constructed through and sustained by language (face-to-face conversations, telephone conversations, letters, memoranda, proposals, reports, contracts, job descriptions, email, in-house newsletters, health and safety regulations and other rulebooks, notice board messages and so on, viewed as forms of discourse); that Information Systems (IS) are fundamentally communication tools rooted in language, and as such are inextricably embedded in the patterns of discourse that largely define an IS-user organization; and that therefore an understanding of the role of language in organizational behaviour generally may be critical to the design of systems, irrespective of whether one's interests lie with "simple" computer mediated communication for the purpose of sharing and distributing information between members of a group (e.g. email, bulletin boards) or with specialized computer based tools for the co-development of documents or the co-management of activities (e.g. collaborative writing tools, multi-user idea generation and organizing tools, collaborative design, project management and such like). Perhaps controversially, I would want to suggest that all computer information systems, whether "single-user" or "group-user", are media for dialogues between producers and consumers of information, and that recognition of this fact must therefore put language issues high on the designer's priorities.

The underlying concern of this chapter is rather to set out an agenda for research than to report results of research, although Hutchison and Rosenberg (1992, 1993) summarize related preliminary studies we have undertaken to date. The research agenda will have the three main goals of:

1. Rigorously examining the roles that language, at all levels of linguistic analysis, appears to play within organizational behaviour. Much of the initial work would be purely descriptive, endeavouring to produce as rich a description as possible of the actual use of language by members of the organization.
2. Using the results of the first stage to suggest and test models of communicative behaviour – and "communicative competence" (Hymes 1972) – in organizations.
3. Investigating the applicability of successful models from the second stage to the design and use of software (including groupware) for the mediation of information between agents within organizations.

The main body of the chapter outlines only some of the key levels of analysis for stage 1 above. For reasons of space, there is no attempt at exhaustiveness. The principal purpose of the survey is to point up contrasting forms of analysis (summarized in Table 5.1) and to assess the usefulness of each for understanding intergroup and intragroup behaviour.

In the following pages I first briefly outline the relevance of theories of language to information system design, then, with reference to the levels of description identified in Table 5.1, endeavour to clarify the nature of the

Table 5.1. Levels and types of linguistic analysis

Level	Type of analysis
Sociolinguistic	Sociometric
Stylistic	Content-free surface–structural
Syntactico-semantic	Systemic functional
Pragmatic	Belief modelling/speech acts

role that language appears to play in organizations. I show, where relevant, how each of these levels of analysis could lead to a better understanding of cooperative behaviour (and, incidentally, communicational failure and conflictual behaviour). To set the context of the work I am currently involved in, I also present in outline a theoretical framework for a more fine grained understanding of the behaviour of organizations, particularly relevant to a discussion of the fourth level of description (this is presented in much fuller detail in Hutchison (1992)). Finally, I sketch a programme for further research.

5.1.2 The Sopwith Case Study

To set the discussion within a more concrete framework, reference will be made where appropriate to a study, as yet incomplete, of a specific group discussion, in large part mediated through email. The discussion is of interest, not because email is considered to be itself an interesting or effective vehicle for CSCW, but because it illustrates the levels of linguistic analysis listed in Table 5.1. The introduction into an organization of information technology has an inevitable influence on the way in which people work, and work together; if designed for some purpose other than that for which it is on some occasion used – in the case of email, designed for the exchange of single messages rather than for collaborative debate, as in the present study – the group that emerges, and the nature and quality of their exchanges, may be merely an accidental product of the use by individuals of the same technology, rather than providing support for an "electronic group" that already exists. This chapter will therefore also show up some of the shortcomings of email as a CSCW medium.

The group of discussants is wholly contained within a School of Information Systems, one of four schools in the technology faculty of a British university. The subject of the discussions, the bulk of which took place over a two-week period (between 17 March and 3 April 1992), was the prospective relocation of the school from its present temporary accommodation, in two separate buildings, to a new building (the "Sopwith Building"), at that time still under construction, on the same site.

The staffing of the school is as follows:

- Academic staff:
  - Head of school: BS
  - Principal lecturers: JL, SM, CLW, PG
  - Senior lecturers: JB, MG, CH, KP, AR, KR, MR, RS, CT, EW, CCW
- Support staff:
  - 2 computing officers: SL, AG
  - 1 technical officer: AH
  - 1 technician: AQ
  - 1 administrative officer: MF
  - 1 full-time secretary (undergraduate): SF
  - 2 part-time secretaries (1 undergraduate; 1 postgraduate): SA, GR
  - 1 full-time postgraduate course coordinator: CA
  - 1 full-time industrial placements secretary (undergraduate): AF

KR, the member of staff responsible for coordinating the move to the new accommodation and for liaising between the staff, the head of school (BS) and the faculty, became involved from July 1991 when he deputized for BS on the "Working Party on New Building (Sopwith) space requirements", initially in his capacity as academic laboratory manager and as such concerned primarily with determining space requirements for laboratories. By the time the email discussions began, his role had expanded to embrace general accommodation requirements for staff. Members of the school perceived the main issues to be:

- The amount of space overall to be made available to the school.

- Poor design of the building, which had been designed and half-built for a different type of use (engineering workshops, laboratories), at a time when it was envisaged that the whole of the technology faculty (including mechanical, aeronautical, production and civil engineering) would be housed there. The second biggest issue for the school was therefore how to recover from that cost effectively.

- The third most important issue was whether the designated area for the school (the whole of the third floor of the building) was to be open-plan or partitioned into offices (and, if the latter, whether these were to be single, two-person or multi-person offices); status versus requirement-based office allocation had become an issue.

- Finally, there was the question of whether the school really wanted to move to the new accommodation or remain in their present buildings.

The school has been Mac-based since around the summer of 1987 when the first "Mac Lab" was created. The machines were on Apple LocalTalk and had a MacPlus running MacServe. Within the following year, all staff had desktop Macintoshes, linked on a local area network, with file server;

the school office was linked to the backbone during the summer of 1988. Microsoft Mail was installed in summer 1991, though most staff probably did not use it until the autumn term. The "Sopwith discussion" was the first major school debate to be conducted in large part via email. The discussants in the email debate were: KR (8 mailings), JL, JB and CCW (4 mailings each), BS and EW (3 mailings each), SM (2 mailings), AR, CT and CA (1 mailing each). All mailings referred to in this chapter were either originally addressed to, or "cc-ed" to, the whole school; other mailings are not included in this study.

Original and previous messages are appended, on Microsoft Mail, to the end of "replies" and "forwards" that they generate, so that any new message will carry as a "tail" the history of earlier mailings. (The network of mailings discussing the projected move to the Sopwith Building is diagrammatically represented in Fig. 5.2.)

Finally, prior to the introduction of Microsoft Mail, only just over half the members of the school had used email before, of whom only eight used it regularly (i.e. at least once a week).

5.2 Four Models of Linguistic Support for Collaborative Work

5.2.1 Language and Information

Lyytinen (1985) argues that:

> The very idea of an information system . . . is to provide a means and an environment for *human communication*. In this sense, information systems are "linguistic communication systems only technically implemented" [Goldkuhl and Lyytinen 1982], and would be useless without a linguistic function. Information systems development involves a language development and formalization process. Thus, development processes, methods, and research programs, explicitly or implicitly, are based on a theory of linguistic phenomena. (p. 61)

In this light, Lyytinen distinguishes and reviews five language perspectives: Fregean denotational (Frege 1952; Montague 1974), Chomskian generative (Chomsky 1986), Piagetian cognitive (Piaget 1936), Skinnerian behaviouristic (Skinner 1957), and the interactionist view of Austin (1962), Searle (1969) and latterly Winograd (Flores and Ludlow 1981; Winograd 1988; Winograd and Flores 1986). Although each linguistic paradigm may have greater relevance than others for some IS applications – a denotational semantics for a database, for example, or a generative grammar for a natural language interface, or an interactionist language model for an expert system (Young 1988) – to the extent that it "can be used to interpret existing design approaches to information systems" and consequently to inform design methodology for the future, Lyytinen concludes that there is no single view that will uniquely and exhaustively account for the linguistic behaviour of the system:

> it is difficult to determine which view, or which views, provide an account for the linguistic phenomena. Each of them serves to explicate some aspect. . . . development methodologies appear often to be based only on one view . . . [which] . . . produces too narrow an understanding of the linguistic behaviour in the IS, because we should be able to abstract language from many points of view. For example, in the order processing application the analysis should perceive the language in terms of behaviour induced, formal inference and validity, syntactic structures, semantic correctness, and the coherency of the social interaction necessary to achieve an adequate specification. Each of these views might add new pieces of understanding to the problem-solving context. However, our problem is that the flexible adoption of views into various development environments is mostly intuitive and carried out in an ad hoc manner. (Lyytinen 1985, p. 71)

Computer based information systems are for the most part, of course, designed to communicate information in rather rigidly specialized ways for quite specific purposes. Thus, a relational database is designed to handle information processing tasks of a very different kind from those of, say, a decision support system. Information may, indeed, just as well be graphical as linguistic, represented in the form of charts or pictures rather than words. Nonetheless, the environments in which such systems are deployed are paradigmatically linguistic: business organizations are above all social entities, in large part created and sustained through continuous interpersonal flows of speech and text, and in that context computer based information systems are in essence merely devices, like their paper based correlatives, for mediating information between language-using human beings. Consequently, it makes little sense to view information systems as autotelic systems performing independently of the broader goals, needs, purposes, linguistic practices and interpretive strategies of the community in which they are functionally embedded.

These are not novel claims. There is a long tradition within sociology that takes language to be fundamental to social understanding and social action (e.g. Cicourel 1974). Thus, Berger and Berger (1976, p. 81), for example, are able to claim that:

> The state, the economy and the educational system, whatever else they may be, depend upon a linguistic edifice of classification, concepts and imperatives for individuals' actions – that is, they depend on a world of meanings that was constructed by means of language and can only be kept going by language.

while Halliday (1978, pp. 230–231) cogently argues throughout his many writings that any social institution – "such as a family, a school or a factory" – can, from the linguistic point of view, be thought of:

> as a communication network. Its very existence implies that communication takes place within it; there will be sharing of experience, expression of social

solidarity, decision-making and planning, and, if it is a hierarchical institution, forms of verbal control, transmission of orders and the like. The structure of the institution will be enshrined in the language, in the different types of interaction that take place and the linguistic registers associated with them.

It is not my purpose to defend such views here. It must be intuitively clear, however, that whatever information goes into an information system is "that which can be talked about", "that which can be communicated between individuals through language", "that which can be agreed upon by conversing individuals to constitute information or knowledge"; in short, whatever it is that happens to be communicable (hence verbalizable) information within the human community that uses it. Likewise, the information accessed or output from an information system is *(re)constructed as information* by the appropriate interpretative strategies of the human users. To state that, as Lyytinen for example does, a denotational view of language provides an appropriate model for understanding the use, development and management of databases, is consequently really to say no more than that the information entered into the database is taken to represent objects that are held to exist in the world and facts held to be true of the world. That the medium is a computer system rather than, say, a paper document – or, indeed, human speech – is in that sense immaterial.

In that regard, significant omissions from Lyytinen's survey are, in the first place, conversational analysis (Goodwin 1981; Jefferson and Schenkein 1978; Sacks et al. 1978) and, in the second place, functional linguistics, in particular systemic functional grammar (Halliday 1978; Halliday and Martin 1981; Kress and Hodge 1979). Of conversational analysis I shall have little to say, as it is discussed elsewhere in this volume (in Chapters 6 and 14) and its relevance to CSCW has been signalled by other authors (e.g. Tatar et al. 1991). Both are likely to be of interest in CSCW in so far as, by contrast with the formal rule based models of language surveyed by Lyytinen, they draw attention to the social contexts of language use, and in consequence bear relevance to the study of interpersonal behaviour and thus to the design of information systems that will mediate meanings between individuals.

5.2.2 Sociometric Analysis

Organizations specify formal paths of communication – who reports to whom, who delegates what to whom, who liaises with whom for what purpose – and these paths are enshrined in, for example, standard chain-of-command organizational charts and a concomitant background meta-discourse that includes such formulae as "going through (the proper) channels" or "bypassing" them.

It may very well happen, and is in fact probably the normal state of affairs, that there is at least a partial mismatch between the paths represented in the organizational chart and those that are ongoingly negotiated between actual individuals. Formal relationships of authority and responsibility will still ordinarily be – indeed, must be – observed if the organization is to maintain its internal integrity. However, by virtue of the fact that the organization is constituted of individuals with their own personalities, interests and goals, the actual (and usually unintended) structure that emerges naturally from the dynamics of interpersonal behaviour will be far richer and denser than that formally represented in the organizational chart.

Sociometry originated in the 1930s (Moreno 1934; Moreno and Jennings 1960) as a technique for "displaying patterns of human relationships that exist within groups" (Huczynski and Buchanan 1991, p. 193), and has since been developed into a method for capturing and analysing communication patterns in organizations. The output of an application of the technique to a group is called a *sociogram*, which graphically represents links between organization members based on their own assessment of the frequency, importance and content of their interactions with other specific individuals. Although the original method was used for the analysis of small groups of people, the availability of current sophisticated database and graphics techniques now enables large and complex formal/informal communication networks to be investigated and analysed. One major software package for doing so is Netmap®, designed by John J. Galloway (see Anonymous 1988; Granberg 1987; Jamieson 1989; Lucas 1987; Madlin 1987).

An example of the display of a Netmap network is shown in Fig. 5.1. Although appearing here in monochrome, the on-screen colour map uses different colours to represent various groupings of people and types of communication links. Additional information is captured and can be displayed for attributes or supporting information on people and the links.

What does a sociogram show? What information in the sociogram is of relevance to the CSCW designer? The interpretation of sociograms is obviously dependent on the purpose of the study, the selected group size and the data collected, but there are a number of general parameters on which any interpretation will be based, as discussed in the following subsections.

Agreed/Disagreed Communication

An important distinction is made between interactions where individuals agree that the communication between them is of a specific frequency and importance, and a disagreed communication where one party differs in perception of the communication. The latter case indicates either that one

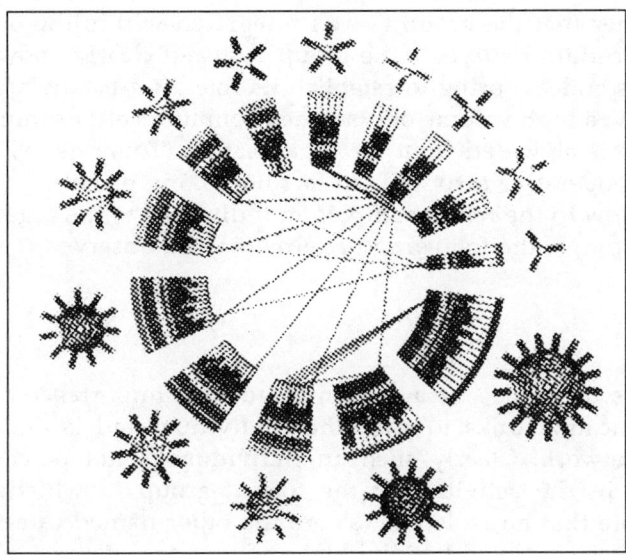

Fig. 5.1. A Netmap network.

of the parties does not believe that the communication happens as often as claimed or that it is of lesser importance than claimed. This difference in perception may show that inappropriate information is being sent, or that important information is being disregarded, or that the format for the transmission of information between the individuals is inadequate. There may even be a degree of conflict. Whatever the reasons may be, a disagreed communication indicates that further investigation is required. The relevance for CSCW is clear: if design is done on the basis of *a priori* assumptions about who, for some activity, talks to whom and those assumptions are ill founded, the software is likely to be of very limited use.

Intergroup and Intragroup

The maps depict two types of communication: those where the interactions are within defined groups (e.g. departments) and those where the interactions are between departments (or members of departments). At a broad level this will show how an individual group is operating; for example, many agreed communications between all members of the group generally means that there is a high degree of cohesion and hence probable cooperation, while a high level of disagreed communications can indicate that the group has not fully formed its own norms and identity or that there is major conflict between group members. Similarly between groups, if there is a high volume of agreed communication links it can indicate either that the group is well integrated within the organization or that – in certain patterns – the group does not clearly know what it is doing and is endeavouring to establish its role *vis-à-vis* the organization. Alternatively, a high volume of disagreed communications might indicate that a group is alienated from the organization (Touraine 1971) and that presumed cooperative activity is in fact not taking place.

Turning now to the relationship of an individual to the organization or to specific groups, the following patterns may be observed.

Isolates

An isolate is one who, for a chosen frequency, importance or task, has no communication links to any other individual and is detached from the main network. Clearly such an individual is not perceived to be taking part in the activities of the formal group to which he or she belongs. Note that an isolate is (as are the other named categories here) a specific flesh-and-blood individual and not the abstract role that he or she performs; that there may be a mismatch between the idealized picture of dependencies represented in the organizational chart and the actual patterns of communication between individuals suggests that the formal description of the (abstract) work group will almost certainly be the wrong point of departure in design. Flexibility in design – in a way that will provide potential isolates with a suite of appropriate communication tools rather than a "hard-wired" (and perhaps unmanageable) prescription of role behaviour – is clearly desirable.

Stars and Bleeders

Where a particular individual has many agreed communication links it is apparent that the individual is having an important effect, good or bad, on the behaviour of the organization. Many disagreed links, on the other hand, could indicate delusions of grandeur. Two aspects that may be considered are bottlenecks and gatekeepers. The first is straightforward, in that this individual is adversely affecting the performance of the group or organization by restricting the flow of communication, information or decisions. The second is more complex in that a gatekeeper may be of information and add or detract value (Kanter 1989) or of power (Huczynski and Buchanan 1991).

Emergent Groups

Emergent groups are those where the members share more than half of their links, irrespective of which formal group they belong to. This clustering can be in direct contrast to the formal organization chart. There are many reasons that can explain this. It may be a function of their job, or part of a matrix-managed or team-orientated organization. However it may be that they have been rejected by, isolated from or never really joined their formal group. It could also be a case of their allegiance still lying with a previous group.

Liaisons

These are particular individuals that are not members of a group and serve a linking function between various emergent groups. They do not have a majority of their links with any one group. If such individuals, in the context of non-computerized cooperative work, serve as bona fide "bridges", and if they seem to do so in virtue of the (perhaps non-obvious) nature of the task they perform, this may suggest that computer support for the task should be engineered to support this liaising function.

Descriptively and graphically showing who talks to whom, for what purpose, and therefore who actually works with whom (whatever might be depicted *prescriptively* in the organizational chart), sociometry – and, increasingly, sociometric tools such as Netmap – is able to provide valuable information about group dynamics and organizational evolution that in turn may constitute valuable data for the CSCW designer. Where an effective task-orientated group is identified, and a rich enough description has been made of their manner of coordinating their work through a stable pattern of communication, the resultant description may become datum for the design of software that will support that activity.

In the Sopwith study, the discussion was in part carried out in face-to-face interaction, in part by email. However, the face-to-face interactions were, apart from two informal "full" (but not fully attended) school meetings, *ad hoc* meetings between small numbers of individuals. It was not possible to get staff to log each and every one of their discussions in these sub-meetings (i.e. when? how long? who present? what discussed?). But, in any case, since computer mediated communication (CMC) as a social and psychological process differs significantly from face-to-face interaction, as too from telephone or from paper communication, these meetings were considered, for the purpose of this study, of lesser interest. Fig. 5.2 maps most of the email messaging that took place in the two-week period of the Sopwith discussion.

A complete audit trail for that period would in effect describe a sociogram for the "cooperative" debate of the issues (see Section 5.1.2) in the move, of which Fig. 5.2 is a fragment. Consequently, the parameters "agreed/disagreed communication", "Isolates" and "Stars and bleeders" are already pre-given. An "emergent group" is likewise described by the complete audit trail for the period.

Significantly absent in CMC, in contrast to face-to-face talk, are various forms of visual (facial expressions, eye contact, body language) and aural

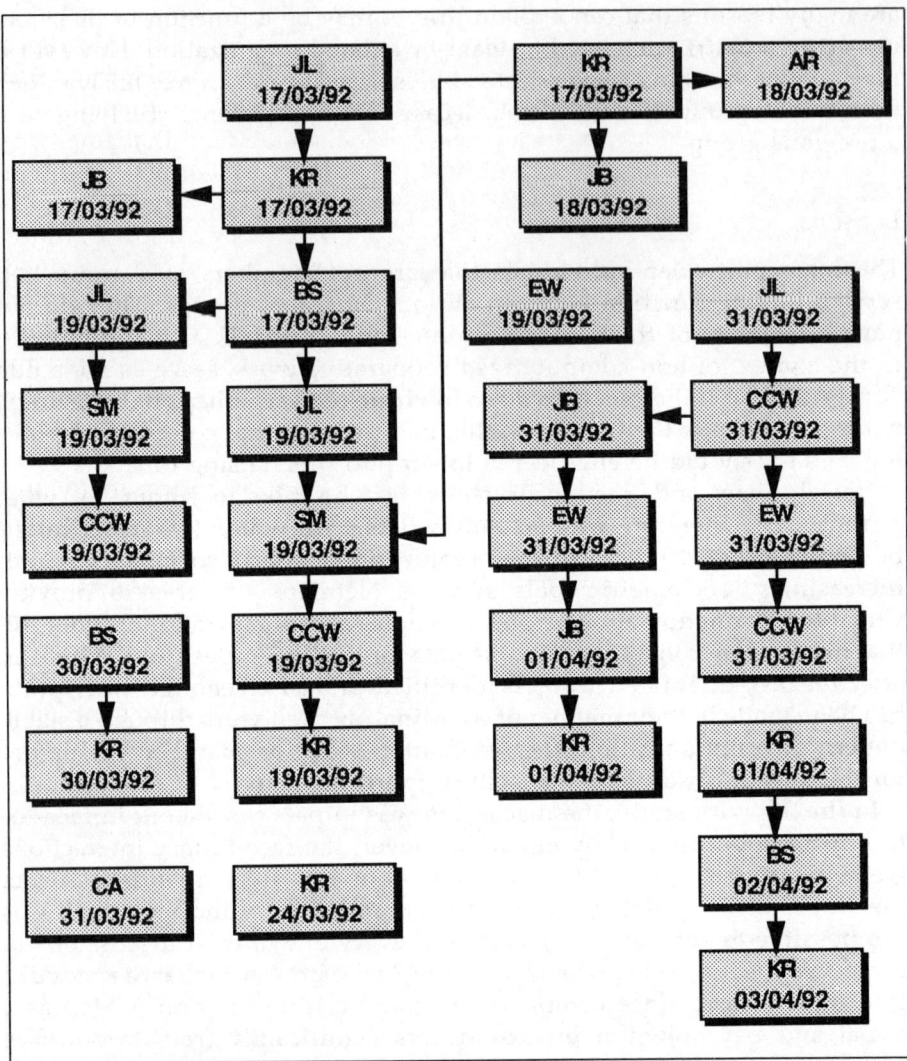

Fig. 5.2. An email network for the Sopwith discussion.

(paralinguistic features, gap-fillers, "vocalizations" such as groans and laughter) information. Also absent are: (i) the "competing-for-the-floor" characteristic of face-to-face conversation, and (ii) immediate feedback and frequent re-orientation of the talk as jointly constructed discourse. Features of verbal behaviour across email include: uninterrupted access to the channel; effectively unlimited "floor time" (mailings can be as long as the writer wishes, although excessively long mailings are a disincentive to others to read); ability to draft, compose and edit email contributions before sending; some loss of inhibitions (people are likely to say things in email broadcasts to the group that they might hesitate to say face-to-face); and persistence of the message after sending (in contrast with the "rapid fading" characteristic of the vocal–auditory channel). (See Sproull and Kiesler 1986, for a discussion of the specific social features of email.)

The distinctive characteristics of electronic mail are such that emergent groups are likely to be different in membership and style from those that emerge in face-to-face interaction. Since temporary groups – working parties, committees, task forces, for example, as well as informal social groups – may come into existence within an organization, and be sustained through ongoing goal-driven or interest-driven talk (paradigmatically, the collaborative generation, organization and exchange of information), the design implication here must be that communication mediated by email must be of a format that will support rather than disrupt the intragroup communication taking place face-to-face. Fig. 5.3 shows a brief extract from another email debate. An initial Word5 text, broadcast as an enclosure to a Microsoft Mail message, was responded to by the insertion, into the text, of comments in different fonts, typefaces and colours (unfortunately the colours cannot be reproduced here). The result was that, although initially the persistence of earlier messages after sending enabled accurate reference to other speakers' contributions, in the longer term the text became so cluttered as to be almost unreadable, and later contributors in any case were faced with the additional burden of finding unused fonts and styles by which to insert their own comments. These obstacles led to a fracture between the face-to-face

---

What, for the end user, is the difference between a KBS and a non-KBS product? The label apart, probably none — simply knowing that it's a KBS product doesn't make it perform any differently, and it should work just the same even if one doesn't know it's a KBS product (just as knowing that my Zanussi washing machine is based on 'advanced logic' — or even understanding the 'logic' — doesn't make my clothes any whiter). KBS Systems potentially widen the applications of IT (eg into law, medicine, 'advice giving') and change user expectations of such systems - look at the terms of the Japanese Fifth Gen/Human Frontiers Program. *[Any technological advance, KBS or not, may "potentially widen the applications of IT", and by virtue of that fact "change user expectations"]* Why, then, market a KBS course, as described? Well, maybe just as the pseudo-mathematical nonsense about Zanussi washing machines helps sell them, so going with a label like 'KBS' may sell the course; i.e., as a pure marketing ploy.

If one substitutes, in the above objectives, another appropriate term (e.g., 'advanced IT') for 'KB(S)', is one saying anything radically different? If not, then what is the justification for singling out KBS for special attention? KBS singles itself out by processing (or claiming to process) 'knowledge'. *[What, at this level of enquiry, is the substantive difference — for the user (rather than for the system) — between 'knowledge' and 'information'?]*

The one salient KBS term in the above objectives is "experts", but 'interaction with experts' is really only germane to the development of Expert Systems which is but one area of KBS. Is this intended to be an Expert Systems course? if so, why not call it that? for the same reason that Alvey used the KBS term. *[I don't understand this comment. KBS for Alvey meant more than expert systems]*

Fig. 5.3. Multi-authored email text.

group and the email group, and eventually to the abandonment of the email debate.

5.2.3 Style Checkers: Form versus Content

In the previous section, I pointed to the webs of communication and affiliation that criss-cross the organization and its subgroups; a more fine grained analysis would examine the substantive linguistic *content* of communicative acts between individuals for a principled description of the interactions out of which a culture of collaborative work practices emerges as a symbolic universe (see Hutchison 1992). This section, and Section 5.2.4, profile two possible analyses of linguistic content.

Communicative failure in an organization can quickly escalate into a major crisis, with potentially serious cost to the organization in the longer term. The critical significance of language use in organizations was dramatically highlighted in an article in the *Sunday Times* business news section, on 20 March 1977, in which it was claimed that industrial disputes may be sparked by poorly composed letters from management to the workforce. Although the article, in itself, has no bearing specifically on CSCW, it does illustrate, as a well-documented case study of organizational disruption, the consequences of a breakdown of communication that is in large part linguistic (see Kress and Trew 1978). In that regard, the study, here and in Section 5.2.4, exemplifies very general issues that are equally relevant to communication in small intragroup collaborative activities.

The author of the *Sunday Times* article rewrote a letter that had been issued by British Leyland's managing director to Leyland employees. The original letter, stating that improvements in productivity were a condition of getting finance for the new Mini project, does not get its message across clearly, claimed the *Sunday Times* writer, because of its preponderance of long sentences and large number of words of more than two syllables. The original British Leyland letter and the *Sunday Times* rewrite are reproduced in Appendix A.

For the *Sunday Times* writer, then, the communicative failure was essentially a result of stylistic infelicities on the part of the author of the British Leyland letter. No consideration is given by the writer to, for example, the uneven distribution of knowledge or authority/power in British Leyland, to histories of previous negotiations between the employers and the unions, or to the context of specific communicative events leading up to issuing of the letter. The writer of the *Sunday Times* article refers to the so-called Clarity Index:

> You calculate the average number of words in each sentence and add the percentage of words of more than two syllables. An article with sentences of 20 words and 10% of the words with more than two syllables has a Clarity Index number of 30. This is the reading standard of the average 16 year old.

The British Leyland letter does not get its message across clearly, claimed the *Sunday Times*, because its sentences, on average, are 35 words long, with 16 out of 100 words over two syllables long, thus giving it a Clarity Index of 51. The *Sunday Times* rewrite, which its author believes "says exactly the same thing" as the original, had a Clarity Index of 21 – "equal to a reading age of $12^1/_2$".

State-of-the-art writing analysis software (e.g. Sensible Grammar, Grammatik, Correct Grammar, Reader, RightWriter and the built-in style checker in Microsoft Word version 5), not available at the time when the original letter and the *Sunday Times* version were written, today make such mechanical analysis straightforward (Deegan 1992; Engelien and McBride 1991; Piller 1991). Checking for "wordy, pretentious, or weak phrases; clichés; and passive verb constructions . . . problems of subject–verb agreement, conflicting tenses, split infinitives, run-on sentences, double negatives" and so forth (Piller 1991, p. 20), these packages both advise authors on the clarity and readability of their documents and also produce statistical analyses of documents read in. When I ran both texts through Grammatik 2.00, the *Sunday Times* version was clearly shown to be the more readable, with a Flesch Reading Ease score of 62 ("Preferred level for most readers") as against 23 for the original ("Difficult for most readers"). Running both texts through the MS Word grammar checker, the original showed a Fog Index of 18.2 as against 8.4 for the rewritten version.

No letter or memorandum was issued by the management of the university in the Sopwith case. The email message that initiated the email discussion, however, contained a two-page enclosure setting out what one member of the school perceived to be the issues and ramifications of the move. (The text of this is reproduced as Appendix B.) The text was run through both Grammatik 2.00 (see Fig. 5.4) and MS Word grammar checker (see Fig. 5.5), and, as the statistics show, there is some inconsistency between the two. The most significant limitation was that, although both packages advise on "style", the stylistic analysis was trivial, addressing surface features of the text rather than matters of substance – what stylistic choices actually "mean". Of course, grammar/style checkers are not intended to do any more than check such surface features; the worrying aspect of such packages is that surface stylistic elegance may be taken for clarity and expressiveness of substance – clearly not the case. Style checkers miss important features of style that reveal something of the background assumptions, beliefs and intent of writers. One can, for example, recognize particular styles of talk, preferred lexicons etc., that characterize the idiolect, and possibly also therefore the "mind-style", of individual writers.

Would, then, an attention to style informed by such software have resulted in a clearer message from British Leyland to its workforce? Would it have influenced the composition process of the writer of the

```
Problems marked/detected:      0/46

Readability Statistics

    Flesch Reading Ease:       48

Paragraph Statistics

    Number of paragraphs:      24
    Average length:            1.2 sentences

Sentence Statistics

    Number of sentences:       31
    Average length:            21.4 words
    End with `?`:              1
    End with `!`:              1
    Passive voice:             0
    Short (< 14 words):        8
    Long (> 40 words):         3

Word Statistics

    Number of words:           665
    Prepositions:              91
    Average length:            4.89 letters
    Syllables per word:        1.62
```

Fig. 5.4. Grammatik 2.00 statistics.

Document Statistics	
Counts:	
Words	700
Characters	4324
Paragraphs	29
Sentences	15
Averages:	
Sentences per Paragraph	0
Words per Sentence	46
Characters per Word	4
Readability:	
Passive Sentences	13%
Flesch Reading Ease	41.5
Flesch Grade Level	14.2
Flesch-Kincaid	12.1
Gunning Fog Index	14.9

OK

Fig. 5.5. MS Word grammar statistics.

"Sopwith" text? In general, would running any text document through a style checker guarantee the clarity of the text? Kress and Trew (1978) do not believe so: the result of the *Sunday Times* rewriting "is not the same as the original. Somehow, what is being said has been changed" – more than a simplification, it "was an ideological transformation of the original text". For Deegan, too, the use of style checkers "has some disturbing implications concerning, in particular, the relationship between form and content, expression and thought. . . . is it possible to separate style from content in this way and, even if it is possible, should one?" (Deegan 1992, p. vi). The answer is undoubtedly: No.

5.2.4 Language and Reality: An Overview of Systemic Functional Linguistics

Although bearing superficial resemblances in certain respects to both the behaviourist and interactionist views described by Lyytinen (1985), systemic functional linguistics, developed by M.A.K. Halliday and his colleagues and students during the late 1950s, is distinguished by its focus on the social embeddedness of the language system in its entirety as systems of networks of behavioural choices representing the socially shared "meaning potential" of language. An individual learning a language:

> is at the same time learning other things through language – building up a picture of the reality that is around him and inside him. In this process, which is also a social process, the construal of reality is inseparable from the construal of the semantic system in which the reality is encoded. In this sense, language is a shared meaning potential, at once both a part of experience and an intersubjective interpretation of experience. . . .
> A social reality (or a "culture") is itself an edifice of meanings – a semiotic construct. In this perspective, language is one of the semiotic systems that constitute a culture; one that is distinctive in that it also serves as an encoding system for many (if not all) of the others. . . .
> . . . [people] do more than understand each other, in the sense of exchanging information and goods-and-services through the dynamic interplay of speech roles. By their everyday acts of meaning, people act out the social structure, affirming their own statuses and roles, and establishing and transmitting the shared systems of value and knowledge. (Halliday 1978, pp. 1–2)

The acts are realized through the simultaneous use of three functions of language: (i) an *ideational* function generally for expressing a speaker's experience of the world (including the world of his or her own consciousness), and in particular the specific content the speaker wishes to transmit to the hearer; (ii) an *interpersonal* function which deals with the communicative purpose of the utterance – to make a request, to express a reaction, for example – or more generally, with those syntactic features of the utterance that bind the speaker and hearer in a communicative event;

and (iii) a *textual* function, concerned with how the content of the message is presented – what the topic is and what is said about it, and how the sentences of the message are woven together as text.

There is not space in this chapter to give a full account of either Kress and Trew's adaptation of systemic grammar (but see Fowler et al. 1979; Halliday 1978; Kress and Hodge 1979) or their analysis of the British Leyland letter and the *Sunday Times* rewrite, but some examples will, I think, illustrate the insightfulness of the method they employ. One instance of the "ideological transformation" of the letter is in the replacement (with denominalization) of the noun "commitment" by the verb "promise": ". . . unless he has commitments to the necessary improvements in productivity" becomes, in the *Sunday Times* rewrite, ". . . must promise to improve output as much as is needed". Kress and Trew, pointing out that "commit" is a reflexive verb while "promise" syntactically requires a following sentence, argue:

> the crunch lies in the fact that the grammar of *promise* demands an action as a complement, and that of *commit* does not. A commitment to some end can remain intact even if the end is never achieved; but the promise is not carried out unless the end is achieved, and unless there are excuses the promise is broken and trust is betrayed.

Consequently, much more is being demanded of employees in the *Sunday Times* version than in the original. Kress and Trew go on to note that:

> In the original letter it was left unresolved who the committers were; further, it was left ambiguous who was to improve productivity. In the rewriting the employees' representatives are identified as the agents of both promise and improve.

Furthermore, the "replacement of *productivity* by the more physical *output* makes the promised action that much more direct and tangible and the obligation even less defeasible". (The same points, incidentally, were also made informally by Sir Richard Dobson, Chairman of British Leyland, in a critical letter to the *Sunday Times* published on 27 March 1977.) Looking further at the expression "improvements in productivity", Kress and Trew point out that:

> the original letter leaves an ambiguity about two things which representatives and managers may do: they may take actions which cause the collective workforce to work in ways which will lead to higher productivity; or they may deliver commitments made by the workforce as a whole – through unions, management committees, etc. – that they, the workforce, will change work patterns. This ambiguity has effects which suit it to this letter; addressed as it is to both employees representatives and to management, maybe both senses are appropriate. In this connection we need to note the more abrasive tone of the rewritten letter, a tone that may be appropriate to a view of industrial relations as more antagonistic than in the original letter, but not to the view embodied in the original. But in a more general way it is suited to reflecting, without expressing, the dual role of a "participation system", as organizer and controller of labour on the one hand and as representative of labour on the other. In the

rewritten letter the first role – organizer and controller – is chosen and the other – representative – removed; that is, the representatives and managers are asked not to represent but to take action to increase output.

Moreover, while the original letter refers to "necessary improvements in productivity", the *Sunday Times* version rewords this as "improve output as much as is needed". As an adjective modifying "improvements", "necessary" suggests some property intrinsic to its noun rather than a process, with presumably in principle some metric for quantifying or at least for reaching agreement on what is "necessary". The intrinsic necessity is divorced from the noun in the rewrite: the change of word class, and the passive structure (from "X needs Y" to "Y is needed by X") with the agent of the verb deleted, allows the "need" to be unilaterally determined by an unnamed agent (the British Leyland Board? the National Enterprise Board? the government?) in a way that – as far as the syntax of the sentence is concerned – need bear no relation to what improvements are intrinsically required.

The analysis could be taken further, but I think the essence of the method will now be clear. Some further processes are summarized in Table 5.2.

The point that should be stressed is that, although each linguistic feature taken alone may not indicate a clear stance on the part of the writer, cumulatively the features of each version of the letter reflect a coherent ideological commitment; the changes that produced the *Sunday Times* version of the letter, taken together, result not only in a formally (and trivially) "more readable" document but also substantially alter the ideological perspective.

The word "commitments", analysed above in the British Leyland text, is also used in the initial email text of the "Sopwith debate":

> If we don't like our working environment we simply don't come in except for commitments.

Ostensibly, the word is being used here as a synonym for "timetabled activities". Yet the use of the word is more significant than this: note, for example, that there is no determiner – it is not *"our* commitments"; we have by default disowned them. Who, then, has committed whom to what? It is unclear. "Commitments" are reified, nominalized as *things* rather than *actions*, dislocated and distanced from the human context of social contracts between *people*. This is consistent with the general tone of the text: that management and teaching staff have conflicting and possibly irreconcilable interests such that *processes* (teaching, meetings, the day-to-day routines of work) are rendered problematic.

The sense of alienation and dislocation is reinforced by other features of the text. Apart from the tellingly high number of nominalizations and use of nominal expressions where verbal paraphrases would have been equally possible and perhaps preferable ("distribution", "development", "workloads", "working conditions", "developments", "accounting procedure", "utilization", "control", "opportunity", "social gatherings can

Table 5.2. Changes by the *Sunday Times* to the British Leyland letter

	Change	Effect
1.	*Denominalization*: an abstract nominal is replaced by the full underlying sentence, with explicit reference to the participants in the process expressed.	The power of the agent of the process is enhanced.
	Example: (i) *his visits* becomes *he visited the* Committees; (ii) *for approval* becomes *to approve*	
2.	*Breaking up complex sentences*: producing shorter sentences, with loss of linguistic expression of casual connection.	A complex of relations is replaced by a set of simple, discrete relations.
	Example: *made it clear . . . in his recent visits* becomes *has just visited . . . He made this point.*	
3.	*Re-ordering units of information (thematization)*: two parts of a complex sentence have been switched in order.	Switches the focus of the sentence, and of the whole letter, from communication to a more physical concrete transaction
	Example: *DW has made it clear* becomes *DW has just visited*	
4.	*Re-wording*:	This changes the effect of DW's speech, making it less communicative and interactive (although an action without regard for other participants may be potentially more forceful).
	Example: *made clear* becomes *made this point*	

occur" rather than, for example, "people can meet", etc.), that ethos is echoed in sentences such as:

> The current spatial distribution of the School and people's workloads are unconducive to the fruitful development of our ideas and teaching and need changing anyhow.

Who is the agent of "fruitful development"? Who is to be the agent of "changing"? Denominalizing the first expression gives us either the transitive "<unspecified agent> develops our ideas and teaching" or the intransitive "Our ideas and teaching develop" – different kinds of process. In the latter case, the process has an internal, quasi-organic, momentum – an illness, for example, might intransitively and hence non-agentively "develop"; likewise, from the Sopwith text itself, "footpaths in parks and cities *develop* over time according to the practices of people": given the appropriate environment, in other words, the "fruitful development" is triggered as a virtually autonomous process. Leaving the transitivity of the process unspecified consequently allows the writer to remain noncommittal as to where the responsibility lies for "the fruitful development of our ideas and teaching" (which might otherwise be held to be the responsibility of the individual teacher).

Actions and processes reified and divorced from human actors then become objects to be manipulated, resources to be controlled:

> we can *gain some control* over the design and management of the allocated space.
> If we increase the effective utilization of space, in a thin, short, light world, we'll *gain negotiable resources* over the thick, long heavy.
> ... where *space is a chargeable resource* negotiated against other costs

The analysis could be extended (there are around 13 000 words of emailed text in all), although the flavour of this kind of analysis has, I think, now been sufficiently well established. Clearly, this type of analysis initially involves some intuitive interpretations, but where the interpretations are mutually supported from across a text, a coherent and cohesive picture emerges of a writer's style and ideology.

5.2.5 Language, Information and Organizations

Pragmatics is the area of linguistics concerned with the relation of utterances to the contexts in which they are uttered, including the identity of the speaker and hearer, their interests and intentions, the state of their knowledge, their physical surroundings, the business in hand, and so on. This section will address some issues in pragmatics by anchoring verbal behaviour in a conceptual model of the organization of organizations. Again, the analysis is intended to be neither profound nor exhaustive, but merely to capture the flavour of a particular approach towards understanding the role of language in cooperative working.

Hutchison (1992) outlines a theoretical framework within the terms of which one might describe the communicative and cooperative activities of people in organizations. A distinction is drawn there between the *organization* of an organization and its *structure*. Whereas the *organization* is the network of formal dependency relationships between *offices* (roughly, job descriptions) that define in the abstract the social collectivity as an organization (as represented in, for example, the standard chain-of-command organization chart), the *structure* is the physical actualization of that network by individuals enacting *roles*. So, for example, if the sales engineer O'Mara leaves and Cohen is recruited to take over his *office*, the *organization* doesn't change, but the *structure* does to the extent that Cohen and O'Mara are two physically distinct individuals, with different personalities, different professional histories and competences, and different biographical paths that have led them into the organization. Similarly, if Cohen spends a great deal of time talking to the service staff, while O'Mara did not, again the *structure* changes, although the *organization* remains the same. Note also that, to the extent that the ultimate locus of the learning process is in the individual learner, the resultant work-specific professional expertise is more properly construed as the property of a *role* than of an *office*.

We might provisionally think of the *structure* then, as the network of *actual* relationships – paths of communication and affiliation – that members of the work group, as individuals enacting *roles* contract with others in the organization. (In Hutchison (1992) the concept of structure is more finely analysed into "overt" and "covert" structure; the distinction is not necessary for the present discussion.) The *organization/office* pair, focusing on non-dynamic formal relations, represents a normative idealization; the *structure*, actualized by cooperative activity between *roles*, captures the dynamic reality of the organization. (Effectively, it is the *structure* that is displayed in sociograms, as described earlier.)

The *office*, defined in terms of the formal contribution it is deemed to make, relative to and in coordination with other offices, to the overall functioning of the organization as *organization*, will have associated with it a core task specification. This will (generally implicitly and, where explicit, almost invariably informally) carry with it a model of the task domain for that specific office and of the functional "fit" of the task domain model within a model of the broader activities of the organization. The model will include an ontology (what the objects in the domain are and of what type, its universe of discourse), a "knowledge base" (how the objects are meaningfully and purposefully ordered into structured representations of the domain), and a process model (a repertoire, partly case-based, of programmes determining the permissable computations on the knowledge base). The "knowledge base" will also include two privileged groups of representations: the one corresponding to possible initial states for tasks (or "templates" for recognizing some situation as a task-instance), the other to acceptable goal states. The three components of the model will have been "designed" to support not only the goal-driven activities of the individual but also, indirectly, the top-level goals of the organization itself. In the framework of cooperative work, the office will be tied to one or more *institutional contexts*, in which talk is in one or more ways regulated by conventions that are known and accepted by the speech participants. These contexts are distinguished by at least the following features:

1. Participants fill pre-assigned *offices*, defined by the context.
2. Participants have both context-specific and *office*-specific knowledge; this would have to include, for example, professional competences.
3. Participants may (be expected to) draw as necessary on a domain-specific lexicon. Using Halliday's functional terminology, such conventions/constraints may extend over both ideational and interpersonal functions; see also Hobbs and Evans (1980, p. 354), who treat these conventions as, respectively, domain goals and social goals.

4. Speech acts (Searle 1969) may have an illocutionary force different from that which their linguistic form would predict them to have in canonical casual conversation, and from that which they might have in other institutional contexts.
5. "Turn-taking is pre-allocated . . . rather than determined on a turn-by-turn basis" (Levinson 1983, p. 301).
6. Talk may be directed towards the achievement of a predetermined agenda; talk in the context of cooperative working at some task will almost inevitably be goal-directed in this way.

The following further observations can be made:

7. The institutional context may influence and even fully determine the kinds of speech act a speaker will utter on an occasion.
8. The institutional context may influence and even fully determine a hearer's interpretation of a speech act on an occasion. This is the corollary of 3, 4 and 7.
9. Therefore, some account of the context should enter into a description of the preconditions for speech acts on such occasions.
10. Institutional contexts in which interactants in pre-assigned *offices* engage in recipe behaviour can be represented as data structures describing the prototype of the context from the perspective of one (or more) of the *offices*. This will be a partial representation of the model of the task domain for that specific *office*.
11. Institutional contexts in which recipe behaviour is directed towards the achievement of some specific task acknowledged and shared by interactants, and for which there exists a more or less well defined sequence of steps or set of subgoals towards its achievement, can be formally represented as "agendas" – checklist relevance structures – for the planning and interpretation of both verbal and non-verbal behaviour.

Typically, the joint acknowledgement by participants of the institutional context, and of the specific conventions and "scriptal" knowledge (e.g. Schank and Abelson 1977) that it implies, can be expected to have as a consequence that participants will behave cooperatively. Or, put differently, given the externality and coerciveness (Durkheim 1966, p. 10ff) of the institutional context, participants act meaningfully only to the extent that they act cooperatively: entry as an actor into the institutional context would be seen as tantamount to a commitment to a tacit contract to respect the relevant conventions.

All this might seem to suggest that a rich enough description of the task-specific model for the *office* might suffice to account for the verbal behaviour of individuals engaged together in a collaborative task: ontologies for the domain are pre-given, belief models and process models are pre-given, speech act types are prescribed. It seems, however, that the *office*, by virtue of its being an idealization, underdetermines the cultural knowledge that enables the individual to perform his or her *role* successfully. This is so for at least four kinds of reasons. Consider that, in the first place, the *office* specifies for the individual actor some initial information about the task domain, including the form of idealized inputs, resource (including time) constraints, a prescriptive repertoire of actions that the actor may select from according to some decision function to transform the inputs into outputs, and an evaluation function for assessing the "goodness" of the outputs. However, the actual model used by interacting agents is likely, by virtue of the form and quality of the information that actually presents itself, to diverge to some significant degree from the idealized model specified for the *office*. For example, the influx of information necessary for deciding action is likely to be asynchronous (not all the information necessary for acting will arrive at the same time, or even in time), the information may likewise be incomplete, inconsistent, corrupted and "noisy". Also, individual tasks may be interrupted (e.g. while awaiting information) and interleaved.

In the second place, the individual brings to the execution of his or her organizational duties a wealth of unique professional experience acquired both from other *offices* prior to assuming the present one and also from the day-to-day practice of working, including feedback from others in the work group. Actors' internal representation of themselves, their activities and their environment, as well as the team culture that emerges through the routinization of their collective cooperative activities, need bear little more than superficial resemblance to the abstract representation of the *office*.

In the third place, work is likely to become routinized in fairly determinate ways as, through numerous decision–action–outcome–feedback–decision cycles, the pattern of action on tasks tends to "settle" into repetitive sequences, quasi-atomic in the sense that they are not perceived by the worker as orderings of discrete actions.

Fourthly, and finally, the individual, in interpreting and executing the duties and responsibilities tied to the *office*, beyond observing the task-specific operational rules for jobs as well as general rules of conduct, develops meta-rules of various kinds. Some of these may pertain to the organization and ordering of tasks; some to integrating the performance of tasks within personal goal agendas; some to engaging the help of, or coordinating activity with, other people, and so on.

The Sopwith study is too extensive to cite at length here. A selection of annotated quotes from the email exchanges will give the flavour of some of the points made above. In the first place, decision making turned out not to be an easy process. It was not that members of staff lacked the information to make a decision so much as that the making of *that kind of decision* seemed premature and problematic. Note in the following mailing, from BS to KR, the request for "commitments":

you will have to move fast! Please sound out –ALL– colleagues about the open-plan plan. It may be that some will want sep (2-person) rooms and I think we will have to respect that. We could specify different sorts of environment, but you will have to assess the balance and get –commitments– from "open plan" people that they are not going to change their minds! Note that they will have no choice about who they share with!!!

To effect any change, [AOK] will need revised schedules and pro-formas by Thurs pm – he has a meeting 8:30am Friday 20th with consultants when we think specs will be frozen.

This generated personal responses such as:

I am angry and fed up that we are being bounced into this at a few days notice [SM]

Why are we being required to make a decision which will affect the quality of our working lives for years to come so quickly? [CCW]

In any case, the decision making process, involving the coordination of information from multiple sources, was potentially hampered by other commitments:

I am now out Wed & Thurs but will aim to come in for about 6:00/6:30pm Thursday (I doubt I'll manage to get in Wed evening) [BS]

Personal (*role*-related) goals further complicated the decision-making process:

My experience of sharing with others, even people with whom I have a lot in common is that my ability to work is hampered by my own natural gregariousness and need to chat. I have also been in a type C situation where one of my room-mates (not JB) made every attempt possible to "dominate" the shared space that made it very uncomfortable for everyone else. [SM]

In the ongoing Sopwith study an attempt is being made to model *roles* and interactions on the basis of the textual cues and in terms of what was already known (from participant observation and interview) of the *roles* and *offices* of the actors concerned. The study is still incomplete, although tentative belief models are being constructed.

In conclusion, to understand how individuals really work, and work with others, one needs to observe the concrete *structure* rather than the abstract *organization*. Sociometry provides us with a set of conceptual and computational tools with which to map the communication networks within an organization, but it does not give us more than superficial access to the content of communicational events. Even less does it give us access to the mental structures that underlie and motivate verbal behaviour. We need to generate cognitive models of task domains for each of the *offices* associated with a cooperative task; most importantly, as we have seen, we will need to consider how actual behaviour may, for the reasons given, diverge from the canonical behaviour predicted by the models. Until we understand how, and the extent to which, teamwork is managed through talk, we cannot begin to build the technologies that will not only support the accomplishment of the cooperative task but will also support the active engagement of the task participants as social and communicative beings.

5.3 Conclusions

Apart from Lyytinen (1985), little attention has been paid to language as a design issue in information systems development. Though there has been a good deal of interest in some aspects of language in CSCW (e.g. Tatar et al. 1991; Winograd, 1988), it has in general been narrowly focused on some quite small area, for example, speech acts or conversational turn-taking. It is clearly a good sign to witness such interest emerging; what is lacking is a comprehensive and globally coherent picture of language in cooperative working.

As I stated at the beginning, the present chapter arose out of concern to set out an agenda for future research into the full range of roles that language, at all levels of linguistic analysis, appears to play within group behaviour. Much of the initial work will inevitably be purely descriptive, endeavouring to produce as rich a description as possible of the actual use of language by members of the organization. That part of the work is now under way, and this chapter has outlined in brief four of the many possible levels of linguistic analysis.

Acknowledgements My thanks are due to Roger Stewart for informative discussions about sociometry and for a demonstration of Netmap, and to Duska Rosenberg, with whom I have enjoyed many productive hours of cooperative work, computer supported and otherwise.

Appendix A

A.1 The Message from Leyland

For the attention of plant directors and for communication to employees as appropriate.

Derek Whittaker has made it clear to all Plant Participation Committees in his recent visits that neither he nor his directors will be submitting any major capital expenditure for final approval to either the British Leyland board or the National Enterprise Board unless he has commitments to the necessary improvements in productivity from employee representatives of all sections and all management involved in the respective project.

After full discussion of the ADO 88 project at Leyland Cars Joint Management Council and at the special Sub-committee the Council set up to study it, the programme was agreed. The Council also agreed that the programme be presented to the Joint Management Committees and senior representatives in the plants concerned to obtain their endorsement.

Endorsement has been obtained from all plants except Longbridge where meetings are being held today at shop floor level seeking a commitment satisfactory to everyone.

At meetings there earlier this week it was emphasized that commitment was required by 4 pm Thursday 7 October as the NEB and the Company were meeting on Friday 8 October; without that commitment no submission could be made. A Mini replacement is essential to the marketing strategy of Leyland Cars endorsed by both Government and the Participation System as without such a model for first time buyers our range will be incomplete and other parts of that range endangered, with obvious consequences to the numbers employed in the Company. The timing of this project cannot be delayed without considerable increase in investment cost and adverse consequences in the market place.

Mr Whittaker stated that there had to be a significant improvement in performance immediately for any commitment to be credible and acceptable.

A.2 How the *Sunday Times* Rewrote It

Derek Whittaker has just visited all Plant Participation Committees. He made this point. All employee representatives and all management involved in the new Mini project must promise to improve output as much as is needed. If not, neither he nor his directors will ask the British Leyland board or the National Enterprise Board to approve any major capital spending plans.

There were full talks about the ADO 88 project by Leyland Cars Joint Management Council – and by the special sub-committee set up by the council to study it. The programme was agreed by both. The council also agreed that the joint management committees and senior representatives in the plants concerned should be shown the programme and asked for their backing. All plants have endorsed the plans except Longbridge. Shop-floor meetings are being held today at Longbridge seeking a deal which will satisfy everyone.

At meetings earlier this week at Longbridge people were told they must promise to give their support by 4 pm Thursday, October 7. The NEB and the company meet next day (Friday, October 8). Without this promise no request for money will be made. A new Mini is essential if Leyland is to sell as many cars as it wants. The Government agrees with this. So does everyone in the participation system. Without an up-to-date Mini to attract new first-time buyers, our range will not be complete and other models will be threatened. The effect on jobs is obvious. Delay will increase costs and play into the hands of our rivals.

Mr Whittaker said output had to improve immediately. If it does not, who will believe any promises made in the future?

Appendix B

B.1 Alcatraz on the Third Floor or Communications and Information Free of Time and Space (CIFTS!)

It was rather useful the visit to Sopwith coming immediately after the MAI Board of Study. It seems to me that we have a choice: we can either resist the move to Sopwith, a possibly bruising battle but with no evidence we'll come out of it any better off, or we can regard the move as an opportunity to purge some problems in the School and end up with a more interesting working environment.

Hypotheses

1) SSR & FTE will continue to decline.
2) The current spatial distribution of the School and people's workloads are unconducive to the fruitful development of our ideas and teaching and need changing anyhow.
3) Management couldn't give a bugger about our working conditions as long as we generate the surplus for them to continue playing their little games.
4) In the foreseeable future we will have about twenty core staff servicing about sixty M.Sc. and one hundred B.Sc. students per year, with a fluctuating number of PhD, part time, visitors etc.
5) Quite a number of us do considerable amounts of our work with other departments, in other institutions and at home. If we don't like our working environment we simply don't come in except for commitments.
6) Our mission as a School is to investigate the relations between developments in new information and communication technologies and the productive activities of human being, and to provide courses based on these investigations. These courses are capable of generating incomes and outputs higher than the average.
7) The [University] will move towards an accounting procedure where space is a chargeable resource negotiated against other costs.

Theses

1) The move to Sopwith gives us the opportunity of a forced change in our working conditions to examine the relationship between time and space in the activities of a group the size defined in 4 above.
2) If we move positively we can gain some control over the design and management of the allocated space.
3) If we increase the effective utilization of space, in a thin, short, light world, we'll gain negotiable resources over the thick, long heavy.

4) We must abolish the idea of personal space in our working conditions.

5) The third floor of Sopwith must be kitted out as deliciously as we can imagine.

6) The staircase, entrance and whole environment must state and echo a place where the most exiting things are going on in communications and information free of time and space, and be in stark contrast with the floors below and rest of the [University].

7) Architects cannot plan beforehand how people will use social spaces – footpaths in parks and cities develop over time according to the practices of people.

Here are some of my suggestions on this:

a) There must be no doors – that corridor without the natural light from all windows will be horrendous.

b) There must be a high level of security at the entrance – a medieval gateway to a city.

c) Some spaces must be for relatively formal meetings, some for informal meetings, some where equipment which is relatively unstable or needs to be in close conjunction can be fitted together, some where people can be quite private, some where social gatherings can occur.

d) The technical infrastructure requires a high capacity LAN, substantial gateways to WANs, and everyone has a personal object directory server (PODS) which is completely portable. (See my earlier paper on our technical architecture and my Information retrieval and networks for summaries of these ideas – I also gave a research seminar on the topics last year, which some people were at.)

e) There needs to be developed a SWIS (School Wide Information Server), for which one person is responsible. New office automation techniques will need to be implemented to separate documents and information.

f) There must always (oops – not quite – say 9–6pm Mon–Fri?) be one person from the administration available at the entrance as a human interface.

g) There must be high quality soundproofing carpets and lots of soft furnishing on a completely bald set of surfaces.

h) My remarks from 1985 on an information strategy for the School, using the [University] as a laboratory still stand. ([BS] probably still has a copy filed somewhere).

Chapter *6*

Coordination Issues in Tools for CSCW

R. Procter, A. McKinlay, R. Woodburn and O. Masting

6.1 Introduction

Neither group-based work nor its associated technologies are exactly new. Computer Supported Cooperative Work (CSCW), however, makes it necessary to reconsider many aspects of the design of technologies for group work. In particular, it raises questions about the support for the maintenance of common ground within the group (McCarthy et al. 1991), and the coordination of their activities – who can do what, where and when. We refer to these two aspects of group work collectively as "collaboration awareness".

In conventional multi-user computer system applications, the design philosophy is to conceal the fact that resources (both system and information) are being shared between tens, hundreds or even thousands of users. For example, a database provides support for common ground, but ignores the whole issue of coordination in group work by making the actions of its users anonymous, and assumes for itself the responsibility for their fine-grain coordination. Should coordination between activities be necessary at any other level, then users must achieve this themselves using whatever mechanisms and resources are available, external to the system.

Groups of people can perform routine work without the need for collaboration awareness. Where group tasks have significant intellectual and problem solving content, however, the need to share information and coordinate activities interactively becomes paramount (Olson and Bly 1991).

In general, the study of Human–Computer Interaction (HCI) has focused on the factors underlying users' competence in communicating with computers. In making the interaction between user and computer its principal focus, however, HCI has largely discounted factors that are important at the group level. The design of CSCW tools must also address factors influencing people's competence in communicating with others, and the mediating influence that technology may have on both the process and the outcome.

We consider some of the problems of maintaining common ground and achieving coordination in CSCW, and contrast different approaches. To understand these issues, we turn to conversation analysis, and consider the extent to which, with the insights it is able to provide concerning the mechanisms and protocols of turn management in the practical accomplishment of conversational work, it may be applied to the problems of coordination in CSCW. We begin by briefly reviewing some of the more significant issues that have been unearthed through practical experience of CSCW.

6.2 Early Experiences with CSCW

Many examples of CSCW have been documented in the literature over the past five years (Ellis et al. 1991; Mantei 1988; Stefik et al. 1987b; Tang and Minneman 1990; Tatar et al. 1991; Watabe et al. 1990). The earliest were tools for distributed, asynchronous computer conferencing, such as email. These facilitate the sharing of information and the coordination of tasks, but stop short of direct, interactive support of the work itself. They have since been followed by computerized meeting rooms, which augment conventional face- to-face group work with tools such as the "electronic chalkboard" (Stefik et al. 1987b).

Most recently, various tools have been developed which attempt to recreate for physically dispersed groups the kinds of opportunities for collaboration that are normally only enjoyed when meeting face-to-face. It is this category of CSCW that generally goes under the name of groupware. Examples include group editors of various kinds (Beaudouin-Lafon and Karsenty 1992; Ellis et al. 1991; Leland et al. 1988; Srinivas et al. 1992; Tang and Minneman 1990). In contrast with the first category of CSCW, collaboration with these tools is tightly coupled and synchronous, adding new dimensions to the problems of information sharing and coordination.

Despite the many tools described in the literature, successful examples of CSCW are difficult to find. The reasons for this embrace a wide range of issues, some of which lie beyond the immediate scope of this particular discussion (Grudin 1988; Kling 1991). By and large, early CSCW tools were designed as simple multi-user extensions of single-user software. It has now become clear that simply scaling up single-user interfaces in this way cannot meet the demands of group work, other than that of a very routine nature (Minneman and Bly 1991).

6.3 Cognitive Issues in CSCW

CSCW introduces a set of design issues that are absent in conventional single-user and multi-user systems, and that emphasize the complexities of group processes. Understanding of what factors influence the effectiveness of group processes in CSCW is still incomplete, but it is evident that one major factor is the difficulty of maintaining adequate collaboration awareness.

The use of computer based tools demands additional mental effort, and this itself may interfere with normal group processes. Studies suggest that CSCW users may cope with this additional cognitive load not by serializing their actions, but simply by paying less attention to the contributions of others (Kiesler et al. 1985; Mantei 1988). One result is that it can be more difficult for the group to maintain a common focus of attention, and thus behaviour becomes divergent.

Similarly, the actions of group members may make it difficult for individuals to concentrate on their own tasks. This problem was revealed in some early WYSIWIS (What You See Is What I See) computer-augmented meeting tools, such as Boardnoter (Stefik et al. 1987a; Tatar et al. 1991). Collaborators found it difficult to sustain a common focus of activity, since the enforcement of the WYSIWIS principle made the effects of all inputs visible at all times, which was simply too distracting. In the design of Cognoter, one of Boardnoter's successors, the principle of WYSIWIS was relaxed by the provision of private input spaces, providing for the formation of subgroups, and permitting collaborators to make their own decisions about how to manage their individual display areas (Stefik et al. 1987a; Tatar et al. 1991).

The impact of computer systems on personal communication patterns and behaviour is well documented. Studies confirm that Computer Mediated Communications (CMC) fail on numerous criteria to match the quality of face-to-face communication (Kiesler et al. 1985; Sproull and Kiesler 1986). The prevailing explanation is that CMC attenuates people's sense of social presence, which normally serves to help resolve ambiguities and regulate behaviour (Kiesler et al. 1985; Sproull and Kiesler 1986). Perhaps the best documented consequence is the phenomenon known as "flaming", i.e. the tendency to violate social conventions, and become aggressive and abusive (Kiesler et al. 1985). Less well known, but equally important, effects include changes in the decision making behaviour of groups (Dubrovsky et al. 1991; Lea and Spears 1991; Murrel 1983).

In face-to-face communication, social presence is conveyed by the rich variety of verbal and non-verbal contextual cues, such as intonation, facial expressions, hand gestures and so forth (Sproull and Kiesler 1986). Social presence constitutes a "back channel" of communication which is constantly active, and assists not only with maintaining common ground, but also in the management of the process. Social "turn management" protocols regulate the contributions of participants and so prevent long pauses or continual interruptions.

Where group members are copresent, they can exploit the information conveyed through social presence to supplement explicit channels of communication. Social presence provides a low cost means to signal intentions, and to anticipate and resolve conflicts. In combination with the affordances of the physical workspace, and the opportunities this presents for the casual monitoring of one another's activities, social presence is a very effective mechanism for sustaining collaboration awareness.

From practical experience, it is evident that collaboration awareness is harder to sustain in CSCW, and that this has important implications for usability and acceptance. A conservative response would be to limit the application of CSCW tools to tasks and situations where the common ground and coordination can be established before work commences (Waern 1992). Increasingly, however, CSCW is being targeted at tasks with substantial intellectual and problem solving content, where a rigid division of roles may be inappropriate. In these circumstances, communication becomes a continuous and essential background activity which establishes and maintains the conditions necessary for effective group performance. Group members must not only respond to the cognitive demands of their individual roles, but also cope with the demands of communicating with others.

Conversation is a natural starting point from which to begin the study of group processes (Bowers and Churcher 1988). Conversational behaviour is situated, i.e. it is contingent upon a continual process of interpretation of the context, and its coordination is typically fine grained and dynamic (Suchman 1987). In Section 6.4, we examine how conversation analysis can help to identify some of the important constituents of collaboration awareness.

6.4 Conversation Analysis

Conversation analysis is an established tool for describing the processes that underlie the competence partners display in the management of conversations (Garfinkel 1967; Sacks et al. 1978). Central to it is the notion that the utterances which make up conversations are orientated to each other in a series of successive steps, and so take the form of *turns* in a sequence of actions. The structure of orderly conversation is accomplished by participants' orientation to simple turn management protocols, which come into effect periodically at points – "transition relevant places" – where it would seem natural for one speaker to break off and another to take over.

In part, turn-taking behaviour relies on expectancies generated by the semantic content of the preceding turn. A simple example of this is found in *adjacency pairs*: pairs of utterances made by separate speakers which are adjacent to one another in conversation and which "go together" because the second utterance is made in response to the first (e.g. questions and answers, greetings and responses). More generally, turn management depends also upon the appraisal of the back channel signals that accompany the turn. Together, these two factors are usually sufficient to limit switching pauses between turns to around 0.7 seconds (Beattie 1983).

6.4.1 Turn Management in Conversations

A conversation in progress can be thought of as a cyclical process, as first one, then another speaker "holds the floor". A representation of a conversation between two partners is shown in Fig. 6.1 (Woodburn et al. 1991). Following basic turn management protocols, this depicts, in simplified form, the process in terms of the main conversational states, and the major events that cause a progression from one state to another. These events are instances of the mechanisms – the informal acts of communication – by which partners signal their conversational intentions.

In conversations, turns are negotiated smoothly, quickly and without much apparent effort on the part of the partners (Levinson 1983). Duncan describes three basic signals which are employed to effect this (Duncan 1972, 1975):

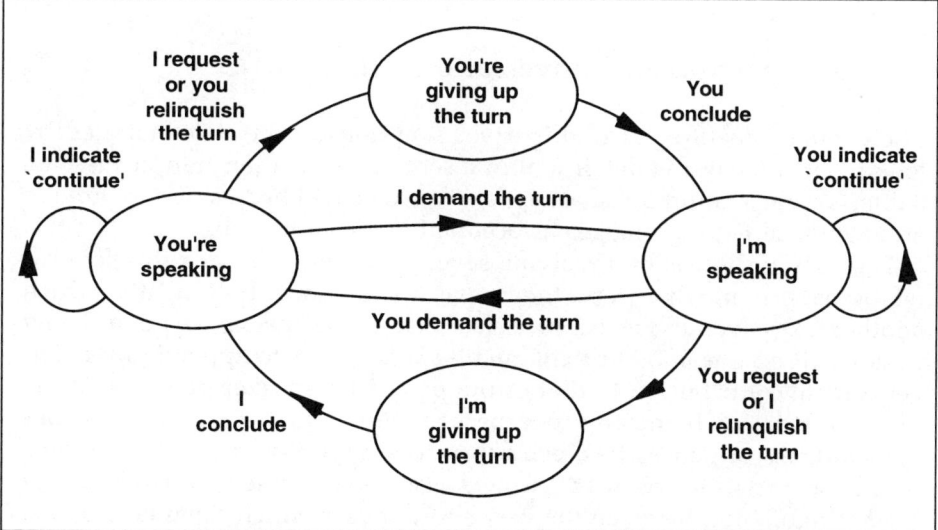

Fig. 6.1. A simplified model of the turn management process.

1. Turn-yielding signals by the speaker, for instance changes in loudness, intonation and pronunciation; particular body movements; and the use of stereotyped phrases.
2. Interruption-suppressing signals by the speaker, particularly hand gestures.
3. Back channel signals (feedback) by the listener, the purpose of which is to enhance the speaker's contribution, rather than interrupt it.

Sacks et al. propose that, at the point where a speaking turn could change, one of three fundamental turn management options comes into play (Sacks et al. 1978):

1. The current speaker selects the next speaker (e.g. by looking at a particular person.
2. The next speaker self-selects (e.g. by being the first to utter an opening signal such as "Well . . .").
3. The current speaker continues.

All of this happens in the absence of any formal coordination. Responsibility for coordinating a conversation is distributed between all partners. It is this which gives conversation its flexible structure:

> What is notable about [conversation] is the extent to which mastery of its constraints localises and thereby leaves open questions of control and direction, while providing built-in mechanisms for recovery from error. The constraints on interaction in this sense are not determinants of, but are rather "production resources" for, shared understanding. (Suchman 1987, p. 95)

The resource upon which the achievement of this "situated action" ultimately depends is social presence.

6.4.2 An Example of Conversation Analysis

The common features of multiparty discussion can be demonstrated by looking at some of the detail within a set of conversation transcripts. The subjects were a group of fishermen's wives who had been asked to provide an account of fishing villages as occupational communities.

Typically, a discussion involving several partners follows a simple turn-taking pattern, in which a partner makes a short contribution, after which another takes over. In Fig. 6.2, it is clear that the partners have no difficulty in dovetailing one another's comments. This ability to append one's conversational contribution to that of the preceding speaker depends, at the semantic level, on being able to recognize utterances that are complete. But the shortness of pauses between utterances, typically measurable in tens of milliseconds, means that partners also have a finely tuned capacity for distinguishing between the very short pauses which separate one of a speaker's utterances from the next, and those other pauses which signal

1	AD:	Are people in fishing communities just the same as
2		everybody else
3	AM:	just the same as everybody else
4	M:	maybe the older people
5	AM:	aye the older people the older ones would
6	M:	I don't know if it's just fishing but up here I mean you
7		don't go into pubs I mean no old women went into pubs
8	AD:	that's right
9	M:	you didn't do that you know but now
10	AM:	It's more just you know the younger generation

Fig. 6.2. Turn-taking.

the speaker's intention to stop talking. This is aided by vocal and non-vocal, non-verbal cues. A conversation without overlaps or long gaps is a joint achievement in which partners bring semantic knowledge and highly tuned non-verbal signal recognition capacities into play.

The signalling is not, moreover, always in the direction of conversation turn holder to listener. Those listening are also able to provide feedback to give assurance to the current turn holder that the conversation is proceeding smoothly. This is achieved via short vocalizations or single word statements, which often take the form of vocal agreements. In Fig. 6.3, the agreement token is "aye". Note that while the agreement token can be used to provide an affirmative answer (line 3), or to express agreement (line 5), its main use here is to act as a single-word reassurance to the speaker that the conversation is proceeding smoothly (lines 7 and 14).

Of course, interruptions can occur, with one partner speaking before the other has concluded. But in such cases, there are standard means by which this potential disruption is managed. In Fig. 6.4, PM interrupts VB's turn at line 5. VB recovers from this by repeating the closing part of her previous turn ("left at home") before continuing. This is a common means of establishing that, whatever was said in the interruption phase, the conversation is to continue on the route it was following prior to the interruption. The effect of using this repetition is to signal to the interrupter that the current conversation turn holder is not yet ready to give way. Its effectiveness as a conversation management strategy lies in the way it precludes an extended period of overlapped talking.

Sometimes people are less willing to give up their attempts to gain the conversational turn by interrupting. In Fig. 6.5, VB wishes to interrupt PM. The strategy used is to quickly insert into PM's contribution several

1	*AD*:	Did that mean that fishermen when they were older
2		and retired were actually viewed as quite important
3	*MM*:	**Aye**, they were
4	*MC*:	And they passed on their knowledge
5	*MM*:	**Aye**. They had no radar or anything. It was far better
6		than the radar that they use now
7	*MR*:	**Aye**
8	*MM*:	They were sure
9	*MC*:	The father passed down their knowledge to their sons.
10		And I know one of my older brothers who was lost five
11		years ago he always said that his father told him to
12		study the moon and that and not to go just by the
13		forecast and true enough he always did it
14	*MM*:	**Aye**

Fig. 6.3. Agreement tokens.

1	*VB*:	We have a very good social life here we are totally
2		used to being without men
3	*AD*:	Yes
4	*VB*:	whereas in a city a woman left at home=
5	*PM*:	=Yes it's different=
6	*VB*:	=left at home on her own it would be a very
7		lonely life
8	*AD*:	what kind of things do you do with your time
9	*PM*:	Oh lots of things
10	*VB*:	what don't we do
11		Laughter

Fig. 6.4. Turn management with interruption.

short vocalizations ("yes"). Unlike agreement tokens, however, these vocalizations are not inserted at the end of PM's utterances but in the middle – typically, in the middle of a sentence.

Short vocalizations (line 4 and line 8) across the current turn holder's utterance are a method of attempting to "close off" his or her conversational turn. The relative strength of these "closure tokens" can be seen from the fact that although PM attempts to retain the conversational turn by repeating what was said before the closure token (line 5: "college", line 9 "extra"), eventually VB wrests it away (lines 12, 13, 15 and 16).

The importance of this final example is that it demonstrates how carefully partners orientate themselves to specific conversation structuring devices, even when they are competing for the conversational turn. The competition can be seen to take place within an agreed set of turn management strategies so that even though both parties want to speak, the discussion remains ordered and well structured, with no extended bouts of overlapped talking.

These conversation extracts illustrate some of the possible orientations people display to turn-taking rules. They also show how use is made of social presence components – in this case verbal tokens – to achieve situated action. More generally, by sending out and attending to intonation,

1	PM:	The YTS is about the one scheme that has been successful
2	AD:	Really tell me about that
3	PM:	Well I feel that it's maybe ... they go to college=
4	VB:	=Yes=
5	PM:	=college and they get a skipper to take them away and I
6		feel its maybe in a way the pay because there's very few
7		skippers that don't give the YTS lads a bit extra=
8	VB:	=Yes=
9	PM:	when the crew gets extra and it has been one of the=
10	VB:	the most successful=
11	PM:	the most successful YTS scheme=
12	VB:	=and they're getting em em their fares paid to Aberdeen
13		as well
14	PM:	Yes
15	VB:	They are getting more money they do so much at college
16		and they go away on trips and it seems to have worked

Fig. 6.5. Managed turn competition.

facial expression, gestures and other non-verbal signals, partners are able to ensure that their conversational turns smoothly interleave, even in cases where competition for the next turn occurs.

The insights that conversation analysis provides into basic coordination in conversational work may be applied to CSCW. Conversation analysis identifies a range of turn management behaviours which, by implication, CSCW tools should endeavour to support. The question for CSCW is how support for coordination may best be provided in circumstances where social presence is diminished, and the situatedness which gives face-to-face interaction its potential flexibility is thereby made more difficult to achieve.

6.5 Coordination in CSCW

The generic groupware tool provides multiple users with a common interface to a shared artefact such as a document, which they can work on together. Groupware tools are therefore instances of open systems, in that they must potentially deal with multiple sources of concurrent input, and the chances of interference or contention are real (Miles et al. 1991). For example, if two users attempt to modify the same piece of text simultaneously, the outcome will be unpredictable. Dix has observed that in these circumstances, group members are likely to perceive each other's behaviour as fundamentally non- deterministic (Dix 1990b).

In groupware, without effective coordination at the fine grained level of interaction, orderly collective activity may become impossible. At a more coarse grained level of activity, coordination is essential to ensure that all the necessary tasks get done, and in the appropriate order. At both fine and coarse grained levels, coordination can only be achieved through the imposition (voluntary or involuntary) of constraints – turn management – on group members' actions. Three basic forms of constraint policy can be distinguished (Miles et al. 1991):

- Restricting tasks eliminates multiple inputs by imposing constraints on the roles that users may play.

- Restricting input permits multiple inputs, but imposes some kind of turn-taking rule to serialize inputs where contention in some form would otherwise result.

- Restricting output enables users to focus on strictly relevant information, and so avoid becoming distracted or confused.

Further to the forms of constraint policies themselves, there are choices available concerning the precise manner of their imposition. In essence, constraints may be applied globally (and hence statically), or locally (and hence dynamically).

Where activities are globally constrained, the constraint policy serves as a plan which predetermines the roles played by each participant, their actions and the sequence in which they must be performed (Miles et al. 1991). Group coordination is achieved through the rigid allocation of roles, in the manner of the factory assembly line. The need for coordination as an explicit task (to which everyone must continually attend) is avoided, but at the cost of flexibility. On the other hand, where activities are locally constrained, i.e. situated, participants are able to re-negotiate these constraints, and so adjust to evolving circumstances. Flexibility is gained, though possibly at the expense of greater coordination effort. Conversation analysis emphasizes the reliance of situated, local constraint policies on collaboration awareness.

In the CSCW literature, coordination problems are widely reported (Lauwers and Lantz 1990). Assuming that flexibility is the paramount concern, the underlying question this poses is how collaboration awareness can be provided most effectively, and with least cost, in terms of the effort demanded of participants. Given the predominant form of back channel communication, it would be reasonable to assume that collaboration awareness in synchronous CSCW can be restored by integrating voice and video links within the CSCW tool interface. This expectation has not been borne out by experience, however (Heath and Luff 1990; Hughes et al. 1993; Lauwers and Lantz 1990; Sellen 1992).

Voice introduces its own possibilities for contention, and ability to discriminate between different speakers rapidly falls as the number of collaborators rises (Watabe et al. 1990). Furthermore, a broadcast voice channel does not fully support the range of verbal acts evident in face-to-face meetings. For example, people may make asides, or join in short-lived conversations with a subset of the whole group. Some form of "narrowcast" alternative might be desirable, enabling remarks to be directed at some subset of the group.

The use of video also introduces problems. The importance of visual contact lies in its capacity to convey non-verbal gestures. Recent studies have reported, however, that visual gestures lose their coordinating power in video-mediated environments (Fish et al. 1988; Heath and Luff 1990; Sellen 1992).

Video (and voice) is handicapped by the fact that packet-switched Wide Area Networks (WANs) and contention Local Area Networks (LANs) are ill-suited to meeting the bandwidth requirements of real-time image transmission (and connected speech) (Ellis et al. 1991; Tanenbaum 1988). Delays that result in voice and/or video data losing synchrony with activity within the workspace undermine their value (Tang 1991).

On a different note, there may be grounds in some applications for wishing to preserve the anonymity of collaborators, for example, in order to capitalize on status-equalizing effects (Valacich et al. 1991).

Coordination issues must also be addressed in asynchronous CSCW tools, where, by definition, voice and video can play no role. Given these several limitations of voice and video, therefore, it is important to consider other ways of facilitating collaboration awareness, and whether and how they might be implemented through the CSCW tool interface. One approach is to focus on the processes by which who can do what, where and when is negotiated, and provide explicit protocols to support turn management (Crowley et al. 1990). Conversation analyses of the sort presented in Section 6.4.2 imply the existence of a range of turn management protocols, reflecting different forms of turn-taking behaviour, and, indeed, selections from this range are to be found among examples of current CSCW tools:

- Implicit request and implicit grant is the simplest protocol. An inactive user requests the turn by beginning a contribution (e.g. the user starts to type) and this is granted pre-emptively (Mantei 1988).

- Explicit request and implicit grant protocols require users to give an explicit signal of their intention to take a turn. This is then granted automatically.

- Explicit request and explicit grant protocols are like the previous case, but the currently active user is now required to explicitly hand the turn over. In other words, once a user has the turn, they may hold it for as long as they wish.

- Explicit request with time limit protocols set a maximum time limit for possession of the turn.

Other examples of CSCW tools embody the altogether different view that collaboration awareness is best sustained by the provision of workspace status – the current state of the artefact, together with information about who is doing what, where and when – through the workspace interface. It is argued that embedding formal turn management policies and protocols in the interface is unnecessarily restrictive (Beaudouin-Lafon and Karsenty 1992; Ellis et al. 1991; Hughes et al. 1993). In contrast, reliance on workspace status places no explicit constraints upon how group members coordinate their activities.

A typical example of the workspace status approach can be found in GroupDesign, a group graphical editor. Workspace status is conveyed through the use of colour, graphics and sound (Beaudouin-Lafon and Karsenty 1992). In this way, anyone can find out where within the workspace individual group members are currently active, what they are doing, the age of any changes made to the document and so forth.

Clearly the workspace status approach is more flexible than explicit turn management protocols. The question is whether it alone is sufficient to enable the group to achieve coordination on an effective basis. In Section 6.6, we outline the results of a study of these two contrasting approaches to the support of coordination in CSCW.

6.6 Studies of Turn Management in CSCW

We have been conducting experiments designed to examine the effects of different approaches to the achievement of collaboration awareness. The goal is to investigate which kinds of approaches are best for particular tasks; whether particular turn management constraints are beneficial to the collaborative process; and which are preferred by users. As a first step, we have been examining the relationship between group size, performance and turn management policies and protocols in simple decision making tasks.

In an earlier study of a text-based conversation tool, we found that turn management is not a significant problem for a simple conversational task involving two partners (Woodburn et al. 1991). Subjects had little difficulty in negotiating turns *ad hoc*, either because the conversations contained suggestive adjacency pairs, or because they spontaneously created suitable mechanisms for signalling a change of turn.

More recent experiments have involved subjects in group decision making tasks. They were required to discuss their opinions using a text messaging tool, under a variety of turn management protocols. The task was to rank in order a number of items of survival equipment. The design allowed the estimation of the effect of the turn management protocol, group size and of the interaction (if any) between the two factors. Details of the experimental procedure, and of the results, have been reported elsewhere (McKinlay et al. 1994).

The message tool interface followed the WYSIWIS principle, thereby enabling participants to monitor one another's activities within the workspace. There were three distinct turn management protocols:

- Free-for-all (FFA) was free of any turn-taking constraints; hence all group members could send messages simultaneously, if they so desired. FFA was designed to allow subjects to develop their own *ad hoc* turn-taking procedures. This corresponded to the implicit request and implicit grant protocol described previously.

- Request-and-grant (RAG) allowed only one group member to send messages at a time. Subjects had to signal their desire for a turn, and the turn did not become available until the current turn holder had finished, and had explicitly relinquished the turn. If more than one turn request was pending, they were placed in a queue, and granted in a strict first-come-first-served basis. This corresponded to the explicit request and explicit grant protocol.

- Request-and-capture (RAC) allowed anyone to seize the turn at any time, irrespective of whether the current turn holder wished to keep the turn. It was therefore possible for any group member to invoke this "interruption" process at any time. This corresponded to the explicit request and implicit grant protocol.

The protocols were chosen to be representative of the range of turn management protocols found in CSCW tools. They provided a set of circumstances in which any turn management had to be developed by the subjects themselves (free-for-all); turn management was perforce well ordered (request-and-grant); turn management could be well ordered or disordered, depending on the subjects (request-and-capture). Both the free-for-all and request-and-capture protocols were designed to test the extent to which subjects were able to exploit workspace status to coordinate their activities. The difference was that, in the former, they faced competition for attention, whereas in the latter, they faced competition for the turn.

As measured by movement towards consensus, request-and-grant was the most successful protocol. Like a very well ordered conversation (compare Fig. 6.6 with Fig. 6.2), there was no overlapping of contributions, and the sequence of turn transfer from one person to another was voluntary.

The next best protocol was free-for-all. At the beginning, subjects found it difficult to coordinate the discussion, with the result that any conventional sequential structure broke down (compare Fig. 6.7 with Fig. 6.5). As the task progressed, however, a form of structure emerged which exploited the potential for concurrent activity. Typically, subjects would type a complete message, regardless of what others might be doing. They would then pause to read the contributions of other group members. The semi-permanence of messages enabled participants to delay their responses, and achieve a significant degree of parallel activity. This did not destroy conversational focus, because each subject would pause periodically to read what others had said and then respond. Nevertheless, the fact that free-for-all was less successful than request-and-grant at generating consensus suggests that group focus in the former condition was weaker.

1	*Subject#1:*	If the river is 5 miles wide then would we
2		be able to cross it not knowing its depth
3	*Subject#2:*	Also even if we had crashed in the day, we would
4		need a full day to walk the 20 miles to the shelter.
5		We would be better to stay the night
6	*Subject#3:*	I agree, especially since 10 of those miles are
7		through hills, 5 is swimming or wading through a
8		COLD river and the last 5 you'll be wet and COLD
9		from the river...

Fig. 6.6. Request-and-grant condition.

1	*Subject#1*:	Shona what=
2	*Subject#2*:	are these=
3	*Subject#1*:	=is all=
4	*Subject#2*:	=rabbits=
5	*Subject#3*:	Are we=
6	*Subject#2*:	=alive any=
7	*Subject#1*:	=the laughter=
8	*Subject#2*:	=way=
9	*Subject#3*:	=all=
10	*Subject#1*:	=about
11	*Subject#3*:	=agreed?=
12	*Subject#2*:	=what!

Fig. 6.7. Free-for-all condition.

The least successful protocol was request-and-capture, which bore a close resemblance to a very disorderly conversation, dominated by turn competition. Instead of acquiescing to an involuntary change of turn, subjects often tried to re-capture it immediately. This oscillation of turns was quite unlike the other two conditions – turns of only one or two characters' duration were quite common. Not unexpectedly, subjects found it difficult to harness the information about one another's activity, which was available through the tool workspace, to the goal of the more orderly turn competition typical of face-to-face conversation (see Fig. 6.5). Clearly, in these particular circumstances, workspace status cannot, by itself, compensate for the diminished social presence.

6.7 Discussion

In conversation, there are compelling cognitive reasons for serializing turns at all times. The problem of coordination maps on to a single dimension of group activity – time. In CSCW, however, concurrent turns become possible because (unlike speech) the medium can serve as a semi-permanent record of each partner's contribution. Our studies substantiate the view that such media may afford users of CSCW tools the opportunity to depart from the normal serial unfolding typical of speech (Whittaker et al. 1991), while replicating the function – if not the form – of face-to-face communication. There will also still be situations, however, where the productivity advantages of concurrent turns are outweighed by other considerations. One example would be where there is a need to maintain a common focus (Tang 1991). The results of our studies also provide some corroboration of this point.

There are many CSCW applications (e.g. groupware editors) where it is undesirable to adopt a strict conversational model of turn management. In the typical groupware tool, coordination issues map on to two dimensions – time *and* space. The extra dimension of space introduces the possibility for concurrent turns within the group workspace, as long as the concurrency is in either time *or* space (same time, different space; or different time, same space), but not both. Viewed from the perspective of the fine-grain structure of group activity, the imposition of strict serial turn management might then only be a measure of last resort for coping with contention (same time and same place), rather than the default.

More generally, the case for adopting coordination through workspace status over turn management protocols rests on two claims. The first is that it enables coordination to be achieved essentially effortlessly, whereas explicit turn protocols require additional actions to be performed. Taken literally, effortless access to the workspace status implies the use of a WYSIWIS interface, and we have already noted that this is susceptible to problems of its own. Relaxing WYSIWIS means that while users remain unburdened by the necessity of providing status information, they will now have to expend some additional effort in order to find it. In this respect, therefore, the difference between the two approaches may be rather less than it might at first seem.

The second claim is that workspace status provides collaborators with the greater flexibility, because it leaves open questions of control, and so better satisfies the needs of situated, local constraint policies. Where the workspace status approach has been applied in practice, the evidence of its effectiveness is inconclusive (see, for example, Hughes et al. 1993). Like that of Hughes et al., our studies suggest that while workspace status is quite effective for coordination in the "steady state", it is less effective in circumstances where orderly coordination has broken down, and there is competition for the turn; at the very least there is a case here for providing explicit support for the management of turn interruption and competition.

Underlying the second claim is the premise that situated, local coordination is a sufficient condition for group processes in CSCW. This, however, is open to question. Global structure may also have an important role to play. In studies of computer-augmented meetings, for example, designated scribe policies (where one person has the turn for the duration of the session) have been reported to perform better than more flexible policies such as rotating scribe (where the turn may be passed from one person to another) (Mantei 1988). Bowers and Churcher observe that many kinds of group interaction actually involve a combination of locally and globally determined constraints, and that, of necessity, the two forms often coexist alongside one another (Bowers and Churcher 1988). Work, therefore, is typically less situated than conversation. It may be therefore, that the literal application of a conversational model for turn management may be detrimental to, or inappropriate for, effective CSCW.

In general, turn management in work will depend upon its social and organizational context. As an example, behaviour appropriate for a brainstorming session would be ill-suited to a formal, chaired meeting.

The discussion so far has assumed that work is being performed synchronously. In fact, real group work may involve a combination of synchronous and asynchronous phases (Dourish and Bellotti 1992). When work is performed asynchronously, individual turns may occupy extended time periods. It is unclear whether workspace status can provide an adequate distinction between past and present activity in these circumstances. Viewed from the perspective of the coarse-grain structure of group activity, there may be a need for a more explicit form of turn management in order to guarantee continuity of a turn. An appropriate model to consider here might be the typical program source code management tool, where turn continuity is ensured by users obtaining locks on documents when checking them out of the source library (Tichy 1985).

Software engineering is an example of a work context where other factors override arguments in favour of flexibility. It is not too difficult to envisage other circumstances where collaborators might prefer the security that explicit turn management can provide. Some of these circumstances certainly owe more to sociopolitical factors in group work, than the essentially cognitive ones that we have considered here. Sociopolitical factors are important in CSCW, nevertheless, and designers have been taken to task for giving them insufficient attention (Grudin 1988; Kling 1991). In particular, perceptions of groups at work have been criticized for relying too heavily on the academic peer model and overlooking the implications of conflict and other factors. CSCW tool design must not only achieve an appropriate degree of situatedness in its support for group processes, but must also consider the situatedness of the group within the larger context.

6.8 Concluding Remarks

Our studies provide mixed evidence for the case for supporting coordination through explicit turn management in CSCW. They do not endorse the view that workspace status alone is sufficient for effective coordination under all conditions, however. Rather, they provide evidence that it is ineffective in conditions where, for whatever reasons, orderly coordination has broken down, and there is competition for the turn. Although our studies have focused exclusively on text messaging tasks, the results have significance for other forms of group based work.

From the limited nature of our studies, it would be inappropriate to attempt to draw definitive conclusions about the suitability of workspace status and explicit turn management approaches for facilitating coordination in CSCW. In real work, there are many variables that might have a bearing on the outcome. Nor, of course, is it necessary to treat the two approaches as being mutually exclusive. It is more fruitful to view them as complementary, and consider them as practical options for use when and where they would be most appropriate. Indeed, some examples of groupware already exhibit features of both approaches. ShrEdit, for example, provides workspace status through the tool interface, but also supports an explicit form of turn management by enabling users to lock areas of the workspace for their exclusive use.

Support for explicit turn management should be understood to be part of – rather than distinct from – a wider repertoire of resources for maintaining collaboration awareness. Although this may require greater effort on the part of collaborators than the reliance on workspace status, there are circumstances where the benefits of explicit turn management policies outweigh their drawbacks. Workspace status enables group members to identify potential opportunities for activity; turn management support provides the means to move in an orderly and predictable fashion from potential to action. Turn management protocols are not inimical to flexibility, but a possible "production resource" for effective collaboration awareness and coordination in CSCW.

Appendix A

A.1 Annotated Bibliography

Bowers J and Churcher J (1988) Local and global structuring of computer mediated communication: developing linguistic perspectives on CSCW in COSMOS. In: Proceedings of the Conference on Computer Supported Cooperative Work (CSCW-88) Portland, OR, September. ACM, New York, pp 125–139

The authors' objective is to demonstrate the relevance of concepts derived from the analysis of conversations for computer mediated communication in general, and cooperative work in particular. They distinguish between local and global structuring of communication, and argue that many group working situations combine both sorts.

Ellis CA, Gibbs SJ and Rein GL (1991) Groupware: some issues and experiences. Communications of the ACM 34(1): 39–58

This outlines categories and examples of groupware, and discusses some underlying research and development issues. GROVE, an example groupware editor, is described in some detail.

Kiesler S, Zubrow D, Moses A and Geller V (1985) Affect in computer-mediated communication: an experiment in synchronous terminal-to-terminal discussion. Human–Computer Interaction 1: 77–104

This describes an experimental study of synchronous text-based messaging involving subjects who had not met before. The results indicated that asocial and unregulated behaviour was more pronounced in CMC compared to face-to-face settings.

McCarthy JC, Miles VC and Monk AF (1991) An experimental study of common ground in text-based communication. In: Robertson S, Olson G and Olson J (ed) Proceedings of the Human Factors in Computing Systems Conference, CHI-91, New Orleans. ACM, New York, pp 209–215

This describes the results of experiments designed to assess the effort required to maintain common ground in group based tasks. Clark's contribution theory of discourse predicts that in a text-only messaging system, common ground will be difficult to achieve. The addition of a common report space was found to reduce these problems.

Stefik M, Bobrow DG, Foster G, Lanning K and Tatar DG (1987) WYSIWIS revised: early experiences with multi-user interfaces. ACM Transactions on Office Information Systems 5(2): 147–167

Discusses the design issues and choices behind the first generation of meeting tools. Experience with these tools revealed that there are inherent conflicts between the needs of a group and the needs of individuals, since user interfaces compete for the same display space and meeting time.

Tatar DG, Foster G and Bobrow DG (1991) Design for conversation: lessons from Cognoter. International Journal of Man–Machine Studies 34(2): 185–209

Users of Cognoter, a multi-user idea organizing tool were found to experience unexpected communication breakdowns. Many of the problems were subsequently identified with an incorrect model of conversation embedded in the design of the tool. Conversation analysis was used to develop a more realistic model of group communication processes.

Chapter 7

Software Engineering Design: A Paradigm Case of Computer Supported Cooperative Working

C. Boldyreff

7.1 Introduction

Software development as an engineering process can usefully draw upon the results of studies in design theory from general engineering research. From an engineering perspective, the activity of design is itself amenable to being designed (Whitney 1990). Thus, there is the potential to develop theories of design with the possibility of radically changing the nature of existing design practice.

Moreover, it is important to understand that the engineering method is not the same as scientific method: for a far ranging discussion of the differences, see Eekels and Roozenburg (1991). While results from science are relevant, such as those from cognitive science considered below, the development of an improved design process model is best conceived as a meta-level exercise in engineering design.

In considering how software design is to proceed so as to improve the process of software design explicitly, one goal of this research is an improved understanding of current processes and products of software engineering. There is a tension between rationality and creativity in design. On one hand, there is a desire to make explicit and formalize design practice, while on the other, there is a desire to allow freedom of expression and not to restrict the designer. In software engineering, this tension is rarely articulated, although its presence can be deduced by the necessity for proposals on how to rationalize designs *post hoc*, such as that found in Parnas and Clements (1986).

It is increasingly recognized that software engineering is an engineering discipline concerned with the development of large software systems; see, for example, Sommerville's preface (Sommerville 1992).

These large system developments could not be accomplished without the cooperative working of several software engineers. With the advent of computer aided engineering, many process models of development with associated method and tool support have emerged (MIT-JSME 1991; Pahl and Beitz 1988), but comparable models, methods and tools for large-scale software engineering design are lacking (Curtis et al. 1988; Sibley 1989). As McDermid (1990) has pointed out, most improvements in our technology for large-scale software system development have depended upon finding improved abstractions or structuring techniques for describing software. He identifies structuring and abstraction as the two key weapons for mastering the difficulties of building large-scale software systems. The case for the use of abstraction in the design process in general can be found in Hoover et al. (1991). This lack of methods and the weapons of abstraction and structuring have provided starting points for the research reported here. Our principal insight has been to link the need for abstraction in design with the development of common design concepts among designers working cooperatively and building up a common understanding on which to base their work.

7.1.1 What is Design Theory?

Design theory brings together results from the engineering sciences and the practice of engineering, from systems theory, computer science and cognitive science. It examines the roles that knowledge representation, mathematics and computation play in design from both a practical and a theoretical standpoint. The National Science Foundation study on design theory and methodology defined design theory as:

> systematic statements of principles and experimentally verified relationships that explain the design process and provide the fundamental understanding necessary to create a useful methodology for design.

where design methodology is:

> the collection of procedures, tools and techniques that the designer can use in applying design theory to design. (Rabins et al. 1986)

We can distinguish two main approaches to design theory; broadly, these are descriptive and prescriptive. The descriptive approach studies design as a natural phenomena, whereas the prescriptive approach attempts to provide models and theory to control and guide the design process. To contrast these approaches as holistic (descriptive) versus rationalistic (prescriptive) is an oversimplification (compare the account found in Winograd and Flores (1986)). Both the descriptive and the prescriptive approaches look for empirical grounds to support their theory, either directly or indirectly.

The prescriptive approach epitomizes the rationalist tradition. It seeks to give a theory to the process of design by giving reasons why design should proceed in a certain way and not others. It also proposes that experimental evidence be provided to support its case. With respect to descriptive approaches, these also follow the rationalist tradition, citing experimental evidence to support the predictive power of their explanations, and they may draw on experimental results from other disciplines such as cognitive science to support their case indirectly. A philosophical issue underlying these approaches concerns the nature of man's intellectual, social, political, economic and moral behaviour – is such behaviour artificial or natural? The work of Simon raised these questions over 20 years ago in the context of proposing a science of design (Simon 1981).

7.1.2 Is Design a Natural Phenomenon?

An alternative view proposes that the central distinction between the prescriptive methods of design and the descriptive theories of design is the shift towards empirical theories of design, with the development of cognitive science and the application of ethnographical studies to groups of designers. This view welcomes the shift away from the prescriptive towards empirically grounded design theories and practice. To my mind, it is based on a misguided view of the application of scientific method. If we consider the differences between scientific method and design method, then the crucial factor is that scientific theories are looking to uncover universal truths strengthened by experimental evidence whereas the designer aims to advance the state of the art by creating a conceptualization of something and then realizing it. The scientist is a discoverer of reality whereas the designer exploits known theories to create things that are needed or missing from reality. The example of the scientist predicting the existence of a star with reference to a theory of planetary motion and the engineer altering the planetary motion by creating a large satellite and installing it makes this distinction clearer. As Glegg (1969) has remarked:

> A scientist will be lucky if he makes one creative addition to human knowledge in his whole life, and many never do so. A scientist can discover a new star but he cannot make one. He would have to ask an engineer to do it for him.

In fact, a theory of design that simply aimed to describe design as it is would have little practical content other than satisfying the intellectual curiosity of its developers (in this context, see, for example, Whitney (1990)). If we consider that the human activity of design is itself amenable to being designed, then we have the potential to develop theories of design with the potential of radically changing the nature of existing design practice. The fact that an approach is prescriptive does not rule out its having empirical grounds for its theoretical basis. The usefulness of applying results from empirically based research such as cognitive science in developing tools to support design practice is illustrated by the following case.

7.1.3 A View of Design from Cognitive Science

In an interesting study by Newsome and Spillers (1989), results from psychological studies of problem solvers are presented. From these, requirements for tools supporting conceptual design are derived. This approach illustrates how practical results from cognitive science can be brought to bear in consideration of how design ought to be supported.

Three characteristics of the way that experts approach problem solving are identified as follows:

- Breadth-first approach
- Use of abstraction representation
- Expanded memory of problem-related information

It appears that experts in computer programming tend to take a breadth-first approach, in contrast to novices, who use a depth-first approach. These differences were found to be most marked as the complexity of the problem increased. These results were reported by Anderson (1985).

Experts tend to use abstract representations or patterns in problem solving – results from computer programming, chess, Go and electronics support this. Novices in these areas concentrate on smaller, more concrete features of the problem. Experts have a quicker grasp of problems; this is illustrated by their capacity to remember more of the problem-related information. For example, experts in chess are able to reconstruct board layouts to a much greater extent than novices; the results quoted are greater than twenty pieces for experts compared to four or five for novices. Similar results were obtained for computer programmers recalling programs. One might hypothesize that this expanded memory is due to high level encodings of the problem-related information.

As Newsome and Spiller point out, these three characteristics are not independent, and it is the second, the ability to utilize abstract representations, that underlies both the first and the third. The conclusions drawn from these characteristics with respect to Computer Aided Design (CAD) tools for expert designers are as follows:

- From the first characteristic, it can be concluded that the immediate closure of design subtasks is not necessary, nor should it be forced on the designer. The CAD system should allow the designer to formulate rough global sketches of solutions prior to fixing any details in depth.
- From the second, support for only the most basic, or prototypical, representations is needed initially. This allows the designer to use abstract patterns to shape the solution until greater specificity is

desirable. In addition, any prompting queries from the CAD system should be of an abstract nature, e.g. clarifying relations among parts rather than prompting for specific details of parts.

- From the third, the system should present the designer with global representations of information, omitting details (the expert designer can fill these in when required).

7.2 Use of Abstract Representations

The studies reported above are from domains where there already exist quite well-known and developed representations, i.e. chess and computer programming. In computer programming, there are a number of languages at varying degrees of abstraction that designer may employ. This raises the question: what role do these abstract representations play in communication of designs? In particular, one may wish to determine whether or not certain levels of abstraction are more useful than others.

In considering designing as a fundamentally social process, the work by Bucciarelli (1988) consists of exploring the nature of design discourse through which designers communicate under conditions of sustained uncertainty and ambiguity. He has identified the importance of multiple representations of objects-in-the-making, and has shown how multiple representations across the design discourse can both facilitate and inhibit convergence of the description of an artefact.

To my mind, this argues for investigations into the appropriate levels of abstraction in any particular field of design discourse, to ensure that multiple representations are an aid rather than an obstacle to the design process. My work on design frameworks is a first step towards a means whereby the results of such investigations can be expressed (Boldyreff 1990, 1992).

7.2.1 Implications for Design Methods and Tool Support

The technological support for representing design at various level of abstraction is available in hypertext and, more generally, hypermedia systems. However, the use of hypermedia systems in design introduces interfacing problems from a variety of views: intellectual in terms of the process of design and design products, and technical in terms of the incorporation of hypermedia systems into conventional CAD systems, to name two of the most obvious.

The meta-modelling of the design process in terms of a progression from a high level design statement to detailed low level design is a prevailing prescriptive view of design (for example, see Pahl and

Beitz (1988)). Although design research has shown that designers work through a series of stages, it is not clear how conscious designers are of these stages, and whether bringing them to the attention of novices or providing explicit guidance through these stages improves the design produced. Where tools are developed to support design, there should be a theoretical basis for the development; but in lieu of a theory of design, empirical validation of tools is what we must fall back on, for if the benefits of design methods are not demonstrable or subject to testing, then there is no proven basis for choosing one over the others to achieve a given benefit. Some design studies have used the progressive refinement (the other side of the abstraction coin, so to speak) stages as a framework for describing actual design behaviour, which was found to move up and down through these stages quite frequently (Guindon and Curtis 1988); it is unclear whether such a result could in fact be attributable to the models and perhaps tools typically employed in software engineering. As this result is somewhat at variance with the breadth-first approach found to characterize expert problem solvers, it illustrates how difficult it is to support the case for a technological solution based on empirical evidence.

The representations used by designers and supported by methods and tools must provide a sufficient and consistent vocabulary and grammar to enable effective communication at the requisite levels without placing unnecessary restrictions on the designer's expression of ideas. A restrictive or biased design language limits the design possibilities. The designer should employ the most appropriate means of expression within any particular design exercise context – where one means is not self-evidently the most appropriate, a variety may be required to cover different aspects of the design. These points seem obvious, and yet there are always new prophets arriving on the scene advocating new design languages and new approaches to design without any supporting evidence. It is possible to evaluate a language critically, and to determine its properties, especially the scope of its application. Simon called for such efforts as a part of his programme of topics for instruction in the science of design.

7.2.2 Philosophical Issues: Are they relevant?

At the higher levels of abstraction, it has been suggested that "types" may be loosened up to yield "worlds" of objects and relations (Schon and Bucciarelli 1989). Thus, high level design sketches may reflect paradigmatic knowledge within a specialized object world. This brings out the fundamental problems of the relations between logic and language, thought and language, and language and reality – the concerns of philosophical logic.

Zemanek (1974) makes this point quite clearly by recalling the development of Wittgenstein's philosophical studies of language. While it is the case that the computer system perfectly realizes the world of the *Tractatus*, it is only in the context of a particular application domain that a program has a meaning, as Wittgenstein realized later in the *Philosophical Investigations*, with his detailed study of how words are employed in various language games. Wittgenstein's insight here is a development of Frege's motto: "Only in the context of proposition does a word refer" (*Nur im Zusammenhange eines Satzes bedeuten die Worter etwas*) (Frege 1884). Zemanek summarizes this view as follows:

> There will be forever a gap between the formal universe in our systems and the informal reality, between the domain of programs and algorithms and the life of people and communities – a gap which remains to be bridged by the human being, before and outside the mechanical and formal tools.

Are the limits of my world the limits of my language, as claimed by Wittgenstein in the *Tractatus*? Are these theoretical considerations really necessary? Does not experience show that designers are able to use language operationally quite adequately? Should we not examine the roles played by various languages in the context of design to determine their usage, rather than attempt to determine *a priori* the relations of language to thought and reality? We must look more closely at the role of concepts in structuring knowledge, and our starting point to give some realistic content to the work should be an examination of languages used within a particular domain.

7.2.3 The Role of Concepts in Structuring Knowledge

It hardly seems surprising that experts were found to be able to remember chessboard layouts or computer programs respectively depending on their expertise. In both cases, the experts can employ conceptual knowledge to structure the given information.

Of course, in reality, where a variety of professionals participate in the development of a design, consideration must be given to their varied interests, strategies of representation and different languages. In reality, such "layering" of meanings is central to design discourse. And part of the research in design theory must address the provision of conceptual structures in which these experts' structures can be structured.

7.3 The Design Frameworks Approach

The design frameworks method arose out of considering how best to support the reuse of software concepts in design. It is obvious on reflection that all design, here taken in the broad sense, implicitly involves reuse. This work has had the aim of making such reuse explicit and has paid particular attention to the initial stages of design, where the designer is attempting to understand the design problem area, relate known design concepts to the problem, and structure potential solutions in terms of appropriate levels of abstraction and known whole–part decompositions, for example, in terms of standard software components. Here the designer is dependent on the maturity of the domain, and is greatly assisted if the existing knowledge and expertise of previous designers has been codified and is readily accessible. So it follows that a two-step process is required. Firstly, the resources required must be built up through the study of existing software; this step can be described as design-for-reuse. Once these resources are in place, the second step is to incorporate their reuse into the design of new systems, i.e. to support design-with-reuse.

The method of design frameworks has been developed to address these two steps in the reuse process. Design frameworks provide a means for recording the results of domain analysis and a basis for supporting the reuse of architectural as well as component design concepts in the development of new systems.

The research reported here has concentrated on software concepts employed in the domain of steel production. Emphasis has been placed on determining how frameworks can be abstracted from known models, and on determining the role that levels of abstraction play within a framework.

Currently, research in software reuse is focused on the reuse of software components – what might be characterized as "reuse-in-the-small"; the contribution of this research is to show how "reuse-in-the-large" can be supported by providing a methodology that looks beyond components to frameworks within which architectural design concepts relating component concepts can be reused. This approach, far from replacing component composition, allows it to proceed in a more appropriate context.

7.4 An Approach to Design-for-Reuse

In populating the Practitioner REuse Support System (PRESS) (Bisgaard et al. 1990), the established methods that we drew on were those of domain analysis (Prieto-Diaz, 1987, 1990; Prieto-Diaz and Arango 1991). Two important landmark projects were the DRACO project and the CAMP project; their reported experience of domain analysis (Neighbors 1984; MDMSC 1990) was found to be particularly relevant to this research.

An overview of the Practitioner approach to design-for-reuse can be found in (Boldyreff and Krohn 1992). In this approach, particular emphasis has been placed on investigating how language is used in a particular domain. This work has been based on studies of domain literature, resulting in the construction of a thesaurus to record the domain terminology and studies concerning how best to use domain terminology in the indexing of software concepts to support their retrieval (Albrechtsen 1990). Our particular interest is the use of terms in describing software concepts in the domain, and to this end we have applied the techniques of text analysis to software application documentation, ranging from requirements statements, specifications and designs to source code, as well as analysing domain literature. This has not only supported our work on thesaurus construction, but it has also been found that such analysis provides a helpful preliminary overview of material prior to a more in-depth analysis of potentially reusable design concepts realized in the existing domain software.

The analysis of software uses the same source of material as terminology analysis, augmented by expertise in software engineering to gain an understanding of the domain's software concepts. Here, an intermediate step corresponding to thesaurus construction, but less well understood, is the modelling of the domain. Output from domain analysis may take the form of modelling typical domain applications, developing a design framework for relating typical designs or, if possible, determining generic architectures for well-understood application families in the domain. These outputs are used to guide the domain analyst working with domain experts and software engineers in the systematic description of the domain's software concepts. A detailed description of the development of a design framework for software concepts in the domain of steel production can be found in Boldyreff (1992).

7.4.1 Considerations Regarding the Use of Frameworks in Design

In characterizing the design process, Guindon (1990) remarks:

> because design problems are ill-structured, the design process cannot just be the retrieval of known solutions, even in experts. The novelty in design and the incompletely specified requirements force even expert designers to punctuate retrieval of known solutions with the inference of new requirements, the recognition of partial solutions at various levels of abstraction, and the creation of new solutions.

Earlier, following Newell and Nii, Guindon characterizes design as a problem solvable from the application of knowledge in the form of empirical associations or rules derived from past experience. From this point of view, it can be seen that reuse is already assumed to be part of the repertoire of the expert designer, albeit reuse of the individual's own experience. A clear role for design frameworks to record past design expertise can be made in the light of Guindon's study. Guindon argues that retrieval of potential solutions is not sufficient because the designer is actively engaged throughout the process in revising and adding to requirements, if necessary, and attempting to identify partial solutions. His study is limited to designers attempting to understand and elaborate requirements, i.e. Phase 1 (Clarification of the Task) in Pahl and Beitz's (1988) characterization of the design process). An important point made by Guindon is that this phase in software design cannot easily be separated out, since problem understanding and structuring were found to be interleaved with solving the problem throughout the design sessions studied.

It is clear from the account of the lift controller design histories given by Guindon that, in the case of the second designer studied, the ability to recall and use a high level design schema that relates what – in the terminology of Pahl and Beitz – are the classifying criteria to the solution characteristics was decisive in guiding his approach to the design task. In this case, the criteria were those generally found in a resource allocation system: multiple clients, multiple servers, limited resources, asynchronous service requests and routing/scheduling optimization. In the schema used, these mapped on to a design decomposition involving three main characteristics: control, communications and scheduling, with the additional decomposition in design strategies given in figure 8. In considering this case, once the designer had recalled the schema, it is clear that it was the primary determinant that led to his effective solution of the task. As Guindon remarks, "design schemas are one source of knowledge that powerfully constrain the search for a solution".

Further, he concludes that top-down processing induced by the design schema contributed to a systematic design process. He adds the rider that, because of their intrinsic novelty, solutions to design problems were also found to be a combination of applying retrieved software schemas and creating new schemas; however, in his reported study of three designers, there is no firm evidence to support this rider. The way in which the second designer was able to employ a high level design schema supports our envisaged use of the design framework for steel production. Guindon cites examples of design schemas described by Lubars and Harandi (1987); here, the schemas given involve very high level abstracting out of design solutions common to several application domains. Lubars and Harandi identify the encoding of reusable design information into design schemas as one of the key aspects of automated design systems. In our work on a design framework for steel production, we are not aspiring to achieve automation of the design process. Nevertheless, abstraction within the domain has proven to be a useful means of developing a framework supporting reuse of designs on a smaller scale.

From these discussions, it can be concluded that it would seem helpful to advocate that the initial search of the designer is guided by an understanding based on giving structure, possibly via abstraction levels, to the design requirements. This is where the capability of drawing on existing design frameworks identified through similar requirements comes into the design process. Compare here the steps found in Pahl and Beitz's characterization of conceptual design, where the designer is advised to abstract away the details given in the requirements in order to identify the essential problem, and then to establish the functional structure of the solution in abstract terms, initially using these as the basis for identification of known functions to apply in the design. With the development of design frameworks, the designer is offered a basis for identifying known structures, and thus, reuse is promoted earlier on in the design process. The answer to the question, "What is the role of these frameworks relating system models in design?" is as follows: "They are the carriers of very high level design concepts".

The role identified for design frameworks has not yet been investigated extensively with the framework for steel production presented here; in the context of the Practitioner project, it formed a contribution to the development of demonstrations of the PRESS in the preparation of offers that utilized the framework. Empirical studies of designers are problematic and were not possible within the framework of the Practitioner project; however, presentation of this work to practitioners in the domain has been favourably received, which has encouraged the belief that the framework developed has a real role to play in actual design.

These studies within the steel production domain have enabled our earlier domain analysis to be built upon, and a framework for guiding further analysis and relating the designs available for reuse in the development of future steel plant control systems to be refined.

A speculative conclusion of this work turns on the utility of abstraction in design. In the discussions of design models in software reuse, the importance of abstraction has been identified as the keystone to successful software reuse (Freeman 1983; Krueger 1989; Standish 1984).

More generally, in their account of a systematic approach to engineering design, Pahl and Beitz (1988) advocate that the designer initially abstract from the specifics given in the requirements to the general case, in order to achieve a less constrained viewpoint from which to attack the design problem conceptually. In the context, of software engineering, Shaw's remarks on the need for higher levels of abstraction are perhaps the real inspiration behind this work (Shaw 1990a, b); she brings out quite clearly how intellectual progress is purchased through the difficult process of abstraction, citing examples from other engineering areas.

In contrast, it has long been known that the strategy of divide-and-conquer is a successful approach to attacking intellectual problems such as design. This has led many to argue that hierarchical decomposition of design from the standpoint of design tasks – attacking subproblems using known plans – is the way to bring past experience to bear. For example, in a general study of design taken from an artificial intelligence standpoint, a classification of design is given in terms of known problem decompositions (Brown and Chandrasekaran 1989).

Through a vertical decomposition based on levels of abstraction coupled with a horizontal decomposition into a whole–part hierarchy, a design framework such as the one presented here allows these two aspects to be combined and offers the design team a more powerful, conceptual basis for reusing designs.

Through this method, design histories can be recorded over time. This allows the design team to base their work on the accumulated experience of past projects. Thus, it supports cooperative working in the small by recording different levels of development within the team, and cooperative working in the large by recording known solutions for potential design reuse.

7.5 Conclusions

A distinction can be made between observational studies of complex phenomena yielding descriptions forming the basis of descriptive theories of design, and theoretical studies to develop formal models of the design process that can be used to structure and control the complexity of the design process. Each approach has the potential to usefully inform the other and to contribute to the improvement of design practice. Ideally, one might hope for a fruitful conjunction of the creative accounts of what design ought to be and the instrumental accounts of how design works in practice; both are needed in design theory.

Chapter *8*

Where Are Designers? Styles of Design Practice, Objects of Design and Views of Users in CSCW

M. Hales

If the tool you've always used is a hammer, you tend to address everything as if it were a nail (Fig. 8.1). This chapter is about alternatives to "hammering style" for information systems professionals. My reading of Computer Supported Cooperative Work (CSCW) is that, despite the fuzzy edges of the field, work is clearly showing us that it's not a nail we're addressing when we design systems based on Information and Communications Technologies (ICTs). And in that case we may feel that it's, let's say, foolish to use a hammer.

To push the metaphor: what if the material we work on – in this chapter I'll refer to it as the "design object" of CSCW – were not a nail, but (say) a seed (Fig. 8.2)? A seed is a form of material that contains its own developmental principles, has in it forms that seem not to be there in its seed form, interacts with its uncontrollable environment and becomes something of different value and different order. Then maybe the appropriate design style might be facilitation, nurturing and husbandry rather than specification, engineering, fabrication: hammering? Even though you can, these days, engineer a seed, can you engineer a *garden*? If you use a hammer on a seed, do you get anything useful or beautiful? Or do you just get a mess?

The metaphor breaks down, of course. Most significantly, a seed does not have language whereas the CSCW design object (being full of "users", people doing things) is perhaps more language than anything else. Nevertheless, I do not intend that this nail/seed metaphor-level critique should be merely casual. If this chapter had to be written in one line, it would be: "Designers of ICT systems – think seed and garden, not hammer and factory".

My approach in this chapter is as a designer and design methodologist, but not an information systems professional. From this slightly outside,

CSCW AS POST-ENGINEERING?

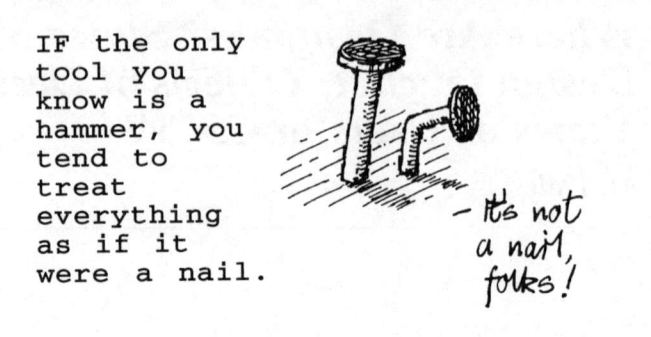

Fig. 8.1. Addressing nails . . .?

Fig. 8.2. . . . or seeds?

but sympathetic and fascinated standpoint, it strikes me that there is a central difficulty in CSCW design methods. And the name I give to that difficulty is "engineering". Just as every carpenter thinks that wood is the greatest thing, so it seems that every information systems professional must strive to be an engineer. The British Computer Society, for example, became "The Society for Information Systems Engineering"; software engineering is the official myth of dominant sections of the would-be profession. This kind of ambition – to render information systems design as an "engineering"-style activity – is addressed by a critical tradition in the social studies of technology. Analyses in this tradition trace the trajectory of systems design work from creative craft to managed labour, and they connect with a broader historical analysis of the modern military–industrial capitalist labour process (Greenbaum 1979; Hacker 1989, chapter 4; Kraft 1977). I have British engineer colleagues who object to my use of "engineering". Part of my response as a social scientist and historian is that British traditions are not the only ones, and that, while British engineers (or any engineers) can define engineering any way they like, globally it is probable that American models of engineering professionalism are the dominant ones (this cultural angle is one way of analysing the notorious "backwardness" of British industry). The critique of routinization and managerial domination in the software process mounted by Kraft and Greenbaum, for example, addresses a historical American model of industrial engineering practice which, as Taylorism/Fordism, is also a dominant industrial paradigm worldwide. Another part of my response – the personal response of an ex-engineer who has left the technical for the practical, political and human disciplines – is that an engineering–technical paradigm is able only to recognize design objects that are too impoverished to be real, and that, myself, I'm more concerned with the managerially real than with the limited project of reducing reality until it fits into the domain of the engineerable.

Basically, in this chapter I am interested in whether the material that we work on when we design ICT systems is engineerable; and if not, what it is.

8.1 Design as Technique, as Social Function and as Politics

I would like us to be able to be more historically, socially and economically concrete about design activity. Thus, this chapter is about where and how designers are situated. I am primarily concerned with CSCW design as a significant and emergent social function and as politics, rather than with current technicalities of how CSCW designers organize themselves to transform their material (for example, integrating the findings and styles of cognitive science into structured development methods, operating usability labs, incorporating ethnographic "thick" data into system specifications and ethnographic styles and values into design teams) or with the production of any specific type of CSCW product–artefact (an electronic conference room, an electronic whiteboard, a workflow management system, or whatever). This is because I am writing from a radical user standpoint. I treat design as a concern and responsibility which rests primarily with users and only *secondarily* with professionalized producers of ICT systems.

After all, whose systems are they? Users live with a system forever; design professionals go away again after sign-off. It would be simplest, and not far wrong, to say that users *are* the material that CSCW designers work on. It is somewhat more complicated, but more precise, to say that *practices* are the design object of CSCW. "Practices" are mental, cultural or behavioural things ("lifeworlds" is convenient shorthand for this aspect), and also have corporeal and objective dimensions ("material culture", the ergonomic dimension, etc.; "apparatuses", for short). From a user standpoint, the central practical–political question has to be: how may their (designers) access to us (users) and our working lives – our apparatuses and lifeworlds – be legitimized and practically, managerially structured?

This is not at all an "outsider" or academic issue, the concern of a sociologist. It is essentially the issue that CSCW has finally succeeded in raising within the ICT design community, as the problem of interpreting the "CW" in CSCW. There are active current debates about the distinctive design object of this fuzzy-edged sphere of practice, CSCW. What is "work"? What is "cooperative" (or "collaborative" and so on: there are many variations here)? What is "support" (as distinct from constraint)? What does this imply for the practice of designing? In common with others in CSCW debates (e.g. Bannon and Schmidt 1989; Kling 1991; Kuutti 1991a; Kyng 1991; Norman 1991), I see the importance and novelty of CSCW as lying in the priority that it gives to the "CW" as distinct from the "CS", and its refusal to see the design object – work – merely as something engineerable (a "system") in the industrial engineering/Taylorist/Fordist tradition.

I should say a little more about social function and politics in relation to design. From one point of view, design is a central economic *function* of high-modern societies. From a different (i.e. non-functionalist) perspective, design is a set of varied *historical* phenomena and practices that emerged under certain conditions and transform and reproduce in certain historical and economic circumstances. (CSCW is a current transformation – still a field of *debate*, in fact, rather than a field of technology or technique; but what are its circumstances, and where is it transforming *to*?) From a further perspective, being about meaning in both product and process, design is clearly a form of *cultural production*, and this, particularly, is where the dominant "engineering" paradigm gets into deep water while CSCW seems determined to swim.

My own interest is, at one level, historical; I am concerned to understand design as a constitutive human capacity – something that makes people *people*, sets us apart from other species. This relates to both the tool making (hammering) and sense making (languaging) capacities of humans. This is not to suggest that anything about people is "timeless", unvarying in actual life. Rather, it is a matter of striving to identify and then, in practice, develop what is characteristic in human action. In a designed world such as we now occupy, some actors have acquired power to close future actions and also to foreclose reflections on our pasts, through the ways in which they configure and position artefacts. Some of these actors are professionalized designers of ICT systems. I am interested in the necessity of these forms of constraint, and the freedoms that they constitute. I am interested in being able to see where design professionals stand in this complex field of freedom and necessity.

The remainder of this chapter goes through three stages. Firstly, I outline three perceptions of users that can be understood as characterizing three self-conscious styles of design activity. They are not ideal types in the sociologist's sense, so much as conceptual clusters that can be mapped on to current practice and that may serve for future practical improvisation by actors in design. We can think of them as *myths* (an anthropologist's or semiologist's technical term, rather than a rationalist's insult) or as roles in a theatrical rather than social–scientific sense. Secondly, I sketch an approach to identifying different objects of design, as they are placed in front of designers by the global, sectoral and occupational division of labour in ICT design. This is in order to reduce the possibility of an excessively voluntaristic interpretation of "style". Finally, I offer some thoughts on taking design with us as we leave the twentieth century; what is happening in CSCW is significant, and where we take it to is important.

8.2 Three Interpretations of the Significance of "Users"

I want to set out briefly a characterization of three styles of design, constructed out of three differing and contradictory, but not mutually exclusive, relationships with users. These characterizations were arrived at both empirically and theoretically. Empirically, I had been aware for some time of the divergences between the first two meanings of "user": the "specify and deliver" style of a user-as-client orientation (as manifested in the strong programme of structured and formal methods, for example), and the "reflect and reinterpret" style of a user-as-codesigner orientation (the Scandinavian traditions of participative design were my main reference here). Then I thought I would try out a conceptual framework from social theory, based on a reading of Habermas (the early Habermas of "Science and technology as 'ideology'" (1971)), which led me to separate out from the second a third style: "enabling and empowering", belonging to a user-as-actor/constructor orientation.

On one hand the third, actor/constructor style highlights much more sharply some of the significant new emphases being introduced into ICT design through the CSCW debate – for example, the ethnographic, anthropological and poststructuralist insights. On the other hand, it enables a necessary historical and political distinction to be made, between politically motivated bottom-up work over the past couple of decades on cooperative design within the Scandinavian "collective resource" tradition, and increasing recent pragmatic excursions into "participation" (e.g. via prototyping) within mainstream Anglo-American system development work: more of this below. Firstly, the three styles and their views of users are summarized in Table 8.1.

Table 8.1. Three views of relationships with users

	1	2	3
Users seen as:	Formal clients	Permitted codesigners	Illegitimate actor/ constructors
Primary problem seen as:	Specify and deliver	Reflect and reinterpret	Enable and empower
Professional identity as:	Technician	"Knowledging" agent/facilitator	Scriptwriter/set designer/voice coach
Managing seen as:	Technique	Task–team building	Struggle for resources and for legitimacy to close the action

8.3 Users as Clients: The "Specify and Deliver" Style

This first interpretation of "users" is dominant within system development practice generally. If users are seen as clients (a legalistic form of relationship, with a start–end, project type or contract type structure) the appropriate designing style appears as that of a technician with skills in taking a specification and "delivering": orchestrating inputs and guaranteeing their transformation into outputs. The managerial presumption is that management too is technique: how to complete a supply transaction, getting from contract to sign-off in one piece, with no litigation. This is the world of "structured methods", "the mythical man month", and all the other apparatus and rhetoric of "professional" system development from the 1970s to the 1990s. It is part of the world of Taylorism. This specify-and-deliver style is what I refer to as "engineering": a practical strategy that constrains itself to see reality as relations between objects. In Habermas's language, engineering, in this sense, can be described as the domain of "technik", technical–instrumental rationality.

It is a natural perspective from the point of view of a twentieth century producer. Our times present us with a *de facto* economic and cultural separation between production and use. In our work world, producers are professionally (i.e. culturally) specialized; to a large extent, system production is located in specialized and distinct sectors and/or geographical locations within an international division of labour. This distanced relationship between producer and user is a datum for professional work; and the distance is often introduced and maintained by legal–economic relations of commodity exchange (between organizations, in the systems and software marketplace), or is treated as if it were (within organizations, constructed through profit centre structures, service level agreements etc.). "Engineering" style – specify/deliver – is the obverse of the commodity production/generic product coin.

Formalized specification and evaluation are central in such a lifeworld. Producer organizations confront specification because they have to get paid for delivering something expensive and complex. They confront evaluation because clients/customers have to agree that what is delivered is worth paying for, and because customer satisfaction determines possibilities for repeat business and future products. They need to formalize because trust is unacceptable as a basis for "cooperation" between conventionally autonomous (i.e. conventionally, self-interested, non-cooperating) social subjects.

Over 30 years of operating within the "delivering" myth, it has become increasingly clear that both specifying and evaluating are problematic because, in a profound sense, users do not know what they need and producers therefore cannot know, with confidence, how to deliver. The technology, and thus the usage, is too new and too complex for the need to be obvious. This is a historic problem, a characteristic learning curve problem of modern (post- traditional) society, located at a broadly social level. It is especially dramatic in ICT domains, which bring us hard up against the limits of modernism and ideologies of progress-through-engineering. Unless there is enough relaxation time between significant innovations, culture (values, stereotypes, custom-and-practice, rationalizations, languages, etc.) cannot keep pace with changing apparatus (geographical organization of work, the information processing capability of machine configurations, the scale, geography and connectivity of communications networks etc.). Reality is too big to know, too strange to act in with confidence.

It is important to note that this argument is not technologically determinist: apparatuses cannot change themselves. They may only be changed through practices, involving agents as well as structures. Precisely what they are when they *have* been changed, however, is in principle unknown, at first, even to the actors who brought the changes. It is in this sense that apparatuses may also lead actors.

In a "delivering" situation it seems appropriate that managerial approaches should have an engineering (machine/bureaucracy) aesthetic (Morgan 1986, chapter 2), one in which production processes have the form of sequences of discrete stages. Kling (1987), for example, characterizes conventional system design practice as being rooted in "discrete entity" models of the systems design object. Although the edges of the discrete-stage methodology model are now considerably blurred, with inter-stage recycles (i.e. learning, as a cognitive and organizational phenomenon) recognized as a characteristic of actual design practice, a prespecified stage model is generally taken as the paradigm of professional design activity. SSADM is the most notorious current British instance of this engineering/bureaucratic ideal.

8.4 Users as Codesigners: The "Reflect and Reinterpret" Style

The second major view of users recognizes them as codesigners with design professionals. This interpretation has professionals as "knowledgers": representers and "languagers", listeners and speakers, formalizers and informalizers, go-betweens and "feedbackers" – in short, facilitators. And management appears as a matter of task-team building. The pivotal vision of the codesigner style is "communication", which includes learning to speak of and listen to and see what was previously unspeakable and unheard and unseen. This is where Habermas seems to come into his own (e.g. in the use that is made of his theory of communicative action); I have my doubts, relating to his deeply liberal rationalism – see below – but his term "praxis" nicely describes the landscape inhabited by the user-as-codesigner style of design practice, and enables a sharp distinction from the "technik" domain of engineering/delivering practice.

Recent trends in system development have included the emergence of collaborative forms of design practice in which both user-side and producer-side actors figure as co-specifiers and co-evaluators (Scandinavian traditions are strong in this aspect, for historical industrial relations reasons). Prototyping (in one of its basic modes, as a specification process, as distinct from an evolutionary system building process) has emerged as a mode of "knowledge extraction" that is increasingly exploited by producers to enable non-technical users to participate more effectively in developing a design specification, bringing to it for explication their concrete but tacit knowledges of the use domain. In its other mode (as an evolutionary system building process) prototyping facilitates more rapid movement of users up a recognizing-and-re-evaluating curve. Elsewhere on the map of system development practice, both "usability" laboratories and a range of user-involving evaluative techniques and cues (mid- and post-project, within the framework of "delivery" methodologies) are increasingly advocated. The "usability" trend, as an approach to the control of product quality, is firmly entrenched by the commodification of systems and software, the penetration of ICTs into routine non-technical activities; suppliers must know whether generic users, in settings which must in their specifics remain unknown to product developers, can use generic products. A consequence of all of these trends is that "final end users" figure increasingly in discussions of design practices, and in day-to-day system development activities. This should be distinguished from the presence of user-side *managers*, whose political–legal project role belongs to the user-as-client, "delivering" lifeworld.

Such trends are generating significant learning among systems professionals about how to work successfully in design with non-technical people. For example, sessions at the ACM CHI'92 conference were dedicated to sharing experience and skills in user centred design practice; "participatory design" was the topic of a biannual conference, held at Cambridge, Massachusetts in November 1992. Greenbaum and Kyng (1991) present some of the Scandinavian experience and related theory derived from "cooperative design"; Namioka and Schuler (1991) address some of the issues in an American cultural context.

Welcome as these techniques, practices, insights and movements are, there remains an indeterminacy, which presents itself as a widely perceived "problem of implementation". At each stage of the systems lifecycle "implementation" has a different local meaning, a fact which seems to go unacknowledged in general discussion; it is as if each sub-profession is only concerned with the handover to the next stage in a production line process. Implementation can simply mean "getting the code to run on a given platform"; rarely does it mean "up and running and everybody is completely comfortable with the new regime – roles, norms, divisions of labour, workstyle and all". Implementation needs to be deconstructed, just like "user" – though not in the present chapter, I'm afraid. The problem of implementation is the inverse – the logical leftover – of the problematic privileging of pre-use design (Hales 1993a).

To the extent that they also focus on pre-use design, codesign practices suffer the problem of implementation along with conventional "delivering" design. Codesign may be enacted as design of an objective, machine-embedded, information processing system, perhaps with phases of codesign as knowledge extraction nested within an overall "delivering" project structure. The question that this forces into attention is: *what* is being designed? What kind of object does design have, and thus what kind of knowledge should we see as being produced in design? The codesign aesthetic recognizes subjectivity in its object (for example, tacit knowledge) in a way that "engineering", by my definition, does not. Some schools of practice stress mutual learning (Kyng 1991) through which professional designers develop knowledge in the users, as a product of design activity in its own right.

Given that practitioners of codesign operate in a world of praxis rather than technik, and are by definition much more aware than "engineers" that they address a social object, a further "distance" dimension becomes important in evaluating design. This is the distance between the knowledge developed in the design process, on one hand, and the social object (the organization, workgroup, user constituencies) of design on the other. To the extent that codesign produces framing-knowledge of a future situation, in only a few actors in that situation, the problem of implementation survives as part of the structure of codesign. Hales (1980, chapter 2) discusses this characteristic of design in chemical process plant.

There are other responses to the problem of knowing and designing social objects, besides the "cooperative design" approach. For example,

recognizing the difference between generic systems and local configurations can lead to an emphasis on "nested" levels of design, through which
a relatively abstract design or architecture may be successively concretized
by layering-on additional local functionality; the interface between levels
may then be determined by "minimum critical specification". This kind of
methodological concept is a coded response to both the general nature of
the design process (a learning/concretizing/objectifying process) and the
specific historical form of organizations (design as a negotiating process
within a social hierarchy). A related approach emphasizes the need to
derive "organizational requirements" at the predesign stage, as distinct
from information processing requirements. A third focuses on the design
of implementation activities. These three strategies, and others, belong to
the "sociotechnical" design tradition (Eason 1988).

Sociotechnical approaches remain similar to engineering/delivering
design approaches in their functionalist assumptions: that the (direct,
significant, intended) products of design are objective; and that the
real design object is a managerially controllable system of externally
knowable, determinate relations. Sociotechnical design approaches are
"organicist" and top-down (dealing with social black boxes within a
hierarchical/managerial perspective) in a way that is not true of the
bottom-up cooperative design tradition. Indeed, in Scandinavia the latter
has been partly founded on a rejection of aspects of the former (Laessøe
and Rasmussen 1989).

Both cooperative and sociotechnical design responses to the "user"
problem support the emergence of final end users within the design
process, with a legitimate status as codesigners who may therefore lay
claim to appropriate facilities and resources (time, training and information, for example). This is a significant shift from conventional practice
in hierarchical, bureaucratic, professionalized milieux. Nevertheless, the
separation of design from use, as distinct moments of a social process,
requires users, at some point, to leave design and simply *use* once more.
Design, as a *prior* phase, is still liable to be conceptually and economically
privileged over use; and design as a *phase* is strongly constituted by design
as a professionally and institutionally specialized form of activity. As long
as there are design professionals, the gap between design and use – and
the concomitant problem of implementation – will be endemic.

Hales (1993a) and Hales and O'Hara (1993) discuss a disappointing
case in which an excellent and surprising practice of cooperative design
(resulting in extraction of good quality design data and a great deal
of mutual learning in a small design subcommunity) seems to have
failed to address organizational and job-design issues. It was strong
on participative ideology and style – interpersonal politics – but weak
on organizational politics. The result may be that a "good design",
"implemented" in appropriate hardware and software, could still fall foul
of industrial relations hangups, managerial fiefdoms, avoidable resource

rigidities and a whole minefield of entrenched subgroup interests and cultures within a large, complex organization. The highly articulated knowledge of the social object that was developed during cooperative design was not effectively shared *with* the object – the full membership of the organization. "Poor management" is one way of describing this. But it is important not to lose sight of this also as a design failure, a weakness of "participation" as a fully adequate characterization of how to do design *and* implementation.

8.5 Users as Actor–Constructors: The "Enable and Empower" Style

The most (methodologically and politically) radical interpretations of design in CSCW recognize that use is *action*. In other words, you can present users with whatever "props" (in the theatrical sense) you want – tools, machines, artefact systems, data and communications architectures, rule systems translated into machine code. But how users act with, through and around these props´ is essentially indeterminate. Actors will act, according to their interpretations of the situation in which they find themselves with the system artefact; design of the artefact, before the fact, cannot fully design use. Thus, design in the conventional professionalized, prior, objectivistic sense becomes just one among a large set of partially determining systemic conditions of use–practice. The whole universe of non-designers and non-design becomes significant in the "live" ongoing outcome of design.

Within such a perspective the problem of design becomes, at one level, the problem of determining a relatively stable reading of the use situation among users – and a lot hangs on that "relatively" and on *who* is doing the determining. The design relation is no longer subject–object, because the object is also recognized as a full subject. My feeling is that it is here, in this problematic sphere of the identical subject–object and the simultaneously self-aware and "natural" actor, that the fascination, excitement and importance of CSCW lie.

Working the metaphor of user as actor a little harder, the professional designer becomes an amalgam of stage designer, scriptwriter and voice coach; and the crux of the difficulty and fascination of computer technology lies in the fact that ICT artefacts can constitute both (physical) "stage" and (textual) "script". Within this metaphor the management function becomes the directorial function, and it can be realized in as many different ways and modes as that function in the theatre. This present discussion is not based on it, but there is a relevant exploration of theatre theory and practice in Mangham and Overington (1987).

One interesting question flowing from the actor metaphor is: who are the audience? Linking with the distinction offered by activity theory (Kuutti 1991b), between active and passive subjects in relation to a design object, we might see the core of users who participate directly in the formal process of pre-use design (e.g. through cooperative design activities) as the cast – the active subjects – and the rest of the user population as the audience – the passive subjects. Then, the purpose of the dramatic action, the self-consciously performed design and implementation process, appears to be to assist the members of the audience in constructing a reading of the action. There is plenty to think about here, for implementation theory and practice.

In a conventional formal, hierarchical organizational setting, the user-–actor view of design is inescapably political. Users "construct" technology; they do this both symbolically, in their "reading" of artefacts, and literally, in the articulation work that is essential before a concrete *configuration* of artefacts (as distinct from the generic system products that emerge from usability labs in Silicon Valley) can serve as an adequate day-by-day supporting structure for a live practice. Formal hierarchies, constructed on the Taylorist machine model, are specifically intended to prevent this kind of "wildcat" action through the strict separation of managerial (knowledgeable) and operational (unknowledgeable) roles; thus in conventional organizations, user-constructors are necessarily *illegitimate* constructors. Designers attempting to perform in a user–actor style find themselves in the middle of a power struggle of not insignificant proportions. Goodbye engineering; hello struggle!

The nature of management within an actor–constructor perspective becomes dual. On one hand, it is about securing and appropriately disposing (in time and space) the resources required by actors to support and present their action. On the other (as in the theatrical director role) it is about structuring users' activity, about closing – however temporarily – the options, in order that a stable mode of practice (performance) may establish itself. In the political world of formal organizations, acquiring resources is a struggle, as is acquiring an appropriate legitimacy that may render the act of closure uncontroversial. Management as well as design becomes politicized if users are seen as actor–constructors.

The distinction between enabling and empowering is crucial. It is tied to the relationship between structure and agency. Enabling is about disposing the resources in a situation. It is possible to pump structure into a situation (notably through installing a technically integrated system of artefacts, but also, for example, by policing formalized communication codes and networks) and still fail to see the expected action emerge, because the user–actors are simply not "in role". Empowering is about role identity, and identity cannot be installed. It is possible (maybe, sometimes) to *call* an identity forth, to invite it to appear. But identities, essentially, have to come out. There are all sorts of good reasons why people at work do not want to "come out", and prefer instead to wear masks, act falsely or simply deny themselves to the organization, refuse to "be present".

This fact of working life alone is enough to make it completely uncertain whether designers (including users as codesigners) can acquire the legitimacy to close use-action. The persons who must bestow legitimacy may simply be withheld from the organizational situation. This is why talk about interface design as "empowering" is simply reckless. At its best – if managers can guarantee necessary resources – good interfaces may be enabling. At its worst, the imminently baroque articulation of usability orientated expertise and apparatus that we currently see in the Human–Computer Interaction (HCI) domain may be just another twist in the pathetic modern tale of professionals (in education, mental health, politics, etc.; Ehrenreich and English 1979) claiming to improve the rest of us by abstracting our world from us and doling it back again. Because they themselves were not at the scene of the crime – Taylorism and its less systematic precursors have been doing the thieving for a long time now – it is possible for members of the HCI community to feel that they are doing humanity a favour by redistributing the spoils of cognitive science. The historical view is a little more complicated and uncomfortable – for all of us in professional occupations. Illich (1975) offers a classic analysis of this syndrome, demonstrating why users' interests are not those of professionals. Empowerment is and will remain the rarest of moments, and it would not be unreasonable to take the view that, when professionals do succeed in having anything to do with empowerment, it will not be because of professionalism.

In a limited way, the codesigner style of design recognizes that what is at stake is "design-*of-use*"; this is signified by the "work" term in CSCW. That is, the eventual outcome is understood to be modified *practices*. In codesign, the internal (largely tacit) knowledges of existing practices, with which a new system must be articulated, become a required part of design knowledge. This itself is enough to take codesigner design beyond "engineering". However, the actor–constructor style also takes in two further aspects of design.

Firstly, the action-aware strand of CSCW design leads ineluctably towards design-*in-use* – recognition of and enabling of articulation work after formal design is complete, before, during and after the formal implementation phase; forever. This kind of focus is beginning to emerge in, for example, Clement (1991), Nardi and Miller (1991) and Gantt and Nardi (1992), which all examine how users in some sense "design" ways of articulating and working cooperatively with conventional, "non-cooperative" technology.

Secondly, out of a greatly enlarged reflective self-consciousness of design, its objects and their mutual relations, comes the *design-of-design*; that is, *management*. The user–actor style makes designing an explicit matter of producing and reproducing social order and social action.

On the design-in-use front, there are plenty of techniques and tactics available. Part II of Greenbaum and Kyng (1991) is mainly concerned with (pre-use) codesign, but also has pointers to design-in-use. Vehviläinen (1986) is a basic reference on "study circles", which should be seen as a design-in-use approach. Clement (1991) describes the design in use of a configuration of equipment and practices, as it occurred among administrative staff in a university. Mostly, the designing in that situation focused on the structuring and securing of user resources for training; Kling (1987) notes that such ancillary practices, articulated with immediate, hands-on, equipment-using practice, are significant in "web" approaches to systems design but marginal in conventional approaches, which he terms "discrete entity" and I would term "engineering".

The techniques and approaches of design-in-use are quite distinct from specification-orientated, up-front ones, though in *redesign* of existing configurations they may work well together (and perhaps most configuration-design situations need to be read and written as redesign). Reverse engineering and other formalizing processes, for example, might be helpful within a framework of user–actor self-redesign. Nonetheless, self-reflexive approaches, by users to their own work, do not necessarily have much to do with the current norms of professionalized, delivery-orientated system development practice. In the profession-structured world of ICT development and research, these differences will inevitably give use-design/design-in-use methods and styles lower status in the pecking order of information systems research.

The deep difficulty, which can be seen emerging in the user-as-actor approach to design, is whether action can be "designed" at all. The meaning of action is relatively stable in this formation; it comes from a well-entrenched (but to Anglo-Americans – especially engineers and natural scientists – often alien) set of traditions including phenomenology, ethnomethodology, interactionism, Hegelianism, some pragmatisms, certain interpretations of dialectical materialism, hermeneutics and various poststructuralisms. Rather than "action", it is "design" that is insecure. On one hand, we find ourselves reluctant to let go of the modern attachment to formal–rational action, to the "plan", to fixing the future through objectified structure (Suchman 1987). But on the other, plans fail and (interpreted as blueprints) must fail, and, as argued above, identities and situations cannot be installed. What the user–actor style within CSCW seems to have taken on – to an extent without recognizing it – is the working-through of "structure" values, archetypally modern values, in a reality in which structures are understood to be mediated by agents, and through inexplicit lifeworlds.

The problem of agency crops up in various guises in CSCW. For example, broaching more issues than they perhaps intend to, Rodden and Blair (1991) criticize or imply criticism of "user friendliness", "transparency", "intuitiveness", etc. as values in user-orientated systems design. All of these require something to be hidden from the user, and the question then is: who hides what from whom, in design? Who is an agent? The designer, who enables fluent use by a user? The user, who acts through a design only partly made obvious in its determinate realization as physical means of production? The design itself (materialized as a system artefact), as an "agent" possibly containing "intelligence"? Are agents consistent or contradictory? And, if contradictory, where does a designer sit in the contradiction?

There is a human centred design tradition within CSCW, surfacing with most methodological rigour in Ehn (1988). This tradition draws on Heideggerian, Marxian and Wittgensteinian roots in explicating a "tool" perspective on systems design; Laessøe and Rasmussen (1989) offer a brief historical discussion of human centred design approaches. Approaches to design under the human centred banner are typically more or less strong on the tool aspect of human action, but weak on the "text" aspect, i.e. the poststructuralist extension of the phenomenology/linguistic philosophy project. Nevertheless, through their humanistic motivation, they do constitute a distinct interest in the technologically structured support of action by human agents.

Research in the anthropology of design/development practices – for example, Woolgar (1991) on "configuring the user" – highlights the "identity" aspect of the problem of agency. In a world of objectively-socialized action, in which arcs of self-acting apparatus (such as computer systems) span increasing domains of time, space, data and logic, what kind of human agent identity can be defined, at a node in an increasingly objectified web of practice, in relation to the (superior? different? indeterminate?) powers of the self-acting apparatus? Can a system properly be called an agent?

8.6 Where are Designers? The Geo-Economic "Location" Problem

Consider three designers at work:

- A designer working for Groupware Inc., Silicon Valley, has limits that determine the views of "the user" that can actually appear in his or her work, regardless of what he or she wills. Most of the eventual worldwide users of the product, and their actual use situations, will be and must remain invisible to the designer. A usability lab is perhaps the best that this designer can do in getting close to users, backed up by the universalized knowledges of cognitive and social science. How close is that? What kind of relationship can designers have with generic users?

- A designer working on a workflow management system configuring project within a user organization, on contract, with a deadline, a certain set of colleagues and a limited range of personal skills, has limits (local and contingent but real) that determine whether anything other than a knowledge-extraction relationship with users can operate in that practice. The designer has a shorter and "thinner" organizational life than the system and its users. While the social relations of the "outsider" analyst role can be liberating (it is sometimes easier to talk to a stranger) they are also tenuous, when it comes to shifting significant resources around in a way that sticks. Funding always constrains the "thickness" of the knowledge of use-practice that can be derived. What kind of relationship can project- and budget-constrained designers have with user–actors?

- A final user, low in the pecking order, overworked and lacking in self-esteem, suffers limits on his or her ability to act as a whole human, both within the large totality of human action, historically, and within the small totality of the development process for configuring an apparatus which he or she deploys at work. In the special setting of design team meetings he or she may become empowered, a distinctive actor. But back on the job, how rapidly the glow can fade. What kind of relationship can user–codesigners have with themselves, and other users, outside the charmed and illuminated circle of the "participatory" design phase?

What I am trying to stress, using these three vignettes, is that there can be no theory or method of design that covers all situations. Each of these situations is objectively different from the others (and there are other cases too, not represented here). The nature of the object being proffered for designers to work on differs, as does the nature of the access that the designer has to it and to objective and subjective resources – tools, time, languages, identities, habitus (Bourdieu's term; 1977). Whether a given design style makes sense depends a great deal on the objective structuring of the design situation and of the object that it presents for designers. The object can certainly be – always is – reappropriated by designers, reread, rewritten (sometimes literally, in revised specifications). But within limits. In this section I want briefly to map out some relevant differences, which lie in multiple divisions of design labour – global, sectoral, occupational.

The distinction between the design of CSCW *products* and the design of the actual *use* of CSCW systems can be developed with the help of ideas from innovation management theory. Fleck (1991) discusses "generic systems" versus "configurations" of technology; this distinction is perhaps best applied in an external market supply context, where the producer organization (which delivers generic implementations of generic designs) is distinct from the user organization (which must configure systems of technology in order to support and constrain specific tasks and activities). In an intra-organizational setting, the equivalent distinction might be better expressed in terms of "standard" designs (corporate, or top-down in the organizational, hierarchical sense) versus negotiated "local" variations of or overlays on the standard system design.

Whether designs come from "out there" (with generic systems) or "up there" (with corporate standard systems) there is always a problem in principle, of what use they are "here", in use. Across the whole range – from generic to standard to local systems – there are clearly many loci of design activity, the practical conditions and norms of which are quite distinct. Depending on the closeness to final users (and the local culture of the producer sector), values may be quite distinct too.

One way to look at the "cascade" process of stepping down the hierarchy, from generic systems to local configurations, is to view it as an active process of "articulation work" (Bannon and Schmidt 1989; Star 1991; Strauss 1985). In what ways must generic artefacts be combined with local design activity to construct working configurations of artefact and identity? Can we – and I mean we *users* – escape the myth of shrink-wrapped "solutions" while continuing to benefit from the falling cost–performance curve of a globally developing software product market? Articulation work is the (bottom-up, action-ist) obverse of the sociotechnical (top-down, structure-ist) coin of "minimum critical specification". Both conceptions are needed in real organizations, integrated within a more self-consciously economic–historical understanding of the significance of articulation in relation to formal definition.

Cultural chasms are a necessary part of the global/sectoral division of labour. If we picture the cascade of design, from suppliers/innovators, down to developers/appliers, down to implementers/final users, at each level there is some activity that should be acknowledged as "design'. And at each interface there is a possibility of communicative fracture, between design and use. This is the "problem of implementation" again. It shows up, for example, in the failure of advanced, Alvey-promoted software engineering methods (Integrated Project Support Environments (ipses), as against stand-alone tools) to be taken up in use within commercial design practice (Quintas 1992). The implementation problem is a matter both of occupational cultures (producer-side/ user-side) and markets (institutional separation of supplier and customer organizations). In a sense, the very purpose of commodity markets is to secure objective economic connection with a minimum of cultural (communicative) connection. We are touching here on some of the problems that get bundled into the CSCW debate on the meaning of the second C in CSCW.

These facts of life pose, in a concrete and commercially serious form, a design-of-design question: what *can* be the relation between product design and use design? How, in practice, can good products be connected with good use? In each sphere of the division of labour, manager-designers will necessarily answer this differently, because of the differences in the resources that they marshal. Their local strategies, and the trade-offs and penalties that these generate, may or may not add up to a "rational" or even a workable connection between the generic and the local.

I have been arguing that style, while a major issue for professional designers, is not just personal. In the context of the global division of labour, for example, we can see that the style appropriate for the kind of work being done in a given location is, to an extent, hostage to the industrial strategies being pursued at a higher structural level. The positioning of the designer's employer and the organization's product determines – although not completely – limits on what designers can take as material for design, and thus the appropriateness of design style. Within organizations, market conditions increasingly apply to the structuring of relations between the practices of different groups (e.g. information systems professionals and users). The professional division of labour and functional division of labour within an organization are further layers of structuring that further determine the limits of style. Issues of this kind are being pursued by Grudin (1991c, d).

A historical–economic approach is important in avoiding excesses of voluntarism. The current "empowerment" rhetoric of some parts of the HCI community seems often to presume that technical professionals are actually in a position to "empower" users. Whether this is true depends on what that volatile word is taken to mean, but, certainly, neither the ownership of certain techniques nor the extent of access to resources and to other people's conditions of work that is normally associated with technician status, are enough to secure empowerment in any sense that I would care to give it.

It *is* important to be talking about empowerment and technical work, and it is a relief that the CSCW ethos is making this legitimate in the hard world of engineering. But it is also important to have a careful understanding of where a given design practice sits, and what are the limitations of being in this location, as regards *any* determinate effect on users, let alone the extremely ambitious outcome of "empowerment". Objects are largely given for design professionals to work on (by a professional discipline, by a market, by an employer or client, by the dynamics of a project or workgroup). And the objects worked on determine appropriate work style. Style is a constrained rather than a free choice, situated within robust, historically prior *structures*. On the other hand, styles, traditions, paradigms or whatever, as situating visions brought by *agents* to specific design settings, call forth, recognize and shape their objects into the kinds of material that they perceive as being workable.

Thus, circles of structure can be broken by agents, and circles of agency can be broken by structure. Locations of design can be shifted, transformed into alternative locations, but not easily, or necessarily in any given case, and not simply by adopting a different style of analysis or communication. Style (as an agent form) lacks weight, to the extent that it passes out of live action and into a "dead" (structure–form) system of hardware and code. Stylish interfaces are fine; maybe even fun. But do we really want to claim that an interface or an interface design practice is "empowering"; or should we reserve that description for stronger, more historically and politically well-situated uses?

Another level of the "location" problem is within the functional division of labour in a given artefact's history. There are many ways of recognizing functions within design and development. The ones that I suggest are most significantly highlighted by CSCW debates are:

- Design of *generic* products and standard systems, in a different time and place from the local configuring of artefacts derived from them.

- Design of use *activities* as a superset of artefact design at the local (configurational) level.

- Design in use; that is, the *articulation work* of recognizing, legitimizing connections with, marshalling the appropriate resources for and actually constructing (performing) the union with allied practices.

- Design of *design*.

This last, complex and fundamentally *managerial* notion embraces a whole ecology of practices, which are often seen as discrete phases. We might identify: the framing, separating-out, elevating and prioritizing, from the mess of everyday activity, of design projects and their resources; the "initial" process of specification and contract making (becoming ever less "initial" as prototyping permeates codesign; and being simultaneously restored, temporally if not logically, by "rapid" prototyping); design as a nominal phase; implementation as another, subsequent nominal phase; organizational learning as an invisible and barely theorized requirement, both on the user-side and the producer-side; evaluation as one more nominal phase of an ideal software life-cycle; redesign as the re-entrant "end" of the software life-cycle (and which actually is the *general* form of design; there really is no design from scratch); and finally, "use", which vanishes from delivery-orientated vision, appearing in conventional life-cycle models only as "maintenance", the *doppelgänger* and poor cousin of professionalized design. If only users didn't exist, the whole messy problem of maintenance could be ditched; it really is a carbuncle on the otherwise neat software life-cycle.

The above is a heterogeneous list: CSCW thinking is not yet able to be sufficiently clear about the mutual relations of the items. The main point to make here is that there is no fixed, necessary relationship between these *functions* and the social distribution of functions embodied in *de facto* personal, occupational and sectoral divisions of *labour* within workgroups, organizations, labour markets and countries. The codesign tradition in system design has notably concerned itself with the redistribution of conventional design roles; the actor–constructor perspective has further, more radical implications. This problem will run and run.

Hales (1993a) uses a simple pictorial schema to represent some aspects of the division of labour in design. In Figs 8.3–8.5 this schema is used to contrast "engineering" with design-of-use, and to locate end use within the global "cascade" of designing/configuring. In Fig. 8.3, the lifeworld of project-based design is contrasted with use: the fundamental problem for the designer is delivering (going from specification to product) and for the user it is changing and staying the same (going from perceived needs to new practices, and round again). In Fig. 8.4, the mutual articulation of design and use is shown, highlighting the differences between the starting and ending points of "engineering" design and the "target" domain. No matter how much designers exercise themselves at the interface – for example, in the current attention being paid to specification – the textured tracks in Fig. 8.4 remain outside of the professional design sphere. Fig. 8.5 shows a cascade of generic-product into local configuration (redrawn, emphasizing upward flows, it would represent the abstraction of actual practices and needs into generic specifications and systems). It emphasizes the cultural "gaps" between spheres of practice within the cascade, and also the marginality and indeterminacy of whether the final user gets to the final use. Each of the tracks in Fig. 8.5 (and also each of the evaluation loops, omitted for clarity) is a significant locus of design activity; but not all of them are legitimate. Each black "blob" is a formal start/end point for the delivering mode of design – the legitimate stuff. And the majority of the diagram's content – the textured tracks – is outside the legitimate domain.

8.7 Taking Design with Us

For me, this discussion of design style is situated historically, in a context of wanting to take design with us as we leave the twentieth century – not literally *leave* (as we start to write dates beginning with "20") but metaphorically. I refer to the norms, values and identities of modern existence and the possibility of future, significantly different forms of social life and work. "Design" is a powerful value of modernism. Large parts of our economies and ideologies are built on it, interpreted and entrenched in forms of professionally specialized activity. As a designer by training and temperament, I value the value. I also (as a turncoat engineer) see profound difficulties in the dominant "engineering" interpretation; also some interesting difficulties in emergent interpretations such as participative codesign. In this final section I will draw attention to some of the challenges implicit in identifying design styles in the way that this chapter has done, and to some sources of practical (i.e. methodological) support.

DESIGN LIFEWORLDS

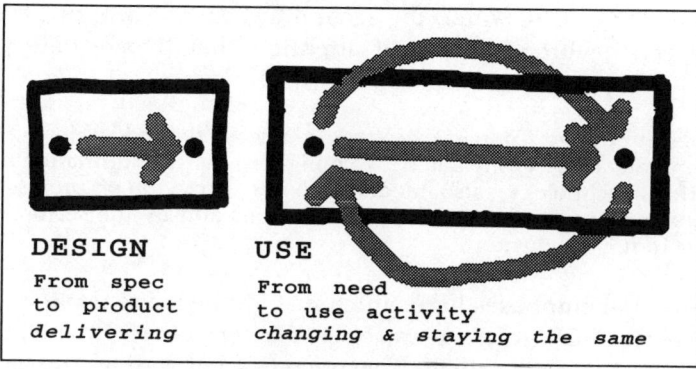

Fig. 8.3. The lifeworlds of design and use.

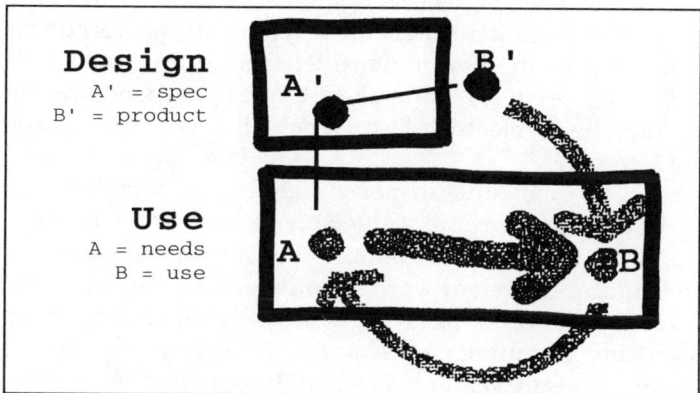

Fig. 8.4. The lifeworlds of design and use.

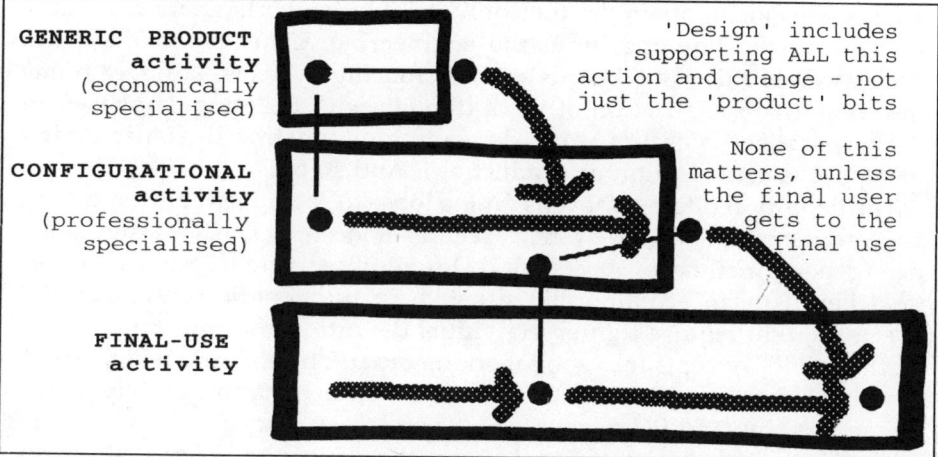

Fig. 8.5. The "cascade" of use development.

Firstly, since this chapter lies within the stream of debate around "the unit of analysis" of CSCW and the second C, here is a working definition that supports the broad sweep of attention that I have here given to CSCW:

> Computer Supported Cooperative Work is objectively and subjectively social-ized economic activity; mediated by configurations of information and com-munications technology; also mediated by the activity of professionalized designers and managers in formal organizations and by the sectoral division of labour in ICT production.

There are several emphases here which need to be made explicit. The first is that the term CSCW refers to an *object of design activity*, that is, *work*, the economic activity of some abstract or concrete set of people. The term refers only indirectly to specific sets of methods for designing or supporting such work, and to specific technologies and classes of systems. In one case that I have in mind, an American academic developer, discussing an electronic meeting room environment, referred to the system throughout as "*a* CSCW'. There is no hope if CSCW researchers use such loose talk, confusing the artefactual design outcome with the design object (transformed *practice*).

Secondly, work (one kind of social activity) is recognized as being something both objective and subjective; a matter of bodies, energy, geometry and physiology, for example, but also of language, intention, identity and culture. Different work situations – and thus different objects for CSCW design attention – differ in the ways in which they are structured in these two complex dimensions, and especially in the articulation of the connections that are made between the two. Workflow management systems, for example, tend to be heavy on the objective socialization – the prespecified trajectory of an objective work item. In this they clearly are late developments in the tradition of Taylorist work organization, the Fordist transfer line and industrial engineering. Other types of system, such as electronic whiteboards or conferencing systems, strongly frame the subjective socialization of work (though with differing emphases on the physicalized object of work, depending on whether the basic design metaphor is conversation or production). And so on.

The definition offered above is far too loose to catch the requirements of any specific type of CSCW system (generic or local), or CSCW design prac-tice (general method or local style). Differently situated design practices (and here I mean economically situated, in the generic–configurational spectrum) will require tighter individual definitions in order to get their methods and concepts into good working order. There clearly will be *many* working definitions of CSCW, because there are many forms of cooperative – that is to say (and it's a *non sequitur*!) social – work.

The final thing to be stressed about the definition is that, although it characterizes an object of design, it also has design within it: "the activity of professionalized designers" and "the sectoral division of labour in ICT production". This reflexiveness is crucial. The single most important thing that I see in CSCW practices and debates, growing out of the accumulated experience in "participation" traditions (and highlighting some of their political and economic weaknesses), is the emergence of "design-of-design" as an issue. It's not just how we design that's at stake, but how we select the ways in which we do the designing, how we learn to go beyond what we've got used to doing when it begins to break down (in the phenomenological sense), as "engineering" is doing.

At this level, I might argue that the single most important contribution of CSCW thinking will be an eventual understanding which might be called *situated design*. This will be an understanding of both the subjective-situatedness ("style") and objective-situatedness (global/sectoral/occupational structure) of choices about how to do design. It will span a huge repertoire of methods, techniques and practical roles, rather than presuming that any style (let alone method) can be universal. It will enable us to find the right mix of deliver, reinterpret and enable/empower; and to do this – because it takes the form of theory-of-practice – on the very cusp of action.

"Situated design" will also be inescapably managerial. Design-of-design is a managerial function, in the strongest *a priori* sense. This is not to presume that "managers", so-called (either producer-side or user-side), do now or exclusively will exercise this function. It is to claim that choices about who does designing, with whom, when, where, and how – and how all of this complicated division of development labour is resourced and socialized – are central in CSCW design's still-emerging agenda. This difficult social function can be parcelled between roles and actors in many ways. But in order for CSCW researchers to get to the place that they're beginning to draw sketch maps of, they will have to address "managerial" and not merely technical or even "communicative" questions. One idea that has begun to help in CSCW design, at the micro level, within analyses of "work", is that of "articulation work". What I am suggesting is that articulation work on a much broader scale – ultimately the global scale of the ICT economy – will need to come within the recognition of design-of-design, before CSCW's self-mapping can be completed. This is quite a challenge for us as designers who, whatever our location, are all "local" in our understanding of the CSCW map.

There is one final point that I want to develop, which is not obvious in the above definition (although it is implicit). The point derives from the three-way characterization of styles that I've used in this chapter. A great deal of CSCW debate at present operates with a two-level model. So I need to explain the significance of the third.

I recognize a certain amount of justified celebration in the CSCW design community at having broken through the one-level "engineering" definition of reality, becoming able to recognize (and thus design for) culture and communicative/hermeneutic/situated action as well as information structure and information processing/technical/plan–instrumental action. For example, Robinson (1989) argues that any effective CSCW system must develop a careful and deliberate relationship between what he calls "formal" (in this chapter, my objective or technik-orientated) and "cultural" (my subjective or praxis-orientated) aspects of language and work-action. The rationale is to support both clarity *and* ambiguity, explicating *and* presuming, delivering *and* reinterpreting.

This seems to me a strong argument and the two-level insight is, I suggest, ground that CSCW can claim to be consolidating, which goes clearly and irretrievably beyond "engineering". The two-level hunch is one that I, and many other methodologists now congregating in the CSCW domain, have been pursuing for some time: for example, it is in the analysis of chemical process design in Hales (1980); it is also central in the definition of CSCW above. It is a hunch that the "participative" stream of CSCW and pre-CSCW work has been following in a particular way and, at a certain level, is related to one of the personal joys that perhaps drives the expanding post-engineering venture along: the momentary exhilaration of successfully deconstructing and expressing what had been tacit in practice, and then putting this insight back to work in design – that is, in objectively reconstructing the reality from which it emerged.

There is another level, however, which does not yet clearly show through in this celebration of the second level. This is the level of articulation, on the large and the small scale, which I referred to above. This is managerial and, because it is about resources and their appropriation by actors, political with at least a small "p". This recognition, too, has been driving much of the participative codesign work for years now. But currently it tends to be marginal in CSCW. Just as the Scandinavian "collective resource" tradition tends to roll together the political and the communicative agendas in cooperative design, Robinson tends to roll this political aspect – the redisposing of real-world (economic *and* symbolic) resources, and the intentional if only temporary closing of discourses (Bourdieu calls this "symbolic violence") – together with the more low-key issues of establishing descriptions and interpretations which are dealt with in "second-level" language.

The third level is not a matter of language at all, in any strict sense, nor discourses, not even "speech acts". It's a matter of materially shifting lumps of the world around: language, artefact, identity, corporeal being, emotion – the lot; not talking about it – doing it. Here we're talking power, and especially, hegemony. CSCW is not yet very good at talking about hegemony. The third level – "politik" as distinct from praxis or technik – is also where Habermas pulls punches. It was sort-of there in his earliest work (as the human interest in "critical-revolutionary practice") but has been thoroughly gagged by "communicative" rationality in his later theory. His theory of communicative action projects a world in which we talk out our problems; fiat, sabotage, even voting with our feet, are beyond his scope. My third view of users is one that acknowledges that, when push comes to shove – even the very hard shove of re-engineering their lifeworlds – people go their own way, and the "language" that operates then is power.

I have earlier and more properly cast this "third-level language" issue as the third style of designing/developing, involving recognition of illegitimate actor/constructors – i.e. it is a practice question, not just a language or discourse question. It may be helpful to briefly review the state of CSCW discussion on this issue in terms of a range of approaches to the "structure/agent" problem.

There is a spectrum, and for brevity I will here concentrate on the poles. One pole is very "structurist": Kling's argument about "web" and "discrete entity" approaches to design (Kling 1987; Kling and Scacci 1982). The picture sketched in this approach is one of ever-extending articulations, of practice with practice, beyond the site of the central processor. There is a steady emphasis on history; but "history" is never well defined, and seems mainly to be mapped at the objective level, by layers of artefact. There does not seem to be the theoretical basis in this work – despite the important emphasis on history and the "social" – to properly recognize how actors and cultures work their constructions. It is short in its ability to deal with both textuality and action. At a stretch, it might be possible to connect the "web" approach with actor–network theory (Latour 1991; Callon and Latour 1981), although this too has its (poststructuralist, deconstruct but don't bother to reconstruct) problems.

The other pole is extremely "de-structurist": the argument from postmodern social theory which denies structure anything other than a transient existence and glorifies the "play" of decentred discourses (Baskerville et al. 1992; Truex and Klein 1991). The difficulty here is that not only do structures vanish from the ontology; so do actors. As a basis for a "user-as-actor/constructor" design style, this type of theory clearly has its limits! Rather than helping to frame situated design, it de-situates activities to the point where functionalism creeps in again by the back door. While a user–actor perspective in principle leaves behind the top-down fetishism of sociotechnical approaches and "engineering", the postmodern analysis of organizational practice as developed by Baskerville et al. leaves actors so unsituated that "The Organization" has to be reinvented to ground any kind of reality; only now it's the "postmodern" organization of post-Fordist restructuring, total quality competition and catch-up-with-Japan culturalist rhetoric. Not far from 1960s sociotechnical theory at all, really! Interesting, this pole; but not well situated except in the domain of high priced Business School "culture consultancy" – too far from most design work to be able to build easy bridges.

Between the poles exists a whole range of interesting possibilities. There's hermeneutics (Boland 1991; Boland and Day 1989), critical theory

(Lyytinen 1990a; Ngwenyama 1991), activity theory (Bødker 1991; Kuutti 1991a, b), structuration theory (Clark et al. 1990; Lyytinen 1990b) and "forces of production" theory, an amalgam of cultural production and labour process theory (Hales 1980). This latter analysis, for example, deconstructs deskilling – one aspect of "the second C" question – and develops the notion of hegemony as a form of power operating through technology design.

Most important of all, I suspect, is the feminist–theoretical literature on situated knowledges, location and articulation work (Haraway 1985, 1987; Star 1991; Suchman 1991b). This is the strongest source of serious reflective work which supports the values of localism rather than universalism, commitment rather than detachment, vocation rather than professionalization, empowering rather than technical-fixing, and facilitation/husbandry rather than engineering/hammering. This is discussed in relation to CSCW and the British tradition of human centred design in Hales (1993b).

Given that third-level "language" (actually, institutional, resource-deploying *practice*) is about *power*, the approaches identified above have varying strengths. I have a hunch that activity theory may be able to talk about hegemony, but present workings of the theory don't do this, staying close to the second-level insight concerning the importance of communication and learning as distinct from transactions and deliveries. Structuration theory claims to be able to handle power, but I am unconvinced. A great deal of feminist theory is about power: both patriarchal power as an anthropological phenomenon and also "decentralist" alternatives to the hegemonic force of centralist, subject–object structures of thought (of which my "engineering" is a classic case). But there isn't sufficient feminist analysis at the level of macroeconomic relations, and hardly any of it (Haraway is an exception) adopts poststructuralist or postmodern approaches, which I suggest are the most powerful, if also the most difficult. Thus, the potential of the various approaches listed above is still to be properly tried, when it comes to analytically (and practically) addressing power.

My own feeling is that Bourdieu's "theory of practice" – which nobody in CSCW is talking about – may be among the best starting points, because of its concern with symbolic violence, symbolic fields and professional politics. Its origins in field anthropology, and its recent application (Bourdieu 1991) to questions of how ethnic/regional boundaries become constituted and how national "voices" emerge, both suggest that this approach would connect with interesting work in CSCW such as Perin (1991), which discusses "electronic social fields" in bureaucracies. Whichever options are pursued, CSCW has a long way to go yet before it can deal with the factual redisposing and reconstituting of power among technology users, as distinct from "better" system designs.

The title of this final section carries a reference to perhaps the first

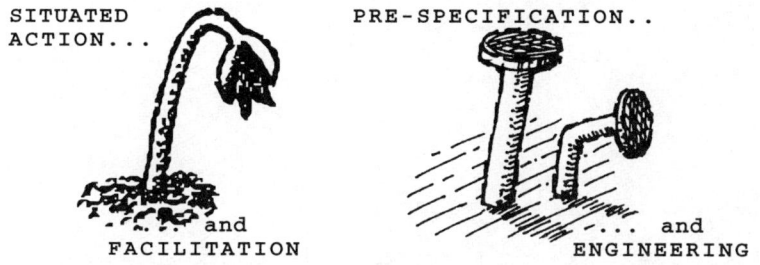

Fig. 8.6. What mix?

postmodern text that I ever happened across, a situationist manifesto (Grey 1974) entitled *Leaving the Twentieth Century*. Feminists are trying hard to do just that and, in the arena of CSCW, are trying also to take design along. CSCW design has already left the high modernism of "engineering" behind. But whether it will learn properly to recognize seeds rather than nails is still open (Fig. 8.6). Really good design will call for a mix of all three of the styles that I have characterized, the last of which is really a style of managing, not simply "designing". And, while interdisciplinarity, flexibility of outlook and other "cultural" and personal responses among professionals will help, some more serious political work, destroying institutional and economic distances, will be required along the way.

Chapter 9

Coping with Complexity and Interference: Design Issues in Multimedia Conferencing Systems

M.A. Sasse, M.J. Handley and N.M. Ismail

9.1 Introduction

Once the concept of Computer Supported Cooperative Work (CSCW) tools was established, many software developers responded enthusiastically, and quite a number of groupware applications were built and released in the space of a few years. Few of these applications, however, were taken up with the same enthusiasm by their intended users. Grudin (1990) studied several of the failed projects and detected a high level of resistance among users against adopting these applications. He attributed this resistance to inadequacies in the design of groupware applications, resulting from the developers' failure to appreciate that technology which aims to support collaborative work groups has to address issues and concerns that are fundamentally different from those encountered in the development of other application software. In Grudin's view, approaches developed in Human–Computer Interaction (HCI) and Human Factors (HF) were ill equipped to tackle these problems, since they were based on experiences and observations of individual users interacting with stand-alone systems. Consequently, they focused on optimizing screen designs and interaction styles. Developing effective and successful groupware applications, however, required approaches that provided an in-depth understanding of the collaborative activities that these applications were trying to support.

Following this approach, the developers of Freestyle,[1] a multimedia groupware system, dedicated resources to in-depth studies of office work and discussing functionality with prospective users (e.g. Ehrlich 1987) prior to developing the system. In a recent report on the post-installation phase of Freestyle, Francik et al. (1991) found that the system was not adopted by many users, simply because adoption required a change in organizational work patterns. They suggest that, in addition to studies on the nature of work, such systems need to develop an adoption strategy in order to be successful. They predict that this will be particularly relevant for multimedia and desktop conferencing systems, which are currently being developed. Such an adoption strategy should include:

- That the system addresses a pressing business problem in the prospective user organization(s).
- Helping users to identify uses of the system in their current work environment.
- Close collaboration during development with a pilot user work group.

When designing a multimedia conferencing system for the automotive industry under the RACE CAR (CAD/CAM for the Automotive Industry under RACE (Research for Advanced Communications in Europe)) project, the design team followed a rationale that closely resembles an adoption strategy as proposed by Francik et al. (1991):

- The system addresses a pressing business problem in the automotive industry (the need to shorten the design cycle for new models).
- The team of developers held trials and workshops involving users (car designers and production engineers) from the target client organizations to help them to identify uses of multimedia conferencing in their work.
- The team of developers collaborated with pilot user groups throughout the project.

The result of this adoption strategy was a pilot system whose functionality closely matched the requirements of the intended users. In addition, the semi-formal trials with members of the pilot user groups helped the developers to identify usability issues specific to multimedia conferencing systems that could pose an obstacle to adoption of the system. This chapter reports the usability issues identified, and discusses how they can be resolved.

9.2 The CAR Multimedia Conferencing System

The CAR multimedia conferencing system was developed in the Department of Computer Science at University College, London, as part of the RACE CAR project. The goal of the project was to develop a multimedia conferencing system that would help to shorten the design cycle for new cars. It was aimed at assisting car designers at different sites to interactively discuss design decisions – something that currently involves much travel and courier transport of drawings and documents. The idea was that designers could have design sessions without leaving their desks, via their workstation.

The design of the system is based on providing a conferencing platform that can support both applications written specifically for the platform (collaboration-aware applications), and existing applications written as stand-alone software (collaboration transparent applications). As an example of a collaborative-aware application, a distributed sketchpad application was developed by one of the CAR partners, which has been fully integrated with the conferencing system. CAD packages running under X Windows are an example of collaboration transparent applications that can be included in the conferencing system. This is done by using a shared window system, which is based on Shared X, developed by Digital. The conferencing system also encompasses video and audio communication. Typically, there is one video channel for a conference, which is controlled by the floor holder, while the audio channel is an open one, independent of the floor mechanisms. Fig. 9.1 gives an overview of a CAR multimedia conference.

Most of the observations reported in this chapter took place during a week-long semi-formal evaluation of the system with a group of sixteen

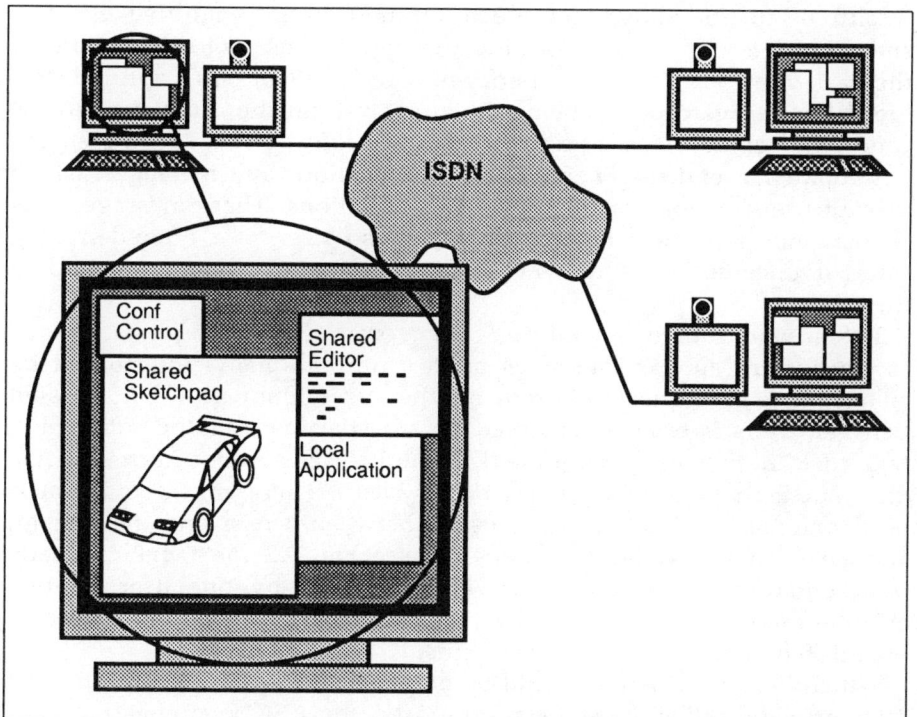

Fig. 9.1. CAR multimedia conference: audio, video and shared applications.

users, car designers and production engineers from an automotive design company and two car manufacturers. The users were introduced to the functionality of the system in a two-hour training session. They were then asked, two users at a time, to complete a series of interactive design tasks using the system. They were also free to experiment with the system. The sessions were recorded on videotape, and the users were de-briefed for about one hour each following the session. Additional observations were made by members of the project team when using the CAR system for a collaborative writing project (Baydere et al. 1993).

9.3 Design Principles

The usability problems observed in the CAR user trials stemmed in the main from two sources. The first is the overwhelming *complexity* of this sort of multi-user system: users of multimedia conferencing systems tend to work with more than one application and use multiple workspaces. In applications such as collaborative drawing tools, more than one layer is generated for each image (for a detailed description of such an application see Ishii and Miyake 1991). Multimedia conferencing systems offer a wealth of functionality, and much of their users' cognitive effort is spent on determining and locating the appropriate tool or function for the task they are trying to perform. Green (1990) has captured this idea of cognitive capacity being taken away from the actual task in the concept of *viscosity*. In addition to being highly viscous, conferencing environments tend to generate many notifications and messages, which disrupt users' actions or their planning of actions. These messages may or may not require action to be taken, so users are often left in a state of uncertainty as to whether and how they should respond to these events.

The second source is continual *interference*. Performing a task, such as starting up an application, is often (unintentionally) interrupted by an action (e.g. a question) from another user. Similarly, a discussion between users is often interrupted by a system message or notification (e.g. that another user has joined). In multi-user systems such as CAR, *users interact with each other, via their systems*. There are three channels of communication: between the users, between a user and the system, and between the system components (see Fig. 9.2 for a diagrammatic representation).[2] Frequently, activities initiated by one user on one channel interfere with an activity that another user is trying to perform on a different channel at the same time.

Which design principles could be employed to avoid these problems? Two principles that have been proposed for CSCW applications are WYSIWIS and seamlessness.

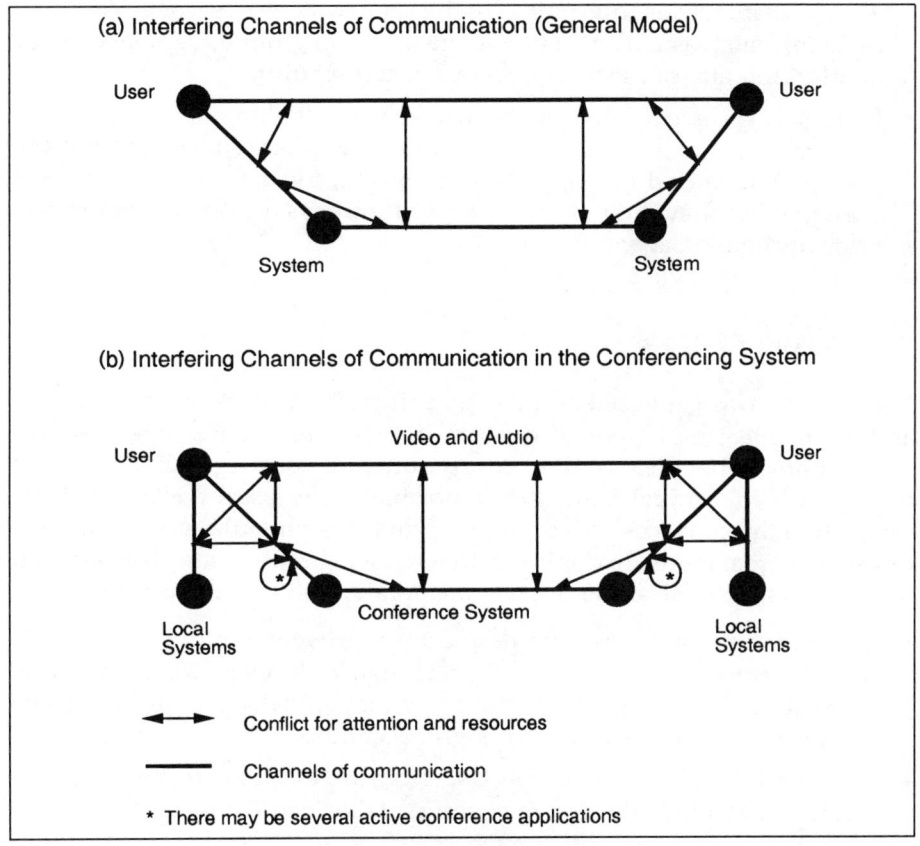

Fig. 9.2. Interfering channels of communication.

9.3.1 WYSIWIS

WYSIWIS (What You See Is What I See) has been proposed as a principle for displaying shared information in CSCW applications. Shared information in a system should be presented to all users in the same way (Elwart-Keys et al. 1990). This means that users cannot, for instance, resize or iconize a window in which shared information is displayed. The main reason is to avoid referencing problems (e.g. "on that second spike from the top"). These could cause distortion of information and subsequent breakdown in communication between users.

However, even with strict application of WYSIWIS, distortion and breakdowns still occur; for example:

- *What you see is what I see:* but does it mean to you what it means to me? Displaying the same information to all users does not guarantee that what is displayed is interpreted in the same way by everyone. Variation in factors such as a user's knowledge and background, vigilance, focus of attention etc. can lead to different interpretation.

- *What you see is only part of the action:* users looking at shared information share the display being changed by another user, but not the actions that caused the change. They might, for instance, see an error message, but they did not see which button/keys the other user pressed prior to the message.

9.3.2 Seamlessness

Seamlessness was proposed as a design principle by Mark Stefik (in Foster and Tatar 1988) as a way of overcoming user resistance to groupware applications. The idea is that group software tools (groupware) must merge with individual tools. While not having to learn additional tools certainly reduces viscosity, and thereby reduces potential user resistance to some degree, there are doubts as to whether complete seamlessness can be achieved, or is desirable for all collaborative tasks; for example:

- A "mindshift" might be essential. Collaboratively working on a task is very different from working on your own task, even when the same software tools are employed. Strategies that are effective for individual work might be less effective in a group context.
- Security and privacy concerns. Users can be expected to be wary of a system that would allow them to accidentally "drift" into a collaborative situation.

Applying WYSIWIS and seamlessness as design principles can solve some problems, but may create others in the process.

9.4 Design and Usability Issues

In a conventional multitasking windows environment (such as SunView or X Windows), a user has many channels of communication with the system using many applications. Several of these applications may be active simultaneously, but typically only one holds the user's attention at any time. The user provides input to a single application, and that application produces a reply – all the window system is used for is a simple way to switch applications and/or context. Any system response is a result of the user's interaction with it.

A multimedia conference windows environment also provides many channels of communication with the system, but these channels now also communicate with multiple users. A user's focus of attention is now not only determined by the desired interaction with the system, but also by unexpected events caused by other conferees. Rather than being able to focus on one channel of communication (with the system), the user communicates with other users at the same time. In addition to receiving replies from his or her own application to known input, the user receives replies to unknown input from other users. This can lead to problems with screen clutter, handling of events, notifications, floor control and pointers. These problems are described in this section, and available design solutions and their – potentially undesirable – side effects are discussed.

9.4.1 Screen Clutter

In a single-user environment, a user has all the necessary information to perform screen management. In a shared environment, users try to keep all applications visible on screen at once, as they feel that iconizing or hiding them will lead to confusion, as outlined below. They rapidly run out of screen space, the display becomes cluttered and information that is needed to manage the interaction with the system successfully (e.g. the conference manager) becomes difficult to locate because windows cove, or overlap with other windows (see Fig. 9.3).

Traditional window managers offer three basic methods for controlling screen clutter in single-user environments:

* *Resize* windows to fit.

* *Iconize* windows not currently being used.

* *Hide* windows not currently being used behind those that are.

In a conferencing windows environment, the display contains windows that can be controlled by other users. These users' actions have to be taken into account before trying to reduce the complexity of the screen. Here, conventional screen management tools such as those provided by window managers do not help, and can easily complicate the situation further.

Resizing a local copy of a shared window, for instance, can lead to problems because the application is then not strictly WYSIWIS. This is a problem with both collaboration transparent applications and collaboration-aware applications, but is much easier to deal with if the application is aware of the existence of the conference. Resizing a window can result in missing some part of another's user drawing. This can occur without users noticing: they assume that they are looking at the same application, but in fact what they see depends on the size of the window.

Iconizing and hiding windows are essentially two ways of performing the same task: temporarily removing an application from the workspace. Users are reluctant to do either, since if another user revives an unused application, they might not notice. They usually attempt to tile the screen

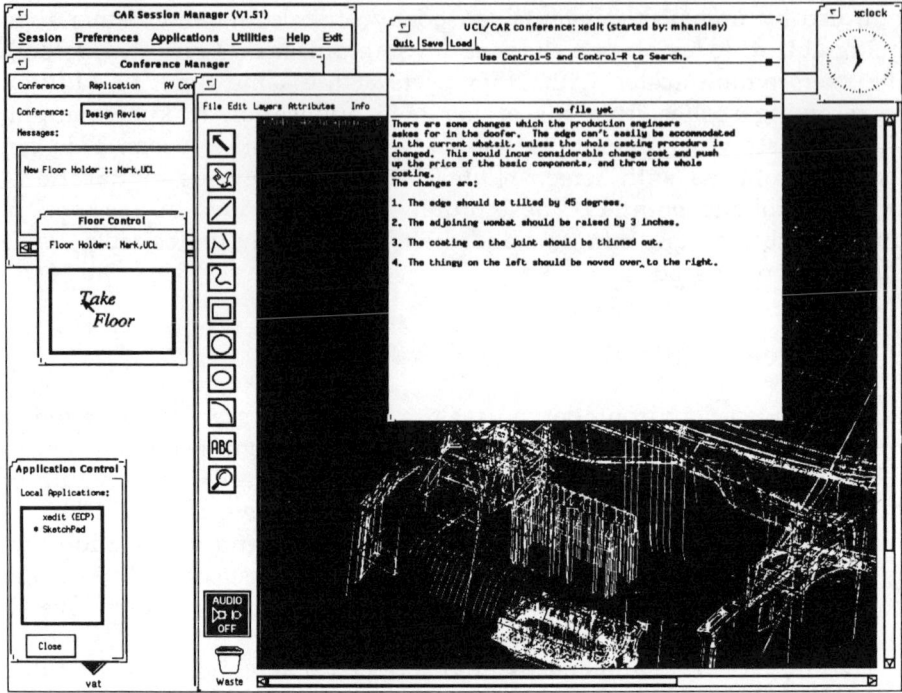

Fig. 9.3. Shared screen with overlapping windows.

to enable them to see as much of the shared applications as possible, even if this involves covering up applications such as conference control. Clearly, this is inefficient use of screen space, which is a scarce resource. Broadly speaking, there are three main strategies for addressing this problem:

- Notify the user when someone starts to modify a hidden or iconized window. This inevitably leads to more notification messages (and hence interference) or more implied symbolic meaning (and hence complexity) and more distractions (although they may be very relevant). This may be a good solution for experienced users who can cope with extra feedback, but for inexperienced users there may already be too much going on at once, so they will still avoid hiding shared windows.

- Let the system take control. A "clean screen" policy can be enforced, in which applications that have not been used for a certain period of time are automatically iconized, and are de-iconized when they become active again. This might result in the user experiencing a certain lack of control. There is also the additional problem that the system cannot tell if the user is only using an application for reference (i.e. just looking at it). The latter problem can be solved if the user tells the system they are interested in an application (cf. OpenLook pushpins), but this requires extra user input for what should be a passive activity.

- Out of band communication: let the users sort it out verbally. This can work quite well if only one or two applications are involved and the conference is very small – the user holding the floor can get verbal feedback on any problems. This approach becomes increasingly ineffective as conferences become larger.

9.4.2 Unexpected Events

In a single-user windows environment, events should be determined by the users' actions, and thus should for the most part be predictable, or at least self-explanatory. Even if the user makes a mistake, the result should explain what that mistake was, but most importantly, the error message is in response to the user's known input or request.

In a shared windows environment, this is often no longer the case. If a mistake is made, it may be another user that makes it, and so any warnings or messages are viewed out of context. This causes confusion, and makes users wonder what they did wrong. The manipulation of applications by other participants causes events that the user does not expect, such as excluding an application from the conference. This leads to a feeling of *lack of control*, especially if one user is less familiar with the system than the others.

In fact, this problem does not only apply to errors and error messages – perfectly legitimate requests, such as to de-replicate an application that you have introduced can cause similar problems. Such events should be accompanied by a notification message saying what has happened, but if you are considering an application when someone else terminates it, this is little consolation. This problem could be avoided if everyone has to agree to an event, but such rigidity would greatly interfere with the intended purpose of the conference – communication. Administrative tasks should be kept to a minimum if conferencing systems are to become "natural" to use. The simplest way of avoiding problems of this sort is to leave it to a *human protocol*; i. e. let the users notify each other verbally (see also Baydere et al. 1993). If this is to be the case, it must be stressed during training that such protocols have to be agreed and followed.

9.4.3 Notification of Events

In a multimedia conference, events will occur that users should be informed about. If a new user joins the conference, all the existing participants should be notified immediately that this has occurred, because it may affect the way they behave. This is a high priority event, and so users should be distracted sufficiently from whatever they are doing to take notice of the event. The CAR system does this by sounding an audible warning, and popping-up a new window containing the information.

This sort of warning proves too distracting for users if it is used for lower priority notifications, such as change of floor holder (on the other hand, this will be a fairly high priority warning if you are the current floor holder). The CAR system has an area set aside for these notifications. We experienced a situation in the trials where users covered this with applications, and were then confused.

Sometimes implicit notification can be used. An example of this is the video communication channel in the CAR system, which switches to show the floor holder when the floor changes. However this default can be overridden, and thus confusion can easily be created.

A example of a low priority event is the resizing of a shared window by the floor holder. Here the notification received needs to be ignored until it becomes relevant, i.e. when the floor holder starts drawing in an area that cannot be seen. Clearly, there is a need to provide communication between conference sites of this information, but irrespective of whether this is done using a shared window manager or aware applications, the presentation of this information to the user causes some problems. In order to lessen the uncertainty, and therefore confusion, of a user, more information needs to be given, which may result in increasing confusion. The question is how to present this information in a way that will reduce the complexity, not increase it.

Many asynchronous events are known about by the system, but a user is usually concentrating on one of the shared applications. If users are not to be confused later, the system should notify them of the event, but if it does this in an obtrusive way, users become irritated by the notifications because they cause distraction.

Which notification method is used for which event should depend on the user. High priority events should always be intrusive, but lower priority events should depend on the user's level of expertise.

In simple cases it is possible to avoid presenting low priority information to the users at all. We tried this method recently when a team of experienced users (the authors among them) used the CAR system to write a chapter collaboratively. Although there was some confusion from time to time, the task was accomplished very smoothly. However most of the time there were no more than two simple shared applications, controlled by one active user (floor holder). As conference complexity increases, or with less experienced users, this is a less satisfactory solution.

Some users may not wish to spend time learning how to use the system, or may just use it on a one-off basis. Such users may just want to *sit back and watch*. In this case they may require active windows to raise themselves and resize themselves in line with those of the floor holder, but would not want to be explicitly told of application inclusion or change of floor as the screen is already changing out of their control.

A user skilled in the use of the system will want to be in control of the environment. Events such as window resizing by the floor holder should be flagged visibly, but as simply as possible. For example, changing the border colour of the window may imply that it has been resized. The environment is already complex, and so complicating it further with unnecessary labelling is undesirable. However, merely changing the border colour has no visible indication of meaning. It may work well at a subconscious level, but only with experienced users.

In between these skill levels come inexperienced users who use the system occasionally, but for whom it is not yet intuitive. It is these people who will have most difficulty. Simple visible flags are only enough to inform such a user that some unknown event has occurred, and so need to be accompanied by an associated icon or label. However, the appearance of a label can be distracting in itself – any change in the state of the system that is not triggered by the user should be self-explanatory. Care should be taken that any notification can be recognized immediately, but ignored until the user wants to act on it. Simply changing a label will be noticed, but the user may not have seen exactly what it was that changed, and so will waste time checking.

9.4.4 Floor Control

In a conferencing environment where more than one person can interact with the shared applications, floor control mechanisms are needed to organize these interactions. These mechanisms can vary from a totally open floor mechanism, in which all users can interact with all applications at the same time, to a strict mechanism, in which only one user can interact with all the applications at any time. An *open floor* gives users more control and flexibility but increases the uncertainty about what is happening and who is doing what. The amount of information that the user needs to know in order to reduce this uncertainty is huge, and displaying all this information increases the complexity of the system. While a single floor is less flexible, as it prevents concurrent activities from taking place, it does not provide the same degree of uncertainty, and accordingly it is not so confusing.

One can think of many other schemes of floor control between these two extremes. In all cases, the more people that can hold the floor simultaneously, the more communication channels can be created between users and thus more parallel events can happen. It is a trade-off between flexibility (number of concurrent activities) and complexity of use (uncertainty).

Different floor mechanisms can be assigned for different applications. Although this concept can exploit the different natures of different applications, it can complicate the user's model of the system. It is not possible to design a single floor control mechanism that can suit all users and all tasks. It is desirable to give users the ability to tailor the floor control mechanism according to their needs and experience, as well as to allow them to switch between different mechanisms easily. A simple floor control mechanism can be used for conferences that include inexperienced users. Once more experience is gained another more open (more flexible) mechanism can be used, but it is important that users can find out who is doing what without disrupting the progress of the real task.

9.4.5 Pointers

Enabling users to share applications in a conference is the first step towards enabling meaningful interactive collaborative work. Still, users do need other means of communication in order to help them to share these applications on a conceptual level as well as on a visual level. One of these tools is a mechanism that enables users to point to objects of interest in a way that everyone else can see.

There are many different policies for designing such a tool. These policies can be categorized along four dimensions.

What to Echo?

There are three main possibilities:

- Echo the local pointer of the floor holder on all other users' workstations. This policy is very intuitive as the floor holder does not have to do or use anything additional. However, it can be distracting for the other users, as the local pointer is used not only for collaborative work but also for other local purposes. The system cannot filter out these local movements from the ones that the user intends to communicate.

- Echo the local pointer on other users' screens if the user has explicitly decided to do so. This method is used by MMConf (Crowley et al. 1990). A user has to click on the middle button of the mouse to cause the pointer to be echoed to the other users. The pointer then changes shape to a big arrow, indicating that it is now a shared pointer. A problem with this method is that once the user releases the mouse button his pointer disappears and then cannot be referred to while further tasks progress.

- Create a separate shared pointer that can be grabbed by the local pointer, moved and then released. This is the policy used in the CAR system. A user can move the pointer to a certain position, leave it and refer to it later.

During trials, users sometimes subconsciously assumed that their pointer was echoed on all other users' screens. They tended to use it to point to things while explaining them verbally, even though there was a real shared pointer facility.

How Many Pointers?

There are two possibilities:

- One per conference. Only one user (usually the floor holder) can move the pointer at a time. This tends to tie discussions to the floor mechanism. This is rather unnatural and can be frustrating at times. It interrupts the flow of discussion, as you have to take the floor to reply. It has the advantage that there is just one pointer echoed to each user's screen, which is simple and not confusing. Having one pointer that anyone can grab solves some of these problems, but introduces the problem of identifying who has control of the pointer.

- One per user. Having one pointer per user gives the users the ability to move their pointers free from any floor mechanism. This gives a greater flexibility and more natural feeling, especially during discussions. However, having several pointers visible at once can become confusing (too many channels of communication). Pointers need to be identified with users, either by colour coding or by labelling.

When to Echo a Pointer?

There are three possibilities:

- Continuously. Leaving pointers echoed at all times can cause confusion and distraction, especially if there is one pointer per user. It also deprives users of controlling their own screen, which is contradictory to what usually happens in stand-alone environments. This is simplest for inexperienced users, because they do not need to do anything.

- Let the person who is viewing decide. This can cause problems when a user is moving a pointer that another user has made invisible. However, pointing is usually done in conjunction with verbal communication, so users should be able to make the relevant pointer visible in due time. This can still be a problem with inexperienced users, but if they echo continuously, it allows a good mix between users with different experience levels.

- Let the person who is pointing decide. This is probably the most natural approach, and is the approach taken by CAR. However, we still found problems when inexperienced users attempted to point with a local pointer.

Who Controls a Pointer?

If we only have one pointer per conference, it makes sense to tie the pointer to the floor mechanism: this way, everyone knows who has control. However, this means that continuous changes of floor are required for a discussion.

If we have the pointer allocated on demand, then interactive discussion is facilitated, but at the cost of requiring the users to know about extra state information – who has control.

There are many more issues involved, such as what happens when a user moves a pointer across a local window. One strategy adapted by the CAR system is to change the pointer shape on the user's workstation to an empty hand whenever the pointer is moving across a local space. Another issue is what to do when the pointer is moving on a shared window that is hidden or iconized on a certain user's workstation. Should the system inform the user that a pointer is out of sight because this window is iconized, small or hidden?

9.5 Discussion: Design Principles for Multimedia Conferencing

As outlined in Section 9.4, the trade-off between simplicity of use and flexibility of communication between users is a recurrent issue. We can provide a system that is simple to understand, but cumbersome to use, or we can provide a system that is powerful and flexible, but that causes inexperienced users to be overwhelmed with information from many parallel communication channels. Our experience shows that even simple systems can cause users many problems because they are not accustomed to working in this way. Clearly, the lesson to be learned is that system designers must not fix these design decisions, but should allow the users to reconfigure their system depending on their task and their expertise.

It is desirable to support both *collaboration-aware* and *collaboration transparent* applications. Whichever approach is taken, some degree of information on what the other users have done is required. Strict WYSIWIS is generally too restrictive, and the resulting events can cause users to become confused because their local environment can change (e.g. raising or resizing windows) outside of their control. If strict WYSIWIS is not implemented, many events triggered by other conferees must be communicated to a user.

From our observations, we conclude that the following set of design heuristics should be considered:

1. If the interaction is simple (few users, few applications), human protocols (verbal communication) may be sufficient, and are less

intrusive. If the interaction is complex, human protocols will not suffice on their own.

2. A set of options should be provided for notification display – not all users can cope with the same level of complexity.

3. The notification set should be consistent, so that users can progress from one level to another gracefully as they learn.

4. As users become more expert, more abstract notifications can be used. The environment is already complex. If the user can cope, reduce the display complexity as far as possible.

5. Users will notice that even small changes have occurred on screen, but if the changes are subtle they will spent time trying to figure out what has happened. Notifications should be obvious enough to be noticed and recognized, so that users can get on with their tasks.

6. Unless a notification is really important, it should not be intrusive (for example windows that pop up). It is worth considering reserving a small area of screen for notifications that do not apply to a specific window. Ideally, it should not be possible to cover up such an area.

7. Only very high priority notifications should require acknowledgement from the user. Users' attention may not be constant, so high priority notifications should usually remain until acknowledged.

8. Users should only be notified of something that is relevant to them. For example, another user resizing a window is not relevant unless that user is the floor holder.

9. The appearance and behaviour of pointers (and related tools) should be chosen by the users to best support the task in hand. The method of control does not have to be uniform throughout the working group.

10. The larger the working group, the simpler the method of floor control that should be employed.

11. If strict WYSIWIS is not implemented, users will not have a constant frame of reference. They should be made aware of this, and a way of synchronizing views (within restrictions imposed by the hardware) with other users, and particularly with the floor holder, should be provided.

This last point is part of a wider issue – who controls what you see? Two extremes are possible:

- *Centralized:* the floor holder controls what the application does and how you see it.

- *Distributed:* every user can control the application, and their own view of it (usually with collaboration-aware applications).

Most of the time neither of these extremes is desirable. Often it is meaningless to have more than one input to an application. Usually, you wish to be able to control your own workstation environment. If a compromise has to be made, then you allow users control over their view, but with a method of synchronizing with other users. However, it would be much more desirable to allow users the possibility of imposing their view on other users when required. It should be emphasized that the authors think this feature should be used with restraint, because it will tend to lead to a conflict of power and confusion when contexts change without warning. Whether you allow free-for-all control of an application must depend on the application itself, but becomes increasingly undesirable as conference size and number of shared applications increases.

9.6 Conclusions

There is no comprehensive set of design principles that would lead to a satisfactory solution of all of the problems we have observed for all users and tasks. Recommendations can be made for individual features such as shared pointers and floor control, depending on the nature of the task and the experience of the user group. At this stage we recommend that the following points should be observed:

- Designers of multimedia conferencing systems should not determine the nature of interaction between users, but should support many possible interaction styles and let the users decide which is most appropriate.
- The decisions about style of interaction should be made in line with user (group) and task characteristics.
- System designers and user groups should be aware that some interaction styles need to be supported by an agreed set of appropriate human protocols in order to be successful.
- A critical part of system design is choosing a set of defaults suitable for novice users.
- Interaction styles should support a process of "graceful evolution" from inexperienced to expert user.
- A "shorthand" system should be provided for experienced users: not just keyboard accelerators, but also for style of notification.
- Users should be kept aware of all relevant events that can affect them, but notifications must be adapted to their level of expertise.

Acknowledgements The CAR project was initiated and is managed by Professor Steve Wilbur, to whom we owe many thanks. We would like to thank all our colleagues on the CAR project, and especially Sue Joyner and Caroline Parker from HUSAT, and users from Ford, IAD and Peugeot, who participated in the trials.

This work was funded by the CAR project of the CEC RACE Programme and the Department of Computer Science, University College, London.

Notes

1 Freestyle is a trademark of Wang Laboratories.
2 The idea of taking users and systems as dialogue partners, and distinguishing possible interactions into user–user, system–system and user–system interaction is taken from Gaines and Shaw (1986).

Chapter *10*

The Role of Replication in the Development of Remote CSCW Systems

S. Scrivener, S. Clark and N. Keen

10.1 Designing for the Future

10.1.1 The System Designer as Creative Problem Solver

The idea that interactive human–computer systems should enhance or augment existing work practices appears frequently in the Human–Computer Interaction (HCI) literature. Jonathan Grudin, when reporting on Douglas Engelbart's address to the CSCW '88 conference, observed that "his [Engelbart's] principal interest lies in describing or identifying the vanguard communities that will drive the field forward and in building systems that augment the work of these groups" (Grudin 1989). Such appeals to augment and enhance the human's experience of work imply novelty and invention in human–computer system design.

A quotation in a newsletter commenting on events at the recent HCI '91 conference in Edinburgh reflects this continuing drive for innovation: "the most important issue raised by the conference . . . was the debate between designers and system engineers. There are two completely different views in training and approach. Designing a system is a creative activity. . . . To take an example, the big mistake as a systems designer is to take what is someone's messy desk and try and interpret that in order to produce a system that looks like it" (HCI 1991).

But who has the responsibility for this innovation? According to those cited above, it would appear to be the system designer. The responsibility for the creative element in redesigning work through the intervention of information technology has become associated with, and accepted by, the computer system designer. According to Shneiderman (1987), "Every designer wants to build a high quality interactive system that is admired by colleagues, celebrated by users, circulated widely, and frequently imitated". Surely it is only a matter of time before the computer industry will have its own heroes, its own icons to admire, like those of architecture?

From this egocentric position the success or failure of a system is attributed to the powers of the designer or design team that produced it. It is then possible to attribute system failure to the lack of suitable training in creative thinking, hence the "messy desk" mistake. Product designers, say, would not make such a mistake. They are trained to question the problem as given, to be creative and inventive, to look beyond what is immediately given, and, implicitly, by virtue of the special skills acquired thereby, the right to impose solutions on people.

10.1.2 The Difficulty of Exchanging Creation for Facilitation

This designer-centred view of the computer system design process is obviously at odds with the notion that the user has a central role to play in the development process (Norman and Draper 1986). User-centred and participative design methods alter the role of the system designer from that of one who offers solutions for consideration and evaluation by users, to that of the facilitator of a solution generation process that involves users and other agents likely to be affected by the introduction of technology. However, this role is difficult for the designer to accept – having had the possibility of greatness thrust upon you, it is not easy to give it up. The preferred stance seems to be one in which user requirements are taken seriously but where the designer nevertheless remains in control of the production of solutions. Shneiderman (1987) endorses this view when he writes, "Designers must decide whether the improvements they offer are enough to offset the disruption to the users". Perhaps part of the system engineer's difficulty in adopting a more facilatory role is due to the received notion of the designer as the creative agent who provides products that enhance and augment the user's experience of work.

10.1.3 Single-User Product Innovation

Why is there such a strong compulsion to provide systems that augment and enhance work practices? In our view, the emphasis within the HCI community on the development of single-user systems provides part of the answer. In general, single-user applications are products that support elements of an individual's working practice. Grudin (1991a) has noted how, "with the emergence of interactive systems, product development has attracted more attention, particularly in the United States. Many of the successful new companies of the 1980's – Ashton-Tate, Borland, Lotus, Microsoft, etc. – primarily sell software intended for the individual user". If such products merely replicated existing methods, if they merely allowed the user to achieve with a new medium what it is already possible to achieve with an existing medium, there would be no compelling reason for companies to produce them or for consumers to purchase them. Hence, designers of such products are compelled to be creative, inventive and innovative, and to look beyond what already exists.

Our proposition is that this product orientated, designer-centred view of system development reinforces designers' belief in their responsibility and fitness to innovate, and makes it difficult for them to accept the idea of user involvement. The problem with this approach is that it places little value on the creativity and inventiveness of the people who understand best the work domain into which the new technology is to be placed. Why should it be assumed that these people are less able than the system designer to recognize ways in which technology can be exploited to enhance and augment their work?

Recognition of the right and value of an organization, however small or large, to be prominent in the designing of its own future would mean that the system designer would have to give up the role of "creator of futures". A new role would be required; that of a facilitator and co-participant in organizational change. The first significant step in stimulating this change might be the introduction of new technology. Bannon and Schmidt (1989) have argued that, "to an extent, any software application project involves the design not just of a technical system, but it also embodies – implicitly if not explicitly – assumptions about how this system will be used within organisations. The system is an organisational change agent". Clearly, it is important that the responses stimulated by the introduction of such a system are positive and conducive to change. Providing systems that merely allow users to achieve with new media what is already possible to achieve with existing media is one way of minimizing the imposition of external constraints on change while providing an initial impetus for internally generated change.

10.2 Designing for the Present: Replication

In practice, the opportunities for pure replication as the first instantiation of a system in the development process would seem limited. It does not look a viable approach to the development of single-user applications because the results would be difficult to market and the cost of evolving the system as new user requirements emerged would be too great. More generally, replication would be seen as a redundant step when new projects are commissioned as a result of perceived problems in computer or non-computer supported systems. However, the benefits of replication in the development of systems that support remote group work are easier to identify. For example, circumstances might arise that require members of a successful team to work from different locations, and yet continue to function as a team. In developing a system to support them it is not unreasonable to argue that the primary goal should be to provide technology that facilitates the group working, and that in doing this one should aim not to disrupt or impoverish the collaborative activity that previously took place. In other words there are benefits in simply allowing a collaborative activity established in a proximal setting to continue in a remote setting. The primary benefit is the continuation of valued work that could not easily continue without the intervention of technology. The replicated workspace would be useful by allowing pre-established group work practice to persist, or occur where it would otherwise not have been possible, rather than because it enhances or augments work practices.

The primary goal of replication in this context would be to provide an immediate substitute for face-to-face working. The replicated workspace should be directly usable, make use of previously learned skills, require the learning of few new skills and involve minimal loss of skills. Finally the experience of work in the replicated workspace should appear similar to that encountered in the original workspace: in other words, there should be a feeling of familiarity.

10.3 An Experiment in Replication

The Remote Cooperation and Communication (ROCOCO) project has been studying the collaborative workspace activity (verbal, non-verbal and shared drawing) of product designers with the aim of establishing the communication requirements of computer systems that support remote working.

The first phase of this study (Scrivener et al. 1992a, b) involved recording and analysing six one-hour design sessions. Pairs of designers were seated at either side of a table and asked to develop a joint solution to a design brief. They were given a large pad of paper and allowed to use their own pens. The only restriction on their behaviour was that they should not erase any of the drawings they produced. MacLean et al. (1990) have likened this to being "in the zoo", in that designers work on realistic problems chosen for them by the experimenter and conducted in the experimenter's laboratory. They describe such a setting as being halfway between an artificial laboratory task and uncontrolled free behaviour "in the wild". All subjects in the study appeared comfortable working in this way.

Using audio and video recordings, the communication occurring in each session has been analysed in great detail. Some of the results of the analysis are described elsewhere (Garner et al. 1991; Scrivener and Palmen 1991).

10.3.1 The ROCOCO Station

On the basis of this analysis of the workspace and workspace activity a replication of the workspace, known as the ROCOCO Station, was produced. The ROCOCO Station supplies pairs of geographically separated designers with an eye-to-eye video link, a high-quality audio link and a shared drawing surface. The principle of replication dictated that, wherever possible, only the communication channels and media available in the face-to-face setting were included.

Each user of the ROCOCO Station is provided with a Sun SPARC Station 1+. A central feature of the ROCOCO Station is the ROCOCO Sketchpad, a computer based Distributed Shared Drawing Surface (DSDS). It allows persons sitting at different computer workstations to share a drawing surface. The surface takes the form of a large "shared window", which is displayed on each workstation screen. Users have simultaneous access to the drawing surface. They are able to draw with a selection of "pen-types" and can point to existing drawings with a "telepointer". The drawing surface can, in principle, be shared by any number of users. However, we are primarily interested in studying its use by two persons.

The sketchpad is operated via a digitizer and pen. To one side of the workstation screen is a VideoTunnel video link (incorporating a video camera and monitor). This arrangement, developed by Smith et al. (1991), uses half-silvered glass and mirrors to allow eye-to-eye contact to be made over the video link. Users have a high quality headset audio link. At present, both the video and the audio are sent along cables. It is realistic to assume that it will be possible to transmit this data over computer networks in the near future. The software was written using the X Window system (Scheifler and Gettys 1986). It uses a centralized software architecture; that is, a single copy of the application maintains all copies of the shared drawing surface. No significant performance problems have been found when the system is being used by up to four persons. If it were to be used by larger groups, it is likely that performance would suffer and a replicated software architecture would be more appropriate. The advantages and disadvantages of application replication have been discussed in detail by Lauwers et al. (1990) and Scrivener et al. (1992c).

The software has been successfully ported to other X platforms and is

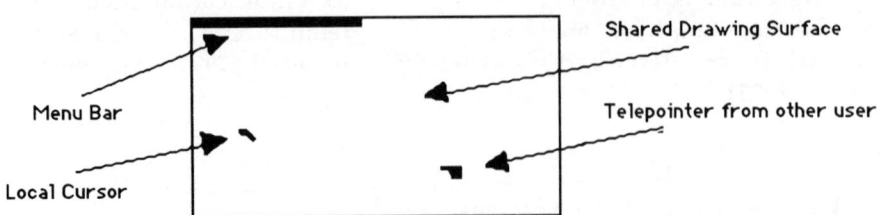

Fig. 10.1. The ROCOCO Sketchpad shared window.

currently being used as part of an Apple Macintosh II based system known as the LookingGlass, which is described later.

10.3.2 User Interface

The ROCOCO Sketchpad is displayed as a large 1200 × 800 pixel shared window on each workstation screen. All users may draw and point in the shared window. The software ensures that each user's input is distributed almost simultaneously to all other users. The local cursors are displayed as telepointers on the remote screens. Hence, there is no need for the user to explicitly select the telepointer function. The format of the shared window is shown in Fig. 10.1.

It is possible for users to position the window anywhere on their workstation screen. However, within the shared window (excluding the local cursors and the telepointers) the system adheres to the WYSIWIS – What You See Is What I See – principle (Stefik et al. 1987b).

Tang and Leifer (1988) have shown that the role of the drawing surface in collaborative settings goes beyond simply acting as a mechanism for storing and conveying ideas graphically or textually. Indeed, Bly (1988) suggests that the process of creating drawings may be as important to the design process as the drawings themselves. Similarly, Tang and Leifer (1988) have highlighted the role of the drawing surface in mediating interactions between groups of designers.

Following observational studies of face-to-face collaboration, Bly and Minneman identify four requirements for systems that attempt to support shared drawing activity (1990):

- Marks and gestures should be made visible to all participants without significant delay.

- Rapid switching between drawing, writing and gesturing should be possible.

- Users should be able to mark, erase and gesture in the same space simultaneously.

• Familiar mechanisms for drawing space activity should be maintained.

By replicating the drawing surface features present in the face-to-face setting we believe that the ROCOCO Sketchpad satisfies these requirements. The guiding principle governing the development of the sketchpad was that it should appear "familiar", by resembling the medium of pen and paper. As such, it was intended to draw on existing skills, require the learning of few new skills and possess high guessability and learnability (Jordan et al. 1991).

These intentions sometimes led to the exclusion of features that existed in the face-to-face setting. For example, sometimes designers used rulers and other templates as drawing aids (e.g. to draw straight lines). The designers were highly skilled in using these devices and manipulated them with great dexterity. There was no immediately obvious way of replicating these tools, with the electronic media available to us, that would come near to providing the manual control achievable with their physical counterparts. It was concluded that the cost in terms of the guessability and learnability of any electronic aids we could provide would exceed their practical benefits, and as a consequence they were left out of the ROCOCO Sketchpad.

In summary, the ROCOCO Station currently allows two product designers to work in geographically separate locations. They are able to talk freely, observe a head and shoulder view of their partner, establish eye-to-eye contact and draw simultaneously on a shared drawing surface.

10.4 Evaluating the System

The success or otherwise of the ROCOCO Station will be determined by the extent to which it is seen as an acceptable substitute for face-to-face working by its users. At present the ROCOCO station is in the process of being formally evaluated (see Scrivener et al. 1992b). Preliminary user reports and observations of the system in use indicate that it is highly guessable and learnable, and does support group activity that closely resembles the face-to-face activity on which it is based. An investigation of a variant of the ROCOCO Station, called the LookingGlass, has been conducted, and this is discussed below.

10.4.1 The LookingGlass

The ROCOCO Station replicates many of the features of the face-to-face workspace. However, gesturing at and over the drawing surface is only

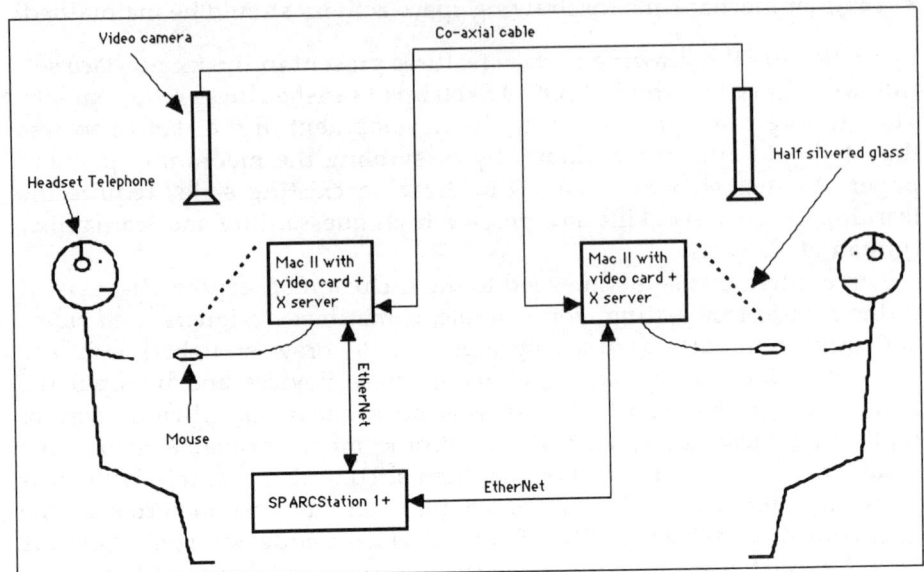

Fig. 10.2. The configuration of the LookingGlass system.

partially supported by telepointing. Similarly, the telepointer provides the only cue to one's partner's focus of attention in relation to the drawing surface, whereas in the face-to-face situation it is possible to observe, simultaneously, the gaze of your partner as its moves over the drawing surface, gross movements of the body and the locations of drawing acts. The LookingGlass configuration aimed to replicate these features of the workspace by using video-overlay technology to integrate the shared drawing surface and the video link.

Unlike the ROCOCO Station, where the shared drawing surface and partner image are displayed on separate monitors, the LookingGlass displays the shared drawing surface and the video image of the remote partner on the same screen. The LookingGlass displays the full-screen ROCOCO Sketchpad window over a full- screen semi-transparent video image of the remote partner. In many respects it is analogous to two people drawing on either side of a ground glass sheet.

The LookingGlass uses two Apple Macintosh computers to display the ROCOCO Sketchpad. They are configured to act as X display servers, and the software client executes on a Sun SPARC Station. All three computers communicate via 10 Mb Ethernet. The sketchpad window fills the entire Macintosh screen and the users are prevented from moving it. The video image of the remote partner is displayed on the screen by using a VideoLogic DVA4000 video card. At present, video is sent along coaxial cables. Audio communication is via a headset telephone link. Currently, mice are being used as the sketching devices, although digitizers will be used in the future. The configuration of the LookingGlass is shown in Fig. 10.2.

10.4.2 An Investigation of the LookingGlass in Use

An investigation was carried out to establish the effectiveness of the LookingGlass as a tool for shared drawing. To do this, pairs of designers were asked to carry out a design task using the LookingGlass. One pair of product designers, one pair of graphic designers and one pair of artists were used to perform a pilot study. The goal of this pilot study was to produce a general indication of how well the LookingGlass might meet its aims, how effective it might be as a shared drawing tool, and as a basis for comparison with further studies.

Owing to the fact that the three pairs of subjects were all from different fields of design, three different briefs were used. The tasks were carefully selected to suit the needs of the subjects since the aim was to determine the effectiveness of the system, not their ability to design. The subjects were given 55 minutes to complete the task, enabling them to use the system fully without feeling pressured to produce anything more than a preliminary solution.

A questionnaire was used to find out the opinions of the users on various aspects of the system. Subjects were guided through the questionnaire by the investigator to ensure that they were fully aware of the meaning of each question. To analyse the overall effectiveness of the system, questions were grouped into seven categories. To establish the effectiveness of different aspects of the system, each category was assigned a percentage efficiency value. To assign this value the number of user responses that were positive towards the system had to be calculated. The percentage of positive replies was then calculated using the total, to give an overall efficiency value for that category. Table 10.1 lists the percentage efficiency figures for each of the seven categories selected. This method of assigning values was not designed to be statistically rigorous

Table 10.1. Percentage efficiency values for the categories of the LookingGlass system

Category	Efficiency (%)
Hardware	74
Software	50
Utterances	100
Vision	73
Gesture	65
Drawing	100
Task	87

but merely to give an indication as to which aspects of the system required improvement.

From the table it can be seen that the utterance, drawing and task categories were very effective. This means that the responses from users were positive in these three areas; i.e. the users found that spoken communication was well supported by the system; they were able to draw cooperatively with their partner; they had sufficient time to complete the task; and the LookingGlass supported task completion. The figures for hardware and software were affected (as expected) by the use of the mouse as a drawing tool, with all users finding it difficult to draw and write using this tool. In the vision category, users were able to alter their attention from the partner to the work surface using the combined video and graphic image. They also believed the image of their partner to be a natural one, not noticing that in fact the image had been reversed. However, responses were mixed in relation to the ability to detect direction of gaze and maintain eye contact. In the gesture category, subjects felt that they were able to gesture naturally using arms and head, and that the gestures of partners were clearly visible. In general, body movements were also noted. Users found the drawing package features easy to understand, but would have liked additional features.

An additional section of the questionnaire concerned the professions of subjects. This was used to establish whether subjects would have reason to use the system within their work area. Three of the six subjects claimed to work remotely with other designers, with two of these being over long distances. These two were very enthusiastic about the system, believing that it had great potential in their field of work, provided that the software matched their needs. It is interesting to note that one user claimed never to have used a computer system before.

One question asked subjects to comment on the system as a shared drawing tool. Two subjects simply responded "great"; the other comments are cited below:

> More effective than it sounds! Easy to use bar the clumsiness of the mouse and no erase facility. Communication very good – it was in many ways like a face-to-face session. Took a little while to relax into it, and to recognize certain features – like the pen changing colour – but familiarity came quickly and made it easier to use. Unaware of the technology – unobtrusive and not physically restrictive (except the [drawing device]).

> It would be useful for designers working at a distance from each other, but I think the range of colours and marks that can be made is not versatile enough. It is suitable for people that aren't used to using computers. If there was no distance it would be easier just to use pen and paper. Communication between users may be better if they could see more of each other's hand gestures.

> Shared designing and negotiation took place. Partner image transparency is just about OK (caused no problems).

> Seeing other designer of little assistance. Drawing surface of far more importance as this became the dominant communication interface.

Clearly, the system needs improvement, mainly in areas where the replication is incomplete, leading to impoverishments in communication, expression and representation. However, it is also clear that in general the LookingGlass systems meets the aims of replication. It does appear to be directly usable, exploiting existing skills and minimizing the learning of new skills. Overall, we can conclude that the system appears familiar to its users and closely resembles face-to-face working. Furthermore, the experience of using the system elicited additional requirements from the user, primarily ones characteristic of the conventional workspace that had not been replicated. However, over longer use we would anticipate users envisioning entirely new features; in other words, actively contributing to the evolution of the workspace they inhabit.

10.5 Conclusion

In this chapter we have argued that the requirement to innovate has driven computer system development, and that the responsibility for being innovative has become associated with the system designer. We have suggested that this designer-centred view of system development makes it difficult for users – who have more at stake, more knowledge of the application domain and the potential for insight and creativity – to actively contribute during system development. We have proposed that one way of minimizing externally defined change and stimulating an internally regulated change process would be for system designers to initially provide a replication that allows users to achieve with new media what is already possible with existing media. We have further suggested that remote CSCW applications are ones where investigating the potential of replication is arguably more obviously worthwhile, since it would allow pre-established group work practice to persist, or occur where it would otherwise not have been possible.

We have identified the usability goals of replication and described the development of a system that aimed to replicate a workspace in which product designers worked face-to-face using pen and paper. A preliminary evaluation of the replication suggest that it meets its design objectives, by providing a workspace that is accessible, useful and stimulating for designers to inhabit.

The challenge for the system designer is to be creative and inventive in finding ways of stimulating and supporting the evolution of the workspace as new opportunities for augmentation and enhancement are recognized by its inhabitants. This might be achieved through the continuing direct support of the system designer (i.e. by making modifications to the system) or through the provision of a flexible and adaptable workspace that can be modified by its inhabitants (i.e. some form of user programming or demonstrable system, e.g. Myers 1991). In either case, it shifts the designer's role from one who defines new workspaces and work practices, to one who creates environments in which new workspaces and work practices can be defined.

Acknowledgements The work described in this chapter was partially supported by SERC under research grant GR/F35814. We would like to thank our colleagues on the ROCOCO Project – Tony Clarke, John Connolly, Steve Garner, Hilary Palmen, Andre Schappo and Michael Smyth – for their ongoing contributions to the research described in here. Finally, thanks to all our subjects for participating in the experiments.

Chapter *11*

Computer Supported Conflict Management in Design Teams

M. Klein

11.1 The Challenge: Supporting Collaboration in Design Groups

Design has increasingly become a cooperative endeavour carried out by multiple agents with diverse kinds of expertise. The design of a car, for example, requires experts on potential markets, ease of manufacturability, safety regulations, available means for shipping vehicles and so on. Many companies are currently studying or implementing approaches to facilitate cooperative design using so-called "concurrent engineering" techniques (Perry 1990).

Conflict resolution is a critical component of the cooperative design process. Different agents often have different notions concerning what kind of design is best. One design agent may specify that a part have a given shape to maximize strength, while another may prefer a different shape that simplifies the operations needed to manufacture it. Conflict resolution is thus ubiquitous; in one domain studied, roughly 50% of the statements made by a group of collaborating designers involved either the identification or resolution of conflicts (Klein and Lu 1990). Rather than a rare and avoidable occurrence, conflict clearly plays a central role in design cooperation.

The development of tools and underlying theories for supporting conflict resolution in cooperative design has lagged, however, behind the growing needs for such work. While other aspects of cooperative activity have been studied in some depth (e.g. Corkill and Lesser 1983; Smith and Davis 1979; Thorndyke et al. 1981), conflict resolution has been only lightly explored (Klein 1989). Work to date has significant limitations; most notably, these systems do not support task level interaction and embody little or no conflict detection and resolution expertise.

Our own work, which we believe avoids the limitations of previous efforts, has consisted of three major stages. The first stage involved studying how human designers cooperate to design artefacts. This resulted in important insights into how conflict detection and resolution works in actual cooperative design situations (Klein and Lu 1990).

The second stage involved creating a computational model and associated cooperative design "shell" that embodies these insights. This shell was instantiated into a system for Local Area Network (LAN) design that consists of seven machine-based design agents (dealing with available technology, reliability, security and so on). This system successfully designs LANs without human intervention, using a knowledge-intensive approach to detect and resolve conflicts among the design agents as they arise (Klein and Baskin 1990).

The third stage involved extending the cooperative design shell to also allow human designers to participate in the design process. This involved developing a task level model of the cooperative design process and then implementing a graphical direct manipulation interface that allows human designers to interact with other agents using this model. The extended shell, called DCSS (the Design Collaboration Support System), has been used successfully to support the cooperative design of LANs with human and machine-based design agents. This work has thus come full circle: insights into human conflict resolution have been embodied into a computer-based system used and evaluated by human designers. Experience with this system has enabled us to cycle through many subsequent iterations of human evaluation and refinement of the computational model. This chapter describes the results of this third stage of work.

The remainder of this chapter is organized as follows. We review existing work on computer support for group conflict resolution, considering both its contributions and limitations. We then describe the theory underlying DCSS, and present examples of its operation. We conclude with an evaluation of our current approach and discuss possible directions for future work.

11.2 Contributions and Limitations of Existing Work

Work relevant to support of group conflict resolution comes from Artificial Intelligence (AI) and related fields as well as from the social sciences. For a comprehensive review, see Klein (1989). A large body of work is devoted to analysing human conflict resolution behaviour (e.g. Coombs and Avrunin 1988; Pruitt 1981). This work highlights the importance of conflict in group interactions, but provides few prescriptions for how conflict resolution can be facilitated. In addition, much of this work focuses on issues specific to the psychology of human participants, rather than on the general nature of conflict resolution.

There is in addition work on supporting human interaction. This includes research on group consensus building and Group Decision Support Systems (GDSSs), and ranges from work on simple conferencing systems (e.g. Johansen et al. 1979), special-purpose systems that support cooperation for a particular task type (e.g. Pferd and Peralta 1979; Sarin 1985) and general-purpose systems (e.g. Chang 1987; Nunamaker et al. 1987; Stefik 1986). This work provides some structure for interactions among group members, but the conflict detection and resolution expertise is expected to reside in the human participants. This is an inevitable consequence of the level of interaction of the users with the collaboration support system: since the system has at best a very shallow understanding of the contents of the participant's interactions, it can offer relatively little meaningful support.

To find work on systems that directly support conflict resolution, we need to turn to AI and related fields such as planning and design. Such work uses expertise encoded in the system itself to detect and resolve conflicts among design participants. This work can be categorized according to the extent to which conflict resolution expertise is given "first-class" status, i.e. is represented and reasoned with explicitly using formalisms as robust as those used for other kinds of expertise, and ranges from "development-time conflict resolution", where potential conflicts are "compiled" out of a system by virtue of exhaustive discussions when it is developed (Bezem 1987; Nguyen et al. 1985), "knowledge-poor runtime conflict resolution", where conflicts are resolved at runtime using a "second-class" conflict resolution mechanism (Brown 1986; Descotte and Latombe 1985; Fox and Smith 1984; Marcus et al. 1987; Sussman and Steele 1980) and "general conflict resolution", where some attempt is made to provide conflict resolution with first-class status (Goldstein 1975; Hewitt 1986; Lander and Lesser 1988; Sussman 1973; Wilensky 1983).

Work on conflict resolution has thus evolved towards making conflict resolution expertise more explicit and using it to support cooperative problem solving. The approaches used to date, however, face in general the following two fundamental limitations:

- The system is unable to "understand" the statements made by the human participants, thereby limiting the role of the computer to little more than a communication channel; the system can participate at a semantic level in only a restricted way.

- The system stores little or no expertise concerning how to detect and resolve conflicts, or else represents this expertise using formalisms that seriously reduce its efficacy. Thus, even if the system could understand the interactions of the participants, it does not have the expertise to make meaningful contributions.

In Section 11.3 we describe our own approach to supporting conflict resolution among design agents, which we believe avoids the limitations of previous work in this area.

11.3 The Design Collaboration Support System

The overall goal of DCSS is to help human and machine-based designers interact effectively. Our current work focuses on the challenges of conflict detection and resolution. Developing a comprehensive approach to conflict management, however, is clearly an extremely ambitious task. We consider in this work an important subset of the problem:

- *Competition versus cooperation:* in competitive conflict situations each party has solely their own benefit in mind, while in cooperative situations the parties are united by the superordinate goal of achieving a globally optimal solution. Cooperative design is (generally) characterized by cooperative conflict resolution.

- *Domain level versus control level conflicts:* domain level conflicts concern conflicting recommendations about the actual form of the design, while control level conflicts concern conflicting recommendations about the direction the design process should take in trying to create a design. Our work focuses on domain conflicts; good general theories of control are still lacking.

DCSS has a distributed architecture consisting of a collection of design agent/assistant pairs (Fig. 11.1). Agents work by refining and critiquing a shared representation of the design, and can be either human or machine-based. Assistants are computer programs that mediate the interaction of their agents with other agents over a communication channel. In the current implementation, human designers work in front of dedicated workstations executing their assistant, while machine-based design agents are independent processes with associated assistant code. The interface of assistants to human designers is graphical and uses pointer-based direct manipulation techniques. Agents can be based on different machines, work asynchronously and communicate with each other over a network. The code currently runs on networked Symbolics Lisp Machines and is written in Common Lisp.

In order to support conflict management, an assistant clearly must provide at least the following services:

- Allowing design agents to express their design actions and rationale.
- Helping design agents to detect conflicts between these design actions.
- Suggesting potential resolutions to conflicts once detected.

Sections 11.3.1–11.3.3 discuss, in turn, how assistants provide each of these services.

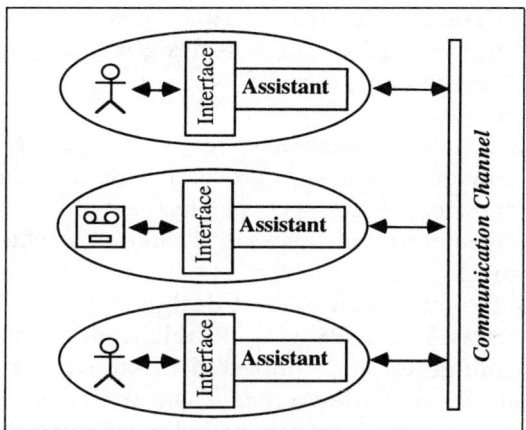

Fig. 11.1. The architecture of DCSS.

11.3.1 Describing Design Actions and Rationale

A key role of design assistants is to allow design agents to express their design actions and reasoning in a way that a design collaboration support system can understand. Expressing design actions is of course a minimal requirement for communicating these actions to other agents. Expressing design rationale is useful for a number of tasks, such as explanation, learning and redesign (Mostow 1985). Of particular relevance to this work, representing rationale also allows assistants to support conflict resolution (Klein 1989).

Describing design actions and rationale requires an effective *interface* between agents and their assistants, which implies that the interfaces should be based on a *task* rather than an *implementation* level model of the problem domain (Gruber 1989). Implementation level interfaces, used in many knowledge based systems, allow the user to interact with the system only in terms of the entities (e.g. rules, facts, assumption-based truth maintenance system contexts) that the system is implemented in. Task level interfaces, by contrast, allow the user to interact with the system in terms of entities (e.g. resources, components, diagnoses) appropriate to the task being performed. If design agents express their actions using a task level model, then to the extent that the model is accurate, it allows these agents to describe their actions and reasoning naturally in a formal way understandable by a computer based system. In the following subsections we describe DCSS's task level model of cooperative design, as well as the interface to design agents based on this model.

The DCSS Design Model

Much research on developing task level models of single-agent design and cooperative activity has already taken place. DCSS's cooperative design model synthesizes elements of this work with novel features involving conflict detection and resolution, and was designed from the ground up to be consonant with the insights derived from our studies of human design group cooperation.

DCSS uses a *routine least-commitment refine-and-evaluate* design model. In brief, this model views the design process as the incremental adding of detail to designs described as connected collections of known components, interleaved with evaluation that checks for design problems and fortuitous design opportunities.

DCSS supports the important class of design tasks called *routine design* (Brown and Chandrasekaran 1986), applicable to domains where known components are configured and connected in known ways. Designs are represented as collections of known *components* with characteristic *features* connected to each other via *connections* between *interfaces* with known properties. Components may provide, as well as use up, different kinds of *resources*. Components, resources, interfaces, connections and features are all typed. A component's class and features can both be indefinitely described. The former is supported by building an abstraction hierarchy of components that ranges from abstract components at the top to existing (e.g. buyable) "primitive" components at the bottom. An indefinite component class description thus involves selecting a non-primitive (i.e. non-leaf) component class. The latter is supported by using a *constraint* language (Sussman and Steele 1980), that currently includes ranges, inequalities and sets as well as algebraic and Boolean equations. Fig. 11.2 gives an example of an indefinitely described abstract component (as displayed by the DCSS interface).

Note that indefinite design descriptions support *least-commitment* design (Stefik 1981), which has the important advantages of avoiding unnecessary conflicts from arbitrary design commitments and allowing early conflict detection, thereby minimizing the amount of design effort expended on unviable design alternatives.

Initial design *specifications* are expressed as one or more initial components with given desired properties. For example, for the LAN domain the initial component would represent the entire site for which the LAN is to be designed, and the component properties would specify the number of workstations to be connected, desired performance and so on. Design agents iteratively *refine* these specifications until eventually the design consists of definitely-specified available components. For the LAN domain a complete design would thus consist of commercially available cable segments, connectors, file servers and so on with specific properties and interconnections. Refinement actions include configuring a component by constraining the value of its features (perhaps relative to other features), connecting the interfaces of two components, decomposing a component into newly created subcomponents, or specializing a component or connection to a more specific type.

```
Component <TRUNK-SEGMENT 88>
In World W-1

Interfaces
    I1                        isa <ELECTRICAL-INTERFACE>
        CURRENT
        VOLTAGE
            Values
                (RANGE -10 10)

Resources
    COST                      isa <Frame RESOURCE>
        COMMITS
        USES
            Values
                (* (SLOT LENGTH OF <TRUNK-SEGMENT 88>) 25)
        PROVIDES

Synthesis Features
    LENGTH                    isa <SV SYNTHESIS-FEATURE>
            Values
                (RANGE 10 15)

Analysis Features
    RF-INTERFERENCE           isa <SV ANALYSIS-FEATURE>
            Values
                (<= 23)
```

Fig. 11.2. An indefinitely described component.

Design agents follow a *refine–evaluate* cycle (Fig. 11.3) based on Wilensky's meta-planning model (Wilensky 1983). All design actions are made in response to explicit *goals*. Whenever a component is generated, the goal to refine the component is automatically asserted. A *plan* triggered by that goal executes refinement actions intended to achieve the goal. Plans may also create subgoals. The evolving design produced by such plans is constantly *evaluated* by the design agents to check for problems affecting their interests. Entities known as *themes* look at the design (with the help of *analysers* that produce design state analyses) for situations that represent problems or fortuitous opportunities, and create goals accordingly.

The design process iterates through successive refinement and evaluation cycles until a specifically-described design satisfactory from all of the design agent's perspectives has been produced.

This same formalism is also used for reasoning at the meta-level, i.e. for reasoning about the state of the *designer* as opposed to the state of the *design*. When a meta-level task appears (e.g. to make a control choice), meta-level versions of goals, plans, themes and actions are used. Actions at the meta-level include the control actions "pick plan for goal", "order goals" and "order design states" (Gruber 1989) as well as conflict resolution actions.

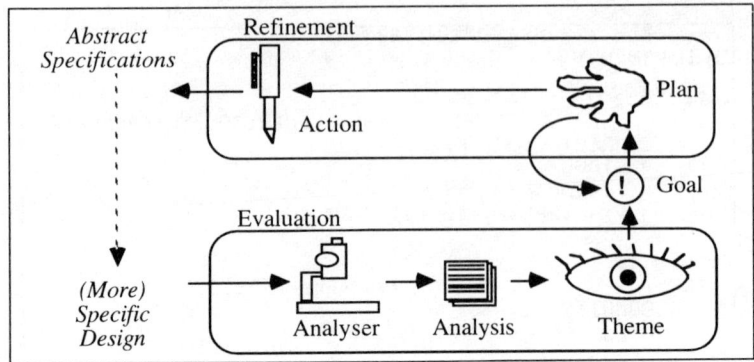

Fig. 11.3. The refine and evaluate cycle.

There are often several alternative ways of achieving any given design goal; as a result, design becomes a search process with a tree of *design states* being generated and explored by the design agents. Some design branches will lead to conflicts (i.e. unviable designs); these branches will be abandoned and other branches suggested by the conflict resolution process will be pursued.

Table 11.1 summarizes the DCSS design model primitives used for describing actions and their rationale, distinguished by role and problem solving level.

These primitives underlie the design agent interface, described in the following subsection.

The DCSS Interface

The DCSS design agent interface allows agents to express their actions and reasoning in terms of the task level model described above. In the current implementation of DCSS, all machine-based design agents execute this

Table 11.1. The DCSS design model primitives

Level	State description	Rationale description
Domain level	Components, connections, interfaces and resources, interface and resource features, synthesis and analysis features, design states, feature constraints	Domain-level goals, plans, themes and analysers
Meta-level	Conflict, stalled-designer, designer-state-analysis, choice-for-plan, goal-ordering, design-state-ordering	Meta-level goals, plans, themes and analysers

model directly. As a result, the assistant interface to such agents need only inspect the working memory of the agent to get a task level view of what the agent did and why. For human agents, of course, we do not have this luxury, and need to define an interface that allows human users to describe their actions and reasoning to the assistant explicitly. In addition to providing a task-appropriate set of communication primitives, moreover, this interface should:

- Make it easy to perform common operations. This maximizes ease and speed of operation.
- Make it impossible to perform nonsensical operations. This does not ensure that the design actions are *correct*, but it does help to avoid needless errors.

Our approach has been to develop a graphical interface where human designers inspect and manipulate task level entities using direct manipulation techniques. The interface consists of four panes plus a display of the current mode (Fig. 11.4).

The activity trace presents a running record of the actions taken by the design agents collaborating with the interface's user. The design state display provides a graph of the design states that have been explored, as well as indicating what the current design state is. The design display describes the contents of a given design state. The interaction pane is used for dialogue between the assistant and the designer, e.g. to allow the user to describe a constraint on a feature. The printed representation for any task level primitive entity (component, design state, etc.) in any pane produces a menu of available operations when selected by the pointing device (the current implementation uses a three-button mouse). For example, options available when selecting a component include describing its

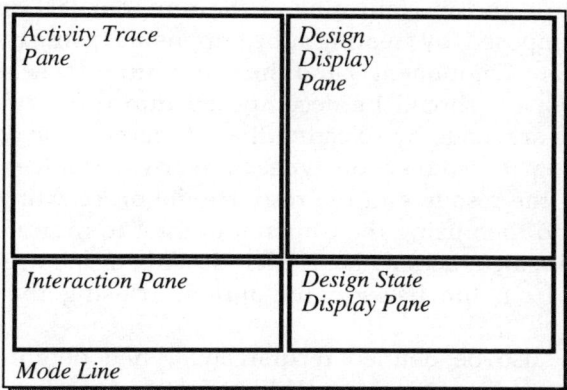

Fig. 11.4. The layout of the DCSS human interface.

features or refining it. There are in addition several "background" options available when clicking on the background of any pane. The background and primitive entity options available at any given time depend on the current mode, which is shown in the mode line display.

The options available for each primitive were selected so that common patterns of activity can be described quickly. The following patterns are basic:

- *Design specification:* design specifications can be asserted at any time. Creating the initial abstract component representing the artefact to be designed is performed by selecting the "Create Initial Component" background option. The user then navigates a component definition database using a hierarchical menu approach to select the type of component to create (every assistant is assumed to include a database describing the components in the design domain). A description of the component is then automatically presented in the design display window. To add a specification, the user selects the "Add-Spec" option, available by clicking on one of the displayed component's design features. The user is then queried in the interaction pane for a constraint to post on that feature; a constraint editor uses knowledge of the constraint language syntax to ensure that the constraint posted is well formed.

- *Design refinement:* design refinement actions can only occur in the context of a plan created to achieve a design goal. To define such a plan the user picks the "Define Plan" option, available when selecting a goal. A new design state to store the new plan's design actions is automatically generated and made current. While a plan is being defined, options for refining the design become available for design entities. Selecting a feature allows one to constrain the feature, create a goal to find the value of the feature, or create a goal to constrain the feature to a given value. Components can be specialized by asserting a constraint on the specialization of the component. Components can also be decomposed, by creating subcomponents (using the background option "Create Component") and then indicating by selection that the given component should be decomposed into these subcomponents. Connections are made by selecting the interfaces to be connected, and then selecting the connection type. Similarly, resources are allocated by selecting the resource in the resource donor, selecting the resource recipient, and then using the constraint editor to indicate the amount. Once all refinement actions have been described, the user selects "End Definition" from the background options, closing the current plan definition.

  Plans can also be defined recursively. When defining a plan, for example, a user may create a goal to constrain a design feature value, and wish to immediately enter a plan to achieve this new goal so the feature value will be available when the designer finishes defining the original plan. The interface supports this straightforwardly by recursively entering a mode where the new plan's actions are defined, and then returning to defining the original plan once the new plan is completed. The mode line display indicates what plan is currently being defined.

- *Design evaluation:* design evaluations are defined in the context of a theme or analyser. Recall that themes generate goals to remedy problems or take advantage of fortuitous circumstances in the current design state. To generate a theme, one selects "Define Theme" from the set of design state options, describes the actions that make up the body of the theme, and then selects the background option "End Definition". Themes often generate goals to analyse some relevant property of the current design state; analysers to satisfy these goals can be defined by selecting the "Define Plan" option for the goal. As with refinement plans, themes and analysers generate new design states and can be defined recursively.

When plans, themes and analysers are being defined, the user is asked to indicate which aspects of the design state represent required preconditions. Selecting the "Add As Support" option on any fact will add that fact as a precondition for the current plan, theme or analyser. Support can also be added after plan definition using the "Add Support" option for plans. Meta-level versions of the above activities are also possible. For example, a meta-level commitment (e.g. to choose a plan for a goal) is expressed by selecting "Define Plan" for a meta-level "make control choice" goal. Meta-level actions such as pick-plan-for-goal and order-goals are available only while a meta-plan is being defined. Meta-themes and meta-analysers are similarly defined, like their domain level counterparts. The net effect is that domain and meta-level actions as well as their rationale are recorded automatically as the interface is used.

11.3.2 Detecting Conflicts

Another important part of the DCSS assistant's role is to help to detect conflicts between design agents. In general, when different agents give incompatible specifications for a given design component, or one agent has a negative critique of specifications asserted by another agent, we can say that a conflict has occurred. Support for conflict detection is provided in two ways (Fig. 11.5).

Some conflicts can be detected in a domain-independent fashion: for example, incompatible constraints on a given component feature immediately imply a conflict. Domain-specific conflict detection is also supported. Design experts are, in general, very knowledgeable about

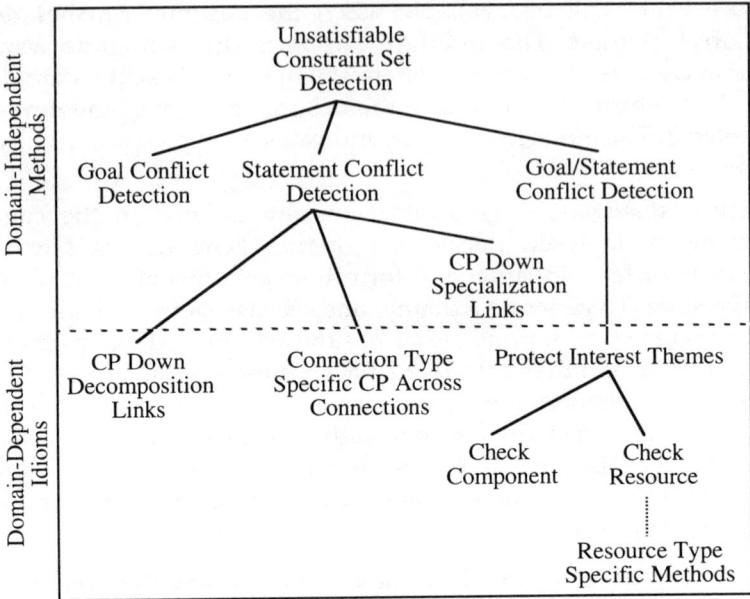

Fig. 11.5. Conflict detection methods provided by DCSS.

situations that represent problems with a design from their particular perspectives. We have found that the techniques used by human designers to detect such conflicts are often instantiations of a relatively small set of stereotyped Conflict Detection (CD) methods that we call CD "idioms" (Klein 1989). DCSS allows designers to quickly instantiate CD idioms with situation-specific values rather than having to enter such CD expertise "long-hand". Whatever technique is used, the assistant automatically updates the design rationale so that the design decisions underlying a conflict can be readily determined.

Domain-Independent Methods

In a least-commitment design model like that of DCSS, all conflicts eventually manifest as unsatisfiable constraints on a given feature. Underlying all CD methods, therefore, is an unsatisfiable constraint set detection mechanism. This is implemented as constraint combination (i.e. simplifying constraint sets by finding their consequences) coupled with detection of individual unsatisfiable constraints. For example, the range constraints (from 10 to 12) and (from 14 to 18) intersect to produce an unsatisfiable constraint. Similar techniques are available for other constraint types.

Built on top of this is support for detecting conflicts between the two kinds of assertions made by design agents: constraints on component features ("statements") and goals. There are three kinds of conflicts at this level: conflicts between achieve-value goals (inconsistent desired constraints on a component feature), conflicts between statements (inconsistent constraints on a component feature), and conflicts between achieve-value goals and statements (inconsistent desired and actual constraints on a component feature).

Constraints asserted by design agents can propagate along the links created during the design process and cause conflict over design features involving some other portion of the design. To find the complete set of constraints implied by a given design description on a component feature, one unions the constraints asserted directly on the component feature with those that propagated over links with related design features. In the DCSS design model, configuration and specialization links propagate constraints domain-independently:

- *Configuration links:* configuration links interrelate component features within or between components. For example, the constraint on the voltage drop across a resistor is related by a configuration link to the constraint on the current through the resistor. This kind of link is used widely in constraint network systems (e.g. Marcus et al. 1987; Sussman and Steele 1980).

- *Specialization links:* specialization links connect components and their specializations. All constraints that apply to an abstract component apply to its specialization, so all constraints are propagated down.

Domain-Dependent Idioms

Built on top of the domain-independent CD methods are the CD idioms. A design agent who wishes to describe a piece of CD expertise, can often simply use a pre-existing idiom, filling in the domain-specific details needed to instantiate the idiom into an active entity. CD idioms found useful to date include:

- *Propagation across connection links:* connection links connect the interfaces of components to each other. The constraints that propagate through a connection depend on the kind of connection. An electrical connection, for example, propagates constraints on voltage and current. A physical connection between rotating axles propagates constraints on rotation speed and torque. Since DCSS includes the notion of typed connections, it can use type information to determine what constraints to propagate.

- *Propagation down decomposition links:* decomposition links connect abstract components and the several components that realize them. While the propagation of constraints down decomposition links is domain-dependent, one can often use the mapping between abstract and more specific connections to simplify describing such propagation.

For example, an abstract LAN trunk component is usually connected to abstract LAN trunk connector components. When the abstract LAN trunk is refined to a particular trunk technology, the constraints that propagate over connections to the abstract component's interfaces also apply to the corresponding connections in the specific trunk instance. Domain-specific knowledge of how connections are mapped over a decomposition step is called "structural" knowledge in MICON (Birmingham and Siewiorek 1989).

- *Protect interests themes:* protect interests themes monitor the current design state for a state threatening to the interests of the design agent, and make assertions that lead to a conflict being asserted if the threatening design state should ever come to pass. We have identified two useful protect interest CD idioms to date: *check-component* and *check-resource*.
  - Check-component idioms check that interests relating to individual components are satisfied, and have the following general template:
    IF there is an instance of <component> THEN create goals to achieve <desired value> for <feature> of <component> and to find the actual value for <feature> of <component>
    To instantiate such an idiom, one simply selects "Create Check Component Theme" from the options for the component feature of interest and enters the value desired for that feature.
  - Check-resource idioms look for situations where some kind of resource budget is exceeded. Resources in most design situations are limited in some way, and it is useful to create budgets representing limits on how much of a given kind of resource should be utilized for a given portion of the design. This idiom works by creating a goal to summarize the total usage of a given resource, as well as the constraint that the actual utilization should not exceed the budget:
    IF there is a <resource> provided by <component> THEN assert the constrain that the amount of <resource> committed by <component> is less than or equal to the amount of <resource> provided and create a goal to find the amount of<resource> committed by <component>
    To instantiate such an idiom, a design agent need merely specify a budget and select the "Create Check Resource Theme" option for the resource of interest. From that point on, if resource utilization exceeds the budget, a conflict will occur.

Resource over-utilization, however, is found differently depending on the kind of resource involved. For example, over-utilization of a monetary budget can be found simply by summing individual expenditures and comparing them with the budget. Detecting space over-utilization is somewhat more complicated; even in the two-dimensional case (i.e. checking for adequate floor space), equipment whose total area does not exceed the available floor space may not fit in a given area due to the shapes of the equipment involved. A functional resource that is not used up over time but can only support a finite number of simultaneous users (e.g. a computer terminal) has resource over-utilization detected in yet a third way. DCSS supports this by typing resources and providing appropriate CD idioms and analysers for each type.

CD idioms can be heuristic in nature. For example, analyser rules used by themes to check for threatening design states may perform analysis based on a shallow model. This can be useful if more exhaustive analysis is computationally expensive, but raises the possibility that the conflict may be spurious, resulting from the limitations of the analysis procedure. For this reason, when a CD idiom is run the results are always asserted in a new design state so that the design state can be abandoned if the CD idiom proves faulty. The methods described above represent a superset of the CD methods utilized in the other approaches to conflict management (e.g. those incorporated in systems such as TROPIC, VT, AIR-CYL, MOLGEN or BARGAINER), and provide a complete set of basic mechanisms for conflict detection, given the nature of DCSS's cooperative design model. The notion of an abstract resource type hierarchy has been discussed previously (Wilensky 1983), as has the conflict detection advantages of using a least-commitment design model (Stefik 1981). Previous work has not discussed, however, the use of domain-independent connection type and resource hierarchies to support conflict detection, or the notion of instantiable CD idioms.

11.3.3 Resolving Conflicts

The third of the services provided by DCSS design assistants involves generating suggestions for resolving conflicts, once they have been detected. The conflict resolution model used is heuristic-classification based (see Klein (1990) for a more complete description). Assistants store domain-independent conflict resolution expertise consisting of a taxonomy of abstract conflict classes, as well as general advice potentially useful for resolving conflicts in each class. When a conflict occurs, the assistants map the conflict to the matching conflict classes and instantiate the associated strategies into specific suggestions expressed in domain level terms. A given conflict may lead to the instantiation of many alternative conflict resolution suggestions; domain-independent heuristics try the one that appears most likely to be effective first.

Both the classification and instantiation processes occur via a dialogue with the design agents, wherein the assistant asks abstract questions about the conflict and the agent responds with situation-specific details. The complete set of possible abstract question types makes up what we call the "query language". Suggestions for resolving a conflict are expressed using a different set of primitives known as the "action language". For design agents to participate effectively in the conflict resolution process, they thus must be able to respond appropriately to query and action language statements.

In the current implementation of DCSS, each assistant incorporates a knowledge base consisting of roughly 100 conflict classes and Conflict Resolution (CR) strategies. Consider the following examples:

1. CLASS: the conflict is supported by a goal with untried alternate plans.
   STRATEGY: try one of the untried plans for this goal (i.e. backtrack).
2. CLASS: the conflict is supported by a plan that searched a database for a component that satisfies some design specifications, but failed.
   STRATEGY: find a relaxation of the design specification that will allow the agent to return a component from the database, and ask that the responsible agents change their specifications to subsume these relaxed constraints if possible.

The machine-based design agents used in the current DCSS implementation, as noted earlier, execute the DCSS model of design directly. As a result, the design assistants for such agents can answer many query language questions about a conflict simply by inspecting the design agent's working memory. The supports for any given assertion can be found by examining the design rationale, and one can easily find assertion types because the DCSS design model includes the notion of typed design and rationale description entities. The "try plan for goal" action language primitive can also be realized straightforwardly. However, DCSS does not as yet have a domain-independent view of the different kinds of models, so machine-based design agents now use domain-idiosyncratic code to answer questions concerning the types of models, whether they can relax their output constraints, whether a deeper version exists, and so on. The "relax value" and "try modified model" actions are also implemented domain-idiosyncratically.

The interface for human design agents supports the query/action dialogue between assistants and human designers. Queries and suggestions are passed on to the designer when the assistant cannot produce the proper responses by inspection of the actions already described by the human designers. Questions that require human intervention appear in the interaction pane, and are responded to using the same direct manipulation techniques used for describing design actions and rationale.

Consider the following example. Imagine that a human designer asserts specifications for a LAN with thin baseband trunk media and a token ring protocol. The hardware machine-based design agent is unable to satisfy these specifications because no LAN technology known to it (i.e. described in its database) matches these constraints, leading eventually to a conflict. The assistant that first notices the conflict then begins searching for suggestions that may help to resolve the conflict, using a series of query language questions. The assistant eventually finds that the second

```
Can you relax constraint on slot PROTOCOL
Of component <LAN 137>
To subsume (INCLUDES <ETHERNET>)
Yes No
```

Choose Yes or No

Fig. 11.6. An example of conflict resolution.

CR class given above matches the conflict, and tries to instantiate the associated general strategy into a specific suggestion. The assistant finds, by querying the hardware agent, that relaxing the protocol specification to include the "Ethernet" option will allow the hardware agent to find an existing LAN technology. The next step is to check if the protocol specification can indeed be relaxed in that way. Since this specification was asserted by the human designer, the question is passed on to the designer's interaction pane (Fig. 11.6).

The designer selects "yes", leading to the generation of the suggestion that the protocol constraint be relaxed. Since the human designer produced the original constraint, he is asked to produce a new plan that asserts the relaxed specification, using the interface's standard plan definition techniques. In general, if an agent is asked to modify a plan's outputs or model, it actually creates a new version of the plan with the desired changes implemented. This action successfully resolves the conflict and allows the agents to continue the LAN design process. Although the conflict resolution dialogue in this example involved nearly a hundred questions and responses, only two had to be passed on to the human user. The DCSS interface automatically records design rationale, so many query language questions can be answered without further interaction with the human user.

11.4 Evaluation and Future Work

Experience with using DCSS has led to a number of insights into the strengths and weaknesses of this approach. The DCSS interface to designers provides a natural and easy to follow approach for expressing design actions and rationale. Typically, a human designer can express a given design action with just a few mouse actions. Since the interface consistently supports (and enforces) a task level model of cooperative design based on studies of human cooperative design, it is intuitive to use and makes nonsensical design actions impossible. The DCSS conflict detection mechanism makes effective use of domain-independent

CD expertise as well as agent-specified domain-dependent CD idioms. The conflict resolution mechanism uses its knowledge of the types and possible resolutions for conflicts to provide meaningful conflict resolution suggestions to the design agents, usually with relatively little burden on the human design agents. To this extent, the efficacy of the basic philosophy underlying the DCSS approach appears to be supported.

The volume of interaction needed in a typical design session, however, can be burdensome for human designers. Even though primitive design actions and their rationale can be expressed quickly, a design session typically involves many such actions, so the overall process can be slow. This problem is exacerbated by the fact that a designer can currently describe specific instances but not general descriptions of domain expertise; every instantiation of a piece of thematic knowledge, for example, has to be described individually. We are currently evaluating a number of schemes for alleviating this problem, including:

- Allowing design assistants to provide high-level domain-specific default templates for expressing design and evaluation knowledge. This allows a designer to express a set of design actions as instantiation (with optional modification) of a template rather than as a possibly large set of primitive design actions. For the LAN domain, for example, the assistant might include a template for the typical layout of a small office LAN.

- Allowing designers to enter general domain expertise (e.g. general themes) that is used from then on for all similar situations. This avoids repetitive description of domain expertise but requires that care be taken to ensure that the general expertise is in fact correct; this approach in effect introduces many of the problems inherent in knowledge acquisition.

- Allowing design agents to describe design rationale only as needed (e.g. by the conflict resolution component) rather than as design actions are described. If only a relatively small fraction of a design's rationale is actually needed in a typical design session, this can result in significant savings in the amount of interaction required of design agents. It may, however, be difficult for design agents to provide accurate *post hoc* explanations for their design actions.

- Allowing design assistants to *infer* design rationale rather than forcing the design agents to express it explicitly (Kellog et al. 1989). This requires that the assistants have significant domain-specific expertise.

Another direction for further work in DCSS is towards provision of further services by the design assistants to their associated design agents. The long-term goal of our research is to build computer systems that effectively support all aspects of cooperative design with both human and machine-based participants, supporting individual agents (i.e. as a "personal assistant") as well as the group as a whole (i.e. as a "facili-tator" or "manager"). Services that could be provided by such a system include:

- Allowing the design agents to offload simple design tasks to their assistants.
- Supporting task decomposition and allocation.
- Supporting cooperative control of the design space search, including resolution of control level conflicts among design agents.

Providing such services requires task level models for these tasks in the same way that support for conflict management requires such models. As noted in Section 11.1, work in this area has already begun.

A collaboration support system ideally should improve with use; this can reduce the knowledge acquisition burden and avoid obsolescence due to technological progress in the domain. As has been noted in a number of contexts (e.g. Ehn 1988; Mumford 1983b), learning about group activity appears to be most effectively pursued by participating in the process and learning from examples as they occur. This can include learning domain level (for performing routine design tasks and inferring design rationale) as well as meta-level (for control and conflict resolution) expertise. We are currently exploring this challenge.

The design model incorporated in DCSS should be expanded in both breadth and depth. The current model seems well suited to some domains (e.g. design of digital electrical systems) but may be inappropriate for other domains where individual components are difficult to distinguish and/or interactions between components do not occur over well-defined interfaces. For such domains a different task level model probably holds; the DCSS model thus will have to be *broadened* to allow the provision of appropriate support for such tasks. The DCSS design model should also be *deepened* to better allow users to explicitly describe the rationale underlying design actions, thereby allowing design assistants to do a better job of diagnosing and resolving conflicts.

Finally, the conflict resolution model incorporated in DCSS should be further refined. Some areas for future work in this regard include expanding the knowledge base of conflict resolution expertise, minimizing diagnostic overhead by selective search of the conflict taxonomy, and allowing machine-based design agents not implemented in terms of the DCSS design model to participate effectively in a DCSS-based system.

Chapter 12

ShareLib: A Toolkit for CSCW Applications Programming Using X Windows

M. Winnett, R. Malyan and P. Barnwell

12.1 Introduction

The need to take user requirements into account is especially important in designing Computer Supported Cooperative Work (CSCW) systems, because CSCW involves not only people interacting with computers but also people interacting with one another, bringing into play a whole new set of design issues. Designers need to be able to incorporate these human factors into a system, while at the same time addressing a variety of the technical issues of implementation.

ShareLib is a toolkit designed to provide programming support for designers of CSCW systems. By making the technical implementation issues transparent to the designer, it aims to allow them to concentrate on the human factors issues, thus producing a better designed and more effective CSCW system.

The focus of this chapter, and of the ShareLib toolkit, is on distributed, synchronous CSCW. A typical application would allow two or more users to jointly view and discuss the contents of a file in real time. They would be able to view a shared window on their screens, enter the contents of a file, e.g. a design diagram, into the shared window, edit the contents of the window, point to it using shared cursors (telepointers), and store the updated versions of the file. They would also typically use an audio link (either by telephone or using the data network) for discussion and coordination, although this is not included in the toolkit.

The design of ShareLib involves the development of a novel architecture, where programming support for CSCW is viewed as a separate layer of functionality above the underlying system.

12.2 Existing Applications

Because CSCW is still an evolving technology, there are not very many commercially available systems or software packages for synchronous, distributed CSCW. A number of packages exist as the result of research projects rather than as commercial products, but even these are few in number.

For workstations running X Windows there is a package called Shared X, developed by Hewlett-Packard. Shared X allows multiple users to use a single-user application by replicating the application's output on several screens and receiving input from those screens.

XTconfer, developed by Nottingham University and Xtel Limited (Cook and Lunt 1992), comprises a number of "tools" for CSCW (although these are not tools in the same sense as those provided by ShareLib). XTconfer's tools are a set of multi-user application programs running under X Windows, and include a shared text editor, a shared drawing area, a shared sketchpad, a shared voting tool and a shared calendar. Each of these applications includes telepointers for each participant in the conference and variable floor control settings, and there is also a "conference manager" program, which allows users to set up new conferences and to join and leave existing conferences.

ROCOCO is a CSCW system developed at Loughborough University designed to investigate group working, which consists of a shared sketchpad in which participants can draw and write, with different colours available to distinguish input from different users. ROCOCO has in fact been used in trials across a data link between the UK and Australia.

Finally, GROVE (Ellis et al. 1991), built as an experimental prototype, is a text editor designed for use by a group of people simultaneously editing a text document. It allows users to see and manipulate one or more "views" of the text being worked on in multiple windows on their screen, where a view is a subset of the overall text. GROVE allows different users to have different permissions on certain parts of the text. Items of text that cannot be edited by a particular user are shown in grey rather than black on that user's screen.

12.3 Other Similar Work

Some systems that provide various forms of programming support for CSCW already exist. MMConf (Crowley et al. 1990) is a project to explore how computers can support distributed, real-time group interaction. It includes the design of an architecture that supports shared, real-time multimedia applications, and the implementation of this architecture and a number of applications. The implementation of the MMConf architecture, under UNIX, comprises a user interface toolkit and a "conference manager", a runtime process that handles all communication between participants in a conference and provides the user interface through which they join and leave the conference and initiate new conversations. MMConf supports a replicated architecture: a separate application program and conference manager operate for each participant. Using code within the toolkit, applications send all conference traffic to the conference manager, which writes copies to each of the remote conference managers. MMConf supports real-time multimedia applications, i.e. graphical, highly interactive applications that include video as well as text and graphics. Some of the applications built with it include a video editor to control remote video resources from a workstation, a map browser that overlays images of maps recorded on videodisc, and a shared graphical editor that allows users to sketch in a shared window. Obviously, video applications require a wide bandwidth network and cannot be run on conventional data networks.

Rendezvous (Patterson et al. 1990) is an architecture for creating synchronous multi-user applications. It consists of a "runtime architecture", which manages communication between users during a session, and a "start-up architecture" which allows users to join and leave a conference session. The runtime architecture consists of a single underlying process, which manages communication between users, together with an interaction process for each user, which manages the user interface to each individual and provides an interface between an individual user's terminal and the underlying process. Rendezvous is implemented using UNIX and X Windows, and applications are written using a user interface management system called MEL, which is a language extension to Common Lisp.

12.4 What Programming Support Should Provide

12.4.1 Features of CSCW

A review of research in synchronous, distributed CSCW reveals a number of general characteristics of these systems in terms of their functionality. Firstly, systems generally need to include a shared workspace or shared window. This is a means by which each user has a view of the shared document under discussion, in a window on their own screen. The information in this window needs to be kept consistent in real time with any changes made by the other users. In some cases the shared window may exhibit WYSIWIS ("What You See Is What I See"), while in other cases each user may see a different view of the shared data which is specifically suited to their needs.

Secondly, users need to be able to point to particular parts of a document. Telepointers can be used for this purpose: a telepointer is a shared cursor that can be seen simultaneously by everyone in the conference. Thirdly, users need to transfer data to and fro between the shared workspace and their own private files on their workstation.

12.4.2 Tailorability

While the features described above indicate elements of a common functionality in distributed, synchronous CSCW, what also emerges is that *tailorability* of design is required. This arises from two factors. Firstly, CSCW is used in a variety of situations and applications, and there is no single design rule that applies equally well to every group working situation. Secondly, it is yet to be fully understood how to design CSCW applications in order to provide the optimum environment for group working, and this is an ongoing research area.

Tailorability arises in a variety of aspects of design. The type of information to be communicated between users during a group working session varies from text through to simple sketches, complex CAD-produced diagrams and even video. Another variable is the style of interaction, which takes the form of floor control or turn-taking policy. In the situation where several users are discussing some shared data that they can all see, for example, a text file, which one of them is allowed to speak, edit and point to the data at any given time? Floor control policy is a complex issue and applies to a number of functions, including control over telepointers, data editing and updating, and data storage. In some systems a "chairperson" is appointed, who can control the meeting facilities; in other systems users are given independent control and there is no restraint on who does what. No one style of interaction is suitable for all situations. As an illustration of this, experiments carried out as part of the EuroCoOp project tested the hypothesis that no system floor control is needed, but concluded that "the 'No Floor Control' . . . [hypothesis was] true only under 'ideal' circumstances and not so under (more pervasive) other circumstances" (Hughes et al. 1991). These observations clearly indicate that tailorability is required in floor control. In addition, systems often need to be tailorable not just by the designer or application programmer but also by the user. For example, users may wish to alter the floor control policy during a session.

12.5 Design of ShareLib: Architecture

12.5.1 A New Level of Abstraction

The aim of ShareLib is to provide programming support to allow the designer to think in terms of CSCW features such as shared windows and

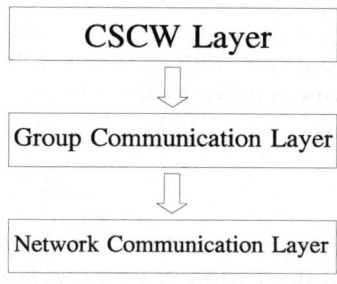

Fig. 12.1. Toolkit architecture.

telepointers, and (i) to allow them to tailor these features to the requirements of the specific application and (ii) to allow tailorability to the user.

This leads to an architecture as shown in Fig. 12.1, which views the CSCW system as a layered model, each layer providing a different level of functionality. The CSCW layer forms a new level of abstraction above the underlying technology. The following subsections describe each of the layers.

Network Communication Layer

The underlying data communication network provides the link between the different users of a CSCW application. For synchronous, distributed CSCW the network needs to provide not just basic data transfer facilities, but services with the following characteristics:

- Real-time communication

- Multimedia communication

- Multicast or group communication

Existing data networks provide only some of these characteristics. For example, small amounts of data, e.g. cursor movement or text entry, can be transferred between two stations on a Local Area Network (LAN) in what appears to be real time to the users. But transferring a graphical image would take several seconds or more. Over a wide area network these data transfer times would be considerably increased.

Group Communication Layer

The above section describes the network requirements in terms of transferring packets of data. But CSCW applications require communication between users, between windows and between remote screen objects. A CSCW application should not have to be concerned with virtual circuits, socket numbers etc., but needs support for direct communication between members of the group. CSCW applications often have to implement this group communication directly, by using networking software such as UNIX sockets, AppleTalk etc. Alternatively, windowing systems such as X Windows provide support for writing to multiple windows on different hosts. As with the network communication layer, current systems do not provide adequate support at this level.

CSCW Layer

The CSCW layer forms the interface between the services offered by the underlying network communication or window sharing, and the requirements of the application programmer. It offers a toolkit of library routines and defines the terms in which the application program is written. In other words it forms the Application Program Interface (API).

12.5.2 Features and Tailorability Provided by the CSCW Layer

This section describes in detail the CSCW features provided by the CSCW layer and the tailorability of these features.

Shared Workspace

A shared workspace, identified by Wilbur (1990) as one of the three "dimensions" of sharing, is a feature of most CSCW systems. It is a mechanism whereby all of the users in the group have access to the same piece of data. In distributed, synchronous systems this normally takes the form of a shared window. The variables of a shared workspace are:

1. *Members of the group:* some method is required of specifying which particular users on the network are participating in the CSCW session. Each of these users has to have access to the shared workspace, e.g. in the case of a shared window, it must be replicated on each user's screen.
2. *Contents of the shared workspace:* a mechanism is required for transferring data (a text file, diagram etc.) into the shared workspace and distributing it to all members of the group. Mechanisms will also be required to allow scrolling through a file, enlarging an area of a diagram etc.
3. *Floor control:* floor control policy determines which member or members of the group have control of the shared workspace at any particular time. A mechanism is required whereby control can be given to one participant or to a subset of participants; or all members of the group can have equal control.

Telepointers

A telepointer is a shared cursor or other object that can be seen by the whole group, and is used to point to areas of the shared workspace for reference in order to assist communication between users. The variables of telepointers are:

1. *Graphical representation:* a telepointer may take the form of an "arrow", an underscore (cursor) etc.
2. *Control:* the shared pointer might be controlled by a single member of the group, or one at a time by several different people in turn, or by everybody in a first-come, first-served manner.

Data Storage and Data Ownership

There are many potential problems in an application where, for example, a user can copy a file to the shared workspace, which can then be edited by other users. At what point is the amended file stored? Does it overwrite the old version? Can another member of the group store a copy of the shared version in their own storage area, or can only the original owner of the file determine where and when it is stored? If anyone can save a copy of a shared file, then there will soon be numerous inconsistent copies of the information stored in numerous locations.

These issues can be thought of as dealing with the interface between "private data", i.e. data owned by each individual user, and shared data. The variables of data storage are:

1. Ownership of files
2. Updating

Data in a shared workspace may be associated with a particular user. For example, that user may have originally owned the file and have copied it to the shared workspace. They might want to have control over the editing and updating of the file, or alternatively they might want to keep an original copy, and free another copy for editing by the group. Another possibility is that a shared file is created, owned by no one member of the group, but subject to rules governing who can write to and edit it, and so on.

12.6 Design of ShareLib: Implementation

12.6.1 The X Windows System

The X Windows system (Scheifler et al. 1988) is a good platform on which to develop CSCW applications, because it provides both a graphical user interface and support for multiple-display applications. X consists of a library of routines with which application programs, or *clients*, are written, and the X *server*, a program kept continuously running on the host being used as the display.

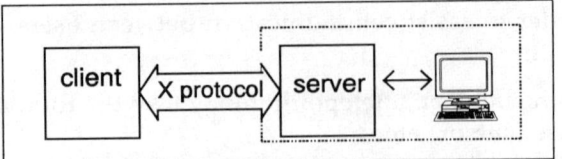

Fig. 12.2. The X client–server architecture.

The client–server architecture of X means that the client and server can run on different machines without any alteration to the client program: the X programming library, Xlib, makes communications transparent to the client. The client simply sets up a connection to the required display and then uses calls to Xlib functions such as XCreateWindow. Xlib translates these function calls into messages sent to the X server on the appropriate display, using the X protocol (see Fig. 12.2). The server then creates the correct screen output. The server also sends "event" messages to the client whenever the user performs an action such as typing or moving the mouse, and the client can then take the appropriate action, for example, telling the server to draw a character in a window.

To create a multi-display application, therefore, the client program can simply set up connections to several displays, as shown in Fig. 12.3. The client then has to send output to each of these displays and process input events from all of them.

12.6.2 ShareLib as a Layer above X Windows

ShareLib is implemented as a number of functions above Xlib (see Fig. 12.4). These functions allow the creation and manipulation of shared objects such as shared windows and telepointers.

ShareLib is still under development: the telepointer object and part of

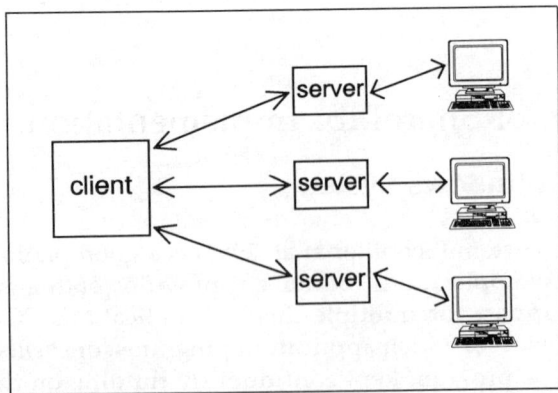

Fig. 12.3. A multi-user application using X.

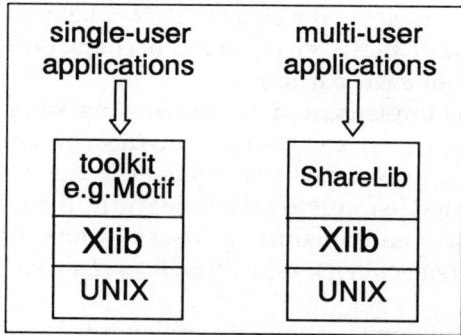

Fig. 12.4. Comparison of single-user and multi-user applications.

the shared window object have so far been implemented. ShareLib is not currently intended to provide an exhaustive set of shared objects, or support all of the functionality required by applications programmers. However, its architecture means that it is expandable, so new objects and functions can be added as the need for them arises.

Section 12.7 provides an example of the way in which the toolkit is being implemented, by discussing the telepointer object.

12.7 Example Implementation: The Telepointer

12.7.1 Writing Xlib Applications

An X application written using Xlib consists mainly of two sections: an initialization section in which connections to displays are set up, windows are created, defaults are set and so on, followed by an event processing section. Events in X are messages sent by the X server to the application program in response to input from the user, such as mouse button clicks, mouse movement, typing on the keyboard etc. The application program waits in a loop for events to occur, and as each event arrives it does the appropriate processing and sends the appropriate output to be displayed to the X server. For example, if the server sends an event message to say that the character "a" was pressed on the keyboard, the application program would probably, among other things, send a message to the server to print the letter "a" on the screen, telling the server which window to print it in and the position of the letter within the window.

12.7.2 The Telepointer Type

ShareLib defines a telepointer data type. This is a data structure containing all of the information pertaining to a single telepointer, i.e. a single pointer displayed on several screens. It is likely that an application would have several of these telepointers, perhaps one to respond to the mouse movements of each participant.

The telepointer is implemented by drawing a pixmap of the telepointer image (e.g. an arrow) on each screen in the conference, and redrawing this pixmap in a new position whenever the mouse is moved. A telepointer is "created" simply by declaring it in the main program. This telepointer is subsequently manipulated using three ShareLib functions: *cscwAddDisplayToTelepointer()*, *cscwTelepointerFloorControl()* and *cscwProcessTelepointer()*.

In the current implementation, the telepointer is implemented as a structure definition:

```
typedef struct {

        int   number_of_displays;

        int   old_x_position;

        int   old_y_position;

        int   floor_control;

        Display_info   display_info[MAX_USERS];

        } Telepointer;
```

In fact, the application program does not need to know the structure of a telepointer, since all interaction with it is done using the ShareLib functions. The telepointer structure contains the floor control policy, together with information about each of the displays on which it is to be drawn: this information, such as the display and window IDs, graphics context and pixmap height and width, is required by the X functions that draw the telepointer pixmap on each screen. The *old–x–position* and *old–y–position* members are used in updating the pixmap image, and are explained below.

12.7.3 Initializing the Telepointer

In order to use a telepointer the data structure has to be initialized or "filled in". This is done using *cscwAddDisplayToTelepointer()*, which has to be called for each display on which the telepointer is to be visible. It initializes the *display–info* data for each display, so that the telepointer structure contains the relevant display IDs, window IDs and pixmaps.

12.7.4 Processing Telepointer Events

Once the application program has created any required windows and has initialized the telepointer, it enters an event processing loop, where it waits for incoming events and processes them when they occur. Event gathering becomes complex when there are several screens involved, and ShareLib includes a function to gather events from multiple screens, although this is optional and another method could be used. Then, when a *MotionNotify* event occurs, the application calls *cscwProcessTelepointer()*, and this moves the telepointer on all the screens to the new mouse position by redrawing the telepointer pixmap in the new position.

12.7.5 Floor Control

The floor control policy is set to either *ALL–USERS* or *OWNER–ONLY* using *cscwTelepointerFloorControl()*. The floor control variable is then used by *cscwProcessTelepointer()* to determine the subsequent response of the telepointer to mouse movement from different users. When a *MotionNotify* event occurs, *cscwProcessTelepointer()* checks to see if it comes from a valid user according to the current floor control value. This is possible because each *MotionNotify* event returns an *XMotionEvent* structure (see Scheifler et al. 1988), which contains the display ID on which the event occurred. In this way the telepointer can be moved either in response to any *MotionNotify* event or just in response to those originating from a particular user's screen, and so on.

12.7.6 Drawing the Telepointer Pixmap

In addition to redrawing the telepointer pixmap each time the mouse is moved, the previous position of the pixmap has to be redrawn with the information that was originally in the window. This can be achieved by copying the contents of the window that will be overwritten into a special pixmap *before* drawing the telepointer image in that position. Then, after the telepointer has been moved to its next position in the window, the contents of the pixmap can be copied back to their original position. The coordinates of this overwritten portion of the window are stored in the *old–x–position* and *old–y–position* fields of the data structure.

12.8 Summary and Further Work

The toolkit, when completed, will provide programming support for applications programmers, enabling them to concentrate their design effort on the human factors issues that are so important in CSCW systems.

The toolkit provides a suitable level of abstraction for CSCW, and hides the details of implementation without removing the ability to tailor the system as required.

There are still many issues to be addressed in the implementation of the toolkit, such as how to extend the functionality of the shared window to meet the needs of a variety of applications, and what other shared objects could usefully be developed. A demonstrator is currently being developed in order to demonstrate the use of the toolkit and also to give practical insight into its use. Investigations will also be carried out into the real-time performance of the toolkit and its use over both local and wide area networks.

Chapter 13

Adapting a Design History Editor for Concurrent Engineering

D. Jenkins

13.1 Introduction

13.1.1 Motivation

As indicated in Chapter 1, it is evident that two forces shape the provision of Computer Supported Cooperative Work (CSCW):

1. What can be done with computer technology at the time, or reasonably foreseen.
2. What is needed by those engaged in the cooperative work situation.

It is also true that it is easier to focus on the former that the latter. Even when attention is directed to users' needs, the temptation is to assume that all cooperative work has the same general form and requirements and to create an abstract user requirement from a general understanding of how individuals cooperate in the work situation.

This has its attractions. The need to get inside a particular work situation is avoided, but this is a less than optimal approach to the system design task where work groups are involved.

Different work groups have different needs, arising from both the organizational culture in which they work and from the disciplines that they bring to bear upon the task in hand.

Konda et al. (1992) argue that shared memory, seen as both vertical (within a discipline) and horizontal (between disciplines) is needed both to enable reuse of design, cooperation over time, and "simultaneous design" or "concurrent engineering". They see shared memory as a unifying theme both for design research and design practice. It is also true that computer support for engineering design must not hinder the application of design theory or design insight to design practice. If this is true, then shared memory must be facilitated and supported, even created, by CSCW applied to engineering design practice.

Indeed, a rereading of Chapter 1 shows the relevance of this observation to the design of CSCW systems. Thus, while this chapter focuses on the needs of the engineering designer, shared memory may well be a useful model by which to understand what has to be done generally in CSCW research.

Further useful context can be given by the observations in Ferguson (1992), where it is seen that continuity in engineering practice exists in the face of radical change in design technology. Yet the underlying substance of engineering is unchanged. It is grounded in specialized knowledge, part of which is found in books but much of which can only be gained through sensory experience but which – through reflection and through joint experience – results in both an individual worldview (*Weltanschauung*) and a shared one that belongs to the profession as a whole, in its shared memory.

13.1.2 Starting Point

The author has been on secondment from Paisley College (now the University of Paisley) from early in the life of the Engineering Design Research Centre (EDRC). He has worked closely over the last year or so with the developer of a Design History Editor (DHE).

One of the concerns at the Centre has been the definition and description of the "Design Infrastructure". Clearly, such an infrastructure has to take account of the need to employ concurrent or simultaneous engineering to reduce cradle-to-launch time.

In the context of discussions regarding the EDRC Phase Two programme, the following points were made about concurrency in design. Concurrency is the concept of running design activities and reflecting the effects of design influences simultaneously. It should provide the most efficient design process as measured, for example, by the time and cost from cradle to launch. Each design factor has its own rate of change and degree of influence within the design process. It is necessary to confirm the impact that design factors have on the balance between design as a sequential process and design as a simultaneous process (see below). The connections between design factors need to be categorized on the basis of the nature of the interactions between them, the extent to which they are linked by feedback, handshaking and interaction, rather than by linear progression. In short, it was believed that the cost and benefits of concurrency needed to be understood, quantified and demonstrated to engineering and business management, as well as within the research community.

An early account (Streveler 1978) describes "design by committee", which, although the term is not used, seems to be an early account of concurrent engineering, although from a "management of the project" viewpoint. Here, group or cooperative work is seen as essential in achieving the timeliness and quality goals of the design process, so that computer support for concurrent engineering is domain-specific CSCW.

The DHE follows the line taken by the developers of the desktop metaphor, and, in CSCW, by the developers of a distributed cooperative work environment (Madsen 1989), of modelling the familiar objects of the workplace within the world maintained within the computer system, or, rather, distributed information system. In the case of the DHE, these familiar objects are the *design journal*, the *page*, the *sketch* and the *label*.

13.1.3 Outline of the DHE Work

Initially the DHE had to support the objectives of an EDRC project, Knowledge and Information Relationships in the Engineering Design Environment (KIREDE). The implicit relationships used by the designer as he or she sketches the design, and their development over time, were to be captured and made available on replay to guide redesign, to correct errors or to produce variants of products or components. This facility implied close connection with a feature based modeller, which had been extended to allow the organization and use of information about the production and materials aspects of design. These are often tackled in a sequential manner since, so often, the information is only accessible and usable within or via different tools, if at all.

The DHE also had to be extensible to produce design protocol information for analysis within design research more generally, and within a proposed Design In Severely Constrained Situations (DISCS) project (Jenkins 1991).

Clearly, the KIREDE extension from the conventional base has one form of concurrent engineering built in. The individual designer can deal with materials or production aspects in a way consistent with the hunting model (see below) of the design process. But still untackled is the problem of making information available at the earlier, sketch based, more conceptual phase of design, where the major cost and value decisions are made.

Dealing with Concurrency

Here, too, after Streveler (1978), we can say that concurrency must also be enabled. The subcontract model of the design process, implied in Streveler, makes concurrency possible. But, particularly at early stages of design, individuals must be free to resile from the (implied) contract if they realize that the (implied) terms make a solution within the (inherited) constraints impossible or excessively costly. Hence, the DHE must be made reactive *between* open design journals, ones in which design is still being elaborated, as well as *within* an (open) design journal, so that interaction can take place between concurrent work on subcontracts.

With the increasing interaction between system integrators (e.g. car manufacturers) and components suppliers (e.g. within the car industry) in the search for higher quality, then this reactiveness has to be achieved at a distance, both up and down the supply chain, and across dispersed design groups.

Clearly, CSCW research has promise for the development of the DHE in the direction of distributed design concurrency. On the other hand, this research may be rather distant from the world of CIME, in which it is clear that standards, e.g. from the ISO 10030 process, will have a dominating impact. Attention also needs to be paid to the converging world of CAD and CASE support environments (Weston et al. 1992).

The Role of Group Interaction

Attention is being focused (Greenberg et al. 1992) on the role of the interactions between group members by way of gesture, interjection and so on, in the design process. Here, multimedia conferencing will extend this over distance, and offers the prospect that, since the interactions are mediated technically (Landry 1992), a means can be found of tracking, interpreting and understanding their role, and monitoring effectiveness. This does not yet seem an immediate prospect, however.

The Impact of Design Models

We can see from the hunting model of Mustoe (1991) (Fig. 13.1) the links that indicate the knowledge needed at a prior stage arising from "later" stages. This requires radically different toolsets from those suggested by the sequential model of design. Our attention is drawn to the blackboard computational model in which autonomous, or quasi-autonomous, knowledge agents interact with the designer, the model of the design process, and the model of the product under design, via the knowledge represented on the blackboard. (See also Kitzmiller and Jagannathan 1987; Kloth 1989 for discussions of the appropriateness of the blackboard model for design support.) Design could then be supported as an iterative, or better, hunting process. Ideally, the cost of iteration – breadth of hunt – could be predicted by the toolset so that this could be achieved optimally.

Lehman's Law of System Dynamics states:

> The introduction of a (information) system changes the environment that places demands on the system or the nature of the problem tackled by the system.

We can see that this implies that introducing concurrent engineering toolsets will change the way in which design is done. The quality of the toolset will determine the potential for improvement. If we regard as a design tool any intellectual method that allows a formal approach to handling ideas, then we see that the choice of knowledge representation tool is important. Such tools make some ways of thinking or approach easy, and inhibit, or even eliminate, others. The impact of the Roman as contrasted to the Babylonian, and, later, the Arabic, number systems is well known, with the former not developing mathematics while the Babylonians developed a sophisticated astronomy and the Arabs gave us the algorithm. Here, the adoption of tools suited to concurrent and cooperative working will enable the wider use of, and research into, concurrent design. Thus, the appropriateness of the blackboard architecture is seen as significant.

The Significance of the Blackboard Architecture

How appropriate is the classical Artificial Intelligence (AI) blackboard architecture to concurrent engineering and hence concurrent design?

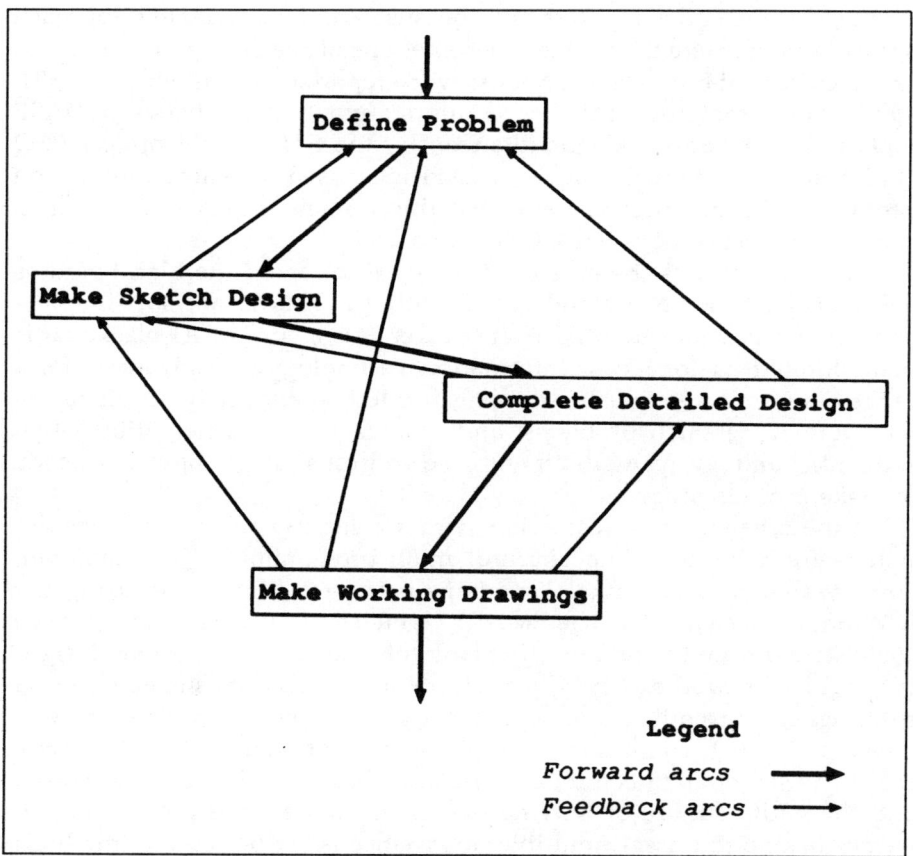

Fig. 13.1. The hunting model of design (Mustoe 1991).

The blackboard architecture may be outlined as having an open repository in which the state of the problem/solution is visible, and knowledge sources, which interact and update the information/knowledge in the repository. Current blackboards have a specific-to-project set of interfaces, which requires that knowledge systems are built on an *ad hoc* basis even where the domain handled is generic. To make practical progress, a blackboard must be partitioned into levels of abstraction, and knowledge systems focused on propagating changes for the better up (or down) the hierarchy of abstractions. The CASSANDRA architecture (Craig 1991), in the interests of real-time efficiency, carries this modularization to an extreme in which domains are more clearly separated. Effectively (although this is not the way Craig (1991) puts it), independent blackboards are set up and composed via message channels to form an overall problem solving machine. If we allow the designer to be one of these, then clearly the architecture of CASSANDRA points a way forward towards a distributed blackboard-style (shall we say) infrastructure for concurrent design in which geographically separate designers cooperate. Again, CASSANDRA is interesting because an object oriented approach seems implied. Here the problem becomes one of specifying the semantics and syntax of the messages. Recent work reported by Rutherford (1991, 1992) shows that the problem of information transfer between CASE tools is being addressed. Simultaneously, the STEP/PDES project (ISO 10030) defines a formal language, EXPRESS, used to define application protocols. The prospect is there that this framework could be used to cause convergence between the domains.

Here a caveat must be entered. It is usual to regard the blackboard as an AI tool which must stand or fall with AI. This is not so, since the architecture is wider than AI in its power. Also, current AI blackboards make limited use of recent Information Technology (IT) advances, for a range of reasons. Obviously, the focus is often on knowledge engineering and pure AI research problems, and a realizable implementation, often sequential and always with an enforced control strategy, has to be made to make projects progress.

On the other hand, a researcher with a computer science background will begin with the time sharing, multi-programming OS paradigm, employ a client–server model, perhaps based (as Khoros) on using the X Window mechanisms. The SMART frame server (Carrasco and Crowe 1990) started from the premise that fault tolerant real-time system designers required a workbench with multiple tools and consistency checkers running concurrently. Thus, an event and frame based system was developed which combined a simple version of frames (Minsky 1980), the client–server architecture, use of plain UNIX text files to store frames, and the notify service of X Windows. Long transactions are supported, frames belong to classes, multiple inheritance is supported and methods are implemented so as to provide facets. Thus, both SMART and IMKA

(1990) technologies provide the asynchronous and potential opportunistic behaviour required by the blackboard paradigm. Consequently, the full power of the blackboard architecture is considered not to have been seen yet.

Knowledge Assets

The value of knowledge assets is seen as considerable, and all the information handled in the domains covered by the foregoing is a knowledge asset. The prospect of vendor-independent standards being set in the way knowledge is handled is the motivation for the work of IMKA. This offers a way of achieving an open blackboard architecture. Even within a CASSANDRA architecture, that is, one in which the links between knowledge systems are predefined, an open blackboard architecture defining interface protocols etc. is attractive since software reuse and knowledge reuse between knowledge systems seems desirable.

13.2 Design History Editor

The approach taken in designing the DHE was based upon what it was considered could be said about designers and design today (Bebbington 1992):

> Most design is evolutionary and iterative; a good design history mechanism is essential to improve this process. Virtually all designers carry out the early stages of design by annotated sketching. They are required to record these sketches in personal logbooks. These logbooks therefore contain the design history. We also know that these logbooks are used for a number of reasons ranging from audit to design modifications and that they make at least some sense to other human designers.

This must be the starting point for designing CSCW support for concurrent engineering/simultaneous design, to which the cooperative aspects, working at a distance aspects and research requirements must be subservient.

13.2.1 Inherent Difficulties with Current Approaches

Bebbington also makes the following points. He sees that much of current design research is devoted to the representation of knowledge within machines and in improving the methods by which this knowledge is gathered and maintained. To date, it has not been possible for a machine to extract useful knowledge from the kind of abstract sketch information that is generated by designers and exists in logbooks, although a few researchers are currently working in this area.

The most successful research in design knowledge representation has been in expert systems and Knowledge Based (KB) systems. These systems, however, suffer from the significant amount of extra work required in describing the base knowledge and its relationships in a form that a KB system can "understand" and use (Tunnicliffe and Scrivener 1991). These relationships have to be extremely well filtered from the mass of information available. The base knowledge has to be extracted from the design. Usually, it has to be described in a system-dependent format. To do this the knowledge must be generalized into rules covering what to apply and when to apply it, together with interdependency rules, which is not an easy task.

Since a designer cannot fully describe something that is not yet designed, this elucidation must be achieved through post analysis. If the relationships are used by the formal system as the structure that the designer must supply as he or she uses it, then the design must be done elsewhere outside the formal design system, so the full detail of the history is lost and a filtered path described on the basis of recollection or paper notes. The design will eventually be completed, and then this (partial) knowledge will be available to the elucidation process. The knowledge is not domain-independent and it must be described in a manner useful to the KB system *post hoc* by inferring general rules from recollections of what was done. This is seen as dangerous, since rules may be left out or be incomplete. Hence, reusing them will result in faulty design if done blindly in a "machine-like" manner, because the description of the filtered path may not contain enough information for the knowledge to be applied successfully to a similar but disparate design. The significant extra workload imposed by knowledge acquisition is only seen as worthwhile when it is known that the design is likely to be repeated often.

13.2.2 Conventional Logbooks and Hypertext

Conventional logbooks, if they could be used as a basis for this work, offer a significant advantage in terms of storing relevant design information for human interpretation, as no additional workload would be imposed on anyone. However, conventional logbooks are extremely difficult to use because a great deal of manual searching is required to find relevant information. Other researchers have recognized the advantages of a logbook based approach and have concentrated efforts on systems such as Hypercard, in which cards containing text etc. are linked via key or sensitive words in the text.

The difficulty in this approach is the formation of the links between the separate cards. The linkage problem is normally overcome by imposing a prescriptive hierarchical approach on the user, so that cards are formed and linked through the use of the process of structured decomposition. There is good evidence that most structured design is carried out in this fashion, although the decision point at which this decomposition takes place is not well understood. That is, the starting point within the final hierarchy, the point where the first decomposition was made, is not known. Thus, the design decisions were not taken in the order implied by a top-down, breadth-first traverse of the final designed structure. We know that structured decomposition of design objects takes place. The act of decomposition into sub-designs is a design decision based on a prior piece (phase, subroutine, sequence of steps, act and so on) of design. Since we do not know what the design is, we do not know when or on what evidence this decomposition will take place. We think that a designer holds in mind an overall view (Suchman 1987), which he or she is free to maintain, without commitment to a (final) object based representation until the last minute. But the designer is free to commit to such a representation in what seems (at least to the observer) to be an arbitrary pattern over what will finally be a tidy tree of sub-objects, neatly decomposed apparently top down. The missing element would be the unexpressed or inexpressible reason for each movement from guddle to structure, a reason that cannot destroy the relationships in the guddle but that may not actually express them explicitly. A system such as GOODS (Ormerod and Bloomfield 1991), which requires decomposition before knowledge capture, is thus seen as putting the cart before the horse, except perhaps in routine design, where the path through the maze, as it were, is well trodden.

13.2.3 The Impact of Prescription

We know that a designer must eventually decompose the design into a description of the individual parts and structure for their assembly before the design can be manufactured. We do not know how the designer will do this, although we may be tempted by the final tidy hierarchic order of the design to be prescriptive. But we recognize the danger that if we prescribe too much the design will be done elsewhere, that is, informally outside of the formal design environment, and then fitted to the prescribed path. The true history will be lost.

A few prescriptive design systems have been researched and implemented, but these are particularly prescriptive in their approach in order to obtain an easily managed hierarchical structure between the cards, that is, within the captured information or knowledge. They also lose the "sequential in time", historical information that a logbook provides since they require that each part of the decomposition is treated as a separate object, in some cases, to provide an engineering change section.

There is also a difficulty with these systems in using parts of previous designs that do not exist as objects in their own right: i.e. no distinction is made between a physical component and a phase in the design process. But this does not allow for common phases that might be embedded in the design process or for components that are different in their final physical form. The concept of subroutining within and between design histories might have to be employed.

13.3 User Requirements of the Design History Editor

It was considered that, to provide a usable and useful tool based around an engineering logbook which contains little prescription and therefore should cater for the majority of designers and design methods in the early concept stages, the following was needed:

1. The ability to draw and write on the page with relative simplicity.
2. The ability to find and modify the page easily with a record of the change.
3. The ability to find related pages.
4. The ability to find and use parts of earlier designs.
5. The ability to have hierarchical designs.
6. The ability to find and use related information from a CAD/CAM system.

Initially, the tool was not intended to provide active help for the designer as he or she is designing, but merely to provide a more useful engineering logbook with access links to enable modification and reuse in the current and future designs.

13.3.1 Page Emulation

As the system is intended to emulate a logbook, the basic requirement is that it should emulate a page. The page must be capable of recording both text and sketch information, and must be capable of being stored in a sequential manner, like pages of a logbook.

If a true freeform sketcher were used to emulate the page based on the light pen principle, then either a pixmap would have to be stored for every sketch or the sketch would have to be preprocessed in order to reduce data storage requirements. At the outset of this work such a capability seemed expensive to acquire, but now, at the time of writing, pen computing systems offer this support to application programmers, and pen input to the DHE is being explored.

Another alternative was to use a CAD sketcher, which would have the advantage of being able to use the sketch information in the final design. The trouble with this was that, by definition, CAD systems expect precise, scaled information – extremely useful for detailing but a significant overhead for a sketcher and unlikely to be used by the designer for that very reason. Another disadvantage of such an approach is that sketches do not always have a physical representation and are merely used as a focus for the designer's thoughts.

Other sketch systems exist in desktop publishing which allow this kind of logbook information to be stored with relative ease but demand that it is carried out within that environment. This is not particularly useful if even sequential links between the pages are to be formed.

13.3.2 Representation of Finer Structure

To decide how to proceed below the level of the page required some consideration of the following.

Design as Hierarchy versus Design as Guddle

Feature based modelling imposes a hierarchy, in the Constructive Solid Model (CSM) sense, on the features within the Designed Product (DP) (Fig. 13.2). There is then the natural tendency to see hierarchy as the way

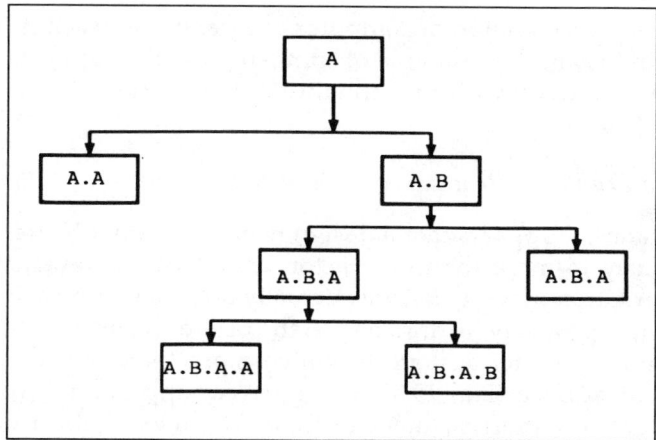

Fig. 13.2. Hierarchy of features within the designed product.

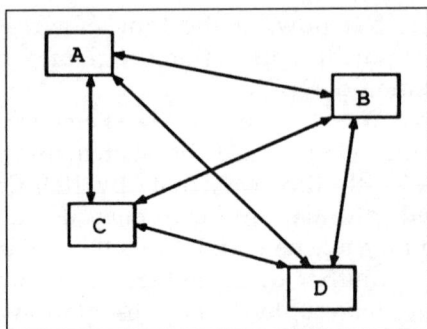

Fig. 13.3. Relationships established as the designer works.

to express design from the outset, since it appears in the final product. Consideration of the process actually carried out by the designer leads to a different picture (Fig. 13.3), in which emerging elements of the design are linked by various relationships. For the moment it is of little interest as to what comprises each relationship. It is enough to know that imposing hierarchy would constrain and distort the design process. For this reason, the DHE did not follow the path taken by GOODS (Ormerod and Bloomfield 1991).

Normative Links

The designer's activity provides the normative links that reveal the reason for the designed product being the way it is. However, each separate evaluative view uses, needs and creates alternative networks, one of which is the CSG/CSM hierarchy or tree. Feature based modelling is another. In general, a feature is comprised of a subtree grouping several elements of the CSM tree.

Again, the preoccupation of computer programming teachers with "top down design" is another example of confusing the final appearance of the program (the product) with the structure of the process.

Design as a Dynamic Process

From a distance, it appears that a design is developed with attention paid simultaneously to more than one factor, aspect or whatever. But it is a simple observation that the designer actually does one thing at a time (Fig. 13.4). A comparison may be drawn with the pseudo-concurrency observed in a real-time computer system, in which more than one real-time task is carried out at once (Fig. 13.5). The program appropriate to each task is actually given a short segment of time. The overall effect of uniform progression is achieved by fair switching between these. So with the

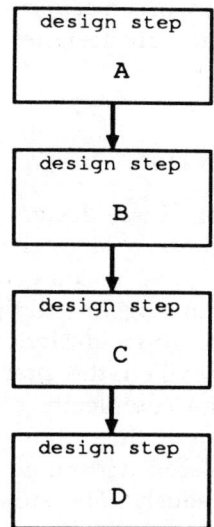

Fig. 13.4. Design steps undertaken in sequence.

human design activity. The designer focuses on one aspect, and deals with that. If more than five or six aspects have to be taken forward together then means are employed to overcome the limits on short-term memory, achieved by chunking and labelling. Labelled sketches are made to record the state of each aspect. The reuse of labels between aspects establishes and is then used to maintain the relationships between the

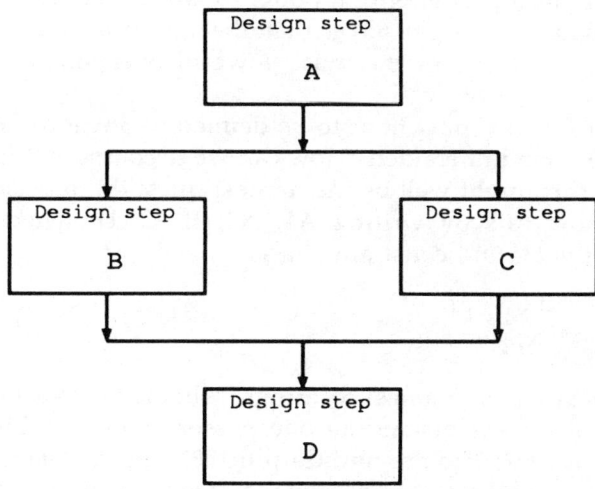

Fig. 13.5. Design steps undertaken concurrently.

aspects. To summarize, the networked aspects of the design are addressed sequentially by the (single) human designer as the final goal is kept in view (Suchman 1987).

Actual Concurrent Design Activity

This is still true when more than one designer is involved, which occurs when the design task becomes so large that more than one designer is required. At this point CSCW becomes an issue. In actuality, the subcontract model is used to manage the design process in this situation (Streveler 1978). Indeed, individual designers need to use it, as well as teams of designers, even when the practical necessity is only the internal one of managing the complexity of ideas. When actions also have to be managed, and here the actions impinge on the ideas as well, then subcontracts are placed with more than one designer to allow activity to proceed simultaneously. The subcontracts are drawn up by subdividing or sharing the requirements and constraints expressed in the specification of the component or system being subdivided; cf. the situation in architecture etc. where a subcontractor is bound by the terms of the original contract in addition to any terms in the subcontract. Since this process involves the manipulation of specifications then the DHE can be referred to as a specification system, but this name focuses more on the *how* than the *what* of the tool and obscures the wider, potential, impact it could have in the total design process.

Two (or more) designers can now generate a stream of design activities in which two, or more, can take place at the same time. So, if A, B, C and D are design activities, we can write (in pseudo Algol 68) instead of A; B; C; D. the radically different, although textually similar, A; B, C; D. A noted weakness of Algol 68 is that the absence of a mere period indicates the use of one of the most powerful weapons in its arsenal, *concurrency*.

The goals of B and C now have to be defined in advance (in A), which introduces the often unheralded "How can we decompose this problem?" problem, and this might well be the hardest question to decide. Perhaps we should show this by writing A1; A2; B, C; D. where A2 is the subdivision of goals and constraints task.

Labels, Labelling and Goals

The attaching of labels (names) to things, whether abstract or concrete, is a measure of the understanding one possesses of the object or of its purpose (Dilnot 1992; Thomas and Carroll 1981). In the DHE, labelling is seen as a fundamental activity. A label may encapsulate a goal or identify an attribute or parameter of something represented in a sketch. We use

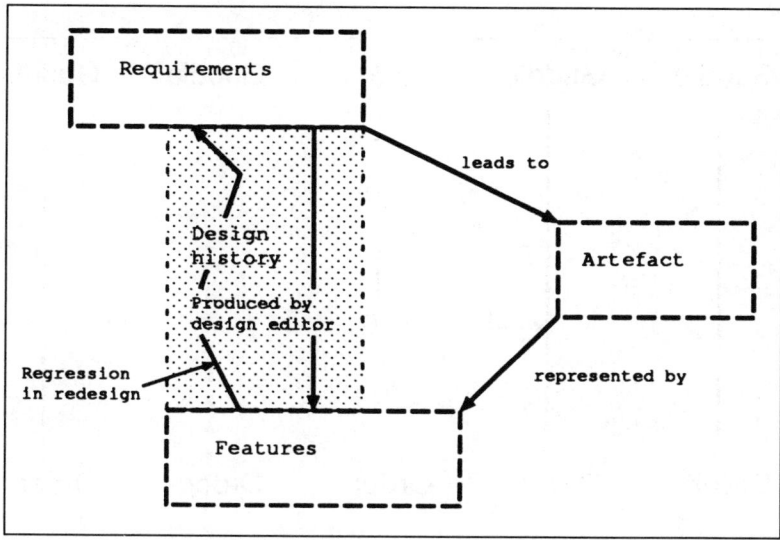

Fig. 13.6. Regression from features to requirements.

sketching rather than drawing to place the emphasis on the idea portrayed, rather than on its (possibly transitory at this stage) physical realization of the moment.

Guddle as a Description of Design

The Scots term "guddle" captures our understanding of the way in which the requirements lead to the designed product, the artefact. It is clear that the artefact is represented by the feature based model (Fig. 13.6), for this is what is used to actually construct it at the time of manufacture. However, redesign, reuse of design and routine design all require that the designer moves away from pure feature based representation towards the requirements (Fig. 13.7). This is not perverse, but necessary to recapture the meaning of the design and cope with diversity since many viewpoints and perceptions of the one designed product, as well as ways of working, exist among designers.

We must retain the intermediate "states of the design" as generated by the initial designer activity (Fig. 13.8). Reworking of any sort involves "unwinding" the design states back to an earlier point, at which all previous design decisions are still accepted as valid for the variant but at which a different decision to that in the original history must now be made. A separate design history will arise from this point of departure, identified in terms of the revised requirement that gave birth to it.

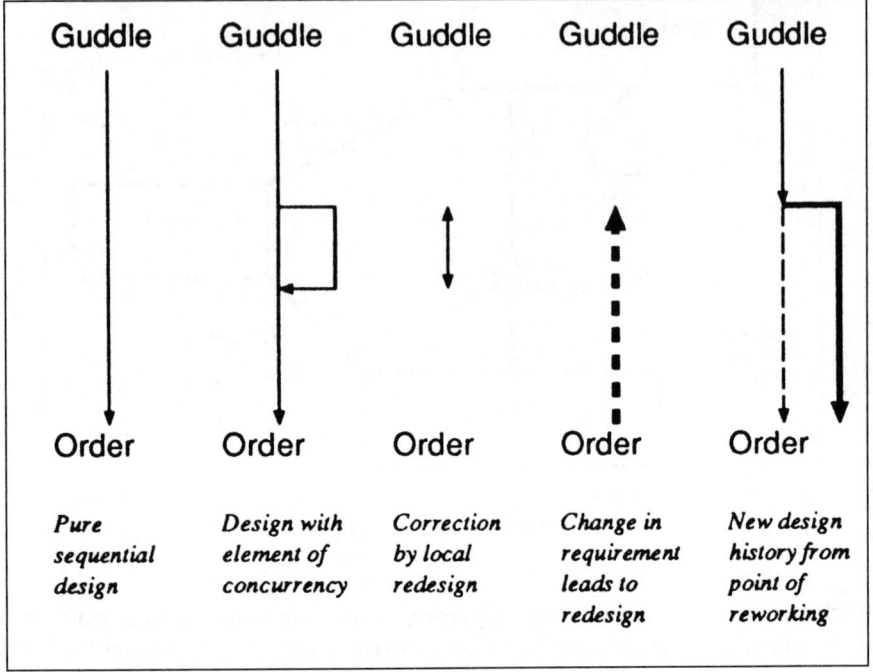

Fig. 13.7. Mappings from guddle to order.

Flexibility in the Subcontract Model

Reworking can take place within the separate decision streams, i.e. within one subcontract, with no constraint. However, a desire to resile from the contracts by restating the problem, goals, constraints, or whatever, associated with each set of subcontracts will generate a set of radical design history changes. Thus, implicit in the subcontracts at design stage, as opposed to manufacture (or execution stage for programs), is the possibility of change in the contract.

13.3.3 The Lemma

The basic premise or lemma of the DHE is that we can use design activity to capture or to organize the relationships between elements or aspects of the design. The choice of the label concept springs partly from programming usage, but also from the need to use a generic or context free term, that is, plain English. "Naming" (Thomas and Carroll

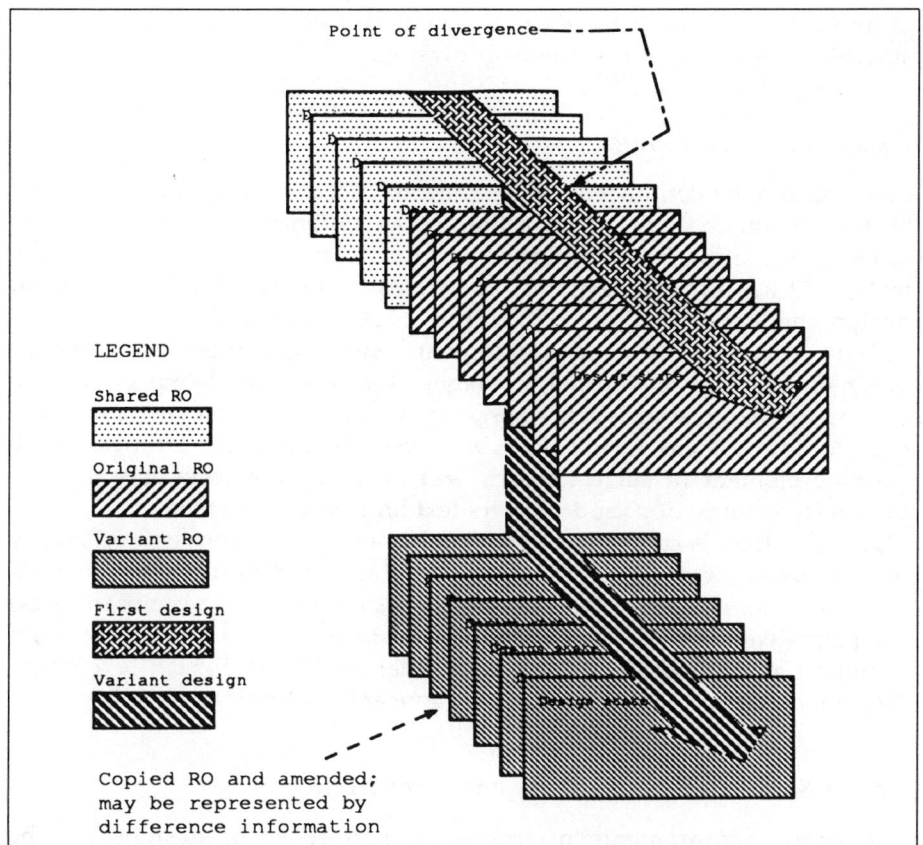

Fig. 13.8. Effect of design variant on design history.

1981) or "labelling" (Dilnot 1992) is a process that moves information from short-term memory into medium-term, and thence into long-term memory, as well as providing the organizational basis for formal management of the complexities of the design task. Labelling is essential to the design task, being associated with the "chunking" which enables the designer's progress through the design process. It is thought that some attempts to produce finer grain protocol information may be self-defeating in a number of ways:

1. Automated techniques may be too intrusive.
2. The volume may limit the number of designs recorded.
3. The tendency to invention has been noted (Stauffer and Ullman 1991).

Thus, the DHE was designed to record all that the designer would have written in his or her design journal, but, vitally, to capture the location of and relationships between these label entries on-line and in a form suitable for subsequent replay or browsing.

Observation versus Interrogation

The two may be contrasted; more could be discovered by interrogation – "Why did you do that?" – but, as Stauffer and Ullman observed, designers often do not know "why" and invent or guess answers. It was also judged to be a "turn off" for designers considering the DHE in the context of design challenges (Jenkins 1991). From observation and experience, the activity of designers could be summarized as: designers jotted things down on pages in the journal; the labels were used to relate page to page via the appearance of labels on sketches etc., or in sketches, equations etc. No doubt labels would have been used before their definition. The primary element of such a sketch was its label, the secondary was its proximity information, and then its text and/or sketch elements.

A page, then, is comprised of labels that are close to (possess proximity to) text by itself, a sketch by itself, or to text and sketch close to each other. A label is a string of characters, a name. Proximity is closeness on the page (leaving the observer to infer relationship). Text is one or more sentences providing description or factual statement. Sketch is a rough two-dimensional picture focusing on concepts rather than detail.

Access Requirements for Reuse and Concurrency

The access requirements of (re)design and reuse of designs can be summarized: an existing design would be available Read-Only (RO) to all users; it could not be changed because it was history. Rework in routine design, revision to eliminate defects, and reuse of (component) designs all required RO access up to the point where the (new) design process rejected a prior design decision and made a new one. The new (trajectory) of design states would represent the new design; while it would appear to be completely separate to its user, it might well actually only exist as a set of editor commands to allow it to be regenerated "on-the-fly", when required, from the mainstream information held in the database. But this is basically an implementation-dependent optimization.

Principles of Implementation

The system is designer driven and records are kept for each designer. Structure within any one design is formed through linked labels. Each log itself has a label. A label that is used within a designer's logbook becomes linked to every other use of the label within that log. By inspection of Fig. 13.9, we can identify the following relationships:

Page (Label(1)) contains: Label (5), Label (6), Label (7) and Label (8) Page (Label(2)) contains: Label (6), Label (9) and Label (10) Page (Label(3)) contains: Label (10), Label (11) and Label (12) Page (Label(4)) contains: Label(6), Label (14), Label (15) and Label (3)

From these we can see that:

1. Page(Label(1)), Page(Label(2)) and Page(Label(4)) are related through Label(6).
2. Page(Label(2)) and Page(Label(3)) are related through Label(10).
3. Page(Label(3)) and Page(label(4)) are related through Label(3).

The logbook can be thought of as pack of linked cards, much as in a hypercard system, formed into a book. The ability to pull, display and alter the relevant pages is as important as the ability to read the log in the order in which it was created. This provides a historical sequential record formed by a stack of page information. These pages are linked both through their sequential history and through the existence of labels. Each page is itself labelled, i.e. it has a label and contains labels together with sketch and text information. If any label is used on more than one page then the pages are interrelated by that common use (Fig. 13.10). Text and

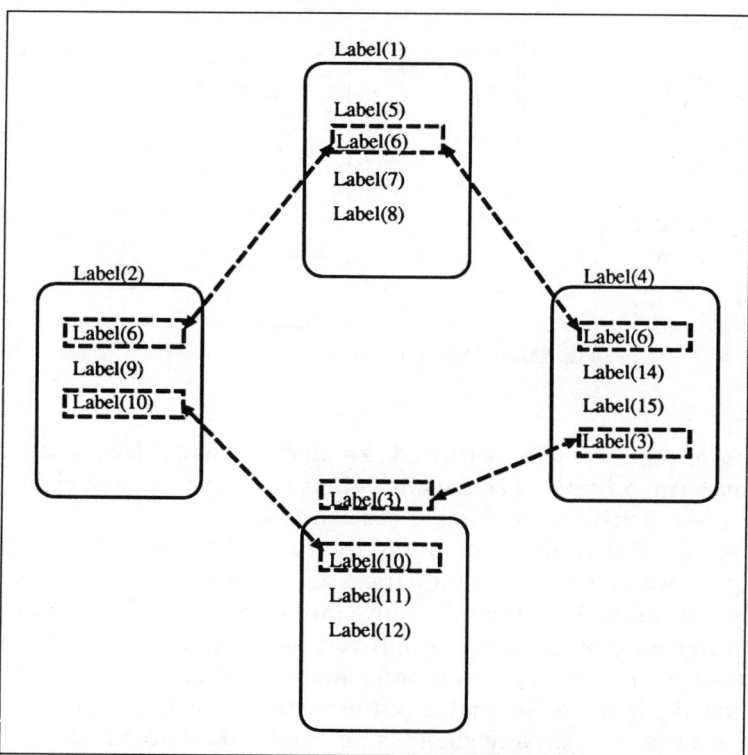

Fig. 13.9. Labels link pages in the logbook.

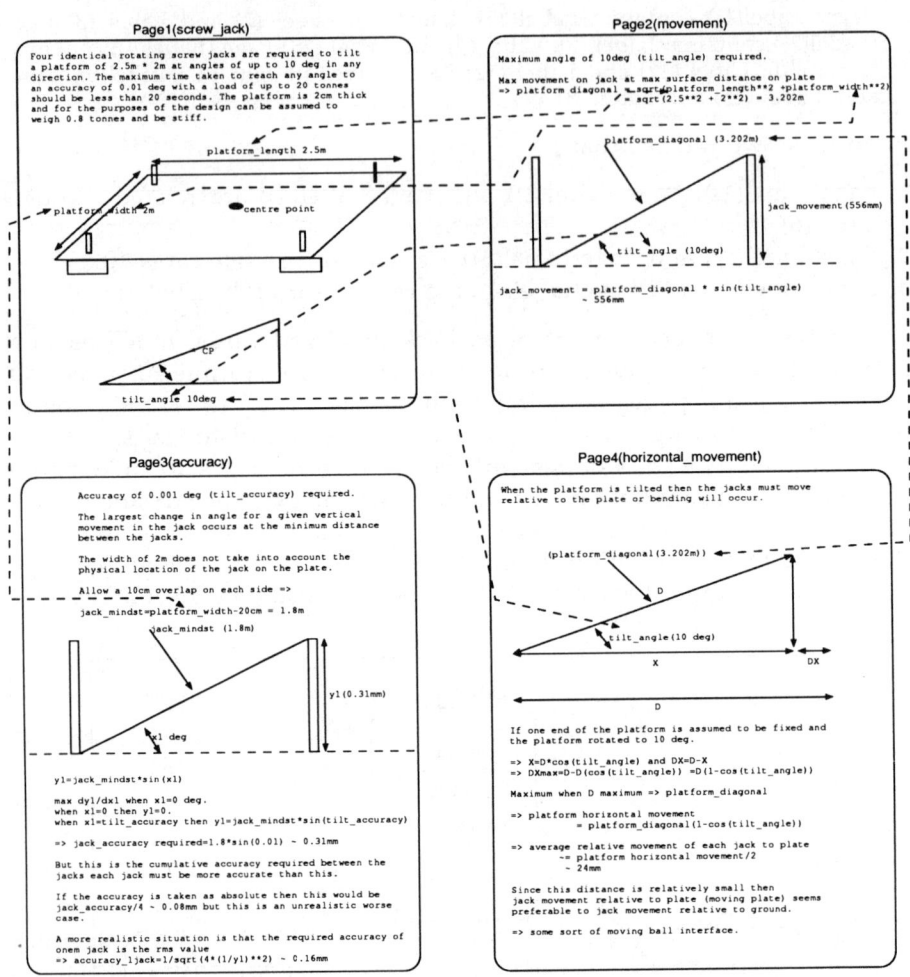

Fig. 13.10. Mutual use of labels links pages.

sketch information is simply treated as a block of data. A label can be active or passive. An example of active labels in use is the relational expression $y = m \times x + c$, where y, m, x and c are active labels.

Changing the definitions of any of the active labels can have repercussions on other pages where the labels are used (Fig. 13.11). A designer must be warned of these repercussions and have the option of retracting or propagating the change. Each design and its designer are both effectively located within a distinct environment, and the design can only be changed while the designer is in that environment. Since the designer cannot change another design, any changes he would like in other designs must be advisory. The designer working on that design must be warned of this

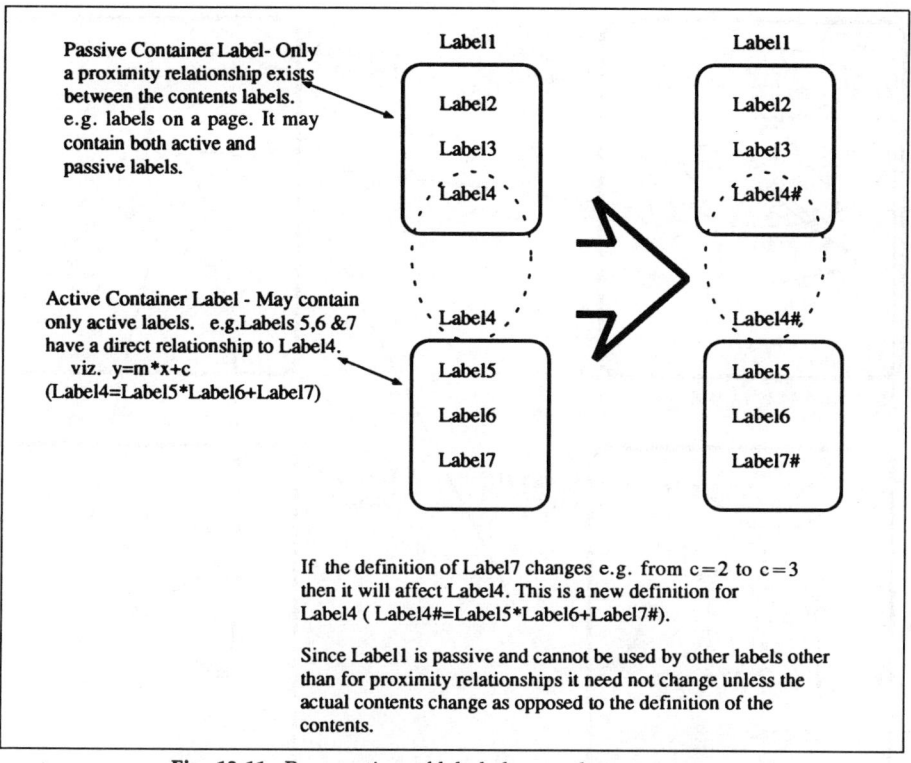

Fig. 13.11. Propagation of label changes between pages.

change and has the authority to accept it, resulting in its propagation, from within the receiving environment.

This interaction takes place in the phase of design in which existing subcontracts are being honoured. Additionally, the design team meetings which draw up these contracts may well use the simultaneous sketching systems designed for this purpose, so that the design record must contain both marks on paper and remarks made between participants. The DHE was not designed for this situation, but rather for that in which individual designers are carrying out work to solve identified problems, as in Streveler (1978). Here, clearly, is an area in which the DHE's capabilities must be extended, perhaps based on Greenberg's GroupKit (Greenberg et al. 1992) or on GO Computing's PenPoint, or on a fusion of these.

A design can be linked to another design (or to the designer's log encapsulating it) by reuse of that piece of design. However, if that piece of design needs to be changed to allow reuse in the new design, an editable copy of the relevant section of the foreign log is entered into the current design logbook, together with a link to the place that the original came from (Fig. 13.12). All pages are managed via a relation in a relational database. Labels and their page occurrences are managed

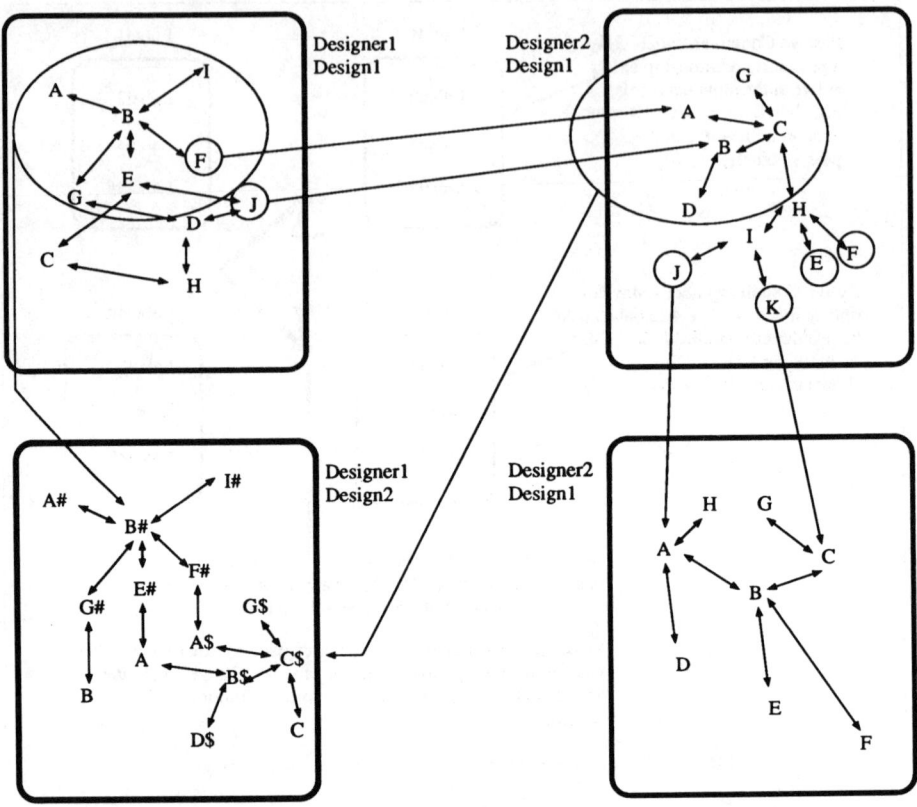

Fig. 13.12. Copying and linking to deal with reuse of designs.

in a separate relation. An expression containing labels that have not been defined is given a null value. The evaluation of the expression label will fail and result in a null value. Labels and their applicable attributes can be used by other tools such as CAD or analysis systems.

13.4 Technology

This section discusses some of the technology currently available and is included to illustrate the approach being taken to the re-implementation of the DHE and its extension to, and integration in, a concurrent engineering or CSCW context. The focus should be seen as being more on the capabilities represented by each technology than on the specific detail of any of them. The emphasis is on the mindset that seeks reuse, rather than re-inventing the wheel.

13.4.1 The SMART Frame Server

The SMART frame server was implemented as part of the SMART project, ESPRIT no. 1609. The frame server provided the infrastructure of the SMART environment. The concept of frame used was rather different from that of Minsky (1980), but provides an extremely general method of describing objects and classes in a similar way. A server–client architecture is used. The server manages a set of independent contexts on behalf of client applications. In each such context, a set of frames is maintained and forms a semantic network, which can be navigated, consulted or updated, by one or more clients. The use of this frame server minimizes access to the disk (except in so far as the virtual memory system of the host is relied on). Furthermore, the server guarantees no back door access to individual objects in the network and notifies any client who has registered an interest when information about the object is updated.

Frames

Frames are typed: the semantics of the frame type is defined in the SMART system by another frame of type *sub-language-specification*, or of a derived type from this. The semantics of an individual frame type can vary between contexts, and appear differently to different applications, each of which may have been started up by preloading a different *sub-language-specification*. or specifications into the context(s) it knows about. That is, its semantic network can be unique to itself even before domain specific knowledge is loaded. Thus, the same frame can be supplied unaltered to various applications, yet appear to be different, presenting only those (in Minsky's terms) slots, facets and methods pertinent to that application. As we have indicated, there are a number of predefined frame types, including *sub-language-specification*, *context* and *window-data*. The last named type is used to define the contents of a window on the display, mapped to a MOTIF widget class. Frames contain attribute value lists. The default type of the value is ASCII text. Repeating attributes are supported; attributes may have sub-attributes.

Semantics

An attribute may have a hook-function associated with it, which leads to a kind of access orientated programming. An important hook-function is make-link: this function makes the attribute value the name of a frame to be installed at that point in the semantic network. Methods associated with a frame type allow the user to define new hook functions. Frame types can specialize other frame types, inheriting their methods and top- level attributes, so that object oriented programming with multiple inheritance is also supported.

Transactions

A transaction mechanism supports graceful error recovery and preserves consistency during complex updates to the semantic network. Frames are stored between sessions of server use in the UNIX filestore in the basic SMART server. A derivative server used in the HERMES project replaces this use of a plain file store by access to relations in a Relational Database (RDB) accessed using Structured Query Language (SQL). Similarly, inquiries to, or via, this server can be made in (extended) SQL.

Frame Browsing and Manipulation

Frame editing and frame browsing tools using the WIMP (Windows, Icons, Mouse, Pointer) style were provided, and, for many applications, the knowledge or information base can be loaded by first defining the domain-specific sub-language, e.g. specifying the frame types, and then creating instances of frames with appropriate values. Application- or domain-specific editors, tools, etc. are easily created. A MOTIF toolset consistent with use of the server has been developed to assist in this.

Context Independence

Management of server sessions is facilitated by the context frame created for each context on its creation. This allows access to internal information about the context, such as the identities of any frames that have been modified but not written to disk.

Open Data Model

It follows from the above that the data model provided by the SMART technology is open. New attributes can be added to existing frame types without any change being needed to existing software. New views of existing frames can be provided simply by using a modified *sub-language-specification*. This makes development of design or other models a simpler matter.

Implementation

Frames (in the original server) were implemented as text files with the names of attributes stored along with their values. The hierarchical structure (within a frame) was controlled by format characters (as in Fortran output files). This proved to be an efficient use of disk space since a single frame could contain a substantial amount of information. When a frame is read into context, the frame type controls the building of efficient data structure in the server's (virtual) memory, which enables efficient access to the frame contents. Linked frames are installed in these structures so that their contents (attributes) appear as sub-attributes of the attributes defined as links. Clients of the frame server issue commands and queries to the server: as in database technology, the queries include the name of the attributes requested. The corresponding retrieval is retained by the server to be the subject of further requests by the client. Typical queries would be update, insert and delete. The server–client communication is built on the reliable transport layer of the UNIX interprocess communication system, and is similar to that of the X Windows system. Applications can thus be remote from the server. Further flexibility is achievable via use of the Sun NFS, or the ECMA-PCTE Open Repository distributed repositories, as in Argento et al. (1992), Harrison et al. (1992) and Duval (1992).

13.4.2 The Blackboard Architecture

The blackboard was introduced thus in 1962:

> Metaphorically we can think of a set of workers all looking at the same blackboard. Each is able to read everything that is on it, and to judge when he has something worthwhile to add to it.

A good account of the architecture is given in Craig (1991). The architecture maintains a globally accessed blackboard database, which records the current state of the emerging solution. Entries in this consist of attribute-value pairs, with the possibility of the values being structures in their own right. Each entry is assigned to one level of abstraction, so that the domain knowledge is segmented to form modules composed of related entities. A correct choice of levels of abstraction is key to the usefulness of any blackboard system. The analogue to the worker in the metaphor is the Knowledge Source (KS), or, more exactly, instantiations of knowledge sources, represented in an internal data structure of the blackboard controller as a KS activation record. Each KS communicates by writing and reading to the blackboard in a format common to all KS, since a KS may read and write at differing levels of abstraction. Ideally, the intervention of each such actor is asynchronous and opportunistic. Achieving this requires a high level of concurrency in the software implementation and one in which recent developments in frame-based technology can be of assistance. The entries on the blackboard are linked together via named relations and frame based technology is appropriate here. The SMART frame server, in fact, provides all the functionality described in Craig (1991). What SMART does not supply is the inference engine, but this is seen as a well-known piece of technology readily implemented.

On the other hand, the IMKA technology (see below) would also appear to have all the functionality required. Since this is involved in a current standardization process, it is seen as an alternative attractive starting point.

The CASSANDRA architecture (Craig 1991) is an attempt to remedy what were seen by its originator as the shortcomings of the blackboard architecture. In addition, it is one form of distributed problem solving architecture, a branch of AI in which the solution of problems is physically or logically distributed across a number of spatially separated problem solvers, a description which fits concurrent engineering well. While both blackboard systems and CASSANDRA systems are capable of considerable parallelism, again essential to concurrent engineering, only CASSANDRA is thought at the time of writing to be capable of effective distribution, although this judgement might well have to be revised in the light of developments such as Khoros. CASSANDRA distributes the problem solving task among a set of level managers. The set may be singleton or it may be a thousand-fold. Each level manager behaves much as the total blackboard did previously, but deals with only one level of abstraction via entries in its local database. Each level manager communicates via a message subsystem employing ports to those level managers, and only to those, who are known to be interested in its solutions or partial solutions. Its knowledge representation and its problem solving method are local to itself. The messages passed between level managers may be in the form of tokens or plain ASCII, requiring parsing by the recipient (in alternatively defining, say, a STEP application protocol, the use of EXPRESS may be appropriate). A CASSANDRA or CASSANDRA-like architecture built using standard technology and protocol definitions seems an exciting prospect, and forms the basis of proposed research (Jenkins 1992). However, the virtual blackboard behaviour requires that the dialogue between the equivalent of CASSANDRA's level manager is established dynamically via Ethernet-like broadcasting of requests for knowledge based assistance, which can be picked up by subscribing distributed KSs. This requirement identifies the crucial area for research for progress. Again, the basic ideas would seem to be found also in the Wide Area Information Service (WAIS) or the X.500 protocol (e.g. the PARADISE project).

13.4.3 Managing Knowledge Assets

Knowledge assets are those ideas, processes and approaches that are used by people to design, manufacture, sell, install and support products and services. Their value may be estimated by comparing the difference between a company's stock value and the book value. In many cases, it has been asserted, the knowledge asset value is over 50% of the total value of a company. The purpose of the Institute for Managing Knowledge Assets (IMKA) initiative is to promote the management of these often isolated pockets of knowledge in order to gain a competitive edge. IMKA supports this mission with appropriate technologies, standards, methodologies and implementations in the areas of knowledge acquisition, knowledge representation and reasoning. The IEEE has established a working group to develop a standard for an Architecture for Knowledge Representation. The functional specification of the IMKA technology is the working document for this group. IEEE members from both IMKA and non-IMKA companies have been invited to participate in the working group. IMKA (1990) addressed 14 basic topics for knowledge management. Phase 2 of the IMKA Technology added, in mid-July 1991, the following: RDB interface, shareable knowledge base (via an Integrated Frame Base (IFB)), Networked Client Server Model (NCSM) and Extended Knowledge Representation (EKR). Knowledge bases can be maintained independently from the applications. The IFB supports multiple simultaneous reads from multiple applications. The NCSM allows an application to use a knowledge base on a separate processor. EKR adds naming of instances, rather than just classes, and user defined types to the Phase 1 capabilities.

13.4.4 Khoros

Khoros is an integrated software development environment for information processing and visualization, based on MIT's X Windows X11R4. Systems developed under Khoros provide multiple users with simultaneous access to the same application via X Windows screens. Khoros components include a visual programming language, code generators for extending the visual language and adding new application packages to the system, an interactive user interface editor, an interactive image display package, an extensive library of image processing, numerical analysis and signal processing routines, and two- and three-dimensional plotting packages. Khoros 1.0 is available as public domain software and version 2 is soon to be released. It supplies seven powerful X Windows applications, over 260 data processing algorithms and five flexible user interface tools, one of which carries out configuration management of distributed source files. Khoros is an open system and is being used by around 1000 sites around the world.

13.5 Technology Transfer

The goal of developed CSCW will produce no practical benefits unless the issue of technology transfer is addressed from the outset. This requires the achievement of two things: the capture of knowledge about design, and the use of this knowledge to guide design. The second implies that we must equip designers with tools that enable or provoke them to improve. Here, the realities of current and near-future technologies will have a fundamental impact on the outcomes of any research programme in concurrent engineering. The rate of technology transfer into small and medium sized enterprises (SMEs) is known to depend on financial standing, cost of the new technology and the attitude of the chief executive officer, in that order. We can do nothing about the first, except via the political process, but the second is within our control, and the way in which we go about reducing that will have an effect on attitudes. The costs of installing the new design technologies will lie, for the user, the receiving enterprise, in three areas: the cost of hardware, the cost of software and the human costs. The cost of hardware is minimized by maximizing the reuse of equipment found in the design offices of SMEs. The use of Open System standards from network technology up to graphical user interfaces will reduce the other costs since the look and feel of software will follow familiar lines as well as, via software reuse, having reduced the cost of producing this new design technology. But the developments within the CSCW field must have taken account of, used and interworked with the standardization processes within ISO 10030 (STEP), which increasingly encapsulate the requirements and knowledge of the leading edge practitioners of engineering design.

These considerations led us to suppose that the computational part of the design infrastructure should consist of a variety of interworking engines, each either an industry standard in its own right, or, where that is not possible, built using standard means, all knowledge/information/data driven. That is, change of behaviour is not achieved by reprogramming, with all of its attendant hazards, but by editing data. This editing process itself might be via engines which are themselves knowledge/information/data driven, so that protection can be given against inadvertent error by researchers themselves. The establishment of a protocol by which these can interwork to create the desired blackboard behaviour is essential to the creation of an open market in design knowledge.

In discussing technology transfer within the ESPRIT ATMOSPHERE project (Lichtenheim 1991), process modelling was seen as a central issue. The software maturity framework of Humphrey (1989) was used as a basis for evaluating the possibilities for technology transfer in systems engineering. In outline, five maturity levels are defined: initial, repeatable, defined, managed and optimizing. The third level, defined, must have been reached for technology transfer to succeed. This is extremely pertinent when considering a programme of research (Jenkins 1991) in which design challenges, in which designers carry out actual design using the toolset, are essential steps in data gathering. It is also significant in considering the situation in which the DHE and concurrent engineering could be introduced. Many firms are wasting millions of pounds trying to implement CASE tools to automate their computer programming. As reported in *The Engineer* (Anonymous 1992), 80% of UK firms who tried CASE have been disappointed by the results. Certain CASE tools are reported to have had a negative impact on productivity and technical quality. It was estimated that many firms have invested upwards of £2 million in CASE but a study of over 800 projects in 75 large enterprises revealed damning evidence against the claims made for CASE. The author of one report emphasized that 95% of companies were not in a position to exploit the potential of integrated CASE. We judge that this is because they lack the necessary process maturity. It is likely that engineering design is in a similar state to software engineering.

13.6 Concluding Remarks

The technical issues facing the re-implementation of the DHE as a tool offering CSCW-style support to concurrent engineering are not the decisive ones. Rather, the cultural, social and design issues will dominate, although the final shape of the DHE will be determined by what is technically feasible. The value of the DHE to an organization will be realized both conceptually and practically only if the value of knowledge assets – the enterprise's shared memory – is given its true worth in the business plan and managerial processes of that enterprise. In this, it shares the challenges faced by all workers in CSCW.

"Nouvelle Design": A Pragmatic Approach to CSCW Systems Building

P.T. Hughes, M.E. Morris and T.A. Plant

14.1 Introduction

Recent growing interest in Computer Supported Cooperative Work (CSCW), is highlighting deficiencies in the classical software development process, and is demanding new tools, processes and techniques. This chapter discusses of some issues involved in designing a CSCW system from an industrial R&D point of view, and will encompass the perspectives of theory, people and pragmatics. As such, we shall be focusing on a novel development process rather than on the product of that process, a detailed description of which can be found in Plant et al. (1991).

The interest in CSCW has been fuelled, at least in part, by a trend towards the development of large global corporations, and the subsequent need for people working within these organizations to consult their colleagues and to collaborate with each other, regardless of their physical location. Global organizations require tools to support the collaborative efforts of distributed groups. These tools must overcome the barriers to interaction between geographically distributed people so that full, effective use can be made of the human and other resources available. The barriers include:

- The cost of global communications
- The time differences between and within continents
- Language barriers
- The time delays inherent in long distance transmissions
- The relative impoverishment of current communications systems
- Users' time and effort costs, e.g. the need to pre-plan videoconferences

The uptake of CSCW will also increase the demand for broadband communications, with changes predicted in both the overall level of communication and in the nature of the transmissions, e.g. to include multimedia data.

We are interested in an area of CSCW concerned with shared window conferencing; examples of previous systems of this type can be found in Greif (1988). The concept of shared window conferencing is so new that most people have great difficulty understanding it. Most people are unable to envisage what the system might look like, what it could do for them, or how they would use it. They therefore have difficulty in expressing any kind of requirements or of seeing the utility of such a system at all. In addition, such requirements are not static and are therefore not capable of being captured in a single pass. As people come to understand the capabilities of the technology provided, they form opinions on what it ought to do for them and how, and their requirements change and develop (Bikson and Eveland 1990). This chapter summarizes our attempts to formulate and practise a rational design process that builds this technology discovery in, resulting in a product whose functionality is largely "designed" by the users of the technology through the process, rather than being determined by non-users in advance. We will sometimes refer to this process as "nouvelle" design in what follows.

Before we examine appropriate design practices for such systems, we will briefly review the background of our current work.

14.2 Background

The work and findings described in this chapter have been carried out as a partner in the EuroCoOp project in the ESPRIT II programme. This project "aims to develop powerful and effective systems for supporting distributed collaborative work" (EuroCoOp Consortium 1990). The consortium includes both industrial and academic partners:

- Triumph Adler (Germany)
- BNR Europe Ltd (UK)
- GMD (Germany)
- Aarhus University (Denmark)
- Jydsk Telefon A.S. (Denmark)
- Great Belt A.S. (Denmark)
- Xtel Services Ltd (UK)
- Empirica (Germany)

The project began in January 1991 and is due to run for two years. The focus of BNR's contribution to this project is a detailed study of the system requirements for synchronous shared window conferencing. In conjunction with voice telephony, shared window conferencing facilities permit groups of users who are not co-located to view and manipulate and discuss, in real time, computer based information (for example, text documents).

Our initial prototype of such a system was developed largely as a technology exercise, not driven by specific user needs. This sort of technology emphasis still appears to be a common failing with many current CSCW systems. A special issue of the *ACM SIGCHI Bulletin* on CSCW systems bemoaned, ". . . the main problem . . . was a lack of analysis of work environments to motivate the need for systems. In the systems work, there seems to be a focus on technology for the sake of technology, without much thought about what people actually need" (Henninger 1991). Our current work is seeking to redress this imbalance by concentrating primarily on the user-centred requirements for CSCW systems design and building. This has resulted in the development of a prototype system called CoOpLab. The process of this later development is the main concern of this chapter.

14.3 Conversation Analysis

One of the main aims in developing CoOpLab was to provide the *minimal* computer based support necessary to facilitate a natural, conversational style of interaction between geographically distributed people. Our main prototype system design and implementation goal was to be as sympathetic as possible to the ways in which people behave in real life. As a result, we looked for a characterization of conversation that might provide a framework for the work we intended doing. We believe we have found such a characterization in Conversation Analysis (CA). CA is a branch of sociolinguistics based on empirical observation of, for example, face-to-face and telephone conversations in both formal and informal settings. The results are descriptive theories concerned with various aspects of talk, and, in particular, descriptions of the socially-mediated "control" mechanisms observed in natural conversations. Comprehensive surveys of CA can be found in Heritage (1988) and Levinson (1983).

Our work benefited in a number of ways from a study of CA. Primarily, CA provided a useful conceptual model of conversation. We were able to use this knowledge to structure the development programme and to guide the analysis of our data. There is also a considerable body of examples in the CA literature, against which we were able to compare our data to give some measure of its "normality" and to highlight any anomalies arising from our approach. Lastly, we adopted the notation for transcribing conversations used in CA.

Our investigations were orientated towards answering such questions as:

- How do people join into an existing conversation?
- How do people become aware that they have joined an ongoing conversation?
- How do people "tune into" the topic of an ongoing conversation?
- How do people recognize who is participating in an ongoing conversation?
- How do people gracefully leave a multi-party conversation?
- How do people close a multi-party conversation?

Most conversational activity exhibits three distinct phases: an opening, a closing and what we have called the conversation "body" (Schegloff 1979). The socially preferred behaviour is for all parties to *achieve* opening the conversation before establishing and exploring conversation topics in the body. Similarly, terminating a conversation satisfactorily is another social achievement. Normally, people do not simply start and stop talking. Natural conversation requires explicit social engagement and disengagement by the participants before what is commonly referred to as "conversation" may occur.

At a more detailed level, the production of utterances is locally managed by the participants, and exhibits a regular structure based on adjacency pairs (Sacks et al. 1978). Each utterance takes the preceding utterance as context and in turn provides the context for the next utterance; this means that the production of an utterance raises expectations as to the likely response. For example, a question is usually followed by an answer, a request by compliance, an offer by acceptance, etc. Production of these preferred responses normally proceeds quite smoothly. However, the production of a "dispreferred" response is signalled in a variety of ways, including abnormally long pauses and the use of conventional markers such as "... well, ...", and "... but, ..." (Levinson 1983). The preferred opening of a conversation is followed by the introduction of a topic ("first topic slot") (Levinson 1983). The first topic slot allows the speaker to give the main reason for the conversation, and is the only point in the conversation where the choice of topic is not constrained by previous turns. In the main body of a conversation, changes of topic are constrained by the content of prior turns. Changes of topic tend to be linked to previous topics in a smooth fashion, with each topic being related in some way to the previous one. The participants of a conversation actively collaborate to maintain topical coherence across the turns. Topic jumps are unusual, and are signalled by a mixture of, for example, increased amplitude, raised pitch, hesitancy, and evidence of self-editing and discontinuity markers, e.g. "Hey!" (Levinson 1983). Sacks et al. (1978) hypothesized that the relative frequency of marked topic jumps was a measure of a poor conversation. The presence or absence of such jumps can therefore be used as a crude measure of the naturalness of a conversation.

Breakdowns in the smooth production of speech are ubiquitous and can occur for a variety of reasons, e.g. misunderstandings, speech not being heard. There are socially mediated mechanisms for repairing such situations (Schegloff et al. 1977). For example, it is preferred for people to recognize and repair their own mistakes ("self-initiated self-repair"). Rather less preferred is "other-initiated self-repair", with "other-initiated other-repair" being the least preferred because of the potential loss of face involved (Levinson 1983). Again, the occurrence of dispreferred behaviours are marked by changes in the pattern of speech.

14.4 User Centred Design

> Design (noun): 1. Mental plan, scheme of attack. 2. Purpose; end in view; adaptation of means to ends. 3. Preliminary sketch for picture, plan of building, machine, etc.; delineation, pattern; art of making these. 4. Established form of a product; general idea, construction from parts.
> Design (verb): 1. Set (thing) apart for person; destine (person, thing) for a service. 2. Contrive, plan; purpose, intend, (. . . design thing or person to be or do something). 3. Make preliminary sketch (picture); draw plan of (future building, etc.). 4. Be a designer.

The *Concise Oxford Dictionary* definitions given above make it clear that design is more than having a plan for the system, it is also about the process of developing and enacting that plan. As stated above, we have adopted a user centred approach to design. The importance of adopting such a stance has been emphasized by Grudin (1991b):

> User involvement in development is especially important for groupware. To succeed, much groupware will have to be used by most or all group members. This means appealing to people with differing roles, backgrounds and preferences. In addition, group dynamics can be very complex, can vary widely from setting to setting, and are not well understood.

The involvement of intended users in the development of CSCW systems is vital if such systems are to be accepted and used in the real world. The history of CSCW is littered with systems that were functionally capable but that have not been accepted by user communities. CSCW systems have to be acceptable to a broad user base, and have to support the wide variety of social and organizational relationships found in the real world. This requires a degree of flexibility unprecedented in single-user systems.

A useful overview of the user centred design process can be found in Open University/Department of Trade and Industry (1990). User centred design means embracing a number of principles:

- Focus on the user's needs, and make user issues the driving force behind design.
- Investigate how users will use the intended system, as well as investigating the functionality required for it.
- Carry our early testing and evaluation with users.
- Design iteratively, evolve the system as requirements emerge.

One of the obstacles to user centred design highlighted by Grudin (1991b) is in finding a design team willing to undertake a truly user centred design process, with all that entails. Fortunately, the culture within our company has been orientated towards user centred design for many years and the benefits of a user centred approach have been demonstrated on a number of occasions.

Classically, system delivery has been approached through three main steps:

- Obtain user requirements
- Produce a specification
- Design, build and deliver the system to the customers

Our approach, loosely based on the "Scandinavian" school of user centred design (e.g. Kyng and Greenbaum 1991), has been different. We start from the viewpoints, that, in the development of a radically new technology:

- People either do not know what they want or cannot express it discursively.
- Designers do not know exactly what people need.
- The usefulness of specific design features of a system is unknown until people have used them in realistic circumstances.

The development of CSCW systems can encounter problems during a classical requirements capture stage, since the aim of many of the proposed systems is to allow people to interact in ways that are not currently possible. The barriers to interaction listed above mean that it is very rare for groups of people to work together if they are not co-located. Where the members of a work group are geographically separated it is very difficult for them to have the kind of *ad hoc* informal interaction that co- location makes possible, but it is precisely this kind of informal interaction that we hope to support with CoOpLab.

A great deal of work had already been done concerned with the development of shared screen and shared window conferencing systems, but much of this work had been technology driven. A number of assumptions relating to the functionality required from a conferencing system have grown up, e.g. the need for shared pointers and floor control systems. We wished to return to basics and re-address the issues from a user centred perspective to see if the assumptions still held. A review of the CA literature had also suggested a number of potential problem areas, but these high-level hypotheses could not be confirmed or prioritized until a real system had been produced and evaluated.

It is well known that people rarely use technology in quite the way that designers expect them to (Bikson and Eveland 1990; Roemer et al. 1986). The only sure way to discover how a system will be used is to give it to people to use as part of their everyday work, and then to observe its use – so-called "contextual evaluation" (Whiteside et al. 1988). However, before a system can be trialled in the field it has to be progressed to levels of functionality, usability and reliability at which any detrimental effects on users' normal activities are minimized. This is something of a "chicken and egg" situation since the system must be at least partially designed before the needs of its users are fully understood. Because of this, the implementation of the system must remain flexible enough for changes to take place at all levels whenever they are required.

Given these properties, the process of user centred design for CSCW is necessarily iterative: a number of design–test–redesign cycles will be gone through when developing any system. This was the approach we used, and can be characterized by the following steps:

A "Requirements capture" → structured observation
    A.1. If the current system meets the current needs of the users, release it, otherwise
    A.2. (Re)build a minimal, but usable, prototype incorporating the key functionality
    A.3. Evaluate it: allow people to use it under "laboratory conditions" with well-defined tasks for each to do, see what they actually do, and ask them what they think of it
B "Specification" → analyse observations
    B.1. Analyse responses and actions from all the observations
    B.2. Formulate a list of prototype system weaknesses and strengths, without attributing, at this stage, any cause for these effects
C "Build and Release" → interpret, modify, iterate
    C.1. Review the list of weaknesses and strengths from the previous iteration against the current list to produce a merged list
    C.2. Examine potential causes to explain the items on the list, and propose modifications to the prototype (or the observational conditions) which attempt to minimize the breakdowns and strengthen the successes
    C.3. Go to A.1

In practice, the steps are not as distinct or as categorical as portrayed above. However, for the purposes of this discussion they will be treated as if they were entirely separate and will be used to structure the rest of the discussion. We will take each step in turn and discuss our experiences during the development of CoOpLab, highlighting some of the problems we had to overcome. In Section 14.8 we will outline some of the main results of applying this technique in shared window systems design.

14.5 Requirements Capture → Structured Observation

A.1. If the current system meets the current needs of the users, release it, otherwise
A.2. (Re)build a minimal, but usable, prototype incorporating the key functionality
A.3. Evaluate it: allow people to use it under "laboratory conditions" with well-defined tasks for each to do, see what they actually do, and ask them what they think of it

The structured observation phase aims to gather a variety of information, principally to:

- Gain an overview of the current system

- Identify strengths and weaknesses of the current system

- Identify user needs that are not being met

These will be discussed in more detail below. However, before we do this, we will outline some important practical details of the structured observation phase.

14.5.1 Basic System Functionality

A point that is so obvious that it can get overlooked is: what user problems is this system intended to remedy? Hence, what is the basic functionality of the system going to be? This aim gives focus and scope to the design phase, and, properly managed, prevents efforts being dissipated through too diffuse or ambitious activities.

In the development of the BNR Europe shared window system, since much everyday activity involves informal interactions in small groups, we decided to concentrate, during 1991, on developing a system for use by groups of up to four people, geographically separated, and who wished to discuss a problem and/or reach a decision in an informal, *ad hoc*, peer-to-peer meeting.

It was assumed that the group members would already be reasonably familiar with each other, and that the system would be used to *supplement*, rather than *replace*, face-to-face contact.

14.5.2 Prototyping

Prototypes do not have to be fully functional. Indeed, the first prototypes may provide only a very limited subset of the functionality of the final system. The main roles of the prototype are to:

- Validate the functionality provided
- Allow the user to critique the look and feel of the system
- Elicit the need for new functionality
- Provide a concrete illustration of the concept

To allow an evolutionary style of system development, the prototype engineering environment should be extensible and capable of being quickly reconfigured as required. Our first prototype was a minimal functionality system, capable only of supporting WYSIWIS (What You See Is What I See) text editing windows. The opening and closing of conferences was under experimenter, not user, control. A configuration is illustrated in Fig. 14.1.

The details of the implementation of the prototypes were mainly influenced by practical considerations. The programming environment chosen made use of modular, object-oriented, techniques and the CLOS-based LispWorks[1] rapid prototyping environment (Plant et al. 1991). This environment has an industry standard X Windows user interface, and in line with company standards, the OSF/Motif look-and-feel widget set was used. Because LispWorks is available for a variety of vendors' platforms, the prototype can be used in several work environments.

In addition, extra functionality, invisible to the subjects, was provided for instrumenting the prototype. This included a tool for easy configuration of the system prior to an evaluation session, and a component that recorded the user interface and selected system events generated by each user when interacting with the system.

14.5.3 Evaluation

The evaluation of a system can be used to satisfy a number of objectives. For example, it can be used to:

- Compare alternative versions or systems
- Test design decisions
- Test for correct functioning
- Assess Human–Computer Interaction (HCI) issues
- Assess the match between task goals and system functions
- Obtain further requirements

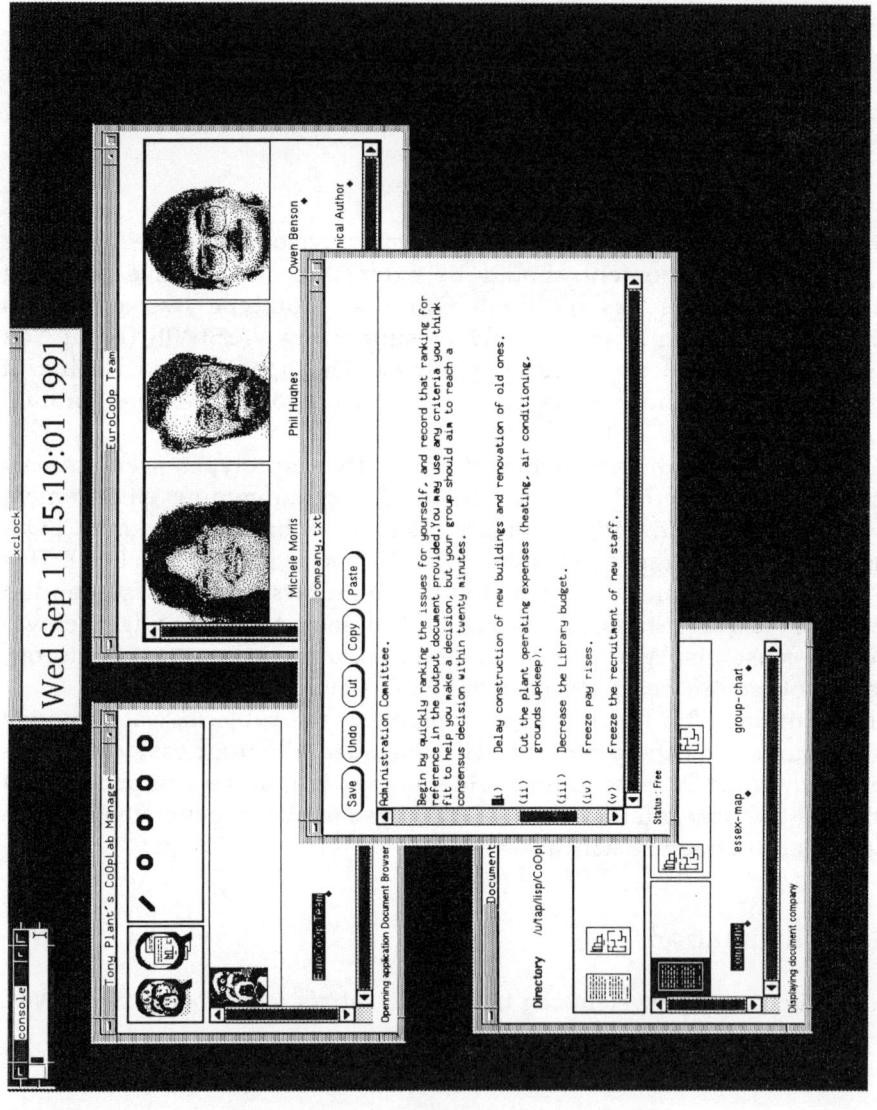

Fig. 14.1. Example experimental screen layout.

One common way to conduct usability evaluations is to guide the user through one or more structured tasks that are intended to test each aspect of the system in turn. The problem with this style of evaluation is that it is all too easy to overlook something, and there is relatively little scope for the user to stretch the system beyond its planned limits. However, this is precisely the kind of usage systems get once released. It was argued above that designers cannot predict how people will use systems, or even who those users may be (Roemer et al. 1986). We agree with Bødker and Grønbaek (1991) over the utility of destructive testing. Destructive testing allows the users to interact with a system in any way they choose to solve a task while observing where the breakdowns occur. As a result of this freedom of action, users will try to use the system in ways not intended by the designers and will try to access functions not yet provided. We believe that destructive testing is not only the best way to create robust systems, but is also a powerful way to elicit user requirements and trigger new design ideas. As such, system "failures" and "user errors" are to be welcomed as sources of inspiration rather than as signs of failure.

Task analysis is intended to examine how people currently perform a task with the aim of working out how to improve this with the new system. It is extremely difficult to perform a task analysis for shared window conferencing since there is no obvious current task to analyse. Shared window conferencing systems provide the *infrastructure* to support a broad range of tasks and applications. Some of these exist and are in use now, but many are currently impossible and/or unforeseen. Indeed, it has been suggested that basing the new systems on the old can have negative consequences on system development and prevent the full utilization of the capabilities of the new technologies (Egido 1990).

Observational evaluation is particularly useful in conjunction with the iterative development process we used. It generates rich qualitative data, but data analysis can be time consuming and demanding on resources. We chose to collect data from several diverse sources:

- System event logging
- Video and audio recording of the subjects
- Questionnaires

In practice, each of these techniques required adaptation for use in a multi-user environment.

In the past there have been attempts to evaluate CSCW systems, but these have either concentrated on strict experiment, or have been concerned with systems that were either asynchronous or where the users were co-located. A number of such evaluations can be found in Greif (1988) and Greenberg (1991). There is *no* widely accepted methodology for evaluating synchronous multi-user systems where the users are geographically separated.

Current evaluation techniques have evolved to assist in the evaluation of single-user systems. Evaluating CSCW systems provides additional challenges to these techniques. The evaluation must cover not only the interactions of multiple users with the system, but also capture and analyse data relating to the social interactions between the users. We believed that it was possible to adapt many of the existing techniques to this situation, but new techniques will undoubtedly also be required to handle multi-user systems, especially where the users are geographically distributed. The development of new techniques will take time and will be based on perceived need. This will come from the failure of standard techniques to adapt to the multiple, distributed-users situation.

14.5.4 Subject Selection

For CSCW systems to be successful, they must actually be used by a wide range of people in their work environment. The potential user group is so broad that identifying a suitably representative set of subjects needs to be done with care. Ideally, user population factors such as age, sex, profession and organizational position all need to be adequately reflected in subject set. Clearly, this is difficult with a small set of subjects. However, these factors should be known and presented for the subject set, so that in the interpretation of the observations any biases are explicitly rather than implicitly treated.

Our approach to this problem has been simply to recruit initially subjects from within a local division of our own company, and then to broaden the subject base as the system has developed.

14.5.6 Types of Data

System Event Data

System event logging is commonly used to capture a user's interaction with the system. In our particular system, we were concerned about conflicting actions performed by users and the need, or lack of need, for formal floor control. We therefore used the time-stamped event log to search for, e.g. simultaneous actions on the same document by different users. A simplified example log is shown in Fig. 14.2.

The main problem with designating events is the minimum resolution to be used. At the fine-grain level of single keystroke capture and the like, far too much data is collected. At coarser levels of resolution more information is lost. We decided not to capture events at the single key press level, but at the level of:

hh:mm:ss	abc	Application	Extend	<filename>	(1) can now see this document
hh:mm:ss	abc	Key-<Return>	Text-input	<filename>	(1) typed: Requirements from the UK
hh:mm:ss	abc	def Trying to connect to def			
hh:mm:ss	abc	def now have screen connection			
hh:mm:ss	abc	def try sharing document			
hh:mm:ss	abc	def shared document <filename> now available			
hh:mm:ss	abc	Application	Extend	<filename>	(2) can now see this document
hh:mm:ss	def	Key-<Return>	Text-input	<filename>	(2) typed: 2 single rooms and 1 double
hh:mm:ss	def	Button-release	Save	<filename>	(2) has saved text to file

Fig. 14.2. Illustration of a log file contents.

- Window opening and closure operations
- Button presses
- Scrollbar movements
- Lines of text input

Users of CSCW systems do not just interact with the system, they also interact among themselves; in the case of dispersed users this social interaction is mediated (or not) by the system itself. Event logging can be extended to record some of this mediated social behaviour. For example:

- Requesting a voice/screen connection
- The refusal of a connection request
- The opening of a connection
- The closing of a connection
- The sharing of a document

Besides recording the action, the system also recorded who performed the action and which document was concerned. Recording the document name is useful when all the logs from a particular session are sorted into a single log. Experience has shown that the two most useful sorts to perform are by time and by user. The former can be used to gain an overall picture of the session, and the latter can be used to trace the actions of an individual.

It is also valuable to record how many people can see a particular document. When only one person can see the document, then there is no potential for conflict, but once two or more people are interacting with a document the potential for conflict increases.

Audio and Video Data

The role of audio recording changes when evaluating multi-user systems that incorporate an audio channel for communication. Instead of being used to collect verbal protocols describing the user's interaction with the system, audio recording is mainly used to record conversation among the users. The conversation is used to mediate the social interactions between the users (e.g. to discuss the allocation of tasks, to negotiate access to computer based resources, to formulate a joint strategy for solving a problem, etc.) and for discussing potential solutions to the problem and the exchange of information. In essence, the audio channel changes emphasis from being solely a source of data about the system, to being also a major source of data on the social and task related aspects of the communication.

Video recording is used to capture the visible aspects of a user's activity with the system. It is normal practice to use two or three cameras for single-subject evaluations. However, this level of surveillance per subject in CSCW systems evaluation becomes difficult and costly. We therefore had to compromise on the degree of surveillance, by using a single camera per subject; this is explained in more detail below.

Questionnaire Data

Questionnaires were designed in-house for our evaluations. They contained a mix of open questions and semantic differential scales assessing a wide variety of issues, including the hardware and its layout, the software, and the users' subjective satisfaction with the task and the conversation.

14.6 System Specification → Analyse Observations

B.1. Analyse responses and actions from all the observations
B.2. Formulate a list of prototype system weaknesses and strengths, without attributing, at this stage, any cause for these effects

14.6.1 Aims of Analysis Phase

The aim of this phase is principally to identify, from the evaluation data, all the system weaknesses and to identify any unforeseen uses which the system supports successfully, or could be modified to do so. In the case of shared window conferencing, we regarded weaknesses in the system as anything that tended to cause breakdowns in the natural flow of conversation. In evaluations, this frequently resulted in users discussing the system itself, rather than using it transparently to progress their assigned tasks.

14.6.2 Data Analysis

System Event Log Analysis

Experience has shown that one of the intended uses for the log data, that of conflict detection, is problematic for the fundamental reason that "conflict" is a term that only has meaning within the current social context defined by the participants. For example, a conflict of action might be assumed when one subject scrolls-up a shared document and, almost simultaneously, another scrolls-down. However, this definition is unsatisfactorily dependent on the period time chosen, and in this case could illustrate finely coordinated cooperation rather than conflict.

In addition, actions that are separated by longer periods of time can actually be conflicting. For example, a user highlights and copies a piece of text to paste into another document, another user then scrolls the document away from the target area before the first user has time to paste the information. Their actions may take several seconds, but they undoubtedly clash in their intentions for the document.

We have found that the best way of identifying real conflict of action is to compare the activity logs with the audio transcripts and the video recordings of the subjects' screens: to judge conflict on the basis of the subjects' interpretations and responses to their activities. The additional contextual information this supplies is usually sufficient to distinguish genuine conflicts from apparent conflicts.

Audio Analysis

A considerable amount of data can be generated from even a few minutes of conversation, and analysing this can be very time consuming. It is therefore necessary to define clearly the aims of the analysis and to have a theoretical framework to give structure to it. Since we were interested in the way that using the CoOpLab system affected the content and structure of informal conversation, we based our analysis on the descriptive theories of CA.

The exact form of data analysis required depends very much on the aims underlying the evaluation. The analysis of the CoOpLab data began with a quantitative analysis of the data. The transcripts were used to generate statistics on the number of utterances produced by each subject. A single utterance was defined as all the words spoken before another subject spoke, including short pauses. Where a subject's utterance was overlapped, the words spoken to the end of the overlap were considered to be one utterance, and any subsequent non-overlapped words were considered to be a second utterance by that subject. This definition is congruent with CA theory. Statistical tests were used to investigate the interaction of variables such as task role and gender on the amount of speech produced by each subject. The data was also searched for correlations between the amount of speech each subject produced and their use of the system as recorded by software logging. Details can be found in Morris (1991).

The transcripts were then subjected to a more qualitative analysis. As summarized above, CA describes the structure of conversations and the management strategies used to control the flow of conversation. This structure provided the framework for the analysis and helped to isolate segments of the transcripts for more detailed investigation. For example, the openings and closings in the transcripts were isolated and compared to the expected pattern – any changes in the patterns were noted.

The transcripts were also used to investigate users' interaction with a system analogously to their interaction with each other. The transcripts were searched for observations on the system, and for signs of problems, e.g. "What happened there?". These incidents received further elaboration by consulting the software logs and, if necessary, the video of the interaction. This ensured the correct interpretation of the incident by providing more context than is available in the transcript alone.

Video Analysis

The main aim of video analysis is to diagnose the problems observed from a user centred perspective, and assess their frequency of occurrence and the likely causes. This information is then used to prioritize the problems and to generate potential solutions. Since we had multiple users for each session, the number of video tapes generated for analysis was large (Phase 2 of CoOpLab generated over 900 minutes of video on twenty tapes). The analysis of each tape can be time consuming and although analysis tools can help to reduce this time, it is still not an exercise to be undertaken lightly. The approach developed for CoOpLab, based on Wright et al. (1989), involves performing a swift overview analysis for each tape to pick up the main usability problems with the system, and in particular problems with the interface. Interesting incidents, worthy of a deeper analysis, are identified from the audio transcripts and the event logs. The video of the incident is then used to provide additional context to enable correct diagnosis of the problem. This pre-selection of potentially useful incidents helps to limit the amount of time spent in detailed analysis.

14.7 Build and Release → Review, Interpret, Modify

14.7.1 Aims of this Phase

The aims of this phase are summarized by the wording of the steps given above:

C.1. Review the list of weaknesses and strengths from the previous iteration against the current list to produce a merged list

C.2. Examine potential causes to explain the items on the list, and propose modifications to the prototype (or the observational conditions) which attempt to minimize the breakdowns and strengthen the successes

and lastly, to re-iterate by redesigning a structured observation phase and proceeding with steps A and B.

It is important to enforce the separation of identifying and discussing problems with the system, from proposing "fixes". This is to allow the design team to be primarily guided by focusing on the needs of the users and their problems with the prototype rather than by their own prejudices and technology concerns.

There are several reasons why we stepped back from providing quick fixes. These are: (i) deeper underlying weaknesses (or strengths) may be swamped by superficial patching, preventing them from being exposed and dealt with (or exploited); (ii) to encourage the development of the system into areas unforeseen by the designers, but for which the users, through their interactions with the prototypes, are expressing a need.

In less focused environments that our own, clearly such findings could spawn whole new subtrees of iterative design work, which ultimately may lie far from the originally formulated goals of the system. This, we feel, is a strength of the process, rather than a weakness.

Having briefly outlined the general features of the iterative design process, the next section discusses our own application of it.

14.8 Application of the Design Process

14.8.1 Programme

A full account of the evaluations we carried out can be found in Morris (1991) and Morris et al. (1992). Because of time constraints we decided to map the iterations of the design process onto the conversational achievements of openings, closings, topicalization and repair in the following way:

- *First phase:* the conversation body:
  - references to textual information
  - turn-taking and repair
  - two-party and four-party conversations
  - computer supported versus voice-only conferences
- *Second phase:* openings and closings:
  - topicalization, integration of document sharing
  - transition from two-party to multi-party

– reference to pictorial and textual information
– user feedback issues
– workstation ergonomics, e.g. headset, telephone configurations

- *Third phase:* repair and other issues (planned at the time of writing):
  – general conversation repair mechanisms
  – broader semantics for document sharing
  – system start-up and close-down
  – integration with current working environment
  – people accessibility issues
  – information access issues

In the first phase, by comparing the results from the minimal prototype with those from voice-only conference calls, we were able to separate the problems resulting from the use of CoOpLab from those concerned with multi-party discourse in general. Having learned much from the first phase, in the second and third phases, we focused on the computer based support and did not look at "control" voice-only and pen-and-paper evaluations.

Questionnaires were designed in-house for all evaluations. They contained a mix of open questions and semantic differential scales assessing a wide variety of issues relating to the hardware, the software, the users' subjective satisfaction with the task and the conversation etc. Since these techniques were not measuring the social aspects of the task directly, they were not adversely affected by the multi-user nature of the system.

14.8.2 Evaluation

The subjects worked on problem solving and decision making tasks based on those found in the literature (e.g. Krueger and Chapanis 1980). The first- and second-phase evaluations were conducted in a large open-plan office at BNR Europe, rather than in a usability laboratory, which ensured that the subjects were distributed and in a familiar environment. In addition, workshops run by a EuroCoOp partner using the first CoOpLab prototype were held in Germany. Participants in the workshops came from the project planning departments of a number of non-consortium companies The workshops validated and expanded the requirements captured at BNR Europe, and exposed the system to users from a different culture working in a different application domain.

The third phase will see a move towards a truly contextual style of evaluation. A number of technology trials are planned, both in-house, small-scale trials on an informal basis, and more structured trials at other company sites. It is hoped to include sites outside the UK. The trials will enable data to be collected relating to the real-life usage of CoOpLab in everyday work by a wide variety of company personnel. The trials should

"Nouvelle Design": A Pragmatic Approach to CSCW Systems Building

P.T. Hughes, M.E. Morris and T.A. Plant

14.1 Introduction

Recent growing interest in Computer Supported Cooperative Work (CSCW), is highlighting deficiencies in the classical software development process, and is demanding new tools, processes and techniques. This chapter discusses of some issues involved in designing a CSCW system from an industrial R&D point of view, and will encompass the perspectives of theory, people and pragmatics. As such, we shall be focusing on a novel development process rather than on the product of that process, a detailed description of which can be found in Plant et al. (1991).

The interest in CSCW has been fuelled, at least in part, by a trend towards the development of large global corporations, and the subsequent need for people working within these organizations to consult their colleagues and to collaborate with each other, regardless of their physical location. Global organizations require tools to support the collaborative efforts of distributed groups. These tools must overcome the barriers to interaction between geographically distributed people so that full, effective use can be made of the human and other resources available. The barriers include:

- The cost of global communications
- The time differences between and within continents
- Language barriers
- The time delays inherent in long distance transmissions
- The relative impoverishment of current communications systems
- Users' time and effort costs, e.g. the need to pre-plan videoconferences

The uptake of CSCW will also increase the demand for broadband communications, with changes predicted in both the overall level of communication and in the nature of the transmissions, e.g. to include multimedia data.

We are interested in an area of CSCW concerned with shared window conferencing; examples of previous systems of this type can be found in Greif (1988). The concept of shared window conferencing is so new that most people have great difficulty understanding it. Most people are unable to envisage what the system might look like, what it could do for them, or how they would use it. They therefore have difficulty in expressing any kind of requirements or of seeing the utility of such a system at all. In addition, such requirements are not static and are therefore not capable of being captured in a single pass. As people come to understand the capabilities of the technology provided, they form opinions on what it ought to do for them and how, and their requirements change and develop (Bikson and Eveland 1990). This chapter summarizes our attempts to formulate and practise a rational design process that builds this technology discovery in, resulting in a product whose functionality is largely "designed" by the users of the technology through the process, rather than being determined by non-users in advance. We will sometimes refer to this process as "nouvelle" design in what follows.

Before we examine appropriate design practices for such systems, we will briefly review the background of our current work.

14.2 Background

The work and findings described in this chapter have been carried out as a partner in the EuroCoOp project in the ESPRIT II programme. This project "aims to develop powerful and effective systems for supporting distributed collaborative work" (EuroCoOp Consortium 1990). The consortium includes both industrial and academic partners:

- Triumph Adler (Germany)
- BNR Europe Ltd (UK)
- GMD (Germany)
- Aarhus University (Denmark)
- Jydsk Telefon A.S. (Denmark)
- Great Belt A.S. (Denmark)
- Xtel Services Ltd (UK)
- Empirica (Germany)

The project began in January 1991 and is due to run for two years. The focus of BNR's contribution to this project is a detailed study of the increase the ecological validity of the data and highlight some of the social and organizational issues relating to the acceptance of CSCW.

Subject Groups

Because of the very limited functionality of the first prototype, it was felt that we could not expose computer-naive personnel to the system. This first system was likely to have a considerable number of usability problems and we wished to avoid alienating such staff, since their cooperation was vital to later stages of the project. Therefore, we initially drew the subject group mainly from engineering staff. As the system began to develop we attempted to extend this to include personnel from all areas of our company, including administration and finance, and from all levels, e.g. managers, secretaries, clerks. So far, we have been only partially successful in achieving this aim. Despite our best efforts to prevent it, our user sample has been somewhat biased towards the young, male IT engineering staff. While this is possibly an accurate reflection of the composition of personnel within the company, it reduces the generalizability of our results to other companies and domains. However, we are continuing our efforts to broaden the user base by means of workshops and technology trials in the field.

Video Capture

As mentioned above, if a similar level of surveillance per subject in single-user evaluations is used for multi-user systems, resourcing becomes costly and difficult. We compromised and used a single camera per subject to record the workstation screen. This meant that we lost some data relating to the subject's non-verbal behaviours, e.g. posture and facial expression, but found that this was not critical for the diagnostic role of the video data. Because our building infrastructure was not specifically set up for the transmission of video signals, we used a video recorder at each subject site.

If multiple tapes are to be synchronized for editing purposes, some form of synchronizing signal from a single source is required. Normally a time code generator is used to produce this signal. However, transporting the signal from the generator to multiple video recorders is subject to the same problems as transporting the camera signal to a central video recorder. The use of a time code generator had to be abandoned for our evaluations. However, a synchronizing signal was still required. Our solution was to synchronize the system clocks on each workstation, and to display the current time to the nearest second in an on-screen digital clock, which was captured on the video tape.

We believed that data relating to the social interaction of the group could be gleaned from the video data if we could replay all four tapes from a session simultaneously. In practice, this proved far from simple. It is impossible to view multiple monitors simultaneously, and so it was decided to edit the four tapes from each session onto a single tape. Even though we had access to professional quality equipment, it was not of a sufficiently high quality to cope with this kind of editing and a number of problems were encountered, including:

- Loss of signal due to the multiple edits involved
- Interference
- Difficulty in synchronously starting multiple tapes
- Difficulty in synchronizing the tapes
- Variable video recorder running speeds
- Image distortion in both horizontal and vertical planes

Once the editing had been completed, the sizes of the four images were so small that it was very difficult to see the cursor movements and other fine details that we wished to analyse. We have had to abandon the use of combined tapes in favour of analysing individual tapes.

Audio Capture

Capturing conversation can prove problematical when users are geographically distributed. The simplest solution is to tap into the system's own audio channel, e.g. by using a telephone answering machine. We found that this introduced a new constraint in that only one conversation could be recorded at a time. Since we had four people collaborating on a task it was possible for two telephone calls to happen simultaneously, with a consequent loss of data. The solution was to prevent more than one call happening by setting up a single conference call, controlled by the experimenter, to which all other participants joined. The advantage of this was that we were able to ensure that we had most of the three- and four-party conversations and were able to investigate the way people managed multi-party conversations. It turned out that the users felt that this arrangement was reasonably natural, and no adverse comments were received. This arrangement also side-stepped a feature of the then PABX, whereby if the initiator of a conference call hung up their phone, the whole call died.

14.9 Summary and Conclusions

The real-world demand for CSCW systems is increasing rapidly but few of the currently available systems have (i) been developed with user needs in mind, or (ii) have any grounding in social theory. We found

that an iterative user-involved design process, with a basis in independent social observation, can be used in a commercial setting, and has given us a number of benefits both in the product of the design process itself and in a logical structure for our development programme.

In this section we review the results of our practising this "novelle" design process during 1991 and the first quarter of 1992. The results have come in several related areas, as discussed in the following subsections.

Better Software

The prototype was more robust in actual use and was much more matched to users' actual needs than could have been expected without user involvement. In particular, we have observed that the structure and management of shared screen conferences are broadly analogous to those used in any informal conversation and that people were easily able to cope with the few differences seen. Both the first- and second-phase evaluations showed that for small groups (i.e. up to four people) the normal conversational protocols were adequate for controlling turn- taking in the conversation. Users were also able to adapt these social protocols to control access to shared documents and no additional turn-taking mechanisms were required.

Users were able to make unambiguous references to people in the group and to people in the task. They were also able to refer successfully to system objects (hardware and software), geographical locations mentioned in the task information, time and aspects of the conversation itself. Additional tools, e.g. shared pointers, are not a prerequisite for successful shared screen conferences where the group size is small. We acknowledge that this finding may break down as the size of the group increases.

Users were comfortable with the functionality provided, which allowed them to initiate and join into multi-party conversations and to share their documents with the rest of the group.

The prototype was flexible enough to allow every subject group to approach the task in a different way, for example with different strategies or different patterns of connectivity between group members. This is an important implicit design objective, since it is not possible to predict how people will use shared window conferencing facilities. The implications of this on the enabling technology are still emerging, for example, the need for communications bandwidth on demand.

Effort was Focused where Needed

By focusing on observed user needs, through the active involvement of users, development effort was deployed much more effectively than in the classical design process.

Prototypes More Easily Productizable

We have developed a prototype system through this process which is a stable basis for re-engineering into product quality software.

The "laboratory"-based evaluations provided much useful data, but to increase the validity of future evaluations, to increase the generalizability of the results, and to broaden the subject base, field-based iterations need to be carried out. This will allow the prototype to be used by people for their everyday tasks, in our case for shared window conferencing. We believe that such trials will inevitably expose many new possibilities, and will greatly facilitate the development of shared window systems in particular and CSCW systems in general.

During the early part of 1992 the system has been extended to form a portable, stand-alone system for use in the field. This has involved the development of modules to handle the launch and shut-down of the system and for the graceful withdrawal of people and documents from an ongoing conference. In addition, the semantics of document sharing have been extended to give people more control over the editing and copying of their documents.

Acknowledgements We would like to acknowledge the partial support of the CEC for this work. Thanks are due to our colleagues at Empirica GmbH for their cooperation in running a workshop in which the CoOpLab system was used.

Note

1   Harlequin Limited, Barrington Hall, Barrington, Cambridge, UK.

References

Albrechtsen H (1990) Software concepts: knowledge organisation and the human interface. In: Proceedings of the ISKO Conference, Darmstadt, August

Anderson JR (1985) Cognitive Psychology and Its Implications. WH Freeman, New York

Anderson RJ and Sharrock WW (1992) Can organisations afford knowledge? Human–Computer Interaction (in press)

Anonymous (1988) Yard investigates gang-busting system. Computer Talk, March, 14–27

Anonymous (1992) This Week. Tools a waste for many buyers. The Engineer 274(7090): 15

Argento A, Bonferini C, Dematte F and Manca S (1992) CMA PCTE, CORBA and ATIS "the easy way to O-O ECMA PCTE services". PCTE Newsletter 10: 20–27

Austin JL (1962) How To Do Things With Words. Oxford University Press, Oxford

Bannon L and Schmidt K (1989) CSCW: four characters in search of a context. In: Proceedings of the First European Conference on Computer Supported Cooperative Work (EC-CSCW '89), Gatwick, 13– 15 September, pp 358–372

Bannon L, Robinson M and Schmidt K (ed) (1991) Proceedings of the Second European Conference on Computer Supported Cooperative Work (EC-CSCW '91), Amsterdam, September. Kluwer, Dordrecht

Barwise J and Etchemendy J (1991) Visual information and valid reasoning. In: Zimmerman W (ed) Visualization in Mathematics. Mathematical Association of America, pp 9–24

Barwise J and Perry J (1983) Situations and Attitudes. MIT Press, Cambridge, MA

Baskerville R, Travis J and Truex D (1992) Intervention – Researching information technology in postmodern organisations, Working Paper 92-214, School of Management, Binghampton, New York

Baydere S, Casey T, Chuang S, Handley M, Ismail N and Sasse A (1993) Multimedia conferencing as a tool for collaborative writing: A case study. In: Sharples M (ed) Computer Supported Collaborative Writing. Springer-Verlag, London, pp 113–135

Beard D, Palaniappan M, Humm A, Banks D, Nair A and Shan Y-P (1990) A visual calendar for scheduling group meetings. In: Proceedings of the Conference on Computer Supported Cooperative Work (CSCW-90), Los Angeles, CA, 7–10 October. ACM, New York, pp 279–291

Beattie F (1983) Talk: An Analysis of Speech and Non-Verbal Behaviour in Conversation. Open University Press, Milton Keynes

Beaudouin-Lafon M and Karsenty A (1992) Transparency and awareness in a real-time groupware system. In: Proceedings of the ACM SIGGRAPH Symposium on User Interface Software and Technologies (UIST-92). ACM Press, New York, pp 171–180

Bebbington J (1992) Research proposal May 1992 to May 1993. In: EDRC Final Report, Engineering Design Research Centre, Glasgow G20 0XA, July

Bentley R, Rodden T, Sawyer P, Sommerville I, Hughes JA, Randall D and Shapiro DZ (1992) Ethnographically-informed systems design for air traffic control. In: Proceedings of the Conference on Computer Supported Cooperative Work (CSCW-92), Toronto, Canada, 31 October–4 November. ACM, New York

Berger PL and Berger B (1976) Sociology: A Biographical Approach. Penguin, Harmondsworth

Bezem M (1987) Consistency of rule-based expert systems, Technical Report, Centre for Mathematics and Computer Science, July

Bikson TK and Eveland JD (1990) The interplay of work group structures and computer support. In: Galegher J, Kraut RE and Egido C (ed) Intellectual Teamwork: The Social and Technological Foundations of Cooperative Work. Lawrence Erlbaum, Hillsdale, NJ, pp 245–290

Birmingham WP and Siewiorek DP (1989) Automated knowledge acquisition for a computer hardware synthesis system. Knowledge Acquisition 1: 321–340

Bisgaard K, Boldyreff C, Elzer P, Hall P, Keilmann J, Kern H, Olsen L, Witt J and Zhang J (1990) The Practitioner REuse Support System (PRESS): a tool supporting software reuse. In: Proceedings of the Third Annual Workshop: Methods and Tools for Reuse, CASE Center, Syracuse University, 13–15 June

Bly SA (1988) A use of drawing surfaces in different collaborative settings. In: Proceedings of the Conference on Computer Supported Cooperative Work (CSCW-88), Portland, OR, September. ACM, New York, pp 250–257

Bly SA and Minneman SL (1990) Commune: a shared drawing surface. In: Proceedings of the Conference on Office Information Systems, Boston, MA, April. ACM, New York, pp 184–192

Bødker S (1991) Activity theory as a challenge to systems design. In: Nissen HE, Klein HK and Hirschheim R (ed) Information Systems Research – Contemporary Approaches and Emergent Traditions. Elsevier, Amsterdam, pp 551–564

Bødker S and Grønbaek K (1991) Cooperative prototyping: users and designers in mutual activity. In: Greenberg S (ed) Computer Supported Cooperative Work and Groupware. Academic Press, London, pp 331–358

Boland RJ (1991) Information system use as a hermeneutic process, In: Nissen HE, Klein HK and Hirschheim R (ed) Information Systems Research – Contemporary Approaches and Emergent Traditions. Elsevier, Amsterdam, pp 439–458

Boland RJ and Day WF (1989) The experience of system design – A hermeneutic of organisational action. Scandinavian Journal of Management 5(2): 87–104

Boldyreff C (1990) Supporting system design from reusable design frameworks. In: Proceedings of the Second International Conference on Information System Developer's Workbench Methodologies, Techniques, Tools and Procedures, University of Gdansk, 25–28 September

Boldyreff C (1992) A design framework for software concepts in the domain of steel production. In: Proceedings of the Third International Conference on Information System Developer's Workbench Methodologies, Techniques, Tools and Procedures, University of Gdansk, 22–24 September

Boldyreff C and Krohn U (1992) The Practitioner REuse Support System (PRESS): a consideration from the standpoint of tool interconnection. In: Proceedings of the Fourth IFAC/IFIP Workshop on Experience with the Management of Software Projects, Austria, 18–19 May

Bourdieu P (1977) Outline of a Theory of Practice. Cambridge University Press, Cambridge

Bourdieu P (1991) Language and Symbolic Power. Polity Press, Cambridge (translated by Thompson JB)

Bowers J and Churcher J (1988) Local and global structuring of computer mediated communication: developing linguistic perspectives on CSCW in COSMOS. In: Proceedings of the Conference on Computer Supported Cooperative Work (CSCW-88) Portland, OR, September. ACM, New York, pp 125–139

Bratman M (1987) Intention, Plans, and Practical Reason. Harvard University Press, Boston, MA

Brown DC (1986) The compilation of routine design knowledge, Technical Report, AI Research Group, CS Department, Worcester Polytechnic Institute, Worcester, MA

Brown DC and Chandrasekaran B (1986) Knowledge and control for a mechanical design expert system. IEEE Computer 19(7): 92–100

Brown DC and Chandrasekaran B (1989) Design Problem Solving, Knowledge Structures and Control Strategies. Pitman, London (Research Notes in Artificial Intelligence)

Bucciarelli LL (1988) An ethnographic perspective on engineering design. Design Studies 9(3)

Button G (ed) (1992) Technology in Working Order: Studies of Work, Innovation and Technology. Routledge, London

Callon M and Latour B (1981) Unscrewing the big Leviathan – How actors macro-structure reality and how sociologists help them to do so. In: Knorr-Cetina KD and Cicourel AV (ed) Advances in Social Theory and Methodology – Towards an Integration of Micro- and Macro-Sociologies. Routledge, London

Carrasco J and Crowe M (1990) System modelling and architecture techniques. In: ESPRIT Technical Week, Brussels. EC, Brussels

Carroll J (ed) (1991) Designing Interaction: Psychology at the Human–Computer Interface. Cambridge University Press, Cambridge

Chang S (1987) Participant systems for cooperative work. In: Huhns MN (ed) Distributed Artificial Intelligence. Morgan Kaufmann, Los Altos, CA, pp 311–339

Chomsky AN (1986) Knowledge of Language: Its Nature, Origin and Use. Praeger, New York

Cicourel AV (1974) Cognitive Sociology: Language and Meaning in Social Interaction. The Free Press, New York

Clark HH and Brennan SE (1991) Grounding in communication. In: Resnick LB, Levine JM and Teasley SD (ed) Perspectives on Socially Shared Cognition. American Psychological Association, Washington, DC, pp 127–149

Clark J, Modgil C and Modgil S (1990) Anthony Giddens – Consensus and Controversy. Falmer Press, London

Clement A (1991) Designing without designers – More hidden skill in office computerization? In: Eriksson IV, Kitchenham BA and Tijdens KG (ed) Women, Work and Computerization – Understanding and Overcoming Bias in Work and Education, Proceedings of the IFIP TC9/WG 9.1 conference, Helsinki, June/July. Elsevier/North-Holland, Amsterdam, pp 15–32

Cook N and Lunt G (1992) XTconfer – Dynamic desktop conferencing. In: Proceedings of the 1992 Conference of the European X User Group (EXUG'92), Brunel University, 24–25 September. EXUG, Cambridge, pp 25–39

Coombs CH and Avrunin GS (1988) The Structure of Conflict. Lawrence Erlbaum, Hillsdale, NJ

Corkill DD and Lesser VR (1983) The use of meta-level control for coordination in a distributed problem solving network. In: Proceedings of IJCAI-83. Morgan Kaufmann, San Mateo, CA, pp 748–756

Craig I (1991) Formal Specification of Advanced AI Architectures. Ellis Horwood, New York

Crowley T, Milazzo P, Baker E, Forsdick H and Tomlinson R (1990) MMConf: an infrastructure for building shared multimedia applications. In: Proceedings of the Conference on Computer Supported Cooperative Work (CSCW-90), Los Angeles, CA, 7–10 October. ACM, New York, pp 329–341

CSMIL (1989) ShrEdit: A multi-user shared text editor: Users manual. Cognitive Science and Machine Intelligence Laboratory, University of Michigan

Curtis B, Krasner H and Iscoe N (1988) A field study of the software design process for large systems. Communications of the ACM 31(11): 1268–1287

Deegan M (1992) Grammatical infelicities. Times Higher Education Supplement, Information Technology supplement, 18 February, p vi

DeMarco T (1978) Structured Analysis and System Specification. Prentice-Hall, Englewood Cliffs, NJ

Descotte Y and Latombe JC (1985) Making compromises among antagonist constraints in a planner. Artificial Intelligence 27: 183–217

Devlin K (1991) Logic and Information. Cambridge University Press, Cambridge

Devlin K (in preparation) Situations and Plans

Devlin K and Rosenberg D (1993) Situation theory and cooperative action. In: Aczel P, Israel D, Katagiri Y and Peters S (ed) Situation Theory and its Applications, vol 3. CSLI Lecture Notes no 37, Stanford University, CA, pp 213–264

Devlin K and Rosenberg D (in preparation) Situation theory and social structure

Dilnot C (1992) Ideas. International Design, March–April, 33, 32

Dix AJ (1990a) Information processing, context and privacy. In: Diaper D, Gilmore D, Cockton G and Shackel B (ed) Human–Computer Interaction: Proceedings of INTERACT '90, Cambridge, 27–31 August. Elsevier, Amsterdam, pp 15–20

Dix AJ (1990b) Non-determinism as a paradigm for understanding the user interface. In: Harrison M and Thimbleby H (ed) Formal Methods in Human–Computer Interaction. Cambridge University Press, Cambridge, pp 97–129

Dix AJ (1991) Formal methods for interactive systems. Academic Press, New York

Dix AJ (1992) Pace and interaction. In: Monk A, Diaper D and Harrison M (ed) People and

Computers VII. Proceedings of the HCI '92 Conference. Cambridge University Press, Cambridge, pp 193– 207

Dix AJ, Finlay J, Abowd G and Beale R (1993) Human–Computer Interaction. Prentice Hall, Englewood Cliffs, NJ

Dourish P and Bellotti V (1992) Awareness and coordination in shared workspaces. In: Proceedings of the Conference on Computer Supported Cooperative Work (CSCW-92), Toronto, Canada, 31 October–4 November. ACM, New York, pp 107–114

Dubinskas F (ed) (1988) Making Time: Ethnographies of Hi Tech Organizations. Temple University Press, Philadelphia

Dubrovsky V, Kiesler S and Sethna B (1991) The equalisation phenomenon: status effects in computer-mediated and face-to-face decision-making groups. Human–Computer Interaction 6(2): 119– 146

Duncan S (1972) Some signals and rules for taking speaking turns in conversations. Journal of Personality and Social Psychology 23(2): 283–292

Duncan S (1975) Interaction units during speaking turns in dyadic, face-to-face conversations In: Kendon A, Harms R and Kei M (ed) Organization of Behaviour in Face-to-Face Interaction. Mouton, The Hague

Durkheim E (1966) Les règles de la méthode sociologique. Presses Universitaires de France, Paris (1st French edition, 1895)

Duval S (1992) PCTE/Oracle, PCTE Newsletter 10, June

Eason K (1988) Information Technology And Organisational Change. Taylor and Francis, London

Eekels J and Roozenburg NFM (1991) A methodological comparison of the structures of scientific research and engineering design: their similarities and differences. Design Studies 12(4): 197– 203

Egido C (1990) Teleconferencing as a technology to support cooperative work: its possibilities and limitations. In: Galegher J, Kraut RE and Egido C (ed) Intellectual Teamwork: The Social and Technological Foundations of Cooperative Work. Lawrence Erlbaum, Hillsdale, NJ, pp 351–372

Ehn P (1988) Work-oriented design of computer artifacts. Lawrence Erlbaum, Hillsdale, NJ

Ehrenreich B and English D (1979) For her own good – Two-hundred-and-fifty years of the experts' advice to women. Pluto Press, London

Ehrlich SF (1987) Strategies for encouraging successful adoption of office communications systems. ACT Transactions on Office Information Systems 5(4): 340–357

Ellis CA, Gibbs SJ and Rein GL (1991) Groupware: some issues and experiences. Communications of the ACM 34(1): 39–58. Also published as MCC Technical Report STP-414-88

Elwart-Keys M, Halonen D, Horton M, Kass R and Scott P (1990) User interface requirements for face to face groupware. In: Chew JC and Whiteside J (ed) Proceedings of the Human Factors in Computing Systems Conference, CHI-90, Seattle, Washington, 1–5 April. ACM, New York, pp 295–302

Engelbart D and Lehtman H (1988) Working together. Byte, December, pp 245–252

Engelien B and McBride R (1991) Natural Language Markets: Commercial Strategies. Ovum, London

EuroCoOp Consortium (Esprit 5303) (1990) EuroCoOp: IT support for distributed cooperative work: technical annexe, EuroCoOp Consortium. Version 1.1

Farace RV, Monge PR and Russell HM (1977) Communicating and Organizing. Addison-Wesley, Reading, MA

Farallon (1987) Timbuktu: The Next Best Thing To Being There. Farallon Computing Inc, Berkeley, CA

Ferguson ES (1992) Designing the world we live in. Research in Engineering Design 4: 3–11

Finkelstein A and Fuks H (1989) Multi-party specification. In: 5th International Workshop of Software Specification and Design. IEEE Computer Society Press, Washington, DC

Fish R, Kraut R and Chalfonte B (1990) The Videowindow system in informal communications. In: Proceedings of the Conference on Computer Supported Cooperative Work (CSCW-90), Los Angeles, CA, 7–10 October. ACM, New York, pp 1–11

Fleck J (1991) Configurations – Crystallizing contingency. International Journal of Human Factors in Manufacturing, Special Issue on Systems, Networks and Configurations inside the Implementation Process, December

Flores F and Ludlow JJ (1981) Doing and speaking in the office. In: Fick G and Sprague R (ed) Decision Support Systems – Issues and Challenges. Pergamon Press, London

Foster G and Tartar D (1988) Video: Experiments in computer support for teamwork – Colab. Xerox PARC

Fowler RG, Hodge RIV, Kress GR and Trew AA (1979) Language and Control. Routledge and Kegan Paul, London

Fox MS and Smith SF (1984) Isis – A knowledge-based system for factory scheduling. Expert Systems

Francik E, Ehrlich Rudman S, Cooper D and Levine S (1991) Putting Innovation to work: multimedia communication systems. Communications of the ACM 34(12): 53–63

Francis D (1987) Unblocking Organisational Communication. Gower, Aldershot

Freeman P (1983) Reusable software engineering: concepts and research directions. In: Proceedings of the ITT Workshop on Reusability in Programming, Stratford, Connecticut, 7–9 September. ITT, Newport, RI

Frege G (1884) Die Grundlagen der Arithmetik, 2nd edn, revised. Basil Blackwell, Oxford (English edition, The Foundations of Arithmetic, translated by JL Austin)

Frege G (1952) On sense and reference. In: Geach PT and Black M (ed) Translations from the Philosophical Writings of Gottlob Frege. Basil Blackwell, Oxford

Gaines BR and Shaw MLG (1986) Foundations of dialog engineering: the development of human–computer interaction. Part II. International Journal of Man–Machine Studies 24: 101–123

Gantt M and Nardi B (1992) Gardeners and gurus – Patterns of cooperation among CAD users. In: Proceedings of the Human Factors in Computing Systems Conference, CHI-92, Monterey, California, May. ACM, New York, pp 107–117

Garfinkel H (1967) Studies in Ethnomethodology. Prentice-Hall, Englewood Cliffs, NJ

Garfinkel H (1972) Remarks on ethnomethodology. In: Gumperz J and Hymes D (ed) Directions in Sociolinguistics: The Ethnography of Communication. Holt, Rinehart and Winston, New York

Garner SW, Scrivener SAR, Clarke AA, Clark S, Connolly J, Palmen H, Schappo A and Smyth M (1991) The use of design activity for research into computer supported cooperative working (CSCW). In: Proceedings of DATER'91, Loughborough, September 1991, pp. 84–96

Gilbert GNG, Hewitt B, Murray D and Wilbur S (1991) TMPI end of year report, University of Surrey

Glegg GL (1969) The Design of Design. Cambridge University Press, Cambridge

Goldkuhl G and Lyytinen K (1982) A language action view of information systems. In: Ginzberg M and Ross C (ed) Proceedings of the 3rd International Conference on Information Systems, Ann Arbor, Michigan, pp 13–30

Goldstein I (1975) Bargaining between goals. In: Proceedings of IJCAI-75. Morgan Kaufmann, San Mateo, CA, pp 175–180

Goodwin C (1981) Conversational Organisation: Interaction between Speakers and Hearers. Academic Press, New York

Granberg A (1987) Corporations reshaped by computer. New York Times, Wednesday 7 January

Green TRG (1990) The cognitive dimension of viscosity: a sticky problem for HCI. In: Diaper D, Gilmore D, Cockton G and Shackel B (ed) Human–Computer Interaction: Proceedings of INTERACT '90, Cambridge, 27–31 August. Elsevier, Amsterdam.

Greenbaum J (1979) In the Name of Efficiency – Management Theory and Shop-Floor Practice in Data-Processing Work. Temple University Press, Philadelphia

Greenbaum J and Kyng M (eds) (1991) Design at Work – Cooperative Design of Computer Systems. Lawrence Erlbaum, Hillsdale, NJ

Greenberg S (ed) (1991) Computer Supported Cooperative Work and Groupware. Academic Press, London

Greenberg S, Roseman M, Webster D and Bohnet R (1992) Human and technical factors of distributed group drawing tools. Interacting with Computers 4(3)

Greif I (ed) (1988) Computer-Supported Cooperative Work: A Book of Readings. Morgan Kaufmann, San Mateo, CA

Grey C (ed) (1974) Leaving the Twentieth Century – The incomplete Work of the Situationist International. Falling Wall Press, London

Gruber TR (1989) A method for acquiring strategic knowledge. Knowledge Acquisition 1(3): 255–277

Grudin J (1988) Why CSCW applications fail: problems in the design and evaluation of organisational interfaces. In: Proceedings of the Conference on Computer-Supported Cooperative Work (CSCW-88), Portland, OR, September. ACM Press, New York, pp 85–93

Grudin J (1989) CSCW '88: Report on the conference and review of the proceedings. SIGCHI Bulletin 20(4): 80–84

Grudin J (1990) Why groupware applications fail. In: Laurel B (ed) The Art of Human–Computer Interaction. Wiley, Chichester

Grudin J (1991a) CSCW: the convergence of two development contexts. In: Robertson S, Olson G and Olson J (ed) Proceedings of the Human Factors in Computing Systems Conference, CHI-91, New Orleans, April. ACM, New York

Grudin J (1991b) Obstacles to user involvement in software product development, with implications for CSCW. International Journal of Man–Machine Studies 34(3)

Grudin J (1991c) Interactive systems – bridging the gaps between developers and users. Computer, April, 59–69

Grudin J (1991d) Systematic sources of suboptimal interface development in large product development organizations. Human–Computer Interaction 6: 147–196

Guindon R (1990) Knowledge exploited by experts during software system design. International Journal of Man–Machine Studies 33: 279–304

Guindon R and Curtis B (1988) Control of cognitive processes during design: What tools would support software designers? In: Soloway E, Frye D and Sheppard SB (ed) Proceedings of the Human Factors in Computing Systems Conference, CHI-88, Washington, May. ACM, New York, pp 263–268

Gust P (1988) SharedX: X in a distributed group work environment, presentation at the 2nd Annual X Conference, MIT, Cambridge, MA

Habermas J (1971) Science and technology as "ideology". In: Habermas J (ed) Towards a Rational Society. Heinemann, London

Hacker S (1989) Pleasure, Power and Technology. Unwin Hyman, London

Hales M (1980) Living Thinkwork – Where do Labour Processes Come From? CSE Books/Free Association Books, London

Hales M (1993a) User participation in design – What it can deliver, what it can't and what this means for management. In: Quintas P (ed) The Social Dimensions of Systems Engineering: People, Processes, Policies and Software Development. Ellis Horwood, London, pp 215–235

Hales M (1993b) Human centred systems, gender and computer supported cooperative work. In: Probert B and Wilson B (eds) Pink Collar Blues: Work, Gender and Technology. Melbourne University Press, Melbourne, pp 101–125

Hales M and O'Hara P (1993) Strengths and weaknesses of participation – Learning by doing in local government. In: Green E, Owen J and Pain D (eds) Gendered by Design? Information Technology and Office Systems. Taylor and Francis, London, pp 153–172

Halliday MAK (1978) Language as Social Semiotic. Edward Arnold, London

Halliday MAK and Martin JR (ed) (1981) Readings in Systemic Linguistics. Batsford, London

Haraway D (1985) A manifesto for cyborgs – Science, technology and socialist-feminism in the 1980s. Reprinted in: Nicholson L (ed) (1991) Feminism/Postmodernism. Routledge, London, pp 190–233

Haraway D (1987) Situated knowledges – The science question in feminism and the privilege of partial perspective. Reprinted in: Haraway D (1991) Simians, Cyborgs and Women. Free Association Books, London, pp 183–201

Harker SDP, Olphert CW and Eason KD (1991) The development of tools to assist in organisational requirements definition for information technology systems. HUSAT Research Institute, Loughborough

Harper RR, Hughes JA and Shapiro DZ (1989) Working in harmony: an examination of computer technology in air traffic control. In: Proceedings of the First European Conference on Computer Supported Cooperative Work (EC-CSCW '89) Gatwick, 13–15 September. Computer Sciences House, Slough

Harrison W, Ossher H and Kavianpour M (1992) OOTIS – Object Oriented Tool Integration Services, PCTE Newsletter, 10, June

HCI (1991) Newssheet of HCI '91, issue 3, Edinburgh, August

Heath C and Luff P (1990) Disembodied conduct: communication through video in a multi-media office environment. In: Chew JC and Whiteside J (ed) Proceedings of the Human Factors in Computing Systems Conference, CHI-90, Seattle, Washington, 1–5 April. ACM, New York, pp 99–103

Henninger S (1991) Computer systems supporting cooperative work: A CSCW90 trip report. ACM SIGCHI Bulletin 23(3): 25–28

Heritage J (1988) Current developments in conversation analysis. In: Concepts of Interpersonal Communication, pp 21–47 (Special Issue on conversation analysis and social psychology)

Hewitt C (1986) Offices are open systems. ACM Transactions on Office Information Systems 4(3): 271–287

Hobbs J and Evans DA (1980) Conversation as planned behaviour. Cognitive Science 4: 349–377

Hoover SP, Rinderle JR and Finger S (1991) Models and abstractions in design. Design Studies 12(4): 237–245

Huczynski A and Buchanan D (1991) Organizational Behaviour (2nd edn). Prentice-Hall, London

Hughes JA, Randall D and Shapiro D (1992a) From ethnographic record to system design: some experiences from the field. Personal communication.

Hughes JA, Sommerville I, Bentley R and Randall D (1992b) Designing with ethnography: making work visible. Interacting with Computers (in press)

Hughes PT, Plant TA, Morris ME and Seel NR (1991) Collaboration media: the problem of design by use and the use of design. In: Proceedings of the Seminar on Computer Supported Cooperative Work – The Multimedia and Networking Paradigm, 16–17 July 1991, Brunel University, UK, Unicom Seminars Ltd

Hughes PT, Morris ME and Plant TA (1993) Understanding and uncovering design issues in synchronous shared-windowed conferencing. Interacting with Computers 5(1): 115–130

Humphrey W (1989) Managing the Software Process. Addison-Wesley, Reading, MA (work carried out at SEI, Carnegie–Mellon)

Hutchison CS (1992) The Organisation of Organisations: Perspectives on People, Cultures, and Information Technology. Kingston University, School of Information Systems

Hutchison CS and Rosenberg D (1992) Human-centred knowledge elicitation, Working Paper, Kingston University, School of Information Systems

Hutchison CS and Rosenberg D (1993) Cooperation and conflict in knowledge-intensive computer supported cooperative work. In: Easterbrook S (ed) CSCW: Cooperation or Conflict? Springer-Verlag, London

Hymes D (1972) On communicative competence. In: Pride J and Holmes J (ed) Sociolinguistics. Penguin, Harmondsworth

Illich I (1975) Tools for Conviviality. Fontana, London

IMKA (1990) IMKA Software Functional Specification phase 1: Knowledge Representation version 2.1 July 1990, Institute for Managing Knowledge Assets, Pittsburgh, PA

Ishii H and Miyake N (1991) Toward an open shared workspace: computer and video fusion approach of teamworkstation. Communications of the ACM 34(12): 37–50

Jamieson W (1989) Plotting a buy-out, Sunday Telegraph, 16 April

Jefferson G and Schenkein J (1978) Some sequential negotiations in conversation: unexpanded and expanded versions of projected action sequences. In: Schenkein J (ed) Studies in the Organisation of Conversational Interaction. Academic Press, New York

Jenkins D (1990) Application of SMART to design of real time fault tolerant systems. In: Velvarsky JF (ed) Proceedings of the 1990 International Conference on Reliability in Computer Science, Jasna pod Chopkom, Czechoslovakia

Jenkins D (1991) Design in the severely constrained situation. In: Proceedings of the 1991 International Conference in Engineering Design (ICED'91), Zurich, August. Heurista, pp 909–917

Jenkins D (1992) Safety critical integrated design support – revised (SCIDS-R), Proposal to the DTI/SERC Safety Critical Systems Programme, Department of Computing Science, University of Paisley, November

Johansen J, Vallee V and Springer S (1979) Electronic Meetings: Technical Alternatives and Social Choices. Addison-Wesley, Reading, MA

Jordan PW, Draper SW, MacFarlane KK and McNulty S (1991) Guessability, learnability, and experienced user performance. In: Diaper D and Hammond N (ed) People and

Computers VI. Proceedings of the HCI '91 Conference, Edinburgh, 20–23 August. Cambridge University Press, Cambridge, pp 237–245

Kanter RM (1989) When Giants Learn to Dance. Simon and Schuster, New York

Kellog C, Gargan RA Jr, Mark W, McGuire JG, Pontecorvo M, Sclossberg JL and Sullivan JW (1989) The acquisition, verification and explanation of design knowledge. SIGART Newsletter 108, pp 163–165

Kiesler S, Zubrow D, Moses A and Geller V (1985) Affect in computer-mediated communication: an experiment in synchronous terminal-to-terminal discussion. Human–Computer Interaction 1: 77–104

Kitzmiller C and Jagannathan V (1987) Design in a distributed blackboard framework. Intelligent CAD 1: 223–233

Klein M (1989) Conflict resolution in cooperative design, Technical Report UIUCDCS-R-89-1557, PhD Thesis, University of Illinois, Urbana-Champaign, IL, December

Klein M (1990) A computational model of conflict resolution in integrated design. In: Proceedings of the ASME Symposium on Integrated Product Design and Manufacturing, November

Klein M and Baskin AA (1990) Computational model for conflict resolution in cooperative design systems. In: Proceedings of the International Working Conference on Cooperating Knowledge Based Systems, Dake Centre, University of Keele, October. Springer- Verlag, London

Klein M and Lu SCY (1990) Conflict resolution in cooperative design. International Journal for Artificial Intelligence in Engineering 4(4): 168–180

Kling R (1987) Defining the boundaries of computing across complex organisations. In: Boland R and Hirschheim R (eds) Critical Issues in Information Systems Research. Wiley, New York, pp 307–367

Kling R (1991) Cooperation, coordination and control in computer supported work. Communications of the ACM 34(12): 83–88 (Special Issue on Groupware/CSCW)

Kling R and Scacchi W (1982) The web of computing: computer technology as social organisation. Advances in Computers 21: 1– 90

Kloth M (1989) Some ideas on a blackboard system for design tasks. In: Blackboard Workshop, Detroit

Knister MJ and Prakash A (1990) DistEdit: A distributed toolkit for supporting multiple group editors. In: Proceedings of the Conference on Computer Supported Cooperative Work (CSCW-90), Los Angeles, CA, 7–10 October. ACM, New York, pp 343–355

Konda S, Monarch I, Sargent P and Subrahmanian E (1992) Shared memory in design: A unifying theme for research and practice. Research in Engineering Design 4: 23–42

Kotter JP (1978) Organisational Dynamics: Diagnosis and Intervention. Addison-Wesley, Reading, MA

Kraft P (1977) Programmers and Managers – The Routinization of Computer Programming in the United States. Springer-Verlag, London

Kraut RE, Fish RS, Root RW and Chalfonte BL (1991) Informal communication in organization: form, function and technology. In: Oskamp S and Spacapan S (ed) Human Reactions to Technology: Claremont Symposium on Applied Social Psychology. Sage, Beverly Hills, CA

Kress GR and Hodge RIV (1979) Language as Ideology. Routledge and Kegan Paul, London

Kress GR and Trew AA (1978) Ideological transformation of discourse; or how the *Sunday Times* got its message across. Sociological Review 26(4): 755–776

Krueger CW (1989) Models of reuse in software engineering, CMU- CS-89-188, Carnegie Mellon University, 14 December

Krueger GP and Chapanis A (1980) Conferencing and teleconferencing in three communication modes as a function of the number of conferees. Ergonomics 23(2): 103–122

Kuutti K (1991a) The concept of activity as a basic unit of analysis for CSCW research. In: Bannon L, Robinson M and Schmidt K (ed) Proceedings of the Second European Conference on Computer Supported Cooperative Work (EC-CSCW '91) Amsterdam, 25–27 September. Kluwer, Dordrecht, pp 249–264

Kuutti K (1991b) Activity theory and its applications to information systems research and development. In: Nissen HE, Klein HK and Hirschheim R (ed) Information Systems Research – Contemporary Approaches and Emergent Traditions. Elsevier, Amsterdam, pp 529–549

Kyng M (1991) Designing for cooperation – Cooperating in design. Communications of the ACM 34(12): 65–73

Kyng M and Greenbaum J (ed) (1991) Design at Work – Cooperative Design of Computer Systems. Lawrence Erlbaum Associates, New York

Laessøe J and Rasmussen LB (1989) Human-centred methods – Development of computer-aided work processes. Deliverable R18, ESPRIT project 1217(1199) Technical University of Denmark, Lyngby

Lakoff G and Johnson M (1980) Metaphors We Live By. University of Chicago Press, Chicago, IL

Lander S and Lesser VR (1988) Negotiation to resolve conflicts among design experts. Technical Report, Department of Computer and Information Science, University of Massachusetts at Amherst, August

Landry J (1992) Working together technology - A new world order. Lotus In View 10: 1-2

Latour B (1991) Technology is society made durable. In: Law J (ed) A Sociology of Monsters – Essays on Power, Technology and Domination. Routledge, London, pp 103–131

Lauwers CJ and Lantz KA (1990) Collaboration awareness in support of collaboration transparency: Requirements for the next generation of shared window systems. In: Chew JC and Whiteside J (ed) Proceedings of the Human Factors in Computing Systems Conference, CHI-90, Seattle, Washington, 1–5 April. ACM, New York, pp 303– 312

Lauwers CJ, Joseph TA, Lantz KA and Romanov AL (1990) Replicated architectures for shared window systems: A critique. In: Proceedings of the Conference on Office Information Systems, Boston, MA, April, pp 249–260

Lave J and Wenger E (1991) Situated Learning: Legitimate Peripheral Participation. Cambridge University Press, Cambridge

Lea M and Spears R (1991) Computer-mediated communication, de- individuation and group decision-making. International Journal of Man–Machine Studies 34(2): 283–301

Leland MDP, Fish RS and Kraut RE (1988) Collaborative document production using Quilt. In: Proceedings of the Conference on Computer Supported Cooperative Work (CSCW-88) Portland, OR, September. ACM, New York, pp 206–215

Levinson SC (1983) Pragmatics. Cambridge University Press, Cambridge

Lichtenheim M (1991) Technology transfer plan: A framework strategy. Atmosphere ID: D3.1-report-2.1-SFGL-ML

Lim FJ and Benbasat I (1991) A communication-based framework for group interfaces in computer-supported collaboration. In: Proceedings of the 24th Hawaii Conference on System Sciences, Kauai, Hawaii

Linde C (1990) Who's in charge here? Co-operative work and authority negotiation in police helicopter missions. In: Proceedings of the 2nd ACM Conference on CSCW, Portland, OR, 25– 27 September. ACM, New York

Lubars MD and Harandi MT (1987) Knowledge-based software design using design schemas. In: Proceedings of the 9th International Conference on Software Engineering, 30 March–2 April, pp. 253– 262

Lucas S (1987) Track real communications for a surprise. Management Review, September

Lyytinen K (1985) Implications of theories of language for information systems. MIS Quarterly, March, 61–74

Lyytinen K (1990a) Information systems and critical theory – A critical assessment, Working Paper WP-13, Department of Computer Science, Jyvaskyla, Finland

Lyytinen K (1990b) Computer supported cooperative work (CSCW) issues and challenges – A structurational analysis, Draft working paper, Department of Computer Science, Jyvaskyla, Finland

MacLean A, Bellotti VME and Young R (1990) What rationale is there in design? In: Proceedings of the IFIP TC 13 3rd International Conference on Human–Computer Interaction, Cambridge, August, pp 213–218

Madlin N (1987) Remapping the corporation. Management Review, September

Madsen CM (1989) Using persistent objects to implement an environment for cooperative work. In: Technology of Object- Oriented Languages and Systems, TOOLS '80, Computer Science Department, Aarhus University, November

Mangham IL and Overington MA (1987) Organisations as Theatre – A Social Psychology of Dramatic Appearances. Wiley, Chichester

Manning PK (1971) Talking and becoming: A view of organisational socialization. In: Douglas JD (ed) Understanding Everyday Life. Routledge and Kegan Paul, London

Mantei M (1988) Capturing the Capture Lab concepts: a case study in the design of computer supported meeting environments. In: Proceedings of the Conference on Computer Supported Cooperative Work (CSCW-88) Portland, OR, September. ACM, New York, pp 257– 270

Marcus S, Stout J and McDermott J (1987) VT: An expert elevator designer. Artificial Intelligence Magazine 8(4): 39–58

McCarthy JC, Miles VC and Monk AF (1991) An experimental study of common ground in text-based communication. In: Robertson S, Olson G and Olson J (ed) Proceedings of the Human Factors in Computing Systems Conference, CHI-91, New Orleans. ACM, New York, pp 209– 215

McDermid JA (1990) Introduction and overview to Part II: Methods, techniques and technology. In: McDermid JA (ed) The Software Engineer's Reference Book. Butterworths, London

McKinlay A, Procter R, Woodburn R and Masting O (1994) Studies of turn-taking in computer-mediated communications. Interacting with Computers 6

MDMSC (1990) Developing and using Ada parts. In: Real-Time Embedded Applications, a manual developed as part of the Common Ada Missile Packages Phase 3 program by McDonnell Douglas Missile Systems Company for the US Air Force, 27 April

Miles VC, Johnson CW, McCarthy JC and Harrison MD (1991) Supporting prediction in complex dynamic systems. In: Diaper D and Hammond N (ed) People and Computers VI. Proceedings of the HCI '91 Conference, Edinburgh, 20–23 August. Cambridge University Press, Cambridge, pp 133–144

Miles VC, McCarthy JC, Dix AJ, Harrison MD and Monk AF (1993) Reviewing designs for a synchronous–asynchronous group editing environment. In: Sharples M (ed) Computer Supported Collaborative Writing. Springer-Verlag, London, pp 137–160

Millar S (1992) Institutional transformation: From fragmentation to discord within consensus, Center for the Study of Higher Education, Pennsylvania State University

Minneman S and Bly S (1991) Managing a trois: a study of a multi-user drawing tool in distributed design work. In: Robertson S, Olson G and Olson J (ed) Proceedings of the Human Factors in Computing Systems Conference, CHI-91, New Orleans. ACM, New York, pp 217–224

Minsky M (1980) A framework for representing knowledge. In: Haugeland J (ed) Mind Design: Philosophy, Psychology, and Artificial Intelligence. MIT Press, Cambridge, MA

Mintzberg H (1979) The Structuring of Organisations. Prentice- Hall, Englewood Cliffs, NJ

MIT-JSME (1991) Computer-aided cooperative product development. In: Proceedings of the MIT-JSME Workshop, MIT, Cambridge, MA, November 1989

Montague R (1974) Formal Philosophy. Yale University Press, New Haven

Moreno J (1934) Who Shall Survive? Nervous and Mental Disease Publishing Company, Washington, DC

Moreno J and Jennings HH (1960) The Sociometry Reader. The Free Press, Glencoe, IL

Morgan G (1986) Images of Organisations. Sage, London

Morris ME (1991) Phase 0 shared screen conferencing system: evaluation report, EuroCoOp Project Document, ECO-BNRE-91-1, BNR Europe Ltd

Morris ME, Plant TA and Hughes PT (1992) CoOpLab: Practical experiences with evaluating a multi-user system. In: Monk A, Diaper D and Harrison M (ed) People and Computers VII. Proceedings of the HCI '92 Conference. Cambridge University Press, Cambridge

Mostow J (1985) Toward better models of the design process. Artificial Intelligence Magazine, spring: 44–57

Mullery GP (1979) CORE – A method for controlled requirement specification, CH1479-5/79/0000, IEEE Computer Society Press, Washington, DC

Mumford E (1983a) Designing Participatively. Manchester Business School

Mumford E (1983b) Designing Human Systems. Cambridge Business School

Murrel S (1983) Computer communication system design affects group decision making. In: Proceedings of the Human Factors in Computing Systems Conference (CHI-83). ACM Press, New York, pp 63–67

Mustoe J (1991) Feedback in design, private communication, April (to clarify an EDRC STAR CHAMBER presentation)

Myers BA (1991) Demonstrational interfaces: A step beyond direct manipulation. In: Diaper D and Hammond N (ed) People and Computers VI. Proceedings of the HCI

'91 Conference, Edinburgh, 20–23 August. Cambridge University Press, Cambridge, pp 11–30

Namioka A and Schuler D (1991) Participatory Design. Lawrence Erlbaum, Hillsdale, NJ

Nardi BA and Miller JR (1990) An ethnographic study of distributed problem solving in spreadsheet development. In: In: Proceedings of the 2nd ACM Conference on CSCW, Portland, OR, 25– 27 September. ACM, New York

Nardi BA and Miller JR (1991) Twinkling lights and nested loops – Distributed problem solving and spreadsheet development. International Journal of Man–Machine Studies 34: 161–184

Neighbors J (1984) The Draco approach to constructing software from reusable components. IEEE Transactions on Software Engineering 10(5): 564–573

Newsome SL and Spillers WR (1989) Tools for expert designers: Supporting conceptual design. In: Finger S (ed) Design Theory '88. Springer-Verlag, London, pp 49–55

Nguyen TA, Perkins WA, Laffey TJ and Pecora D (1985) Checking an expert system's knowledge base For consistency and completeness. In: Proceedings of IJCAI-85. Morgan Kaufmann, San Mateo, CA, pp 375–378

Ngwenyama O (1991) The critical social theory approach to information systems – Problems and challenges. In: Nissen HE, Klein HK and Hirschheim R (ed) Information Systems Research – Contemporary Approaches and Emergent Traditions. Elsevier, Amsterdam, pp 267–280

Nissen HE, Klein HK and Hirschheim R (eds) (1991) Information Systems Research – Contemporary Approaches and Emergent Traditions. Elsevier, Amsterdam

Norman DA (1990) The Design of Everyday Things. Doubleday, New York

Norman DA (1991) Collaborative computing – Collaboration first, computing second. Communications of the ACM 34(12): 88–90

Norman DA and Draper SW (1986) User Centred System Design: New Perspectives on Human–Computer Interaction. Lawrence Erlbaum, Hillsdale, NJ

Nunamaker JF, Applegate A and Konsynski K (1987) Facilitating group creativity: Experience with a group decision support system. In: Proceedings of the 20th Hawaii International Conference on System Sciences, pp 422–430

Olson MH and Bly SA (1991) The Portland experience – a report on a distributed research group. International Journal of Man– Machine Studies 34(2): 211–228

Open University/Department of Trade and Industry (1990) A Guide to Usability. Open University Press, Milton Keynes

Ormerod TC and Bloomfield H (1991) Delivering the GOODS: A system for supporting generic design. PPIG Newsletter 10: 12–14

Pahl G and Beitz W (1988) Engineering Design: A Systematic Approach. Springer-Verlag, London (English edition, translated by A Pomerans and K Wallace, edited by K Wallace)

Parnas DL and Clements PC (1986) A rational design process: How and why to fake it. IEEE Transactions on Software Engineering 12(2)

Patterson JF, Hill RD and Rohall SL (1990) Rendezvous: An architecture for synchronous multi-user applications. In: Proceedings of the Conference on Computer Supported Cooperative Work (CSCW-90), Los Angeles, CA, 7–10 October. ACM, New York

Perin C (1991) Electronic social fields in bureaucracies. Communications of the ACM 34: 75–82

Perry TS (1990) Slashing development time: Combining technology with teamwork. IEEE Spectrum 27(10): 61–78

Pferd P and Peralta P (1979) Interactive graphics teleconferencing. IEEE Computer

Piaget J (1936) The Origin of Intelligence in the Child. Penguin, Harmondsworth

Piller C (1991) Prose and cons. MacWorld, August, 20–26

Plant TA, Morris ME, Hughes PT and Benson ORK (1991) CoOpLab: Computer supported cooperative working by evolution. In: Proceedings of the UK Unix User Group Meeting, Liverpool, July

Prieto-Diaz R (1987) Domain analysis for reusability. In: Proceedings of the COMPSAC-87 Conference, Tokyo, 7–9 October

Prieto-Diaz R (1990) Domain analysis: An introduction. ACM SIGSOFT Software Engineering Notes 15(2): 47–54

Prieto-Diaz R and Arango G (1991) Domain Analysis and Software System Modelling: IEEE Computer Society Press Tutorial. IEEE Computer Society Press, Washington, DC

Pruitt DG (1981) Negotiation Behavior. Academic Press, New York

Putnam L and Pacanowsky M (1983) Communication and Organisations: An Interpretive Approach. Sage, Beverly Hills, CA

Quintas P (1992) Innovation in software development – Lessons from the UK Alvey programme, Working paper no. 16, CICT centre, Science Policy Research Unit, University of Sussex

Rabins M, Ardayfio D, Fenves S, Seireg A, Richardson H and Clark H (1986) Design theory and methodology – A new discipline. Mechanical Engineering, August, 23–27

Reder S and Schwab RG (1990) The temporal structure of co- operative activity. In: Proceedings of the Conference on Computer Supported Cooperative Work (CSCW-90), Los Angeles, CA, 7–10 October. ACM, New York

Robb F (1990) In defence of conversation. Journal of the Society of Management Science and Applied Cybernetics 19

Robinson M (1989) Double-level languages and cooperative working. AI and Society 5: 34–60

Rodden T (1991) A survey of CSCW systems. Interacting with Computers 3(3): 319–353

Rodden T and Blair G (1991) CSCW and distributed systems – The problem of control. In: Bannon L, Robinson M and Schmidt K (ed) Proceedings of the Second European Conference on Computer Supported Cooperative Work (EC-CSCW '91) Amsterdam, 25–27 September. Kluwer, Dordrecht, pp 49–64

Roemer JM, Pendley WL, Stempski MO and Borgstrom MC (1986) Field study of a voice mail system: Design and design-process implications. SIGCHI Bulletin 18(2): 60–61

Rogers Y (1992) Ghosts in the network: distributed troubleshooting in a shared working environment. In: Proceedings of the Conference on Computer Supported Cooperative Work (CSCW- 92), Toronto, Canada, 31 October–4 November. ACM, New York

Rutherford J (1991) Knodes blackboard interface, unpublished

Rutherford J (1992) KNOWDES: knowledge based design decision support. In: Fleming U and Van Wyke S (ed) Proceedings of the 5th International Conference on Computer Aided Architectural Design Futures (CAADF'93), July, Carnegie-Mellon University, Pittsburg, PA. North Holland, Amsterdam, pp 357–374

Sacks H (1972) On the analyzability of stories by children. In: Gumpertz J and Hymes D (ed) Directions in Sociolinguistics: The Ethnography of Communication. Holt, Rinehart and Winston, New York, pp 325–345

Sacks H, Schegloff E and Jefferson G (1978) A simplest systematics for the organisation of turn-taking in conversation. In: Schenkein J (ed) Studies in the Organisation of Conversational Interaction. Academic Press, New York (also published in Language (1974) 50(4): 696–735)

Sarin G (1985) Computer-based real-time conferencing systems. IEEE Computer

Schank RC and Abelson RP (1977) Scripts, Plans, Goals, and Understanding. Lawrence Erlbaum, Hillsdale, NJ

Schegloff EA (1979) Identification and recognition in telephone conversation openings. In: Psathas G (ed) Everyday Language: Studies in Ethnomethodology. Irvington, New York

Schegloff EA, Jefferson GA and Sacks H (1977) The preference for self-correction in the organization of repair in conversation. Language 53(2): 361–382

Scheifler RW and Gettys J (1986) The X window system. ACM Transactions on Graphics 5(2): 79–109

Scheifler RW, Gettys J and Newman R (1988) X Window System: C Library and Protocol. Digital Press, Bedford, MA

Schon D and Bucciarelli LL (1989) Design theory and methods – An interdisciplinary approach. In: Finger S (ed) Design Theory '88. Springer-Verlag, London, pp 29–35

Scrivener SAR and Palmen H (1991) An analysis of face-to-face drawing activity. In: Proceedings of DATER'91, Loughborough, September, pp 200–214

Scrivener SAR, Clarke AA, Connolly J, Garner SW, Clark SM, Palmen H, Schappo A and Smyth M (1992a) ROCOCO Phase I Report, LUTCHI Research Centre, Loughborough University, Leicestershire

Scrivener SAR, Clarke AA, Connolly J, Garner SW, Clark SM, Palmen H, Schappo A and Smyth M (1992b) ROCOCO Phase II Report, LUTCHI Research Centre, Loughborough University, Leicestershire

Scrivener SAR, Clark SM, Smyth MG, Harris D and Rockoff T (1992c) Designing at a distance: Experiments in remote-synchronous design. In: Proceedings of OZCHI'92, Goldcoast, Australia, November, pp 44–53

Searle J (1969) Speech Acts. Cambridge University Press, Cambridge

Sellen A (1992) Speech patterns in video-mediated conversations. In: Proceedings of the Human Factors in Computing Systems Conference, CHI-92, Monterey, California, May. ACM, New York, pp 49–59

Shannon CE and Weaver W (1949) A Mathematical Theory Of Communication. University of Illinois Press

Shaw M (1990a) Elements of a design language for software architecture, Position Paper for IEEE Design Automation Workshop, January

Shaw M (1990b) Informatics for a new century: Computing education for the 1990s and beyond, Carnegie-Mellon University, Software Engineering Institute, Pittsburgh, Technical Report, CMU/SEI-90- TR-15, ESD-90-TR-216, July

Shneiderman B (1987) Designing the User Interface: Strategies for Effective Human–Computer Interaction, Addison-Wesley, Reading, MA

Sibley EH (1989) A layered approach to very large system specification. In: Shriver BD (ed) Proceedings of the 22nd Annual Hawaii International Conference on System Sciences, vol. II: Software Track, Computer Society Press, Washington, DC, pp. 988– 995

Simon HA (1981) The Sciences of the Artificial, 2nd edn. MIT Press, Cambridge, MA

Skinner BF (1957) Verbal Behaviour. Prentice-Hall, New York

Smith RB, O'Shea T, O'Malley C, Scanlon E and Taylor J (1991) Preliminary experiments with a distributed, multi-media problem solving environment. In: Bowers J and Benford S (ed) Studies in Computer Supported Cooperative Work: Theory, Practice and Design. North-Holland, Oxford

Smith RG and Davis R (1979) Cooperation in distributed problem solving. In: Proceedings of the International Conference on Cybernetics and Society. IEEE Computer Society Press, Washington, DC, pp 366–371

Sommerville I (1992) Software Engineering, 4th edn. Addison-Wesley, Wokingham

Sproull L and Kiesler S (1986) Reducing social context cues: electronic mail in organizational communication. Management Science 32(11): 1492–1512

Srinivas K, Reddy R, Babadi A, Kamana S, Kumar V and Dai Z (1992) MONET: A multi-media system for conferencing and application sharing in distributed systems, CERC Technical Report Series, CERC-TR-RN-91-009, West Virginia University

SSADM (1986) Vol 1: Tasks and Techniques: An Introduction to SSADM, SSADM Version 3, NCC, Manchester

Standish TA (1984) An essay on software reuse. IEEE Transactions on Software Engineering 10(5): 494–497

Star SL (1991) The sociology of the invisible – The primacy of work in the writings of Anselm Strauss. In: Maines D (ed) Social Organisation and Social Processes – Essays in Honour of Anselm L Strauss. Aldine de Gruyter, Hawthorne, New York

Stauffer LA and Ullman DG (1991) Fundamental processes of mechanical designers based on empirical data. Journal of Engineering Design 2(2)

Stefik M (1981) Planning with constraints (Molgen: Part 1 and 2). Artificial Intelligence 16(2): 111–170

Stefik M (1986) The next knowledge medium. AI Magazine III(1)

Stefik M, Bobrow DG, Foster G, Lanning K and Tatar DG (1987a) WYSIWIS revised: early experiences with multi-user interfaces. ACM Transactions on Office Information Systems 5(2): 147–167

Stefik M, Foster G, Bobrow DG, Kahn K, Lanning S and Suchman L (1987b) Beyond the chalkboard: computer support for collaboration and problem solving in meetings. Communications of the ACM 30(1): 32–47

Strauss A (1985) Work and the division of labour. Sociological Quarterly 26(1): 320–328

Streveler DJ (1978) Designing by committee works – Sometimes. Datamation, March, 117–120

Suchman L (1987) Plans and Situated Actions: The Problem of Human–Machine Communication. Cambridge University Press, Cambridge

Suchman L (1991a) Inaugural lecture, Lancaster CSCW Centre, University of Lancaster, October

Suchman L (1991b) Identities and differences, Closing remarks. In: Eriksson IV, Kitchenham BA and Tijdens KG (ed) Women, Work and Computerization – Understanding and Overcoming Bias in Work and Education, Proceedings of the IFIP TC9/WG 9.1 conference, Helsinki, June/July. Elsevier/North-Holland, Amsterdam, pp 431–437

Sussman GJ (1973) A computational model of skill acquisition. Technical Report/PhD Thesis, Artificial Intelligence Laboratory, Massachusetts Institute of Technology, Cambridge, MA

Sussman GJ and Steele GL (1980) Constraints – A language for expressing almost-hierarchical descriptions. Artificial Intelligence 14: 1–40

Tanenbaum A (1988) Computer Networks, 2nd edn. Prentice-Hall, Englewood Cliffs, NJ

Tang J (1991) Findings from observational studies of collaborative work. International Journal of Man–Machine Studies 34(2): 143–160

Tang J and Leifer L (1988) A framework for understanding the workspace activity of design teams. In: Proceedings of the Conference on Computer Supported Cooperative Work (CSCW-88) Portland, OR, September. ACM, New York, pp 244–249

Tang J and Minneman S (1990) Videodraw: A video interface for collaborative drawing. In: Chew JC and Whiteside J (ed) Proceedings of the Human Factors in Computing Systems Conference, CHI-90, Seattle, Washington, 1–5 April. ACM, New York, pp 313–320

Tatar DG, Foster G and Bobrow DG (1991) Design for conversation: lessons from Cognoter. International Journal of Man–Machine Studies 34(2): 185–209

Thomas JC and Carroll JM (1981) Human factors in communication. IBM Systems Journal 20(2)

Thorndyke P, McArthur D and Cammarata S (1981) Autopilot: A Distributed Planner For Air Fleet Control. In: Proceedings of IJCAI-81. Morgan Kaufmann, San Mateo, CA, pp 171–177

Tichy W (1985) RCS – A system for version control. Software – Practice and Experience 15(7): 637–654

Touraine A (1971) The Post-Industrial Society. Random House, New York

Truex D and Klein H (1991) A rejection of structure as a basis for information systems. In: Stamper RK, Kerola P, Lee R and Lyytinen K (ed) Collaborative Work, Social Communications and Information Systems. Elsevier, Amsterdam, pp 213–236 Tunnicliffe AJ and Scrivener SAR (1991) Knowledge elicitation in design. Design Studies 12(2): 73–80

Valacich JS, Dennis AR and Nunamaker JF (1991) Electronic meeting support: the GroupSystems concept. International Journal of Man– Machine Studies 34(2): 262–282

Vehviläinen M (1986) A study circle as a method for women to develop their work and computer systems. In: Proceedings of the 2nd IFIP conference on Women, Work and Computerization, Dublin

Waern Y (1992) Modelling group problem solving. Zeitschrift fur Psychologie 200: 157–174

Watabe K, Sakata S, Maeno K, Fukuoka H and Ohmori T (1990) Distributed multiparty desktop conferencing system: Mermaid. In: Proceedings of the Conference on Computer-Supported Cooperative Work (CSCW-90) Los Angeles, CA, 7–10 October. ACM, New York, pp 27–28

Weston RH, Edwards JM and Hodgson A (1992) Model driven CIM: a framework for the design, implementation and management of open CIM systems, Status Report on Current Research funded by the Directorate, ACME Directorate, SERC, Swindon, p 79

Whiteside J, Bennet J and Holtzblatt K (1988) Usability engineering: our experience and evolution. In: Helander M (ed) Handbook of Human–Computer Interaction. North-Holland, Amsterdam, pp 791–817

Whitney DE (1990) Designing the design process. Research in Engineering Design 2(1): 3–13

Whittaker S, Brennan S and Clark H (1991) Coordinating activity: An analysis of interaction in computer supported cooperative work. In: Robertson S, Olson G and Olson J (ed) Proceedings of the Human Factors in Computing Systems Conference, CHI-91, New Orleans. ACM, New York, pp 361–367

Wilbur SB (1990) Dimensions of sharing in multimedia desktop conferencing. In: IEE Colloquium on CSCW, London, 24 October, IEE Digest No. 1990/132

Wilensky R (1983) Planning And Understanding. Addison-Wesley, Reading, MA

Winograd T (1988) A language/action perspective on the design of cooperative work. Human–Computer Interaction 3(1): 3–30

Winograd T and Flores F (1986) Understanding Computers and Cognition: A New Foundation for Design. Addison-Wesley, Wokingham

Woodburn R, Procter R, Arnott J and Newell A (1991) A study of conversational turn-taking in a communication aid for the disabled. In: Diaper D and Hammond N (ed) People and Computers VI. Proceedings of the HCI '91 Conference, Edinburgh, 20–23 August. Cambridge University Press, Cambridge, pp 359–371

Woolgar S (1990) Configuring the user: a look at usability trials, CRICT discussion paper, Brunel University

Woolgar S (1991) Configuring the user – The case of usability trials. In: Law J (ed) A Sociology of Monsters – Essays on Power, Technology and Domination. Routledge, London, pp 57–99

Wright P, Monk A and Carey T (1989) Co-Operative Evaluation: The York Manual. University of York

Young R (1988) Expert systems and expert opinion. In: Moralee DS (ed) Research and Development in Expert Systems IV. Cambridge University Press, Cambridge

Yourdon E (1989) Modern Structured Analysis. Prentice-Hall, Englewood Cliffs, New Jersey

Zemanek H (1974) Formalization: Past, present and future. In: Shaw B (ed) Formal Aspects of Computing Science. Newcastle University, Newcastle upon Tyne.

Subject Index

abstraction 72, 73, 142, 143
accountability 33
activities, classification of 46–55
activity theory 176
agents 164–5, 210, 221, 224
agreed/disagreed communication 96–7, 99
AIR-CYL 223
analysis phase 284
anti-CMC systems 10, 18–19
Apple Macintosh 67
appropriateness conditions 71
archiving 52
argument roles 71
artefacts 11–13, 54, 210
  communication about 22
  communication through 13–14, 18, 20
  communication with 21–2
  computerized 19–21
  non-computerized 21–5
articulation 174
articulation work 169
artificial intelligence (AI) 149, 210, 211,
  245, 246
associative links 75
ATMOSPHERE 268
audio analysis 285–90
audio capture 290
audio data 283–4
authoring 48
automotive industry 180

bar codes 25
BARGAINER 223
basic parameters 72
basic types 72
blackboard architecture 245–7, 265–6
'bleeders' 98, 99
breadth-first approach 142
bulletin boards 90

CAD 142–3, 181
CAD/CAM 180

CAMP 146
CAR system 180–2, 188, 190–2
CASE 268–9
CASSANDRA architecture 246, 247, 266
Clarity Index 102–3
client briefings 57
client-server model 246
cognition 75–9
cognitive science 121–2, 142–3
Cognoter 121, 137
collaboration 209–10
collaboration awareness 119, 122
collaborative activity 48–9
collaborative editing 18
collaborative information 52
collaborative work 31, 34, 93–113
colour printers 55
commitments 107, 112
Common Lisp 231
communication 10–11, 15, 19, 56, 79
  about the artefact 22
  codes 34, 54
  episodes 34
  informal channels of 23
  media 57, 58
  network 94
  out of band communication 187
  through the artefact 13–14, 18, 20
  with artefacts 21–2
  within group 61
Communication and Information Free of
  Time and Space (CIFTS) 116–18
communicative competence 90
communicative failure 102
complexity 179–95
compound infons 70
Computer-aided Design (CAD) 142–3, 181
computer mediated communication
  (CMC) 16–18, 99, 121, 137
computer resources 39–40
computer support 16–19
concurrency 242, 243–4
concurrent design 245
concurrent engineering 209, 241–69
conferencing 120, 179–95, 272, 273, 284

configuration links   221
conflict detection   210, 219–23
  domain-dependent idioms   221–3
  domain-independent methods   220–1
  management   209–27
  resolution   209–11, 223–5
  strategies   224
constraints   37, 72–4, 77, 83, 112, 128, 129,
      134, 221
Constructive Solid Model (CSM)   251
content   102–5, 135
conventional logbooks   248–9
conversation   122–4
conversation analysis (CA)   95, 122–8,
      273–5, 285, 286
cooperation   10–11
  environments for   20
cooperation rooms   20
cooperative behaviour   91
cooperative design   159
cooperative work   10–15, 110
CoOpLab   273, 276, 278, 285, 286, 288
coordination   119–37
CORE   29
corporate style   40
creation   198
critical theory   175
CSCW   1, 2, 16
  asynchronous   120, 129–30, 135, 148, 188
  definition   27–8, 172
  features of   231–2
  framework for   9–26
  implementation   56
  information system   82
  requirements for   27–59
  situation-theoretic network   83
  synchronous   120, 135, 231, 232, 281
CSG/CSM   252

data
  analysis   285
  collection   29, 30
  ownership   235
  storage   235
  types   282–4
Data Processing (DP) department   19
database   19, 20, 23, 24, 46, 69, 94, 119,
      261, 264
DCSS   210, 212–25
  design model   213–16
  evaluation and future work   225–7
  interface   216–19
decision-action-outcome-feedback-decision
      cycles   112
deixis   15–16, 21–2, 25
design   9, 61–87, 119, 120, 139–50, 179–95
  agents   224
  as dynamic process   252–4
  as guddle   251–2

as hierarchy   251–2
as politics   153–5
as social function   153–5
by committee   243
capacities   55
codesign practices   159
concurrent design   254
descriptive theories   141
design actions and rationale   213
design-for-reuse   146–7
design-in-use   163, 164
design-of-design   163, 167, 169, 173
designing for the future   197–9
designing for the present   199–200
empirical theories   141
evaluation   219
factors   242
frameworks   143, 145–6, 147–50
groups   209–10
heuristics   192–3
histories   150
issues   27–31
meta-modelling   143
methodology   140, 143, 152, 198
model   149, 227, 244–5
  design states   216
  goals   215
  least-commitment   223
  refine-evaluate cycle   215
  routine design   214
  routine least-commitment refine-and-
      evaluate   214
  specifications   214
  themes   215
nested levels of   160
object   151
practice
  collaborative forms   158
  styles of   151–77
  user centred   159
prescriptive methods   141
principles   182, 192–4
process   85–6
  application   287–8
(re)design and reuse of designs   258
refinement   218
research   144
schema   148
shell   210
specification   218
style   170–7
teams   209–27
technique, as social function   153–5
theory   140–1
Design Collaboration Support System *see*
      DCSS
Design History Editor (DHE)   242–4,
      247–50
Design Infrastructure   242
Designed Product (DP)   251

designer-user mismatch 64
desktop metaphor 243
development process 198
digitizer 201
discrete entity approaches 175
discussion groups 31
DistEdit 21
Distributed Shared Drawing Surface
    (DSDS) 201
division of labour 170, 173
document production 37–9

echo 190–1
ECMA-PCTE Open Repository 265
editing 36
electronic mail (email) 20, 21, 90, 91, 93,
    99–102, 120
electronic meeting rooms 18
electronic social fields 177
emergent groups 98–9
empowerment 163, 168
engineering 152–3, 157
Engineering Design Research Centre
    (EDRC) 242
error message 64–5
ESPRIT II programme 272
Ethernet 225
Ethics 29
ethnography
    ethnographic modelling 30–1
    ethnographic study of office work 31–3
ethnomethodological analysis 85
EuroCoOp project 232, 272
evaluation 279–82, 288–90
events
    notification of 187–9
    unexpected 187
expert-novice situations 12
expert systems 93, 248
EXPRESS 246, 266
Extended Knowledge Representation
    (EKR) 267
extensional specification 85
eye contact 99
eye-to-eye 201

face-to-face 18, 99–101, 121–2, 133, 202,
    203, 278
facilitation 198
feedback 13, 22, 24, 100
feedthrough 13, 22, 23
filing systems 34, 49
financial information 19
flaming 121
floor control 189–90, 239
floor holder 188
floor time 100
flow charts 67

"forces of production" theory 176
Fordism 153
form 102–5
free-for-all (FFA) 131, 132
Freestyle 179

generic domain 246
generic products 169
generic systems 166–7
global organizations 271
global structure 134
goals 254–5
GOODS 252
grammar checker 103
grammar statistics 104
Grammatik 2.00 103, 104
grounding situation 73
group
    consensus building 211
    coordination 129
    editing environment 20
    editors 120
    graphical editor 130
    interaction 134, 244
    members 122, 128
    memory 49
    processes 122
    user 89, 90
    work 112, 121, 135
Group Decision Support System (GDSS)
    211
GroupDesign 130
GroupKit 261
groupware design 27
groupware editors 134, 136
groupware systems 9, 27, 89, 128, 179
group work 119, 121, 135
GROVE 136, 230
guddle 251–2, 255

help facility 64
hermeneutics 175
HERMES 264
house style 36
Human-Computer Interaction (HCI) 17,
    29, 120, 137, 163, 168, 179, 197, 198
human centred design 165
Human Factors (HF) 179
human-human communication 79
human-machine interaction 65
human protocol 187
Hypercard 248, 259
hypermedia 81
hypertext 248–9

ideational function 105
IMKA 246–7, 265–7

in the wild   200
in the zoo   200
industrial engineering   153
infon   70, 77
informal norms   57, 58
information   62–5, 79–81, 109–13
    information flow   67
    information systems (IS)   61–87, 90
    nature of   63, 66
    technology (IT)   27, 28
    theory   63, 64, 67
Information Age   63, 64
Information and Communications
        Technologies (ICTs)   151
innovation   198–9
institutional contexts   110, 111
Integrated Frame Base (IFB)   267
intellectual-ware   15
interaction episodes   43–6
interactions
    with clients   43–5
    within the company   45–6
interactive information systems   61–87
interactive systems   198
interdisciplinary team   61
interference   179–95
intergroup communication   97–8
interpersonal function   105
interpersonal skills   36
interrogation   258
intragroup communication   97–8
IS-user organization   90
Isolates   98, 99

job conditions   39–42

Khoros   267
KIREDE   243
knowledge
    knowledge assets   247, 266–7
    knowledge base   110
    knowledge based (KB) systems   110, 248
    knowledge extraction   158
    knowledge source (KS)   265
    knowledge structuring   145

labelling   254–5, 257–62
lack of control   187
language   89–117, 146
    action language   223
    body language   99
    natural language conversation   79
    perspectives   93
    philosophical studies of   144

query language   223, 224, 264
laser writers   55
Law of System Dynamics   244
liaisons   99–102
life-cycle framework   30–1
linguistic analysis   91
linguistic behaviour   94
linguistic constraint   74
linguistic support   93–113
LispWorks   279
Local Area Networks (LANs)   129, 210, 214,
        224–6, 233
location   49, 57, 58, 70, 165–70
log analysis   285
logbook   248–9, 259, 261
LookingGlass   202–7

mailbox servers   64
mathematicians   85
mathematics   65–9
meaning   71–2
meetings   44, 45
MEL   231
metaphor   65–9, 86
meta-planning model   215
Microsoft Mail   93, 101
minimality conditions   71
MMConf   230–1
model-theoretic truth   72
MOLGEN   223
Montague semantics   72
MOTIF   264
multimedia   81–3, 179–95
multi-user systems   81–3, 119, 281

Netmap network   96, 97, 99
network based object linking   21
Networked Client Server Model (NCSM)
        267
noise levels   41–2
normative constraints   75–9
norms   57

(object-)type abstraction   73
object-types   73
observation   258, 284–6
office based computer systems   28
office work, ethnographic study of   31–3
Open Systems   268
oracle   76, 77
ORDIT   29
organization vs structure   109–10
organizational context   135
organizational cooperation   49–55
organizational description   35–6
organizational norms   57, 58
organizational strategies   49

organizations   109–13
OSF/Motif   279

page emulation   250–1
PARADISE project   266
participant analysis   30
participant observation   30, 32
participant structures   33
participants   11, 13, 110, 111
participation   155
participatory design   159
PenPoint   261
pen-types   201
personal object directory server (PODS)
      117
philosophical issues   144–5
plans   78, 79
pointers   190–2
politik   174
power   176
Practitioner project   149
Practitioner Reuse Support System
      (PRESS)   146, 149
pragmatics   109
praxis   174
prescription   249–50
privacy   184
problem-related information   142
problem solving   142, 197–8
process control systems   24
processes   107
product development   198
production procedure   32
programming support   231–2
project managers   35
proofing   36
proposition   71
prosthesis   21–3
prototyping   279, 291, 292
publish   21

quality control   37
quality procedures   36
questionnaires   284
Quilt   20

RACE   180
RACE CAR   180
RCA (Requirements capture and analysis)
      28
real-life work situations   32
real-world actions   31
rendezvous   231
replication   197–208
representation   80
request-and-capture (RAC)   131–3
request-and-grant (RAG)   131, 132

requirements
      requirements analysis   28
      requirements capture   28, 277–84
resource allocation system   148
restricted parameters   72
ROCOCO   200–4, 230
      ROCOCO Sketchpad   201, 203, 204
      ROCOCO Station   201–3
roles   109
rules   57, 76, 78

scheme of individuation   70
screen clutter   185–7
screen displays   55
scriptal knowledge   111
seamlessness   184
security   184
sentence meanings   72
shared applications   29
shared data   19
shared editing   25
shared memory   241–2
shared screen   186
shared systems   52
shared window   278, 284
shared workspace   234
SharedX   20, 181, 230
ShareLib   229–40
      architecture   232–5
      CSCW layer   234–5
      design   232–7
      existing applications   230
      group communication layer   233–4
      implementation   235–40
      network communication layer   233
sharing, support for   20
ShrEdit   18, 19
single-agent to single-agent
      communication   79
single-user applications   20, 90, 120, 121,
      198–9, 282
situated action   124
situated design   173
situation   14, 76–8, 79–81
situation theory   61–87
      review   69–74
      role of   83–6
(situation-)type abstraction   73
situation-types   73
small and medium sized enterprises
      (SMEs)   268
SMART frame server   246, 263–5
social context   135
social organization   32–4
social presence   121–2
social systems   30
sociogram   96, 99
sociometric analysis   95–102
sociometry   96, 99, 113

sociopolitical factors 135
sociotechnical design 160
software
  software design 139
  software development 139, 271
  software engineering 135, 139–50, 152
  software life-cycle 169
  software reuse 146, 149
  software systems 67
specialization links 221
specification 157, 277, 284–6
speech acts 110–11
spreadsheets 19, 20
SSADM 157
staff organization 35
'stars' 98, 99
status-equalizing effects 129
Stella 67
STEP/PDES project 246
stock control 19–22, 25
structured observation 278–84
Structured Query Language (SQL) 264
stucturation theory 176
style checkers 102–5
styling 36, 52
subject selection 282
subscribe 21
SunView 184
Support 75–6
SWIS (School Wide Information Server)
    117
synchronous-asynchronous group editor 9
system designer 197–8, 207
system development 158
systemic functional linguistics 105–9
systems analysis 28

tacit knowledge 34
tailorability 232, 234–5
task activity 57, 58
task analysis 29
task domain 112
task-specific model 111
Taylorism 153
technical authoring 35–7, 55, 58
Technical Publications Unit (TPU), case
    study 33–46
technical writing 36
technik 174
technology 262–7
technology transfer 267–9
telepointer 201, 232, 234–5, 237–40
  initializing 238
  pixmap 239
  processing events 239
textual function 106
theory of practice 177
Timbuktu 18

time-space matrix 9
tool support 143
toolkit 229–40
tools 56, 67, 84, 120, 122, 128, 130,
    132, 271
Tractatus 145
TROPIC 223
turn competition 127
turn management 122, 123, 128, 131–6
turn-taking 123, 124, 127
type-abstraction procedures 72
types 83

understanding 10–11, 14–15, 17, 67
uniformities 70
UNIX 69, 230, 231, 246, 264, 265
usability 182, 184–5
user
  interaction 29
  interface 202–3
  involvement 291
  requirements 229, 250–62
  user-as-actor/constructor 155, 161–5
  user-as-client 155, 156–7
  user-as-codesigner 155, 158–61
  user-centred design 275–8
utterances 79

video 129
video analysis 286
video capture 299–300
video data 283–4
VideoTunnel 201
viscosity 182
voice 129
voice links 56
VT 223

waterfall model 30
Wide Area Networks (WANs) 129
WIMP 264
Wind Area Information Service (WAIS)
    266
windows 55, 56, 67, 185, 187
work 11–13, 32
workspace status 130, 134
workstations 55
writing analysis software 103
WYSIWIS 121, 131, 134, 183–5, 192, 202,
    231, 279

X.500 protocol 266
XTconfer 230
X Windows 181, 184, 201, 229–40, 246,
    265, 267

Name Index

Aarhus University 272
Abelson RP 111, 304
Abowd G 296
ACM Transactions 137
AIR-CYL 223
Albrechtsen H 147, 293
Algol 68 254
Alvey 167
Anderson 32, 142
Anderson JR 293
Anderson RJ 293
Apple LocalTalk 92
Apple Macintosh 67, 204
Apple Macintosh II 202
Applegate A 303
Apple's System 7
AppleTalk 234
Arango G 303
Ardayfio D 304
Argento A 265, 293
Arnott J 306
Arrano 146
Ashton-Tate 199
Austin JL 93, 293
Avrunin 210

Babadi A 305
Baker E 295
Banks D 293
Bannon L 34, 154, 167, 199, 293
BARGAINER 223
Barnwell P 229
Barwise J 3, 82, 87, 293
Baskerville R 175, 293
Baskin AA 210, 300
Baydere S 182, 187, 293
Beale R 296
Beard D 21, 293
Beattie F 123, 293
Beaudouin-Lafon M 120, 130, 293
Bebbington J 247, 293
Beitz W 140, 144, 148, 149, 303
Bellotti V 135, 296

Bellotti VME 301
Benbasat I 9, 301
Bennet J 306
Benson ORK 303
Bentley R 31, 32, 293, 299
Berger B 94, 293
Berger PL 293
Bezem M 211, 293
Bikson TK 272, 277, 294
Birmingham WP 222, 294
Bisgaard K 146, 294
Blair G 164, 304
Bloomfield H 249, 252, 303
Bly S 119, 121, 202, 302
Bly SA 294, 303
BNR Europe Ltd 272, 278, 288
Boardnoter 121
Bobrow DG 137, 305, 306
Bødker S 176, 281, 294
Bohnet R 297
Boland RJ 175, 294
Boldyreff C 2, 5, 139, 143, 146, 147, 294
Bonferini C 293
Borgstrom MC 304
Borland 199
Bourdieu P 166, 174, 177, 294
Bowers J 122, 134, 135, 136, 294
Bratman M 76, 294
Brennan S 11, 18, 306
Brennan SE 295
British Computer Society 152
British Leyland 102, 103, 106, 107, 108,
    114, 115
British Telecom 59
Brown DC 149, 211, 214, 294
Bucciarelli LL 143, 144, 294, 304
Buchanan D 96, 98, 299
Button G 32, 294

Callon M 175, 294
Cammarata S 306
CAMP 146
CAR 180, 181, 182, 188, 190, 191, 192,
    194, 195

Carey T   307
Carrasco J   246, 295
Carroll J   61, 62, 254, 257, 295
Carroll JM   306
CASE   269
Casey T   293
CASSANDRA   246, 247, 266
CEC   292
CEC RACE   195
Chalfonte B   296
Chalfonte BL   300
Chandrasekaran B   149, 214, 294
Chang S   211, 295
Chapanis A   288, 300
Chomsky AN   93, 295
Chuang S   293
Churcher J   122, 134, 135, 136, 294
Cicourel AV   94, 295
Clark   137
Clark H   304, 306
Clark HH   11, 18, 295
Clark J   176, 295
Clark S   197, 297
Clark SM   304
Clarke AA   297, 304
Clarke T   208
Clement A   163, 164, 295
Clements PC   139, 303
Cognoter   121, 137
Common Lisp   212, 231
Computer Mediated Communications
     (CMCs)   17, 18, 19, 21, 26, 99, 121
Concise Oxford Dictionary   275
Connolly J   208, 297, 304
Cook N   230, 295
Coombs   210
Cooper D   297
CoOpLab   273, 276, 278, 285, 286, 288, 292
CORE   29
Corkill DD   209, 295
Correct Grammar   103
COSMOS   136
Craig I   246, 265, 266, 295
Crowe M   246, 295
Crowley T   130, 190, 230, 295
CSMIL   18, 295
Curtis B   140, 144, 295, 298

Dai Z   305
Davis R   209, 305
Day WF   175, 294
DCSS (Design Collaboration Support
     System)   6, 7, 210, 212, 213, 214,
     216, 217, 219, 220, 221, 223, 224, 225,
     226, 227
Deegan M   103, 105, 295
DeMarco T   28, 295
Dematte F   293
Dennis AR   306

Department of Trade and Industry   275,
     303
Descotte Y   211, 295
Design In Severely Constrained Situations
     (DISCS)   243
Devlin K   2, 3, 61, 63, 66, 67, 69, 72, 75, 76,
     77, 78, 79, 83, 85, 87, 295
Digital   181
Dilnot C   254, 257, 295
DistEdit   21
Dix AJ   2, 3, 9, 11, 19, 26, 128, 295, 296, 302
Dobson, Sir R   106
DOGE   269
Dourish P   135, 296
DRACO   146
Draper SW   2, 198, 299, 303
Dubinskas F   32, 296
Dubrovsky V   121, 296
Duncan S   124, 296
Durkheim E   111, 296
Duval S   265, 296

Eason K   160, 296
Eason KD   298
ECMA-PCTE Open Repository   265
EDRC   243
Edwards JM   306
Eekels J   139, 296
Egido C   281, 296
Ehn P   165, 227, 296
Ehrenreich B   163, 296
Ehrlich RS   297
Ehrlich SF   179, 296
Ellis CA   120, 129, 130, 136, 230, 296
Elwart-Keys M   183, 296
Elzer P   294
Empirica GmbH   272, 292
Engelbart D   28, 197, 296
Engelien B   103, 296
Engineering Design Research Centre
     (EDRC)   242
English D   163, 296
ESPRIT ATMOSPHERE   268
ESPRIT II   272
Etchemendy J   82, 293
Ethernet   204
Ethics   29
EuroCoOp Consortium   7, 232, 272,
     288, 296
Evans DA   110, 299
Eveland JD   272, 277, 294
EXPRESS   246, 266

Farace RV   89, 296
Farallon   18, 296
Fenves S   304
Ferguson ES   242, 296
Filofax   53

Finger S   299
Finkelstein A   29, 296
Finlay J   296
Fish R   296
Fish RS   129, 300, 301
Fleck J   166, 296
Flores E   10, 64, 140, 306
Flores F   93, 297
Ford   194
Forsdick H   295
Foster G   137, 184, 297, 305, 306
Fowler RG   106, 297
Fox MS   211, 297
Francik E   179, 180, 297
Francis D   89, 297
Freeman P   149, 297
Freestyle   179, 195
Frege G   93, 145, 297
Fuks H   29, 296
Fukuoka H   306

Gaines BR   195, 297
Galloway JJ   96
Gantt M   163, 297
Garfinkel H   84, 122, 297
Gargan RA Jr   300
Garner S   208
Garner SW   201, 297, 304
GDSS   211
Geller V   137, 300
Gettys J   201, 304
Gibbs SJ   136, 296
Gilbert GNG   46, 297
Glegg GL   141, 297
GMD   272
GO Computing   261
Goldkuhl G   93, 297
Goldstein I   211, 297
GOODS   249, 252
Goodwin C   95, 297
Grammatik2.00   103, 104
Granberg A   96, 297
Great Belt AS   272
Green TRG   182, 297
Greenbaum J   152, 153, 159, 164, 276, 297, 301
Greenberg S   27, 89, 244, 261, 281, 297
Greif I   272, 281, 297
Grey C   177, 297
Grønbaek K   281, 294
GroupDesign   130
GroupKit   261
Groupware Inc   136, 165
GROVE   136, 230
Gruber TR   213, 215, 297
Grudin J   120, 135, 168, 179, 197, 198, 275, 276, 298
Guindon R   144, 147, 148, 298
Gust P   21, 298

Habermas J   155, 156, 158, 174, 298
Hacker S   152, 298
Hales M   2, 5, 151, 159, 160, 170, 174, 176, 298
Hall P   294
Halliday MAK   94, 95, 105, 106, 110, 298
Halonen D   296
Handley M   293
Handley MJ   179
Harandi MT   148, 301
Haraway D   176, 177, 298
Harker SDP   29, 298
Harlequin Limited   292
Harper RR   32, 298
Harris D   304
Harrison MD   302
Harrison W   265, 298
HCI   298
Heath C   32, 129, 298
Henninger S   273, 299
Heritage J   273, 299
HERMES   264
Hewitt B   2, 3, 27, 297
Hewitt C   211, 299
Hewlett-Packard   230
Hill RD   303
Hirschheim R   303
Hobbs J   110, 299
Hodge RIV   95, 106, 297, 300
Hodgson A   306
Holtzblatt K   306
Hoover SP   140, 299
Horton M   296
Huczynski A   96, 98, 299
Hughes JA   32, 33, 293, 298, 299
Hughes PT   3, 7, 129, 130, 134, 232, 271, 299, 302, 303
Humm A   293
Humphrey W   268, 299
HUSAT   194
Hutchison CS   1, 2, 4, 89, 90, 91, 102, 109, 110, 299
Hymes D   90, 299
Hyperproof   82

IAD   194
IEEE   267
Illich I   163, 299
IMKA   246, 247, 265, 266, 267, 299
Iscoe N   295
Ishii H   182, 299
Ismail N   293
Ismail NM   179
ISO 10030   246

Jagannathan V   244, 300
Jamieson W   96, 299

Jefferson G   95, 299, 304
Jefferson GA   304
Jenkins D   3, 7, 241, 243, 258, 266, 268, 299
Jennings HH   96, 302
Johansen J   211, 299
Johnson CW   302
Johnson M   87, 301
Jordan PW   203, 299
Joseph TA   301
Joyner S   194
Jydsk Telefon AS   272

Kahn K   305
Kamana S   305
Kanter RM   89, 98, 300
Karsenty A   120, 130, 293
Kass R   296
Kavianpour M   298
Keen N   197
Keilmann J   294
Kellog C   226, 300
Kern H   294
Khoros   266, 267
Khoros 1.0   267
Kiesler S   101, 121, 122, 137, 296, 300, 305
Kitzmiller C   244, 300
Klein H   175, 306
Klein HK   303
Klein M   2, 6, 175, 209, 210, 213, 220,
        223, 300
Kling R   32, 120, 135, 154, 157, 164, 175, 300
Kloth M   244, 300
Knister MJ   21, 300
Knowledge and Information Relationships
        in the Engineering Design
        Environment (KIREDE)   243
Konda S   241, 300
Konsynski K   303
Kotter JP   89, 300
Kraft P   152, 153, 300
Krasner H   295
Kraut R   296
Kraut RE   32, 300, 301
Kress GR   95, 102, 105, 106, 297, 300
Krohn U   146, 294
Krueger CW   149, 300
Krueger GP   288, 300
Kumar V   305
Kuutti K   28, 154, 162, 176, 300
Kyng M   154, 159, 164, 276, 297, 301

Laessøe J   160, 165, 301
Laffey TJ   303
Lakoff G   87, 301
Lander S   211, 301
Landry J   244, 301
Lanning K   137, 305
Lanning S   305

Lantz KA   129, 301
Latombe JC   211, 295
Latour B   175, 294, 301
Lauwers CJ   129, 201, 301
Lave J   31, 301
Lea M   121, 301
Lehman   244
Lehtman H   28, 296
Leifer L   202, 306
Leland MDP   20, 120, 301
Lesser VR   209, 211, 295, 301
Levine S   297
Levinson SC   111, 123, 273, 274, 275, 301
Lichtenheim M   268, 301
Lim FJ   9, 301
Linde C   32, 301
LispWorks   279
LookingGlass   202, 203, 204, 205, 206, 207
Lotus   199
Loughborough University   230
Lu SCY   209, 210, 300
Lubars MD   148, 301
Lucas S   96, 301
Ludlow JJ   93, 297
Luff P   32, 129, 298
Lunt G   230, 295
Lyytinen K   93, 94, 95, 105, 114, 176,
        297, 301

McArthur D   306
McBride R   103, 296
McCarthy JC   119, 137, 302
McDermid JA   140, 302
McDermott J   302
MacFarlane KK   299
McGuire JG   300
Macintosh   68, 92
McKinlay A   119, 131, 302
MacLean A   200, 301
McNulty S   299
MacPlus   92
MacServe   92
Madlin N   96, 301
Madsen CM   243, 301
Maeno K   306
Malyan R   229
Manca S   293
Mangham IL   161, 301
Manning PK   89, 301
Mantei M   120, 121, 130, 134, 302
Marcus S   211, 221, 302
Mark W   300
Martin JR   95, 298
Masting O   119, 302
MDMSC   146, 302
MEL   231
MICON   222
Microsoft   199
Microsoft Mail   93, 101

Microsoft Word   103, 104
Milazzo P   295
Miles VC   9, 20, 128, 129, 137, 302
Millar S   85, 302
Miller JR   32, 163, 303
Minneman S   120, 121, 302, 306
Minneman SL   202, 294
Minsky M   246, 263, 302
Mintzberg H   89, 302
MIT-JSME   140, 302
Miyake N   182, 299
MMConf   190, 230, 231
Modgil C   295
Modgil S   295
MOLGEN   223
Monarch I   300
Monge PR   296
Monk A   307
Monk AF   137, 302
Montague R   72, 93, 302
Moreno J   96, 302
Morgan G   157, 302
Morris ME   10, 271, 286, 287, 299, 302, 303
Moses A   137, 300
Mostow J   213, 302
Mullery GP   29, 302
Multiparty Specification   29
Mumford E   29, 227, 302
Murray D   2, 3, 27, 297
Murrel S   121, 302
Mustoe J   244, 245, 302
Myers BA   208, 302

Nair A   293
Namioka A   159, 303
Nardi B   297
Nardi BA   32, 163, 303
National Science Foundation   140
Neighbors J   146, 303
Netmap   96, 97, 99, 114
Newell A   147, 306
Newman R   304
Newsome SL   142, 303
Nguyen TA   211, 303
Ngwenyama O   176, 303
Nii   147
Nissen HE   303
Norman DA   2, 61, 154, 198, 303
Nottingham University   230
Nunamaker JF   211, 303, 306

O'Hara P   160, 298
Ohmori T   306
Olphert CW   298
Olsen L   294
Olson G   137
Olson J   137
Olson MH   119, 303

O'Malley C   305
Open University   275, 303
OpenLook   187
ORDIT   29
Ormerod TC   249, 252, 303
O'Shea T   305
Ossher H   298
Overington MA   161, 301

Pacanowsky M   89, 304
Pahl G   140, 143, 148, 149, 303
Paisley College   242
Palaniappan M   293
Palmen H   201, 208, 297, 304
PARADISE   266
Parker C   194
Parnas DL   139, 303
Patterson JF   231, 303
Pecora D   303
Pendley WL   304
PenPoint   261
Peralta P   211, 303
Perin C   177, 303
Perkins WA   303
Perry J   3, 87, 293
Perry TS   209, 303
Peugeot   194
Pferd P   211, 303
Piaget J   93, 303
Piller C   103, 303
Plant TA   271, 279, 299, 302, 303
Pontecorvo M   300
Practitioner REuse Support System
    (PRESS)   146, 149
Prakash A   21, 300
PRESS   146, 149
Prieto-Diaz R   146, 303
Procter R   2, 4, 5, 10, 119, 302, 306
Pruitt DG   210, 304
Putnam L   89, 304

Queen Mary and Westfield College   59
Quilt   20
Quintas P   167, 304

Rabins M   140, 304
RACE   180
Randall D   293, 299
Rasmussen LB   160, 165, 301
Reader   103
Reddy R   305
Reder S   32, 304
Rein GL   136, 296
Remote Cooperation and Communication
    (ROCOCO)   200, 201, 202, 203, 204,
    208, 230
Rendezvous   231

Richardson H   304
RightWriter   103
Rinderle JR   299
Robb F   89, 304
Robertson S   137
Robinson M   174, 293, 304
Rockoff T   304
ROCOCO   201, 202, 203, 204, 208, 230
Rodden T   9, 164, 293, 304
Roemer JM   277, 281, 304
Rogers Y   32, 304
Rohall SL   303
Romanov AL   301
Root RW   300
Roozenburg NFM   139, 296
Roseman M   297
Rosenberg D   1, 66, 75, 78, 79, 83, 85, 90,
        114, 295, 299
Russell HM   296
Rutherford J   246, 304

Sacks H   66, 75, 78, 79, 85, 95, 122, 124,
        274, 304
Sakata S   306
Sargent P   300
Sarin G   211, 304
Sasse A   293
Sasse MA   2, 6, 179
Sawyer P   293
Scacchi W   300
Scacci   32, 175
Scanlon E   305
Schank RC   111, 304
Schappo A   208, 297, 304
Schegloff E   304
Schegloff EA   274, 275, 304
Scheifler RW   201, 235, 239, 304
Schenkein J   95, 299
Schmidt K   34, 154, 167, 199, 293
Schon D   144, 304
Schuler D   159, 303
Schwab RG   32, 304
Sclossberg JL   300
Scott P   296
Scrivener S   2, 5, 197, 200, 201, 203, 248
Scrivener SAR   297, 304
Searle J   93, 110, 305
Seel NR   299
Seireg A   304
Sellen A   129, 305
Sensible Grammar   103
SERC   208
SERC Advanced Fellowship   26
Sethna B   296
Shan Y-P   293
Shannon CE   10, 305
Shapiro D   299
Shapiro DZ   293, 298
Shared X   21, 181, 230

ShareLib   229, 230, 232, 235, 236, 237,
        238, 239
Sharrock WW   32, 293
Shaw M   305
Shaw MLG   195, 297
Shneiderman B   197, 198, 305
ShrEdit   18, 19, 136
Sibley EH   140, 305
Siewiorek DP   222, 294
Simon HA   141, 144, 305
Sketchpad   201, 203, 204
Skinner BF   93, 305
SMART   246, 263, 264, 265
Smith RB   201, 305
Smith RG   209, 305
Smith SF   211, 297
Smyth M   208, 297, 304
Smyth MG   304
The Society for Information Systems
        Engineering   152
Sommerville I   139, 293, 299
Spears R   121, 301
Spillers WR   142, 303
Springer S   299
Sproull L   101, 121, 122, 305
Srinivas K   120, 305
SSADM   29, 157, 305
Standish TA   149, 305
Stanford University   87
Star SL   167, 176, 305
Stauffer LA   257, 258, 305
Steele GL   211, 214, 221, 306
Stefik M   18, 120, 121, 137, 184, 202, 211,
        214, 223, 305
Stella   67, 68
Stempski MO   304
STEP/DES   246
Stewart R   114
Stout J   302
Strauss A   167, 305
Streveler DJ   243, 254, 261, 305
Subrahmanian E   300
Suchman L   31, 32, 64, 65, 84, 85, 122, 124,
        164, 176, 249, 254, 305
Sullivan JW   300
Sun NFS   265
Sun SPARC Station   204
Sunday Times   102, 103, 105, 106, 107,
        108, 115
SunView   184
Sussman GJ   211, 214, 221, 306
Symbolics Lisp Machines   212

Tanenbaum A   129, 306
Tang J   120, 129, 134, 202, 306
Tarski   72
Tartar D   297
Tatar DG   95, 114, 120, 121, 137, 184,
        305, 306

Taylor J   305
Theories of Multi-Party Interaction
    project   59
Thomas JC   254, 257, 306
Thorndyke P   209, 306
Tichy W   135, 306
Timbuktu   18
Tomlinson R   295
Touraine A   98, 306
Tractatus   145
Travis J   293
Trew AA   102, 105, 106, 297, 300
Triumph Adler   272
TROPIC   223
Truex D   175, 293, 306
Tunnicliffe   248

Ullman DG   257, 258, 305
University College   180, 195
University of London   59
University of Paisley   242
UNIX   69, 230, 231, 234, 237, 246, 264, 265

Valacich JS   129, 306
Vallee V   299
Vehviløinen M   164, 306
Ventura DTP system   39, 53
VideoLogic   204
VideoTunnel   201
VT   223

Wraern Y   122, 306
Wang Laboratories   195
Watabe K   120, 129, 306

Weaver W   10, 305
Webster D   297
Wenger E   31, 301
Weston RH   244, 306
Whiteside J   277, 306
Whitney DE   139, 141, 306
Whittaker D   115
Whittaker S   133, 306
Wilbur S   194, 297
Wilbur SB   234, 306
Wilensky R   211, 215, 223, 306
Winnett M   3, 7, 229
Winograd T   10, 64, 93, 114, 140, 306
Witt J   294
Wittgenstein   144, 145
Woodburn R   119, 123, 131, 302, 306
Woolgar S   32, 165, 307
Word v.5   101
Wright P   286, 307

X Windows   7, 181, 184, 201, 230, 231, 234,
    235, 246, 265, 267, 279
X Windows X11R4   267
Xlib   236, 237
XTconfer   230
Xtel Services Ltd   230, 272

Young R   93, 301, 307
Yourdon E   29, 307

Zemanek H   144, 145, 307
Zhang J   294
Zubrow D   137, 300